*Modern Studies in Philosophy*

SARTRE

Modern Studies in Philosophy is a series of anthologies presenting contemporary interpretations and evaluations of the works of major philosophers. The editors have selected articles designed to show the systematic structure of the thought of these philosophers, and to reveal the relevance of their views to the problems of current interest. These volumes are intended to be contributions to contemporary debates as well as to the history of philosophy; they not only trace the origins of many problems important to modern philosophy, but also introduce major philosophers as interlocutors in current discussions.

Modern Studies in Philosophy is prepared under the general editorship of Amelie Oksenberg Rorty, Livingston College, Rutgers University

———————

MARY WARNOCK was a fellow of St. Hugh's College, Oxford, from 1952–66. She is now headmistress of the Oxford High School. She is the author of *Ethics Since 1900, The Philosophy of J. P. Sartre, Existentialist Ethics,* and *Existentialism.*

*Modern Studies in Philosophy*

# SARTRE

## A Collection of Critical Essays

EDITED BY

MARY WARNOCK

1971
ANCHOR BOOKS
Doubleday & Company, Inc.
Garden City, New York

# CONTENTS

# PREFACE

Jean-Paul Sartre has been a most prolific and versatile writer; this collection of articles is about some of the more important and fruitful aspects of his work. In no sense does it form a complete analysis or criticism of every contribution he has made to the thought of the twentieth century. The emphasis is obviously on his philosophy, but some explanation may be in order. It is possible that the inclusion of so many articles on topics only marginally philosophical may need justification in a volume in this series. The justification I would offer is this. As a philosopher, Sartre is fluent and illuminating but not particularly original or consistent. Little was known of his philosophy twenty years ago in England or America, and the first discovery of *Being and Nothingness* (which was written in 1943, but translated into English in 1957) was for many people an intellectual adventure and a source of excitement. But strictly as a philosopher, Sartre's main achievement, as we can now see, was to introduce phenomenology to France and to combine some of the insights of phenomenology with the existentialism of Heidegger. His philosophy is essentially German, turned into French. As a result, it is impossible to make a serious study of Sartre's philosophy by itself. One is always aware that one is dealing with ideas which, if not second hand, are at any rate not independent of their original sources. It is for this reason that I have included the comprehensive general account of Existentialism by Alisdair Macintyre from *A Critical History of Western Philosophy* as a general introduction. But though Sartre is philosophically a borrower and interpreter, there is of course much of his work which is highly original. The most impressive and the most original feature of his writing, whether philosophical, critical, or dramatic, is his powerful, concrete imagination. Even in the works of pure philosophy, and especially in *Being and Nothingness,* this concern with the concrete and the particular, which exists as a matter of principle in all Existentialist philosophers, has a new and very characteristic role in which anecdotes and detailed descriptions of actual objects in the world play a specific part in the argument, not as mere illustrations, but as steps. From a concrete description of a situation, an imaginative rather than a strictly cognitive response is produced in the reader, such that when Sartre proceeds to draw a general conclusion from the particular description, the reader assents to the conclusion. Thus there is a well-known passage in *Being and Nothingness* in which Sartre describes a man caught listening at a key-hole, from which the conclusion is drawn that we must necessarily be aware of ourselves as objects for other people, since, if we were not, the situation as described in which the agent feels shame at his discovery could not occur. But that it does occur we are compelled to agree by our imaginative acceptance of the anecdote. Other examples of the same kind could be listed. Again, in a rather different way, from a description of honey dropping off a spoon onto the surface of the remaining honey in the jar, he derives an absolutely general conclusion as to our attitude, necessarily adopted as part of our "original project" as human beings in the world, to everything sticky or viscous. And from the existence of this attitude he derives a further conclusion about the status of consciousness in the world of non-conscious things. It is this kind of attachment to the real world, with a thoroughly romantic interpretation of it as significant for us which has constituted the main attractive force of Existentialist philosophy for those brought up on English philosophy in the last twenty years.

It is, then, in the use of his philosophical imagination, above all, that Sartre shows his genius. And the same power of imagination is shown, perhaps to better advantage, in his writings which are not, or not strictly, philosophical. The most rewarding aspect of the study of Sartre is the drawing together of features of his philosophical, literary, and critical work which comes through the study of his imagination. It is for this reason that I have included certain articles on Sartre as dramatist and critic, some of which may not be easily available elsewhere to students of philosophy.

But it would be completely misleading to think that the author of *Being and Nothingness* and the other early philosophical works, the author of the plays and novels, was the complete Sartre; and it would be misleading simply to say of Sartre that he was an Existentialist. Since *Being and Nothingness,* he has himself undergone a radical conversion toward Marxism, and his later writings have been, to a large extent, concerned with political, historical, and sociological issues. *The Critique of Dialectical Reason* itself, we must remember, is only half complete, and though it is unlikely that a second volume will ever come out exactly as it was projected, there is still no reason to suppose that the first volume contains his last or final thoughts on these subjects. On the evidence that we have at present, one of the most difficult and controversial questions to be answered is that of the interpretation of his philosophy of the group. How are we to relate this to his earlier philosophy of the individual? I have included two essays written especially for this volume which are concerned with this subject, and I am greatly indebted to Professor Manser and Professor Burkle for these original articles. I am also extremely grateful to Professor Weinstein for another previously unpublished article, in which he explores the relation between Sartre's sociological theories and some other traditions in the study of sociology. Here again, though the subject is strictly not pure philosophy, students of Sartre must widen their view and try to follow Sartre into the unfamiliar territory in which he has bravely set out if they are to understand that part of his work which is philosophical. I also wish to thank Dr. Wardman of the University of Lancaster for his article on Sartre as critic, which was also written especially for this volume.

I would like to express my thanks to Mrs. Balhetchet for her work in translating the articles by Otto Hahn and Francis Jeanson into English. I have not, however, adopted a consistent policy about the quotations from Sartre contained within the articles here reprinted. Where the authors of the articles have left the quoted excerpts in French, I have not translated them. There is, therefore, some, but not very much, untranslated French in the book. Thanks are due, too, to all the authors of the published articles for their generosity in allowing me to reprint them here. I am grateful also to the publishers of the books and the editors of the journals in which articles have previously appeared for allowing them to be reprinted.

Finally, I am very greatly indebted to Mr. David Bradby of the Department of French, the University of Kent, not only for his article, but for his help and advice in the selection of articles from non-philosophical journals. He has been an indispensable guide.

# EXISTENTIALISM

## Alisdair Macintyre

Jean-Paul Sartre was born in Paris in 1905. He studied philosophy in Paris and Berlin, taught for a short time in a lycée in Le Havre, and joined the French Army in 1939. It was in the period which culminated in his experiences as a prisoner of war that he resolved to become a writer committed to the causes of democracy. His pre-war philosophical writings and his first novel, *La Nausée,* show the influence both of Heidegger and of Alexandre Kojève's lectures upon Hegel. His war-time and post-war plays express an imaginative concern with problems of guilt, responsibility, and freedom. In the post-war period Sartre's main enterprise has been the journal *Les Temps Modernes.* He was one of the founders of a small independent socialist party, in alliance with the Communist Party, in 1948. But this collapsed under the pressures of the Cold War. He has never been a member of the Communist Party, which he has criticized both for confused theory and for political and moral failure, but he has often seen it as the only radical force in French politics. Sartre's expressed preference has been for a rootless mode of life, the life of the café rather than of the bourgeois hearth. His works are sometimes unfinished: promised second volumes rarely appear, and the announced final book in his sequence of novels *Les Chemins de la*

*Liberté* appears never to have been written. He
was at one time a close friend of Camus, but they
became estranged over the Cold War. An excellent
account of the younger Sartre is contained in
Simone de Beauvoir's memoirs.

---

"I am not an existentialist"—so Jaspers and so also
Heidegger. When the very name is disowned by philosophers as central as these, but is conferred by their
admirers at the same time upon figures as diverse as
St. Augustine and Norman Mailer, Blaise Pascal and
Juliet Greco, one almost despairs of arriving at a useful definition of "existentialism." We could probably
find no single common characteristic shared by all
those who have been called existentialist. We could
certainly find little use even for a brief statement of
doctrine shared by some of the central figures. For
any formula wide enough to include the thought of
Kierkegaard and Sartre, of Heidegger and Marcel, and
pithy enough for our purposes, would be meaningless
apart from the interpretations given to it by individual
thinkers. "Existence precedes essence," for example,
is like those philosophical slogans out of context susceptible of too many interpretations, and the use of
such formulas to define existentialism is what has enabled both Dostoievski and Aquinas to be described
as existentialists for purposes of controversy. But how
then are we to define the field initially?

Some writers—William Barrett, for example—have
wanted to characterize existentialism as part of an an-
tirationalist revolt, against the Enlightenment, against
deductive metaphysics, against Marxism, against positivism. But this is a dangerous half-truth at best. It
stresses differences at the cost of ignoring resemblances. Sartre's social philosophy is one of the heirs
of the Enlightenment, his ethics is first cousin to that
of Anglo-Saxon analytical philosophy, his later writing
is avowedly Marxist. Kierkegaard's hero was Socrates.
Jaspers sees much to be praised in positivism. But it

is not only that this kind of historical characterization irons out and ignores complexity. It is also that each of the leading existentialist philosophers is partly characterized as an existentialist because of his own stress upon what is specific to *his* thought, and not shared with others. "As a man is, so is his philosophy," said Fichte. One criterion of existentialist philosophizing is that the man is brought into the picture; his philosophy is commended partly because it is his. Hence the unfortunate tendency to oracular pronouncements and self-dramatization.

To discuss existentialism it is therefore necessary to be somewhat arbitrary, to select a list of names by most of which to define a particular intellectual continuity. Some of the names choose themselves: Kierkegaard, Jaspers, Heidegger, Sartre. Others fall into place by reason of their relation to the larger names: Bultmann and Camus, for example. Nor at least is there any problem about where and when to begin. The time and place are 1813 and Copenhagen, and the event is the birth of Sören Kierkegaard.

### Kierkegaard's Interpretation of Christianity and of Ethics

Kierkegaard's sense of a unique vocation thrust upon him connects his life with his writings. In his writings he is discharging this vocation by expressing what he has learned in his relationship with his authoritarian and guilt-ridden father, in his broken engagement, and in his dilemmas about Christianity and the church. The form of these dilemmas led him to conclude that truth, so far as it involves human existence, cannot be grasped by objective scrutiny or argument. These are certainly in place in mathematics and natural science. But they have no place in questions about how to live. Here all that rational argument can do is to present alternatives, to pose choices. Kierkegaard's writings take the form in part of such a presentation, the use of pseudonyms concealing the fact that it is one and

the same man who is presenting the rival claims of
contrasting and conflicting alternatives. To acquire the
truth we have to choose between doctrines for which
no logically coercive arguments can be advanced. For
any argument derives its conclusion from premises
which have to be vindicated, and if these premises are
themselves derived as a conclusion from prior premises then these prior premises will in turn stand in
need of vindication. Ineluctably we come to a point
where not argument but decision is necessary.

On Kierkegaard's own view the most important application of this doctrine is to the characterization of
authentic Christianity. Kierkegaard denies "that ob-
jections against Christianity come from doubt." They
come from "insubordination, unwillingness to obey,
rebellion against all authority." It follows that Christian apologetics is a mistake. But it is more than a mistake. It is a falsification of Christianity itself, which
necessarily must appear to the ordinary reasonable
man or to the philosopher as absurd and paradoxical.
It would be a mistake, however, to take this as mere
irrationalism. On the contrary, that Christianity must
appear as absurd and paradoxical he asserts to follow
from one of the two possible views of truth and reason
between which we have to choose. These two views
are outlined in the *Philosophical Fragments,* which
begins from the paradox posed by Socrates in Plato's
*Meno.* How is it possible to come to know anything?
For either one knows already what one is to come to
know or one does not. But if one already knows one
cannot come to know; and if one does not already
know, how can one possibly recognize what one
comes across as being what one desired to know? The
Socratic solution to this paradox is that we never in
fact do come to know that of which before we were
ignorant. Rather, it is that we recall that which we
once knew but had forgotten. Truth lies dormant
within us. We have only to elicit it. In this Socratic
doctrine Kierkegaard sees the assumption of philosophy from Plato to Hegel: that a capacity for grasping

the truth belongs to human reason, that what brings the truth to light for us on a given occasion is accidental (that it was this teacher, rather than that), that teaching is bringing out what was already present. Suppose, however, Kierkegaard argues, that this is not the only possibility. Suppose that we might instead be strangers to the truth, unable to grasp it with the resources of human reason. Then the truth would have to be brought to us from outside by a teacher capable of transforming us so that we can receive the truth from him, and such a teacher *ex hypothesi* must be more than human. But in what form will he have to come if he is to teach us? He will have to come in the form of a man, and of a man who impresses us not by his appearance or his power—for that would be not to teach but to dazzle us—but simply by himself and his teaching. He will have to come in the form of a servant. Thus Kierkegaard deduces from this assumption the necessity of a revelation in the form of God appearing as a man. His ironically veiled allusions to Christian doctrine gain from his emphasis that he is doing nothing but pursuing the consequences of one out of two possible alternative assumptions about the relationship of human reason to the truth. As to whether this assumption is true or not he cannot presume to say; he can only leave us to choose between philosophy in Platonic or Hegelian style on the one hand or the Christian revelation on the other.

It is characteristic of Kierkegaard that the brilliance of his prose style in the *Philosophical Fragments* may induce us to overlook the prosaic point that the truth which furnishes Plato with his central example in the *Meno* is geometrical truth and that this is precisely what Kierkegaard is not concerned with. And merely to notice this is for all the compellingness of Kierkegaard's delineation of the two alternatives to fall away. But this is not all. For when we have chosen Christianity, what on Kierkegaard's view have we chosen? What is Christianity? Christianity is inwardness, and "inwardness is the relationship of the individual to himself before God," and from this derives the kind of suffering which is involved in Christianity. Christianity is a matter of suffering for the believer, for it is to grasp oneself before a God where demands of faith and action invade one's ordinary standards by their absurdity, if judged by those standards. The inward acceptance of the absurd does not show outwardly; the knight of faith looks like a tax-collector. In *Fear and Trembling* Kierkegaard considers the type of action which outrages the public standards of ordinary morality but accords with the inwardness of faith because it is in obedience to a divine commandment. Clearly he has in mind his own breaking of his engagement to Regine Olsen, which he justified by referring to what he took to be his divinely appointed vocation; in fact he discusses the story of Abraham and Isaac. Abraham is commanded by God to sacrifice his son. This command runs counter not only to inclination, but also to duty. God commands the sacrifice of Isaac whom Abraham loves; indeed part of what makes it a sacrifice is that Abraham loves him. But Abraham has to break also with duty; his faith in God can make murder a holy act and not a crime. There is thus a rift between the highest human consciousness and the divine intrusion of the apparently absurd. But if at this point what Kierkegaard stresses is the dividing line between the ethical and the religious, there are other places, especially the book *Either/Or*, where he assimilates the religious and the ethical in order to contrast both or the latter with a category which he calls "the aesthetic." The aesthetic life is the life of the man who has no criterion but that of his own happiness. His enemies are pain and more especially boredom. The ethical life is the life of duty, of moral standards which admit of no exceptions in one's own favor. Romantic love, which lasts only as long as the appropriate feelings persist and is always flying off to new satisfactions, is characteristic of the aesthetic; marriage, with its commitments and obligations of an inescapable kind, is characteristic of the ethical. The case for the aesthetic in *Either/Or* is presented in the papers of an anonymous "A"; that for the ethical in the letters of an older man, Judge Wilhelm. The two cases cannot meet, for the first judges between the aesthetic and the ethical on aesthetic grounds and the second judges between them on ethical grounds. Yet there can be no criteria of judgment of a higher order beyond both the aesthetic and the ethical; all there can be is the reader's own choice. But here a reading of *Either/Or* raises an unavoidable doubt.

For Kierkegaard on the one hand insists that the choice between the ethical and the aesthetic is ultimate. It cannot be governed by criteria, for it is a choice of criteria. But on the other hand his descriptions of the two types of life are not neutral. He portrays the aesthetic life as essentially one in which the pleasures of hopefully traveling are destroyed by actually arriving. Hence the aesthetic life is concerned with possibilities which lose their point when they are actualized. But because they can never be actualized without this happening Kierkegaard could write of the aesthetic state of mind at its highest as "an imaginative inwardness which evokes the possibilities with intensified passion, with sufficient dialectical power to transform all into nothing in despair." The point of the ethical, by contrast, is found not in the future but in the present, not in the possible but in the actual, so that in the same passage Kierkegaard describes the ethical as "a quiet, incorruptible, yet infinite passion of resolve" which "embraces the modest ethical task."[1] Indeed, when Kierkegaard insists that he has made "A" cleverer than "Judge Wilhelm" he inadvertently reveals his conviction that one case can be more cogently presented than the other. But it is not just that the descriptions of the two alternatives are not framed in neutral terms. It is also the case that Kierkegaard explicitly affirms at times that one choice can be more

[1] *Concluding Unscientific Postscript*, translated by W. Lowrie, Princeton, 1941, p. 228.

correct than another. Sometimes he writes that all that one can do is to choose; at other times he writes that if only one chooses with sufficient seriousness and sufficient passion this will assure that one chooses the correct alternative. Thus, Kierkegaard wishes to argue both that there is no criterion for choosing between the aesthetic and the ethical and also that there is some sense in saying that one alternative is to be preferred to the other. We might rescue him from inconsistency by supposing him to be speaking from an ethical point of view when he says that the ethical is to be preferred and from a point of view at once meta-ethical and meta-aesthetic when he says that the choice is criterionless. But it is not clear that this is so —and when Kierkegaard speaks of his own "point of view" he speaks of his motives and not about this—and Kierkegaard's possible inconsistency on this point would in any case be only one instance of a dilemma which must inform the views of all those who hold that truth is subjectivity. This dilemma is as follows.

If I hold that truth is subjectivity, what status am I to give to the denial of the proposition that truth is subjectivity? If I produce arguments to refute this denial I appear committed to the view that there are criteria by appeal to which the truth about truth can be vindicated. If I refuse to produce arguments, on the grounds that there can be neither argument nor criteria in such a case, then I appear committed to the view that any view embraced with sufficient subjective passion is as warranted as any other in respect of truth, including the view that truth is not subjectivity. This inescapable dilemma is never faced by Kierkegaard and consequently he remains trapped by it. One source of this dilemma lies in the confusions consequent upon Kierkegaard's equation of the distinction between the subjective and the objective with the distinction between the standpoint of the agent and that of the critic or spectator.

Kierkegaard is anxious to emphasize that the individual cannot without falsification conceive of his place in the world as that of an impartial spectator, an ideal and impersonal observer. He is always and necessarily a participant. As such his life is a series of decisions. The aesthetic, ethical, and religious stages are not so related that the individual who pursues one finds himself pushed by the very logic of what he does into a transition to another stage. Yet this is precisely how Hegel pictures the successive phases of human life in the *Phenomenology of Mind* and in the *Logic*. And Hegel is able to do this, is forced to do this, so Kierkegaard believes, because he pictures the individual as absorbed by the rational system which constitutes the universe and because he pictures the philosopher as the impartial observer of this rational system, seeing it as a timeless whole. It is clear at once both how Kierkegaard interprets Hegel's thought and why he has to react against it.

## Kierkegaard's Relationship to Hegel

For Kierkegaard Hegel is the Hegel of the mature writings and especially of the Berlin period. Hegelianism is a philosophy which conceives of the universe as the articulation of a set of logic categories. These categories represent different phases in the rational self-development of the absolute idea. Every period in human history is the embodiment of some such phase, and the history of thought, especially the history of philosophy, is the idea coming to self-consciousness of its own rational nature. Nothing that occurs is contingent or arbitrary, once it is understood in the context of the systematic development of the idea, and the Hegelian philosophy is the total rational exposition of that context. Rational argument is the arbiter on every issue, for the coincidence of the rational and the real is complete. Even those individuals who apparently defy reason are by the cunning of reason made to serve its purposes. This explains the sense in which, according to Hegel, the philosopher is committed to envisage reality objectively and as a whole.

For Kierkegaard this concept of philosophy is impossible because the philosopher is situated within the reality of which he speaks. He necessarily speaks from one particular, limited, contingent standpoint; his truths cannot be impersonal, objective or necessary. He cannot both be in the universe of which he speaks as an agent and grasp it as a spectator. But why not? The standpoint of the agent is often one from which it is wise to view the universe as impartially and impersonally as possible. It is simply untrue as a matter of empirical fact that we can never transcend our own immediate viewpoint. Agents who cannot do this are often less successful than those who can. If, then, what Kierkegaard was saying is so obviously false, assuming that he intended his words to be taken in their ordinary senses, how did he come to say it? The answer is surely that his vocabulary is badly infected by the Hegelianism which he is trying to reject and that Kierkegaard's use of such terms as "objective" and "subjective" is not intelligible outside a Hegelian context. But by borrowing a Hegelian vocabulary in order to attack a Hegelian position, Kierkegaard becomes himself involved in a kind of inverted Hegelianism. And this is a matter of substance as well as of vocabulary. For Kierkegaard's concept of human nature is already to be found in that portrait gallery of the varieties of human experience, the *Phenomenology of Mind*. When Kierkegaard depicts man as alien from the truth, forced to seek a truth which is at once an objective reality outside him and which he can only apprehend through experiencing his own subjective inwardness, he reproduces with extraordinary fidelity, although certainly unconsciously, Hegel's picture of what Hegel called "the unhappy consciousness."[2] His attempted refutation of Hegel turns out to rest on a doctrine which Hegel himself had recognized as one stage in the development of philosophy toward Hegelianism. Since Kierkegaard believes that his thought

[2] *The Phenomenology of Mind,* Section IV, B.

expresses the standpoint of genuine Christianity, and since Hegel in this section was describing attitudes which he took to have been historically identified with Christianity, perhaps this coincidence is not surprising. But it is worth dwelling upon it, since the Hegelian view reappears later in existentialist writers and may help to make intelligible some of the instability of existentialist thought.

Hegel's starting point is that human growth in rationality and knowledge is not a simple additive process. It is a process of contradiction and the transcendence of contradiction in which the human subject moves through alienation (*Entfremdung*) to reunification (*Aneignung*). The concept of alienation covers all those cases in which men do not recognize the products of human social life and thought as such, but falsely invest those products with independent power and reality. Whereas they are in fact akin to us, they appear as alien. An example is the attitude men take to the moral law. In reality the moral law expresses human ideals and norms. It is something made by men. But men see it as an objective authority, external to them, against which they are judged. However, as we progress rationally, we recognize the human character of such artifacts, and as we approach the complete appropriation of truth we can see our earlier false consciousness as a necessary moment of estrangement in our progress. These Hegelian concepts have been immensely influential; they are, however, inherently unstable. For they try to combine the possibility of seeing the world as a totally rational system with the possibility of seeing the world as the realm of the contingent and arbitrary where the individual has no guide. Yet to try to envisage both possibilities at once is to destroy the possibility of either. If we try to conceive the universe as a total rational system of which we ourselves are but a finite part, and of which our view is necessarily a finite and partial one, then for that very reason we must abandon any claim to completeness and finality for our own philosophy. But in that case we have not grasped the system as a final whole, and so we have no ground for asserting that there is such a system or that the universe has such a character. If, on the other hand, we try to conceive of ourselves as alienated and estranged in the Hegelian sense, we can only make sense of these predicates if we can assign some sense to the notion of not being or no longer being alienated and estranged. Alienation and estrangement are defined in Hegelian terms as not being or having or knowing what one *could* be or have or know. It follows that estrangement and alienation *can* be overcome; they cannot be the necessarily final word. They can only be moments in a possible progress toward a rational and systematic overcoming of estrangement. Hence, if one embraces those Hegelian concepts which imply a denial of the possibility of systematic, rational knowledge of the universe, one is driven toward the affirmation of such a possibility, just as much as if one affirmed the Hegelian system one would be driven also to affirm that one could not as a finite being be in possession of it.

These Hegelian concepts are therefore unstable in that if one uses them to deny the possibility of rational systematic knowledge one is driven toward something like the Hegelian system by the use of the concepts; whereas if one uses the concepts of system seriously one is forced in the end either to abandon them or to escape, as Hegel does in the *Logic*, by denying the finite limitations of the systematizer as himself only part of the system. A claim to an absolute extra-historical point of view is forced upon the serious Hegelian. When Hegel in the *Logic* explains that the thoughts which he is expressing are the thoughts of God, he develops his own positions in a way that makes him appear as all that Kierkegaard would condemn; but when Kierkegaard makes men totally alien to the truth and to the divine (except by grasping them through nonrational choice) what he is developing is precisely the other side of the Hegelian dilemma. There is thus built into the thought of Kierkegaard and of those who inherit his concept a basic instability about the enterprise of system-building in the Hegelian manner.

In Kierkegaard himself this oscillation is already evident. He professedly abjures system but is in fact one of the most rigidly systematic of thinkers. In spite of his complaint against Hegel that for Hegel Christianity is allowed to say only what the Hegelian world will permit it to say, much the same is true of Kierkegaard himself. Kierkegaard presents Christianity in terms of his own philosophical views and thus becomes all that he wants to abjure. For he wishes to stress the irremovable quality not only of the moral but also of the intellectual offensiveness of Christianity; and he does this by showing that Christianity cannot be rationally justified. To be a Christian is not to have reached a conclusion but to have made a choice. But since all religions and moral belief equally lack ultimate rational justification (including the beliefs both of rival religions and of atheism), the groundlessness of Christianity is not distinctive. It merely belongs to it as a member of the class of religious and moral beliefs. If this claim is made good, it provides a rational answer to the skeptic who has assaulted Christian faith by demonstrating that it is groundless. Of course it is. What else could it be? Thus Kierkegaard's argument renders Christianity easier to believe in than it would otherwise be in an age of skepticism. His hostility to apologetics cannot prevent the objective effect of his writings being quite other than he willed. And this has in general been Kierkegaard's fate. He despised professors and academics; but his writings fell into their hands and were used for purposes quite other than he originally intended.

It is striking, however, that Kierkegaard did not merely fall prey to academic apologists, but also to academic secularizers. This too, however, is easily intelligible. On the one hand, Kierkegaard's own life may have consisted of the kind of religious self-

dramatization which Ibsen portrayed in *Brand*; but on
the other hand, Kierkegaard's type of religion reduces
the content of religion to a minimum, Christianity consists in inwardness; the knight of faith outwardly appears like a tax-collector. What difference does it
make to be a Christian, to be before God inwardly?
The bareness of Kierkegaard's response to this question allows for an easy secularization of his central
thesis.

### Kierkegaard's Analysis of Dread

One major difficulty in understanding what the content of Christianity is for Kierkegaard is that his psychological analysis is of inner states which are, so far
as they are comprehensible, secular. In *The Concept
of Dread*, for example, Kierkegaard's stated theme is
original sin; but he allows that original sin as a fact is
beyond explanation. What he offers is an intercon-
nected analysis of concepts such as freedom, genius,
fate, individuality, and above all dread. Dread enters
the argument from the outset. ("Dread" translates
*"Angst."* Unamuno translated this in French by *"ago-
nie,"* Sartre by *"angoisse."* The psychoanalytic use of
"anxiety" comes close to the meaning.) Before Adam
fell, he was innocent. But—"Innocence is ignorance."
Man in a state of innocence is not yet "determined as
spirit." (That is, he has not a characteristically human
awareness and intelligence.) He is undisturbed and
peaceful, except that—there is something else which
man might be. What is that something else? It does
not yet exist. It is nothing. But this nothing haunts man
and produces dread. Dread is not fear. Fear, so Kierkegaard asserts, always has a definite object. Dread,
by contrast, has no such object; its object is nothing,
"a nothing which is able only to alarm," a nothing
which is "freedom's appearance before itself as a possibility." Kierkegaard describes the object of dread yet
again as "something which is nothing."

So far we have a dramatically convincing description of a recognizable state of mind. But how does Kierkegaard use this to throw light upon his professed theme of original sin? Kierkegaard asserts that when he speaks of original sin, he is not speaking merely of Adam but of the entire human race. He asserts, indeed, that "man is an individual and as such is at once himself and the whole race. . . ." But then it at once occurs to us to ask, must each individual fall? Is sin the only alternative to innocence? Can we not discard our ignorance and remain good? Kierkegaard, who treats very patiently all kinds of abstruse problems about original sin, is completely impatient with these plain questions. Of one such, the question "what would have happened in case Adam had not sinned?" he remarks, "To the innocent man it never can occur to ask such a question, but the guilty man sins when he asks it; for with his aesthetic curiosity he would like to obscure the fact that he himself has brought guilt into the world, has himself lost innocence by guilt." Kierkegaard was presumably ignorant of the fact that he would have to count John Calvin among the aesthetically curious, since Calvin is prepared to speak seriously of what would have happened "*si Adam integer stetisset*" (if Adam had remained whole). The contrast with Calvin serves only to bring out how far Kierkegaard is prepared to go in avoiding awkward questions by treating them as signs not of doubt but of rebellion, not of problems but of sins. This procedure means that so far as the specifically religious content of the notions of sin and dread is concerned we come up against a blank wall of unintelligibility. What remains is an analysis of dread as an inseparable part of the human condition. What are we to make of this analysis?

The difficulty lies in the way in which Kierkegaard moves from treating dread as a highly specific emotion to treating it as something very general indeed. Sometimes dread is sharply contrasted with all other emotions; sometimes all other emotions are in danger of turning out to be forms of dread. When it is the

burdensomeness of dread that is to be emphasized, the
former is the case; when the omnipresence of dread is
to be emphasized, the latter. So we are most implau-
sibly informed by Kierkegaard that in children dread
is found in the form of "a seeking after adventure, a
thirst for the prodigious, the mysterious." The reasons
why dread has to be omnipresent are perhaps two-
fold. First of all, Kierkegaard wishes to establish a
necessary connection between certain very central
features of human life and dread. Freedom and possibility necessarily involve dread, and freedom and
possibility are necessary features of human existence.
We thus find Kierkegaard establishing an *a priori*
framework within which all the actual experiences of
human beings have to be accommodated. There is
nothing disreputable about this enterprise as such; it
is simply that the Kierkegaardian framework is an un-
comfortably and misleadingly constricting one.

We can bring out part of what Kierkegaard is doing
by contrasting his view with that of Hume: "when a
man is in a cheerful disposition, he is fit for business,
or company, or entertainment of any kind; and he
naturally applies himself to these and thinks not of religion. When melancholy and dejected, he has nothing
to do but brood upon the terrors of the invisible world,
and to plunge himself still deeper in affliction." Hume,
like Kierkegaard, connects religion with apprehension.
But whereas Hume wants therefore to connect religion with one particular frame of mind, Kierkegaard
wants to show the pervasiveness of this frame of mind.
That cheerful concern with the affairs of this world
which for Hume constitutes the happy norm is for
Kierkegaard a desperate attempt by men to conceal
their dread from themselves. It is a mask, a disguise,
an escape.

How could we settle the issue between Kierkegaard
and Hume? It is certainly not a straightforward empirical matter. What we would need is a firm criterion
for distinguishing between psychological realities on
the one hand and mere rationalization, pretenses, and

disguises on the other. And this requires a conceptual investigation which has never yet been carried through satisfactorily. It is the lack of such an investigation rather than any clearly established criteria which leaves us in doubt over Kierkegaard's conceptual psychology. Kierkegaard hovers uneasily between an *a priori* elucidation of the concepts necessary to characterize our inner experiences and a transcript of his own private experience. The weakness of his account is that we do not get enough of either. His personal life limited absurdly his sense of the possibilities that were open; Kierkegaard is deeply ignorant of most of human life. His wish to speak of humanity as such forces an air of abstraction on to what could have been a moving personal recital; it is no accident that his *Journals* are often more illuminating than his published works. But if Kierkegaard is almost lost between the Scylla of autobiography and the Charybdis of *a priori* generalization, here also he gathers some of his force. For he does present a narrative which is both dramatic and yet concerns "Everyman." He does at least suggest both an intensity of purpose and a gift of psychological insight, especially when he deals with particular examples. Kierkegaard, as I have argued, is ambiguous in his attitude toward systematic thought. His attention to the individual case rescues him from a possible vulgarity into which some of his followers at once fall. It is therefore worthwhile to examine in turn the vulgarization and the genuine use of Kierkegaardian themes. A prime example of the latter is Heidegger; to view the former we have only to turn to Karl Jaspers.

### Jaspers' Use of Kierkegaard

If the concepts which Kierkegaard used to attack metaphysical system-building in the end betrayed him into the vices which he sought to exterminate, at least he was the unwitting victim of his own, or rather of Hegel's, concepts. But with Karl Jaspers (1883–    )

Kierkegaard's concepts are quite consciously put to
the service of enterprises alien to Kierkegaard. For
Jaspers' interest in Kierkegaard arose out of trying to
solve problems of a kind with which Kierkegaard was
never concerned. Jaspers was a practitioner of psychological medicine who in classifying psychiatric dis-
orders began to connect them with fundamental
attitudes to life and who became simultaneously dissatisfied with what he took to be contemporary philosophy's view of such attitudes—and also with what
he took to be the scientific psychologist's attitude to
mental disorder, and to normal personality. He saw
philosophy as concerned to give an objective account
of the universe, preoccupied with the vindication of
the rationality of this or that *Weltanschauung* as
against all others, and therefore committed to the view
that all questions can be settled at the bar of pure
reason. He saw psychology as concerned to give a
wholly determinist, causal account of the origin of
different types of personality, whether normal or dis-
ordered. Both these accounts share one and the same
omission and both require the same Kierkegaardian
corrective. What both omit is fundamental choice. We
have to choose between different world-views and reason will not make the choice for us. Moreover, the
study of a man's personality as it actually is, which is
all that scientific psychiatry can view, omits what else
that man could have become and omits also the fundamental choices which actualized one possibility for
that man as against others. Jaspers therefore envisages
behind the empirical self a true self whose situation is
essentially Kierkegaardian. This authentic self is revealed to us in what Jaspers calls boundary-situations,
moments of dread, of guilt, of awareness of death.
For these moments force upon us consciousness of the
necessity of choice. So far the development is not too
unlike Kierkegaard's own. But from this point it is not
just that Kierkegaard's thought is put to new uses. It
is rather that while verbal tributes are still paid

to Kierkegaard, everything that Kierkegaard hated
returns.

For Jaspers' attitude to both science and rationalist
metaphysics is really quite different from that of Kierkegaard. Kierkegaard's genuine mistrust of system
leads him to see all thought as necessarily fragmen-
tary and incomplete. Jaspers believes that philosophy
can be an attempt to grasp being as such, "the comprehensive." While he nominally adjures "system," he
does not mind being called systematic. Positivism is
mistaken because it thinks that natural science is all-
inclusive. Idealism makes equally totalitarian claims
for the sphere of *Geist*. But if each will only concede
that its own view is merely part of the truth then there
is room for all in a wider synthesis. No philosophical
view is false unless it claims to be final and exclusive.
At this point, where Kierkegaard placed arbitrary, criterionless choice, Jaspers reintroduces the concept of
an objective transcendent reality with which the
whole history of philosophy is concerned. What does
Jaspers have to say of this reality? The dominant criterion for what to say appears to be the consensus
among other philosophers—but certainly not all other
philosophers. His is a highly selective view of the history of philosophy. By now Kierkegaard is quite left
behind. The "authentic self" is not defined by its acts
of choice; its task is to interpret the signs of a reality
beyond the merely empirical. Two of the key terms
here are "communication" and "transcendence"; the
former indicates an awareness of there being other
people, the latter appears to be a pseudonym for God.
Jaspers himself is a Protestant, but his characterization
of the transcendent is general enough to be ambiguous
between Platonism, Judaism, and Christianity. Yet at
this point it must be confessed that any account of
Jaspers which is lucid is for that very reason necessarily unfaithful. A great deal of Jaspers' thought cannot
be reduced to the kind of religiose platitude to which
I have reduced it because it is written in a high-flown
German that resists decoding altogether. Moreover,

Jaspers explicitly believes that philosophy must finally
express itself in antinomies, in the opposing contrasts
of rival views. He admires Nietzsche precisely for the
contradictory qualities of Nietzsche's thought. Like
other existentialist philosophers, he is extremely neg-
lectful of the formal aspects of thought (Kierkegaard
himself was to a limited extent an exception here; he
was a keen student of Trendelenburg's version of Aristotelian logic) and so does not recognize that to admit contradiction into a system is to license any kind
of utterance at all. It is perhaps partly for these reasons that Jaspers' cultural solutions are so empty of
content. He sees a mediocre, scientistic frame of mind
overwhelming the West; the solution is a spiritual aristocracy that has assimilated inwardly the truths which
the external social world has rejected. But what is the
content of *this* inwardness? Kierkegaard's hidden faith
loses all its particularity. Even with Kierkegaard it is
diffiult to grasp what the sense of being before God
consists in. But to try to secularize and to generalize
this sense is to see it evaporate. In Kierkegaard we
may suspect a final lack of content in the solution,
particularly if we are not ourselves Christians; in Jaspers the lack of content is there for all to see.

## Heidegger's Debt to Phenomenology

If Jaspers vulgarizes Kierkegaard, Heidegger makes
a genuine use of him. But since Kierkegaard is only
one of Heidegger's sources, we cannot begin here.
We can begin only with Heidegger's critique of Husserl's phenomenology. The roots of phenomenology
are in the work of Franz Brentano (1838–1916).
Brentano was a critic of the associationist psychology
which derived from the British empiricists and more
particularly of the view that mental life consists of
mechanically associated individual entities (Lockean
ideas, Humean impressions and ideas). For Locke or
Hume an assertion is a conjunction of ideas, an emotion is an inner occurrence ("Passions are original

existences," wrote Hume), willing is an internal impression. For Brentano this omits the crucial constitu-
ent of mental life, its intentionality. Judging is judging
that such-and-such. It is taking up an attitude toward
an idea. Ideas are always themselves ideas of something. Feelings are feelings toward something. That
something Brentano calls "the intentional object," borrowing the scholastic word "*intentio.*" Brentano's way
of putting the matter suggests that he is accepting the
empiricists' characterization of the mental world, but
both adding to their catalogue of items (ideas are not
the only ultimate constituents of mental life, there are
also judgments) and extending their view of the properties of ideas. But in fact the ascription of intentionality to mental states marks a far more radical breach
with the traditional empiricist position.

Beliefs, emotions, desires are not just inner happenings which occur or do not occur. They have objects
and they are part of an intelligible sequence in which
the connections are not those of constant conjunction,
but those of rules and concepts, reasons, and purposes.
("What led you to believe that?" "Why are you angry
with him?" and "What do you want that for?" do not
require causal answers.) Although beliefs, emotions,
and desires need very different kinds of conceptual
elucidations, it is common to all of them that they are
directed upon objects which may but need not exist,
that they are partially defined by an internal use of
names and descriptions. The belief may be about
something which I wrongly suppose to exist, the emotion concern an event about which I have been mis-
informed, the desire rest on a mistaken belief about
the character of the object. But in each case, in order
for the belief to count as a belief, the emotion as an
emotion, the desire as a desire, something must be
envisaged as an object, and this is what Brentano
meant by an "intentional object." (There is no connection with the ordinary English use of "intentional.")

Brentano's central concern was to investigate the

character of judging, believing, and the like. He was thus in fact engaged upon conceptual investigations, and later phenomenological writing often comes close to the methods of conceptual analysis used by such philosophers as Wittgenstein and Ryle. But Brentano's second theme separates phenomenology from all conceptual analysis. For Wittgenstein and Ryle are both essentially anti-Cartesian philosophers, while Brentano wishes to give a peculiarly Cartesian primacy to the contents of inner consciousness: here we have clarity and certainty, *Evidenz*. Thus, we may be in doubt as to our judgment about the external world, but we can be in no doubt when judging of our own inner selves.

Edmund Husserl (1858–1938) developed both of Brentano's main themes. In his early writings he argued against psychologism in mathematics; in his later he developed a fully fledged account of the "science of essences." Husserl's logical investigations go beyond Brentano both in rigor and in generality. But he retains both of Brentano's central positions, and the appeal to *Evidenz* has its heir in the "transcendental phenomenology" of Husserl's last years. For the earlier Husserl phenomenology does not commit itself to existential assertion. It elucidates essences, not existences; concepts, not objects. It says what anything would have to be like if it were to be of such-and-such a kind, but as to whether there are any beings of this kind it remains uncommitted. For the later Husserl there is an attempt to say what consciousness must be if its intentional acts and objects are what they are. There is an attempt at a new start on the path upon which Descartes set out with the *Cogito*. Husserl's earlier phenomenology had already led him to the doctrine that it is of the essence of objects to be objects "for" consciousness, to be correlative to states of mind. He came to view all that was not immediate experience as constituted by the meanings which are the intentional objects of consciousness. And so, while Brentano's doctrine of intentionality was extremely antisolipsistic, the Husserlian version is increasingly a solipsistic, or at least a Kantian one, in which consciousness somehow makes the perceived world.

This highly inadequate and distorted account of Brentano and Husserl is a necessary prelude to any discussion of Heidegger, both because of what Heidegger accepted from and what he criticized in Husserl. Heidegger begins by trying to go behind the questions posed by Husserl and Descartes. They had asked: "How can consciousness come to know a world outside consciousness?" Husserl had behaved as if it was clear that the investigation of conscious states of mind was one thing, the investigation of consciousness-in-the-world another. But whence this dualism? What makes us dualists? What is the "I" which poses the question "What can I know?" and what must be true of it for it to be able to pose this question? On Heidegger's view, although Descartes claims to be making a new start and Husserl claims that phenomenology is presuppositionless, both men take for granted their dualism of mind and matter, consciousness and the world, from the outset, rather than discover it. Heidegger's own attempt to start genuinely at the beginning with what is authentically primitive leads him to coin a new philosophical vocabulary, and to claim that this vocabulary is uninfected by earlier theorizing. Thus when Heidegger names the "I" which asks the Cartesian question he names it in its most primitive mode of being-in-the-world, "*Dasein*," literally "being there." What is the mode of being-in-the-world? It is a general movement toward things, reaching out after objects. Intentionality characterizes all awareness. But the mode of grasping the world which is knowledge is less basic than a more generalized grasping after things, in which we gradually build up concepts. After *Dasein*, human existence, comes the concept of things which are grasped as having a use, as tools, as instruments, the things which lie to hand. Then we come across things which resist use, which cannot serve our purposes. Thus we build up our categories.

Two philosophical traditions thus have to be disowned and not just one; not only is it wrong to start with consciousness and reach out to the world, but it is also wrong to try and capture the primitive reality of *Dasein* through the derivative concepts which we apply to the world of things, such as the concepts of cause and substance. We grasp *Dasein* as being-in-the-world or not at all. But is this victory over Cartesian dualism more than verbal? The great difficulty with Heidegger's *Sein und Zeit* (which is a far better book than those who have not read it generally allow) is that the perhaps warranted apprehension of traditional philosophical terminology is too often used to permit the invention of a new word (often a compound of hyphenated monosyllables, which thus gives an impression at once of the sophistication of the metaphysician and of the childlike simplicities of the nursery) to be a substitute for a solution to an old problem. But what then, to take up Heidegger's key word, is *Dasein*? Here Heidegger brings in his reading of Kierkegaard, and also of other Christian writers, especially of Augustine.

### The Analysis of Dasein in Sein und Zeit

"*Dasein* ist sorge." *Dasein* is care, concern. (*Sorge* is a translation of the Latin *Cura*.) It is being-concerned-with. But what characterizes our concern is our finitude and the way in which our being is consumed in the moment-to-moment passage of time. We do not exist only for the present moment, however. Human existence is open toward the future. We confront possibility and we are filled with *Angst*. Here Heidegger follows closely Kierkegaard's analysis of dread. I can only avoid *Angst* by retreating to the less than human anonymity of "the One" (Heidegger's coinage from the ordinary use of "one does . . ." in place of "I do . . ." to express impersonality), by attending not to my own existence in its future reality but by envisaging myself as a unit along with other units. I can only overcome *Angst* by facing my existence in its totality, and for human existence that is to face the fact of my own death as the limit of possibility. Both conscience and guilt play their part here, for conscience informs me of what I might be and guilt of what I might have been. I cannot escape an inauthentic, harassed, and consumed existence except by continually living as one who knows that he is going to die. I am therefore confronted with a decision between the inauthentic existence of "the One" and authentic existence. Heidegger's account of *Dasein* is thus a blend of *The Concept of Dread* and *Either/Or*. We are no longer faced with choice as the key to truth; we are faced with a systematic and argued ontology—or at least with the prologue to such an ontology—in which choice has its place. The ontology is that of *The Concept of Dread*—without God. It is not that Heidegger explicitly denies that God exists. It is just that God is absent. Heidegger himself has indignantly repudiated the suggestion that he is an atheist. Nonetheless, all the concepts taken from Augustine and Kierkegaard are secularized, and with that secularization Heidegger frees himself from the problems created by Kierkegaard's theology. What he cannot free himself from, however, are the problems which he inherits from both Husserl and Kierkegaard.

The first of these is the solitariness of Heidegger's human being. The existence of other people in my world is certainly admitted; but it is not allowed to touch the concept of *Dasein*. Yet crucially human existence is social. We learn about ourselves from the mirror-image afforded by other people. We enter upon the use of a language which we did not invent but have to learn. Heidegger's own theory of language is not inconsistent with this; he stresses the context of mutual understanding in which a silence can be as meaningful as a spoken word. But nothing about the relationship to other individuals enters into the difference between authentic and inauthentic existence. And this makes it very difficult to understand what the content of authentic existence is. The concept is empty in the way in which Kierkegaard's concept of inwardness is empty. And the combination of the passionate enjoinder to choose authentic existence with the emptiness of that notion ought to make us ready for any sort of conduct from the Heideggerian which is at least chosen and involves brooding upon death. We should not be surprised that Heidegger was for a short period a Nazi, not because anything in *Sein und Zeit* entails National Socialism but because nothing in *Sein und Zeit* could give one a standpoint from which to criticize it or any other irrationalism.

Secondly, the concept of the logically and anthropologically primitive notion is as laden with philosophical assumptions as Husserl's dualism is. The primacy which Brentano awarded to inner perception is the ancestor of the primacy which Heidegger awards to *Dasein*. Heidegger never makes it clear why some concepts should be primary and others secondary and derivative. If he is claiming that the primary concepts are those that we do (as children, or as members of primitive societies) in fact acquire first, he appears to be simply wrong on points of fact. If he is claiming that his primary concepts *must* be acquired first, not only is his claim odd in the light of the facts (for how can what does not happen be necessary?) but he provides no arguments for his claim. Indeed, *Sein und Zeit* contains relatively few arguments.

What is worse is of course that Heidegger's account of human life, where it is not vacuous, is transparently false. Kierkegaard already had generalized the notion of dread into something difficult to pin down; Heideggerian *Angst* escapes altogether. And had Heidegger not been put by Sartre to quite new uses Heidegger's importance would not be what it is. To Sartre, therefore, we must now turn. But in order to understand Sartre we must place him in the total history which we are recounting.

## Sartrian Ontology

Jean-Paul Sartre was educated in the dull backwaters of Brunschvigian idealism and Bergsonian preoccupations which marked French academic philosophy so badly between the wars. His own successive readings of Heidegger and Hegel, together with the influence of such phenomenological writers as Merleau-Ponty, provided him with the materials for a series of episodes in each of which Sartre reissues an earlier existentialist theme, but in such a new context as to transform it. From Heidegger he takes his basic ontology. The world is divided into two species of being, "*être-en-soi*" (literally, "being-in-itself") and "*être-pour-soi*" (literally, "being-for-itself"). The former is the being of things, the latter that of people. Things simply are; they are complete in themselves. Human beings are incomplete; they are open toward the future, an as yet unmade future. The emptiness of this future has to be filled by the choices of the agent. Confronting the emptiness of his future the agent feels not only Heideggerian anxieties but elementary nausea. But the difference from Heidegger is profounder than this.

In Sartre's first novel, *La Nausée*, the protagonist, Antoine Roquentin, confronts the total meaninglessness of existence. This meaninglessness consists in the fact that things just are; they have no sufficient reason for being as they are. They are contingent. They are absurd. If we try to make sense out of existence we necessarily falsify. We tell stories about the past which impose a coherence that never could have existed. Is there, then, no way to lend life meaning and coherence (and with it perhaps dignity)? We can try to escape the meaninglessness of our lives like the bourgeois notables whose portraits Roquentin sees in the local galleries. They falsify human existence by pretending that it is solid and determinate, a matter of filling pre-existing roles, a matter of existence merely filling out an already determined essence. But the essence of man does not preexist his existence. Existence precedes essence. Is there, then, any way of escaping despair and nausea on the one hand or falsification upon the other? In *La Nausée* only one hint is given. Perhaps a work of art, a song or a book, may exist as geometrical forms exist, free from contingency. No clear sense is assigned to this possibility, and for an amplification of what Sartre might mean we have to turn to *L'Être et Le Néant*. Here it becomes clear that the lack of meaning in life is connected with Sartre's atheism.

The notion of God is self-contradictory, the notion of a being who is an impossible blend of being-in-itself and being-for-itself. As one who makes choices and decisions, God must exist "for-himself"; as one who is complete and self-sufficient, God must exist "in-himself." He must have the freedom of a person and the fullness of a thing. This is a criticism of the concept of God which is very much to the point. It can easily be extracted from Sartre's terminology and posed as the old problem about predestination: how can the traditional concept of God avoid the charge that for God it is necessary that some things shall not yet have been decided and yet that for God it is necessary that everything is already decided? But Sartre is not interested solely in establishing the truth of atheism. He wishes, rather, to show that the concept of God embodies an impossible ideal of self-sufficiency and meaningfulness against which we measure human life and find it contingent and meaningless. Human life has to be without a sufficient reason, because God is impossible. God is what man uselessly and hopelessly aspires to be.

The essential content of human nature for Sartre, then, is that it is an as yet undetermined project. It is open toward the future. It is the form of intentionality which has to be filled out with content. Sartre has in fact made the advance which Husserl attempted by cumbrous and Kantian arguments, but he has done it by simple assertion. Husserl wished to pass from analyzing the intentional form of consciousness to saying how consciousness was, or must be, in actuality. Sartre asserts that the intentional form is precisely what consciousness is. He uses this starting point to criticize both physiological and Freudian theories of emotion. Since emotions are intentional we must explain them by bringing into the picture their intentional objects. We must explain them as directed toward something which is an object of consciousness. What we cannot do is to bring into our explanation either antecedent physiological conditions or unconscious memories and motives, for they do not belong to the realm of consciousness as emotions do.

Man, as Sartre pictures him, is then absolutely undetermined by his physiological constitution. Actions cannot have causes but are the outcome of undetermined choices. There are regularities in human behavior, because a great deal of human behavior consists in living out routines and roles which, like the bourgeois worthies in *La Nausée*, we treat as if they were predetermined grooves along which we had to run. We behave as if we were determined; we present our choices as if they were unavoidable. In so doing we seek to deceive both ourselves and others. We are guilty of bad faith. The omnipresence of bad faith haunts Sartre's world. The waiter in the café, going about his job, is acting a part—the part of a waiter. The girl who refuses to admit to herself her would-be seducer's intentions and treats what she does as a series of happenings, not a series of actions, in which each episode follows the next without any responsibility on her part—she too is offered as a paradigm case of bad faith. So widespread is bad faith that it is difficult to understand the content of the concept of the *"acte gratuit,"* the action not in bad faith. Indeed, in Sartre's series of novels *L'Age de Raison* the first protagonist, Mathieu, pursues with desperate ambiguity the possibility of an act that can truly be his own; when he dies in a hopeless last stand against the Germans in 1940, it is left unclear whether he

achieved it. And this ambiguity in the novel seems to
be a necessary consequence of the ambiguity of the
concept. For on the one hand Sartre appears to treat
bad faith as a purely contingent feature of human
life which could be abolished; indeed, he urges us
to turn from it. But his association of the concept with
that of living out any socially recognized or recognizable role almost turns it into a necessary feature of
human life. And this is entirely coherent with the doctrines of *La Nausée*; if the reality of human existence
is to be meaningless, discontinuous, and incoherent,
then any coherent way of life or action is necessarily
a falsification. If, confronting the reality, we are necessarily to be overcome with anxiety and nausea, the
retreat into falsification will become a central and
characteristic feature of human life. Sartre's problem is
that he is unwilling just to accept this. He wants to
save us from it. The pattern of salvation appears very
slowly in his writings and when it does appear it is
a fascinating combination of Hegel and Kierkegaard.

## Sartre's Picture of Human Relationships

Hegel first appears on the scene as providing a model
for human relationship. Sartre takes with great seriousness Hegel's remark in the *Phenomenology of Mind*
that "Self-consciousness exists in itself and for itself,
in so far as and by virtue of the fact that it exists for
another self-consciousness; that is, it *is* only by being
acknowledged or recognized." He thus breaks with
the solitariness of Heideggerian man. Moreover, he
takes from Hegel the dialectic of master and serf in
the same portion of the *Phenomenology* and uses it to
construct a psychology in which love between people
is always deformed into mastering or being mastered.
He is able to do this because he sees an ultimate distinction between my being a subject (what I necessarily am for myself) and my being an object (what
I necessarily am for others). Sartre has a fascinating
phenomenological analysis of what it is to be turned

into an object by being looked at. If, therefore, I make someone else an object of my regard, I necessarily treat him as something that is now an object for me; in so doing I impose myself on him. I manifest not love but sadism. If, to correct this, I try to make myself an object of the other's regard I equally destroy the possibility of love, for now I substitute masochism. Imprisoned within the cycle of sadism and masochism, what way out can there be? Sartre offers a hint of a possibility of a way out, but in *L'Être et Le Néant* he never specifies what it would be like. It remains as contentless as Kierkegaardian salvation. Or at least it only acquires content when Sartre turns to ethics and sociology.

In *L'Être et Le Néant* what is said of human freedom is ambiguous. Freedom is a burden. "We are condemned to be free." During his time in a German prison camp after 1940 and later in the French Resistance, Sartre decided with immense seriousness to become a writer on behalf of democracy. A major preoccupation from then on is his attempt to link the freedom inherent in human nature with political freedom. In a short essay after the war (*L'Existentialisme est un Humanisme*) Sartre argued that all moral principles rested upon the individual's choice; there are no objective grounds for morality. If I treat some consideration as morally cogent, it is because I have chosen to consider it cogent. There are no criteria governing such choices, and there can be none; for our fundamental choices are choices of criteria. Believers in objectivist theories of morals are yet another example of men in bad faith; they wish to shift the responsibility for decisions that are in fact their own on to someone or something else. Nonetheless, if I choose I choose as one who seeks to legislate not for himself as this particular individual but for himself as any man. I bring myself under some universal principle which I have chosen. In so doing I have to regard myself as legislator for all, and I have to limit the exercise of my own choice to those forms of action in which I do not infringe upon the freedom of others to choose similarly. The universal form of the moral choice determines a content for morality: respect the freedom of everybody. This conjuring of moral content out of moral form is of course more than merely reminiscent of Kant; and it invites all the criticisms to which the Kantian thesis has been subjected. Even if it be the case that any moral judgments, perhaps in order to qualify as moral, must always be of the impersonal form "Anyone in these circumstances ought . . . ," why does it follow that my judgments must have such a content that they enjoin respect for the freedom of all? "One ought always to respect the freedom of the propertied classes, even at the cost of the freedom of other classes" is a perfectly consistent and intelligible judgment which has in fact been advanced by many political theorists. The democratic ideal cannot be made to follow from the existentialist premises.

Sartre continues to remain obscure on this point in his later writings. But he provides a much more explicit account both of what we are to be saved from and of how we are to save ourselves. This account is rooted in Sartre's newly self-proclaimed Marxism, a Marxism surprising to those who remembered the immediate post-war philosophical debates between Sartre and orthodox Marxists. The Sartre of 1946 presents men as exempt from all causal determination, as unconditionally and limitlessly free in their choices. Pierre Naville as a Marxist accused Sartre of trying to separate men from nature altogether and of "a contempt for things." Lukacs argued that Sartre's concept of freedom portrayed not a necessary and essential characteristic of human nature but rather the contemporary indecision of the rootless bourgeois intellectual. Sartre's political agreement with the French Communist Party on many issues never exempted him from philosophical polemic. When, therefore, Sartre calls himself a Marxist, how far is he guilty of a *volte-face*? Only at the most superficial level. The Sartrian individual who is compelled to choose is a secularized version of Kierkegaard's individual, who is in turn perhaps Hegel's unhappy consciousness lifted outside the dialectic of history. Moreover, when the Sartrian individual enters into relationship with others, the patterns of his relationship are drawn, as I already noticed, from Hegel's account of the alienation of the unhappy consciousness. But the concept of alienation is difficult and probably impossible to use without implying something like its Hegelian context. The predicament of Sartrian man is often presented as the necessary predicament of all human nature; but Sartre's descriptions slide all too easily into those of contingent features of one form of human life, features which can be removed. So Sartre in the *Critique de la Raison Dialectique* presents a set of formulations in which bad faith and bad human relationships in general belong to the life of class-divided, and especially of capitalist, society.

The key expression, however, in describing our condition is no longer "bad faith"; it is "serialization." We are serialized by the routines and rigidities of our society: the perfect example of serialization is the member of a queue, who envisaged as such is only a unit in a series. Serialization will be overcome by a group which through its disciplined unity (bound together by a commitment to a rule the infringement of which carries the penalty of death) will break into a new form of society. Sartre's political science-fiction in the *Critique* scarcely deserves notice; what is of real interest is the attempt to construct a sociology which takes seriously the notions of freedom and activity as theoretical concepts. What attracts Sartre in Marx is precisely the notion that "Man makes his own history, but. . . ." What distresses him in later Marxism is the mechanical use of economic determinism. But his sociology suffers immensely from a lack of patience with facts, and there are only two aspects of it to which we need to attend closely.

The first is Sartre's general claim that existentialism

and Marxism are complementary, not opposed. In the
form in which Sartre makes it this claim is dubious, for
all he wants to do is to make existentialism a reminder
of the particularity, the contingency, and the power
of choice annexed to individual human existence to
the Marxist who will otherwise be too *a priori*, too in-
flexible, too determinist. But since Sartre never grap-
ples properly with either the conceptual or the factual
points at issue in controversies over determinism, it
is difficult to assess the value of what he says. He jeers
at attempts to reduce Flaubert to a social product of
the Second Empire, but he does not say at anything
like sufficient length what a renovated Sartrian Marxist would say about Flaubert. Moreover, he never
separates out clearly what most needs distinguishing
in his work, the conceptual and the empirical. The
early Sartre ascribed to human existence as such, a
freedom and a contingency whose almost unavoidable
consequence was bad faith. But although bad faith
appears not to be inevitable, Sartre never appears to
base his claims as to how widespread bad faith is upon
empirical generalization. The later Sartre ascribes our
fate of serialization to contingent features of human
existence which belong to bourgeois society, not to
man as such. But once again he appears not to derive
his assertions from empirical generalizations but rather
from conceptual considerations. In both earlier and
later writings Sartre's plethora of lengthy examples
suffers because he does not analyze with sufficient
clarity the concepts which he is allegedly illustrating.
The clue to the difficulty here perhaps lies in his novels and plays. His examples often tend toward small-
scale works of imagination, and it may be that the
philosophical arguments are better treated as elucidations of points in the novel and plays rather than *vice
versa*. The examples would then appear as the core of
the philosophical writings; and this would exemplify a
constant existentialist theme, that of concreteness as
opposed to abstraction. In France, at least, existentialism has above all informed a literary imagination and

enjoyed a literary vogue. Not only Sartre is in point here but also Camus and Marcel.

## The Vulgarizers: Camus and Marcel

Why should I not commit suicide? Camus' philosophical essay, *The Myth of Sisyphus*, begins with this question and with the claim that this is the most central of all philosophical questions. But any claims that traditional philosophy might have either to assess this claim or to answer this question are disposed of very speedily. A few sentences from Aristotle are misread, the claims of traditional rationalism are disallowed, and characters are various as Don Juan, Kafka, and Dostoievski hold the stage. The essence of Camus' argument is simple; human life confronts an alien universe. The values of human life have no foothold. And therein lies its meaning. In giving way neither to falsely grounded hopes, nor to despair because such hopes are overthrown, we find the significance of human effort. We confront a world of the absurd, where contingency reigns, where there is no sufficient reason. And in the modern world the man who does this, who has been deprived of the false solaces of traditional rationalism, whether religious or antireligious, is the absurd man. He is among Dostoievski's characters, he is Kafka's hero, he is studied in Camus' novels. In fact, Camus' novels are far more interesting than his philosophical writings; but they exhibit just as clearly how the existentialist clothing of Camus' ideas is no more than clothing. The ideas themselves are old and familiar. For Camus is in fact an heir of the Enlightenment, an old-fashioned atheist, but an old-fashioned atheist who writes in a situation where theism can no longer be the main enemy because it was defeated too long ago. So he is preoccupied with old problems in a new setting: the nature of atheistic sanctity and virtue (*La Peste* and *La Chute*) and the dangers which arise from absolutizing and deifying the values of the rebellion against religion and tyranny since the Enlightenment (*L'Homme Revolté*).

If Camus is a conventional atheist behind his existentialist vocabulary, Gabriel Marcel is a conventional theist behind his. Marcel, in fact, would scarcely be counted an existentialist had he not been forced into controversy with Sartre's atheism. He was originally a disciple of Royce's personal idealism, and his phenomenological analyses of such states as hope and despair owe little to Husserl. Marcel's preoccupations have been similar to those of Karl Jaspers, although he has never constructed a system, for his philosophy is seriously antisystematic. Marcel distinguishes between what he calls problems and what he calls mysteries. Problems are characteristic of the natural sciences; they concern matters about which we can be objective, which are outside our personal existence. We can assemble all the data and we can offer a definitive solution. Mysteries are perplexities where we ourselves constitute part of the problem, where we cannot stand apart and be objective. There can be no definitive solutions here, and thus philosophy and religion, where a concern with mysteries is characteristic, are not problem-solving activities.

It is worth mentioning this aspect of Marcel at least because it focusses attention upon an assumption of much existentialist philosophy. It is often asserted by existentialists that problems which involve the character of human life or, more especially, which involve self-knowledge are problems where there can be no objective argument or discussion. This is perhaps partly due to a confusion between the problem of trying to be objective in arriving at self-knowledge (a real but not a philosophical problem) and that of trying to be objective in analyzing the concept of self-knowledge or speaking about self-knowledge (which is surely no special problem at all). But it is also perhaps due to the highly unsatisfactory way in which more orthodox philosophers discuss the problem. There is a real gap at this point in the philosophy of mind which the criticism of Cartesianism has done nothing to fill. And on the whole existentialists rush in where analytical philosophers fail to tread.

## Theological Existentialism

The relation of some theologians to existentialism is much closer than that of Camus or Marcel. If one begins with Kierkegaard himself, one is bound to pass at once to Karl Barth whose commentary on the *Epistle to the Romans* (1918) uses Kierkegaard's concept of fundamental choice and some of Kierkegaard's psychological analyses in order to elucidate St. Paul. Barth here marks a break not merely with the liberal neo-Kantian Protestant theology which he was explicitly attacking but even with the neo-Calvinism which he was avowedly defending. For Calvin, although he would have seen many decisions for the believer to make, would never have thought of decision as our way of coming to know the truth that God exists. When Barth makes all hang upon decision, however, he is at least faithful to traditional Protestant (and Catholic) orthodoxy in his description of the content of the Christian belief to which we have access by our decision. So far as he is a philosopher, Barth is an existentialist philosopher, but to characterize him as a philosopher at all is perhaps a mistake, since Barth derives the necessity of choice from the nature of Pauline Christianity, and although he uses philosophical arguments in the commentary upon *Romans*, he was later to express doubts about his own procedure in so doing. It is quite other with Rudolf Bultmann, who is a Heideggerian existentialist through and through.

Bultmann is a New Testament scholar who believes that the New Testament message stands in need of demythologizing. It is mythological because it presents an existential message, a message to do with *Dasein*, as though it were a cosmology. The prescientific cosmology of the New Testament is Gnostic in content: it pictures a three-story universe and man on the earth poised between God on the one hand and the powers of darkness on the other. This cosmology conceals what is essentially being said, which is that in the person of Jesus men are called upon to choose between authentic human existence in which the limits of our life are faced up to and, more particularly, our death is faced up to, and an inauthentic existence in which we are the prey of our own refusal to face up to *Angst* and *Sorge*. It is difficult to resist the suggestion that for Bultmann Jesus is an early and imperfect anticipator of Heidegger. Bultmann himself would deny this. He would argue that what makes his view distinctively Christian is the contention that we cannot make the transition from inauthentic to authentic existence by our own power. But about this it is clear that Bultmann believes that we can acquire the necessary power simply by a decisive choice. Therefore it is difficult to see what it is that Heidegger asserts we can do which Bultmann denies. At the very least it is clear that Bultmann is vulnerable to every criticism to which Heidegger is vulnerable, or at least to which the Heidegger of *Sein und Zeit* is vulnerable.

Bultmann is perhaps unique in the detail of his existentialist commitment. Many other theologies have plundered the existentialist vocabulary or have used distinctions or concepts which are characteristic of certain trends in existentialism. Particularly unfortunate is the kinship here between certain types of theology, especially perhaps that of Paul Tillich, and Heidegger's revival of ontology in his post-war writings. In those writings Heidegger passes from *Dasein* to *Sein;* he produces an aphoristic and enigmatic yet extended account of being, which while it is unique to him, uses concepts which are present in Sartre, in Kierkegaard, and elsewhere. It is thus perhaps better at this point to examine the themes of being and existence as they appear generally in existentialist writing in order to understand the roots of the confusion with which we are faced, and avoid being distracted overmuch by the details of particular existentialist expositions.

## Existentialist Themes
### BEING AND EXISTENCE

A. J. Ayer has castigated Sartre for the simple misuse of the verb "to be." It is quite true that Sartre, Heidegger, and others all use "being" and "nothing" as if they were the names of subjects which could have predicates ascribed to them. (The mistake is that of the Red King in Alice's world who thought that if nobody had passed the messenger on the road, nobody should have arrived first.) It is true also that they write as if being was a genus of which existence and non-existence were species. But it is untrue that these errors rest on simple confusion. They arise out of deep confusion. The basic existentialist confusion about existence arises perhaps from trying to say too many things at once. When the existentialist asserts that existence cannot be grasped in concepts, that it evades conceptualization, too often he puts the point rhetorically as Kierkegaard did: "What the philosophers say about Reality is often as disappointing as a sign you see in a shop window which reads: Pressing done Here. If you brought your clothes to be pressed, you would be fooled; for only the sign is for sale."[3] The point that philosophers deal in concepts, not in reality, is necessarily ambiguous. For "real" functions well as an adjective, but "reality" functions badly as a noun. When "real" is used significantly it is always in contrast to something else, and the force of "real" varies with what it is being contrasted with. In Madame Tussaud's one may look for a real policeman—rather than a waxwork model. In an argument one may ask whether an alleged exception to a rule is real—or only apparent. In looking at Van Meegeren's work one may ask how one can tell a real Vermeer from a forgery.

[3] *Either-Or*, Part I, "Diapsalmata."

But detach "real" from any such context and turn it
into a noun and one is left without any clear sense.
Among the meanings which existentialists appear to
have intended to give to the contention that reality
or existence cannot be fully conceptualized we can
pick out at least two.

The first is the thesis that human existence evades
conceptualization in a way that the existence of things
does not. What is meant by this is perhaps that our
characterizations of things are accurate or inaccurate,
true or false, adequate or inadequate; we match up
the description of the thing with the thing itself and
there is an end to it. But in the case of people, how
we characterize them, and the adequacy or otherwise
of our characterizations, depends in part on how they
characterize themselves. Moreover, the way in which
we describe a thing will not of itself change the thing,
but the way in which we describe people, if they become aware of it, may well change their behavior. The
well-known phenomena of self-confirming and self-
falsifying predictions are instances of this. That this
is what some existentialists are speaking of when they
speak of the impossibility of conceptualizing existence
is suggested by their stress on the role of consciousness
in human existence. But this is clearly not what Heidegger wishes us to attend to, for example, and the
difficulty lies in explaining what he wishes to attend
to without using his own language and so involving
ourselves in his confusions. But a rational reconstruction might run something like this.

Let us begin with a lucid, even if mistaken, analysis
of the concept of existence. Quine has argued that
"to be is to be the value of a variable." The suggestion
is that we are committed to asserting the existence of
whatever we are committed to assigning as a value to
a variable. The notion of existence is introduced after
we are already familiar with the notion of a language
containing variable expressions for individuals and for
predicates. Such a language, if we take the notion of a
variable seriously, must be a *formal* language. It there-

fore appears to follow from Quine's view that we can understand all that there is to understand about the notion of existence in terms which presuppose that anything that can be said can be formalized. This latter claim, even if true, has, however, to meet the difficulty that formalization is something that we do to and with statements and that we use alternative ways of formalizing statements in order to bring out different logical features of the structure of a given statement. What variables we are committed to, what values we are committed to assigning to them, will depend not just upon what we said in the initial statement (in some natural language) but also upon how we choose to formalize. And we have choices about formalization. There is no one single hidden logical form in a given statement which the logician only has to reveal. Michelangelo envisaged sculpture as chipping away the stone to reveal the form of the statue within; such a view of logical form seems to make the logician a Michelangelo. It follows from this that no one formalization of a given piece of discourse necessarily reveals the extent of our ontological commitments. And because we can never be sure that we have exhausted alternative possible ways of understanding we can never close the door on all further commitments. In other words, the question "What is there?" could never have a final answer.

It follows that no one way of talking (and one can include here with alternative modes of formalization, alternative ways of putting something in a natural language), nor even a number of different ways of talking, about a given subject-matter necessarily exhausts all that we want to say *is*. But it does not follow from this that *being* is a fish which the net of our concepts can never catch, that there *is* something which goes beyond everything our discourse and our concepts can identify, refer to, and characterize, namely existence itself. Because our language may always leave us with more to say it does not follow that there is something we can never say, something that lies beyond expression in conceptual form, something else which the word "existence" or the word "being" names. Yet just to this or to something akin to it most existentialist writers appear to wish to conclude. Sometimes, of course, they are merely making in dramatic form the familiar and correct point that "exists" is not a predicate in the sense that "is red" is a predicate. But whatever the starting point, or the logical force, of the consideration involved, the conclusion is the same, that over and above the existence of particular beings, there is something else, *being itself*.

Kierkegaard, Jaspers, Husserl, Heidegger, and Sartre all speak of being. In the case of Kierkegaard and of Sartre there is a reference back to Hegel's discussions. In the case of Husserl and Heidegger there is a reference back to the medieval scholastics as well. But in both these cases the use of "being" was controlled by a context which the existentialist writers remove. In Hegel's *Logic* the attempt is to set out those categories which are embedded in nature and spirit; the movement from one class of predicates to another is transformed into the self-movement of the absolute, and in the course of this transformation much nonsense gets talked along with some sense. But the original enterprise was not nonsensical or unintelligible. The medievals used and expounded Aristotle's treatment of being *qua* being in the *Metaphysics*, and Aristotle's treatment is at the opposite pole from any claim that being evades conceptualization. The Aristotelian account is an attempt to show the unity and the diversity of uses of the verb "to be." Just because being *qua* being is the most general of concepts it cannot be the name of a single elusive entity. The medieval use of Aristotle is complicated by the attempt to write into an Aristotelian schematism the Christian God. Every finite being exists in a particular mode, under particular limitations. God is not so particularized. Hence he is being without such modal limitations, and the scholastics referred both to this and to the Mosaic meaning of God as "I am that I am" when they spoke of God as *Esse Ipsum Subsistens* (subsistent being itself).

This scholastic willingness to speak of "esse" is entirely harmless so long as it is not detached from the Aristotelian (or earlier, the Platonic) framework in which it has a place. For we can assess the claims made about being in the light of the claims which we want to allow or disallow about the framework. But in the modern neo-Thomist revival Aquinas was turned upside down as radically as Marx inverted Hegel, but unintentionally. For being was now presented as an independent subject-matter, but not as it is in Aristotle's *Metaphysics* as the object of conceptual enquiry. Rather, "being" is treated as the name of a *particular* subject-matter, albeit a very queer one, about which we can ask specific questions. This is not yet true, of course, in the nineteenth century.

The sobriety of the Aristotelian scheme is not lost in Brentano or indeed in Husserl. Kierkegaard's central positions do not depend on any of his Hegelian uses of "being." But with Heidegger and to a lesser extent with Sartre, being comes into its own. In Heidegger's later writings the starting point is from the question posed by Leibniz: why are there the things that there are rather than nothing? In Leibniz the answer to this question was the cosmological argument for the existence of God. In Heidegger the answer is that in the posing of the question we have not taken seriously the relation between being and what it is contrasted with, nothing. Heidegger proceeds to speak of being and nothing as contrasted powers, as well as contrasted realms. He allows that we can only speak of nothing as a thing, as something, at the cost of being unscientific. He concludes that the philosopher and the poet are here in a superior position to the scientific man. Of being and nothing he says that they are not objects; that logic cannot comprehend but presupposes them; that they are things which we scarcely grasp. Nietzsche with almost prophetic anticipation of Heidegger spoke of these concepts as "the last cloudy streak of evaporating reality"; Heidegger quotes him and argues that this bears testimony to the extremely elusive properties of being and nothing. Every accusation as to the indeterminateness of the concept of being is treated as if it were evidence of the indeterminateness of being.

Heidegger distinguishes between *Sein* (being) and *die Seienden* (existents). He in fact treats both terms as if they are names of objects, in spite of all his denials. But this is not his basic mistake, which is to suppose that because an expression is used in some one context with a particular grammatical form it can be transferred without change or loss of sense to any context in the same grammatical form. To take the most simple kind of change, Heidegger takes to be equivalent the assertions "He is afraid of nothing in particular" and "What he is afraid of is nothing." It is not only Heidegger who speaks like this. Tillich does so also, and in Tillich's writings existentialist and scholastic terminology meet in a new way.

For Tillich God is not *a* being, but Being-Itself. The medieval scholastics who spoke like this did so because they had produced proofs of the divine existence of a kind which led them to contrast the divine being with contingent beings in specific ways. Their careful Aristotelianism also restricted them in their use of negatives with the verb "to be." Not so Tillich, who can speak of the power of being to resist non-being, in a manner very similar to that of Heidegger.

Tillich's relationship to Heidegger is in no sense accidental, not so much because of a direct indebtedness but because Tillich like Heidegger begins from and tries to go beyond a Husserlian concept of philosophy. He believes that in analyzing the structure of the categories of thought, as Husserl did, the philosopher is driven to recognize that these are the categories of a finite being, and to recognize further an unconditional ground behind that thought and its objects. Something not unlike the cosmological argument appears in Tillich, but just because Tillich does not present an argument he is all the more difficult to grapple with. The resemblance to Heidegger comes out when Tillich uses his ontological assertions in psychological contexts. The power of being to resist non-being and the fear of the encroachments of non-being upon being are used vividly by Tillich in describing neurotic anxiety. Kierkegaard's Nothing which is the object of our dread is only to be appeased and driven away by a secure hold on our existence. We can all imagine a rendering of this into psychiatric terms at once less dramatic and more susceptible of questions about truth, falsity, and testing. Heidegger, similarly, is at his most convincing in his psychology and at his most wayward in his ontology.

The culmination of this waywardness lies in the kind of dialogue which has been carried on between Heideggerian existentialists and the upholders of degenerate modern versions of scholasticism. The attempt to call Aquinas an existentialist is bad enough in itself; but debates about the character of being and not-being, the treatment of existence as a genus of which these two are species by existentialist writers, the disputes over the relative priority of essence and existence, mark a depth rarely reached in the history of philosophy, which has its counterpart in a systematic misreading of the history of philosophy. So, for example, a contemporary book of readings in metaphysics is able to suggest that there is a single question, "What is being?", to which Parmenides, Plato, Aristotle, and Descartes all give rival answers, Parmenides saying that it is One, Plato that "It is, through the Ideas, One and Many," Aristotle that "It is Substance, or that which *particularly* persists; and thus, both one and many," and Descartes that "It is Substance, but according to the modes of thought and extension."[4] The scholastic author is very easily able to then give Heidegger credit for giving yet another answer to the

---

[4] *A Modern Introduction to Metaphysics,* ed. by D. A. Drenner, New York, 1962, p. 333.

same question. But what matters is that there is no such question, posed just like that. Parmenides, Plato, Aristotle, and Descartes posed different questions and elaborated quite different types of conceptual schemes in each of which "being" or some cognate term or terms has a place. But there is no simple, identifiable use of "being" independent of linguistic or conceptual context which we can use to pose the question "What is being?" with a view to comparing rival answers.

Heidegger is not merely indebted to this version of the history of philosophy; he is himself an important and original contributor to it. To the criticisms of his perversions of language Heidegger's reply would be that he is certainly using language in ways that we are not used to, but this is not because he is an innovator but because he is trying to return to that primal simplicity of language in which alone the truth about being is laid bare. The only philosophical vocabulary pure enough for this task is that of the Greek pre-Socratics, and Heidegger sees this vocabulary as rooted in Homeric Greek. His method is to look for etymologies of the words which became "truth," "being," and the like and then to use his alleged etymological roots are prime evidence of what the word really means. Unfortunately he first mistranslates his authors and makes philological mistakes in his etymologies. But worse still, he never explains how etymologies could be clues to concepts. What Heidegger fails to grasp here is of the first importance.

The pre-Socratic Greek philosophers were not doing just one thing; they were grappling with attempts at physical theories, with religious cosmologies, and with conceptual puzzles. When Parmenides proves that change and multiplicity must be illusory, beginning from such premises as "What is is," he is making the first moves toward producing a logical grammar of the verb "to be." The groping with tenses, participles, and infinitives reflects an assiduous attempt to discover what you must commit yourself to if you are to say anything. Plato follows this up in dialogues such as the *Sophist*, where the problem of negative judgment is already treated in such a way as to enable us to dispose of all Heidegger's problems as to how we can speak of what is not. Heidegger insists upon treating pre-Platonic Greek writers not as making the earliest attempts at elucidations which Plato, Aristotle, and their successors could then use to improve upon, but as expressing final insights by means of definitive concepts. To do this he has to mistranslate at least one of Parmenides' uses of the verb "to be" and produce spurious etymologies for such expressions as "truth" and "to say."

What is unfortunate about these later writings of Heidegger is that they have helped to turn some contemporary Continental philosophy into a shared cult of ritual phrases rather than a serious conceptual enquiry. Heidegger's nonsense is harmful nonsense. But it is in fact not, strictly speaking, existentialist nonsense. Had *Sein und Zeit* remained Heidegger's testament, had we otherwise only Sartre's developments of Heidegger's thought and not Heidegger's own development of it, we would have had for criticism a much tougher and more interesting task. For the crucial *existentialist* thesis is not that existence is a realm beyond particular existents, but that existence, and especially human existence, is simply absurd. To this theme therefore we must now turn.

### THE ABSURD

"The Absurd" has been the preoccupation of French, rather than German, existentialism. When Sartre calls existence absurd he appears to combine two main contentions. The first is that things have no sufficient reason for being as they are and not otherwise. The second is that things are contingent and not necessary. We can begin by considering the latter. An Anglo-Saxon analytical philosopher might be inclined to argue as follows. That the existence of material ob-

jects, including people, is contingent, that "Such-and-
such an object exists" is always a contingent truth and
not a necessary one, is itself a necessary truth. To wish
that it were otherwise is therefore to wish that the
denial of a necessary truth could be asserted as true.
But the denial of a necessary truth expresses a logical
impossibility, and just as we cannot make sense of
that which is logically impossible, we cannot make
sense of wishing that what is logically impossible
should be so. For we cannot say what it is we would
be wishing for. This argument, however, contains two
important mistakes. The first is that it contains a very
crude notion of what it is for an expression to have
meaning or to make sense. Because an expression apparently denotes what it is logically impossible should
be the case or exist, it does not follow that the expression does not have meaning. Indeed, it is a condition
of our characterizing the expression as we do, it is a
condition of our detecting the logical impossibility involved, that we should understand its meaning. This
is true both in simple cases, like "round square," and
in complex cases like those where a mathematician
understands a formula as a preliminary to proving
that it cannot be a theorem of a system because it is internally inconsistent. Such a proof may be long and la-
borious, and at a stage when the mathematician does
not yet know whether the formula is or is not inconsistent he may well hope that it is consistent and can
be proved to be a theorem, because, if it can be, certain other mathematical and even physical possibilities will be opened up. When he discovers the inconsistency he may then lament that it is so, and we
should all understand him. So that there is nothing
nonsensical about lamenting that necessary truths are
what they are and not otherwise. Hence when Sartre
laments the contingency of things, so far he does not
violate sense. But to have shown this is not enough
to vindicate Sartre.

When the mathematician lamented his inconsistency
proof, the point of his lament was that were there not

inconsistencies, other possibilities would open up. But for these, we might understand the words which the mathematician used to lament, but we would not understand his lament. We would not know what he had to regret. We should understand what he said, but not what he did. How are we to understand what Sartre does when he laments contingency? What possibilities are closed to him which would otherwise be open? What was the point of writing *La Nausée* or the relevant parts of *L'Être et Le Néant*?

A reading of *La Nausée* suggests strongly that the contingency of things is lamentable precisely because they lack *therefore* a sufficient reason for being as they are. That this is so affects things and people differently. Things just *are* in all their nauseating fullness. They do not point beyond or outside themselves as do the contingent beings of Aquinas' "Third Way." Their being contingent is not a lack for them. Here there is nothing to lament. But with human existence the lack of a sufficient reason for oneself *and* for things being as they are means an imperfection, a Sartrian rendering of what Heidegger calls "fallenness." We are in a senseless world, of which we ceaselessly and inevitably try to make sense. This is the absurdity both of things and of ourselves. Can we make sense of lamenting the lack of a sufficient reason? Only if we suppose that if the universe were what Leibniz, or Hegel in his more rationalist metaphysical moods, said it was should we have possibilities opened to us which are now denied to us. But on Sartre's own showing, if Leibniz or Hegel were right we should cease to be free. Sartre of course speaks of us as condemned to freedom, so perhaps it is right to lament a state of affairs which entails our freedom. Yet at the same time Sartre clearly shows that all the possibilities of characteristically human life are bound up with the possession of freedom. So that about the Sartrian lament there is something false. What it is comes out very clearly if we compare the Sartrian picture of human nature in *La Nausée* with what Simone de Beauvoir says in her memoir about Sartre's life and attitudes at the time at which he was writing it. Sartre is there pictured as leading an eager, meaningful life, with many friends and projects. His fictional creature, Antoine Roquentin, has a meaningless, empty existence by contrast, and the power of Sartre's portrayal is in the claim that Roquentin is discovering the reality beneath the surface, the false solidity of social life hiding the metaphysical void. Yet Sartre does not behave as though this were true. His confidence in his own novel reaches far beyond Roquentin's desperate hope that writing a book might rescue him from contingency. What then induced Sartre's bad faith? (For Sartre's own behavior and its lack of coherence with his professed doctrines is a striking example of bad faith.) At least two reasons can be suggested.

The first is that Sartre is a disappointed rationalist. I do not by saying this point only to Sartre's well-known Cartesian tendencies. I mean, rather, that he continuously writes as if he expects something like the Cartesian or the Leibnizian or the Hegelian view of the world to be true, and is disappointed that it is not. Everything ought to be necessarily as it is, the parts all finite manifestations of a single rational whole, each with a sufficient reason for being what and as it is, which if we only knew it would provide a rational justification and explanation of a totally satisfying kind. The importance in Sartre's scheme of the human aspiration to the condition of God is only intelligible on this view. This also explains why when Sartre makes conceptual points long familiar from the writings of the British empiricists he does so with a sense of drama or even melodrama which is notably absent in Locke, Berkeley, and Hume. Or is this always true? When at the end of Book I of *A Treatise of Human Nature* Hume describes his experience of epistemological vertigo we are very close to the world of *La Nausée*: "I am confounded with all these questions, and begin to fancy myself in the most deplorable condition imaginable, environed with the deepest darkness, and

utterly deprived of the use of every member and faculty."[5] What questions? Questions that make Hume
"look upon no opinion even as more probable or likely
than another." Why? Because all questions of likelihood rest upon inductive generalizations, and Hume
has argued that we cannot justify inductive arguments.
The arguments which Hume uses here amount, as has
often been noticed, to pointing out that inductive arguments cannot be justified deductively, that we
can find no clear and certain self-authenticating first
principle from which to deduce what we need for inductive argument. In other words, the empiricist failure to justify induction rests upon an acceptance of
rationalist standards of justification. Hume's empiricism is that of a disappointed rationalist. But at this
point Hume turns to the solaces of friendship and
backgammon; he invokes nature and the force of custom and habit. We argue inductively from custom and
habit and there's an end on't. No amount of skeptical
doubt can prevail against nature. This is the move that
is not open to Sartre. For him custom and habit are
falsifications, disguises. His discovery that the expectations of metaphysical rationalism are necessarily disappointed leaves him characterizing the world as lacking something. Where he ought to go a stage further
back in the argument, and question the whole rationalist use of such terms as "sufficient reason," he retains
this language and characterizes the world by saying
that the world is such that the rationalist descriptions
do not and cannot be applied to it. This is like supposing that when one has shown that animist forms of
description do not apply to trees and rocks, one has
adequately characterized trees and rocks. The refutation of primitive religion is no substitute for botany or
geology; the refutation of metaphysical rationalism is
no substitute for an adequate logic and conceptual
psychology. But this is not the whole story. There is
another and a complicating factor. This is that the

[5] *A Treatise of Human Nature,* I, iv, 7.

shock of the discovery that there are no sufficient reasons, no ultimate justifications (in the sense intended
by rationalist metaphysics and also by a certain kind
of theology which closely resembles it) is not private
to Sartre. The question of ultimate justification for beliefs and standards remains relatively unimportant for
most people when social forms are stable and social
conflict is minimal. When, however, the support of
custom and habit, which constitute civilized social
life and are neither the work of nature as Hume
thought or of self-deception as Sartre thinks, is with-
drawn, as it has been in periods of rapid industrial
change, of war, of prison camps and torture, of Nazism
and the totalitarian state, people are forced to ask
questions about justification which normally just do
not arise. Moreover all their normal responses are
put in question by extreme situations. What were socially approved and praised public acts, having familiar utilitarian justifications, become private gestures
in a social void. The question "But what would happen
if everybody acted like you?" has no more force when
everybody has been acting much worse than you for a
very long time. And something like this was the case
in a large part of Europe from 1933 until 1945, to go
no further afield.

In this situation the psychology of the absurd man,
of the man who gestures in the void, becomes crucial.
But Sartre's study of this man is defective in an important way. Consider two other studies of the psychology of the absurd or the extreme situation. The
psychoanalyst Bruno Bettelheim, when put in Dachau
and Buchenwald by Hitler, found that the way the
prisoners reacted to the extremity of their situation
was not what he would have expected on the basis of
his past experience of and theorizing about ordinary
life. So that when he began to theorize about the psychology of extreme situations it was in a context where
concentration camp behavior was contrasted with
"normal" behavior. Or take instead as even closer to
Sartre's preoccupations the central character of Camus'

novel *L'Étranger*. He has no normal human emotions or responses. Things happen to him and he performs actions, but all in an emotional vacuum. He neither hopes nor despairs. He is neither interested nor uninterested. He just is. The death of a mother, the wishes of a girl-friend, the chance killing of an unknown person—these are all the kind of events which have normal and standard, though not uniform, responses of various types. What are we to make of someone not characterized by these responses, and so radically lacking them that it is not enough to say that he is not sad or repentant? For him these are attributes that he scarcely understands. The words lack meaning for him. Why are we deeply moved by Camus' novel? In part, at least, by the contrast with ordinary human life. The meaning and point of the normal responses are thrown into sharp relief by this picture of a man who lacks them. But it is essential both to the structure of the novel and to our understanding of its central character that he should be abnormal and exceptional. Without this contrast with the normal we should be at a loss and the novel would be deprived of its point, just as Bettelheim's explanations of concentration camp behavior would lose their point if the backcloth of ordinary life were taken away. Yet this is the backcloth which is lacking in Sartre's philosophical writings, though it is certainly not lacking, at least by implication and sometimes by statement, in his novels after *La Nausée* and above all in his plays. And thus the absurdity which infects Sartrian man's existence is deprived of its point. But at the same time the vogue of Sartre is easily explained. He provides a picture of human existence which can easily be accepted by many uprooted and displaced people; he offers an explanation of why others do not see themselves like this, when he cites bad faith. Curiously, Sartre in his social philosophy identifies the deceptions of custom and habit with the social life of the bourgeoisie—curiously because probably the majority of those who recognize the application of Sartre's picture to themselves are rootless members of the bourgeois class. I do not think many French workers are Sartrians.

In Hegel "the unhappy consciousness" belongs to one historical phase, to one psychological type. It is the clue to one sort of man, not to men. It cannot be the clue to human nature, just because the problems of the unhappy consciousness can be resolved. Equally, when modern psychoanalysts recognize the experience of the absurd or Kierkegaardian dread or Sartrian nausea in their patients, they see these as symptoms of a condition that can be or needs to be cured. But in Sartre we are faced with a description of the human condition which suggests no alternative but the drastic, conceptually confused, political alternatives of the *Critique*.

## CHOICE

To all this the reply might be that what is being underestimated is the extent to which Sartre in fact proves his points. For independent testimony can be adduced to support Sartre in such contentions as that no one else can choose moral principles for me, that in the end I can only stand firm on my choice of principles, and the like. Neither David Hume nor R. M. Hare are usually taken for existentialists, but Sartre leans heavily not only on Hume's thesis that we cannot deduce an "ought" from an "is," but even more upon a view of justification fundamentally similar to that of Hare. For Hare, when we have specified the consequences of acting upon the sort of principle we have chosen, when we have specified the way of life of which this principle is a part, the justification for principles is at an end.[6] Here we can no longer argue, we can only decide. But this is apparently Sartre's ethical position also, and even Kierkegaard's. The view is the opposite of Aristotle's that deliberation and choice belong together—for Hare and Sartre alike, where there

[6] *The Language of Morals*, Oxford, 1952, pp. 68–69.

is no further room for deliberation, choice is in place. This choice is necessarily criterionless.

One reason why a point apparently of cold logic in Hume or in Hare becomes a dramatic point of controversy in Sartre is that Hume and even Hare are able to assume a social context of widespread moral agreement and Sartre is not. When we know what to choose morally, to be told that our choices have no further justification will not disturb us as it will when we do not know what to choose, and are looking for reasons to turn one way rather than another. But are Hare and Sartre in fact right? Are there criterionless choices and do they underlie moral principles? One could approach this in a number of ways. One would be to ask for examples of choices and to study the relationship of choice to criteria. Here it would perhaps turn out actual examples of apparently criterionless choices seem always to be special and misleading cases, such as the choice of a number ticket from a hat in a raffle, where there must be no criterion for deciding between one ticket and another, because the whole point is that the selection shall be random. And this is to say that the choice is governed by a criterion, namely that each ticket shall have an equal chance of selection. In any case, choice of moral principles does not appear to be like *that*. Moreover, it follows from the Sartre-Hare view that a moral principle can (logically) have any content whatsoever. What moral principles one has depends on one's choices, and these, being not restricted by criteria of choice, can be of anything at all. But we are strongly inclined to say that if a man avowedly made it a moral principle that one ought always to walk about with one's hand on one's head we should find what he said unintelligible. If we discovered that he had a belief that doing this prevented some disease, or gave pleasure to himself or others, or was connected with some other recognizable human good, we should begin to understand. And this suggests strongly that the content of moral principles is not open for us to choose, just like that; that we are limited by the character of the concept of a good. But to admit this would involve Sartre in admitting his *bête-noire*, an objective moral order of some sort.

We can understand in any case an oddity in Sartre's position when we consider the fact that desires appear to play no role in providing criteria of choice. The reason for this is simple. Sartre thinks that desires and emotions themselves are chosen. If I am sad, he argues, it is because I choose to be. He pictures a man in a state of melancholy, who rouses himself to a state of interest and cheerfulness when someone else enters the room. But it does not follow from this, as Sartre supposes, that the man can be sad or not as he chooses. It would be much more natural to say that he can rouse himself from his sadness, if he wants something else badly enough, such as not to show his sadness to someone else. This absence of an account of desires and emotions as unchosen is linked, of course, to Sartre's unwillingness to give causal explanations of human behavior. The merit of Kierkegaard, Heidegger, and Sartre is that they do not omit the intentional element from their account of affective life; but insofar as they suggest that this is incompatible with giving a causal account, what they say is difficult to understand.

## Existentialism A Possible Explanation

It is, however, not so difficult to understand how the existentialist position was arrived at historically. Consider the period in philosophy which began with Descartes and ended with Kant. In this period certain epistemological problems were posed but not solved. They could not be solved because of the assumptions which dominated the conceptual framework within which they were posed. There is the isolated, single knowing subject out of whose epistemological resources the whole of knowledge has to be reconstructed. There is the use of a deductive model in setting out the organization of our knowledge with the consequent search for logically guaranteed axioms, or for the hard data of sense-experience. There is the assumption that skeptical difficulties can be overcome, and a willingness to invoke God to overcome them when argument breaks down. Descartes' God bridges the gap between my ideas and the physical world. Kant's God bridges the gulf between duty and inclination. Hume's nature is very much a *deus ex machina.*

Hegel abandoned the epistemological assumptions of the Descartes to Kant era. But he appeared to make the price of a solution to the philosophical problems the acceptance of his system. And those who rejected the system were apt to retreat to the assumptions of an earlier age. With Kierkegaard this is at best implicit. Certainly we can see the choice between the ethical and the aesthetic as a replica of Kant's choice between duty and inclination, but with the rational basis removed. And more generally, the Kierkegaardian individual resembles the Cartesian "I" without the *Cogito.* This resemblance is reinforced by the explicit Cartesianism of Husserl which Sartre inherits. Sartrian man is Cartesian man in his theory of knowledge, and Kantian man in his ethics, with rational first principles having been replaced by criterionless choices. There is no God or nature to guarantee the rationality of the universe; and there is the same absence of a background of socially established and recognized criteria, which is necessary to make the knowledge we possess and the way we come to possess it intelligible. Sartrian man is the heir of Descartes' lonely epistemological hero.

Is, then, existentialism a series of mistakes and nothing more? Even if this were all it would not be valueless. The saying that to be ignorant of the history of philosophy is to be doomed to repeat it is relevant here. In one sense, and quite another than that intended by the existentialists, a great deal of existentialism constitutes a *reductio ad absurdum* of certain philosophical theories. By forcing them to an unacceptable conclusion we obtain a much clearer view of what is wrong with them and also therefore of what we ought to say instead. But embedded in Sartre and Heidegger and Kierkegaard there are certain paramount insights, especially in the philosophy of mind. Disentangling them from the confines in which they are embedded belongs to the future history of philosophy rather than to the past history of existentialism. Sartre, for example, in his early essay on the emotions does not merely say of them that they are intentional: he expounds a whole theory of them as purposive attempts to change the world by quasimagical means. My horror is an attempt to get rid of what horrifies me. Kierkegaard's analysis, in the course of his discussion of the aesthetic, of tragic pain and why we feel it, is a brilliant analysis of the difference between seeing what happens to a man as due to a flaw in him and seeing what happens to him as due to a flaw in the universe. Heidegger's secularization of Augustine on temporality and the experience of temporality is not inextricably bound up with his ontology. In every case there is a serious, if not a final, contribution to those studies which lie on the margin of philosophy and psychology.

The paradox of existentialism is that one of the great existentialist slogans has been to deny the possibility of constructing a philosophical system; that not one of the major existentialists has escaped doing this; and that with all of them the systematic form has done just what they said it would do, tortured and distorted their individual conceptual insights into less acceptable forms than they would otherwise have had. The lesson to be learnt is that in philosophy system is almost unavoidable; that to recognize this is to be able to use systematic forms without too much danger, but that to fail to recognize it is almost inevitably to fall victim to that which one professes to despise so much.

# SARTRE THE PHILOSOPHER

## *Stuart Hampshire*

---

To read this long and important book, every word to
the end, calls for dogged determination. M. Sartre's
philosophical style, formed by Hegel and Heidegger,
is ugly and discouraging. . . . Here is a typical sentence, chosen at random: "It is necessary that there
be a being 'I-and-the-other' which has to be the reciprocal scissiparity of the for-others just as the totality 'reflective-reflected on' is a being which has to
be its own nothingness."

It will be admitted that this thought, so expressed,
is not entirely easy and straightforward. Yet it is a de-
cipherable link in an interesting argument. Perhaps it
is better to be misunderstood than not to be understood at all. Any short guide must involve misunderstanding, but I shall state a few points in this closely
knit system in rather easier words.

* * *

To exist as a man is to have intentions in the light of
which the world, otherwise mere undifferentiated Being, is divided for me into instruments that I need.
While I am conscious, I am always imagining and
contriving that things should be other than they are.
I am always pursuing possibilities. My nature and
character at any moment are identical with the plans
that I am freely pursuing; I have no real nature apart
from my own renewed choices of what I am to be. I
am in this sense empty, and my actions are a perpetual
flight from this nothingness inside me.

"Sartre the Philosopher," a review of *Being and Nothingness*
by Stuart Hampshire, is from the *Observer*, May 12, 1957. Reprinted by permission of the *Observer*, London.

It follows that I am responsible for every phase of my consciousness, including my emotions. Emotions are a form of arrested action, a kind of magical behaviour to which I resort when practical manipulations are unavailing. Through my active intentions I become conscious of myself as separated from other things. But, as an embodied consciousness, I am always acting and observing only from one particular standpoint within a world of which I am part. I find that I have come to the surface, as a consciousness, at a particular point in the ocean of Being, the whole world being for me arranged around this casual position.

This idea of my own existence as an object within the world involves the idea that I might be observed by other free and conscious beings; their meaningful looks, directed at me from their point of view, will situate me as an object in a particular place. If a Robinson Crusoe, finding himself alone in the world, did not realise the possibility of being present to the consciousness of another, he would have the illusion that the order in which objects presented themselves to him was the only possible order. He would then think of himself as a God-like observer outside the world of things and not as immersed in it.

Sartre accuses Descartes of representing men as metaphysical Robinson Crusoes, outside the world of things which their consciousness impartially reconstructs. Descartes ignored the fact of man's "engagement" in the world, a fact which becomes plain to anyone, together with his consciousness of himself, as soon as he finds himself the object of meanings and intentions that he has not originated himself. Each man is to every both an object in the path of his intentions and a rival free consciousness of a world from another point of view. This leads to that grim dialectic in personal relations described in Sartre's plays and novels. When I fall in love, I am trying to capture for myself a free consciousness which is making me into an object for itself. But I can never finally succeed in

this self-contradictory project; either the other becomes wholly an object for me, or his freedom remains beyond my grasp, and therefore there can never
be an identity of viewpoint.

Sartre ingeniously explains various types of personal
feeling and of sexual behaviour as following from this
central contradiction. All my patterns of feeling and
behaviour have been chosen by me to serve my overriding intentions; there is always a motive behind the
character traits which I may dishonestly represent as
given facts in my nature. If I am to describe myself
honestly, I must describe myself as the man who is
trying to do and to be such and such things in the future. Conventional morality is founded on the pretence that my consciousness can be divided down the
middle: on the one side, that which I do at will and
am responsible for: on the other, the passions and impulses that occur to me through natural causes. But
this is to regard part of my consciousness as a thing
external to myself. A consciousness cannot be divided,
and intentions can be explained only by motives and
reasons, and not by external causes. Therefore the ex-
cuse "Being the man that I am, I could not help trying
to do this" always shows "bad faith," since the only
limit to my freedom is the world of resisting things.

Competing with Freud, Sartre has his own psycho-
pathology of everyday life, which shows the real
motives behind involuntary behaviour. He criticises
Freud for clinging to a simple determinist's idea of the
mind, as being like a machine governed by natural
forces, while fully admitting the motives and intentions behind unconscious behaviour; Sartre therefore
dismisses the subconscious mind as an impossible hy-
brid. An Existentialist knows that he always has a plan
to find for himself a definite character or role by his
actions in the world. He knows that only when he is
dead, and the story of his efforts is told, will his nature
be known, and that even then the story cannot be told
without alien meanings being imposed on it. If he
stops to reflect on this emptiness and nothingness of

his nature at any particular moment, he will feel anguish, the consequence of realising his freedom without exercising it. If, ignoring his freedom, he realises only his immersion in the world of undifferentiated things, he will feel nausea, the nausea that we feel in front of any viscous, shapeless substance that extends meaninglessly in all directions. He is therefore wise if he never dwells on one aspect of his being to the exclusion of the other; he will continually exercise his freedom in concrete projects in the world.

*  *  *

This bald and partial summary of course makes Sartre's philosophy seem more banal than it is. But it may at least suggest the continuity between his philosophy and his politics. Born into a particular position in the social fabric and starting with a language and habits of thought that I did not make, I unavoidably take sides in trying to rearrange or to preserve that fabric of human relations in which I am always embedded. I can never say in good faith either "I am an artist and outside society" or "Society has made me what I am."

At the end one may wonder whether these conclusions are just commonplaces disguised by the sophistries of Hegelian logic. I think not. Sartre's criticism of traditional theories of mind is at too many points convincing for his whole system to be ignored. And in detail he is extraordinarily sharp, clever and enlightening. But is it true that "nobody can be vulgar all alone"? There are many simple observations of this kind.

# THE PHENOMENOLOGICAL PHILOSOPHY IN FRANCE. AN ANALYSIS OF ITS THEMES, SIGNIFICANCE AND IMPLICATIONS

*Ian W. Alexander*

---

All familiar with the development of philosophy in France during the present century are aware of the dominant role of phenomenology in this development. Indeed, it would not be too much to say that the influence of Husserl in reorientating philosophical speculation in France has been as powerful as that of Wittgenstein in Britain during the same period, and that the result in both cases has been to revolutionize the philosophical perspective.

The year 1930 may be considered a starting-point, for that year saw the publication of Levinas's *La Théorie de l'intuition dans la phénoménologie de Husserl* and Gurvitch's *Les Tendances actuelles de la philosophie allemande*. The resultant interest in German phenomenology was canalized, and the first applications centred, in the journal *Recherches philosophiques*, five numbers of which appeared from 1931, although it must be noted that one French thinker antedates this period, namely Gabriel Marcel, France's first phenomenologist in his own right. His article, *Existence et Objectivité*, published in the *Revue de métaphysique et de morale* in 1925, might well be classed as the first application, quite independent of Husserlian influence, of that phenomenological method which he brought to perfection later.

This essay, first published in *Currents of Thought in French Literature: Essays in Memory of G. T. Clapton*, Oxford: Basil Blackwell, New York: Barnes & Noble, 1966, is reprinted by permission of the editor and publisher.

It was, however, in the immediate post-war years that phenomenology invaded the whole field of philosophical thought, leaving not one of its disciplines untouched, permeating literature itself and moulding a certain *style* which we have come to recognize and even to take for granted as a mode of thinking characteristically French.

Any study of the later issues raised by phenomenology must of necessity go back to Edmund Husserl, the founder of the 'phenomenological philosophy'. The development of Husserl's thought is highly complex and critics are by no means unanimous in their interpretations of it.[1] The account of experience that he offers in his earlier period, from the *Logische Untersuchungen* (1900–1) to the *Ideen zu einer reiner Phänomenologie* (1913), would seem to preserve strong traces of both Cartesian and Kantian idealism, accounted for largely by the particular use made at that stage of the *epoche* or 'bracketing' of existence. The *epoche* or 'phenomenological reduction' is said to have for object to transcend all actual experience and to place us before the activity of a pure, transcendental ego. And there is a distinct reminiscence of the Cartesian *cogito* in that attention would seem to be concentrated on 'internal experience'. Much the same strain is continued in the middle period—the period of the 'constitutive' phenomenology—where, in Kantian manner, Husserl treats of phenomenology as a transcendental theory of knowledge, the object of which is said to be to bring to light the sense-giving operations of consciousness that lead to the constitution of a possible world and whose synthesis is the transcendental ego.

It would seem that we are still somewhat embedded

[1] For two interesting treatments of this problem see A. de Waelhens, *De la phénoménologie à l'existentialisme*, in *Le Choix, le Monde, l'Existence*, Arthaud, 1947; M. Farber, *The Foundation of Phenomenology*, Harvard, 1943, pp. 15 ff.

in a cognitive idealism or a philosophy of pure consciousness.[2] The true, revolutionary nature of Husserl's thought becomes apparent, however, in the light of his later works. Already in the *Ideen* he made it clear (and decisively so in the *Méditations Cartésiennes* of 1931) that the bracketing of existence or 'suspension of the thesis' is a purely methodological device:

> *Ce que nous mettons hors de jeu, c'est la thèse générale qui tient à l'essence de l'attitude naturelle;* nous mettons entre parenthèses absolument tout ce qu'elle embrasse dans l'ordre ontique: *par conséquent tout ce monde naturel* qui est constamment 'là pour nous', *'présent'*, et ne cesse de rester là à titre de 'réalité' pour la conscience, lors même qu'il nous plaît de le mettre entre parenthèses.
>
> Quand je procède ainsi, comme il est pleinement au pouvoir de ma liberté, je ne *nie* donc *pas* ce 'Monde', comme si j'étais sophiste; *je ne mets pas son existence en doute,* comme si j'étais sceptique;

[2] Farber notes the 'pitfalls' involved in Husserl's use of the phenomenological method: 'Husserl's very language betrays his predisposition to treat the transcendent realm of existence, in which belief was suspended as a matter of method, as something reducible to pure consciousness' (op. cit., p. 520). But he claims, we believe rightly, that Husserl overcame this leaning and that a proper understanding of the nature and function of the phenomenological reduction, as Husserl came to see it, exculpates him on this score. Jean Wahl does, however, suggest that the resemblances between Husserl and both Descartes and Kant are greater than the former imagined (*L'Ouvrage posthume de Husserl: La Krisis*, Cours de Sorbonne, 1957, p. 123). There is, indeed, a latent ambiguity in Husserl's thought as a whole that lays it open to both an 'idealist' and a 'realist' interpretation according to the emphasis of the interpreter. (Cf. H. Kuhn, *The Phenomenological Concept of 'Horizon'*, in *Philosophical Essays in Memory of Edmund Husserl*, Harvard, 1940; R. Ingarden, *L'Idéalisme transcendantal de Husserl*, in *Husserl et la pensée moderne*, The Hague, Martinus Nijhoff, 1959).

mais j'opère l'ἐποχή 'phénoménologique' *qui m'inter-
dit absolument tout jugement portant sur l'existence
spatio-temporelle.*[3]

What Husserl indeed is seeking is an absolute foundation, which will 'make clear the presuppositions
of experience', in short, reveal itself as both the logical
ground of meaning and the ontic root of experience,
to which all particular modes of experience and all
particular meanings must be referred and which determines their sense radically and absolutely. Phenomenology is the science of meanings: it is not concerned
with a mere realistic description of the world, but with
making explicit the fundamental structures whereby
the world is constituted as meaningful for consciousness. The *epoche* and transcendental reduction do not
deny the existence of the world. What they do is to
suspend the 'natural' attitude with all particular modes
of intentional experience so as to leave visible within
the transcendental *cogito*' a residual *a priori*—the intentional relation between consciousness and the
world *in se*, now revealed in its essentiality as a *vécu*
of which the subjective and the objective poles are
correlates:

La suspension phénoménologique fait apparaître
immédiatement la corrélation à priori de la constitution et du constitué, de la noèse et du noème, de la

[3] *Idées directrices pour une phénoménologie,* Gallimard,
1950, p. 102. Cf. Farber: 'It is essential that the phenomenological reduction be viewed as a purely methodological device. . . . It is radical in the sense of helping us to make clear
the ultimate presuppositions of experience. . . . But it must
never forget its own 'mother-earth', its own actual ('natural-
istic') genetic foundation, if it is to constitute a world which
will satisfy experience. To do so, and to go the way of cognitive
idealism, would mean that the phenomenological quest would
have to rest content with the pale shadow of reality, depending
upon a hypostatized *logos* in an ethereal absolute consciousness' (op. cit., p. 536).

conscience et du monde. Elle manifeste immédiatement la bilatéralité de la recherche transcendantale.
Il s'agit d'une bilatéralité *à l'intérieur* de la réduction
transcendantale, car la recherche transcendantale est
à la fois noématique et noétique.[4]

The transcendental reduction works *within* the
*vécu*, and its purpose is not to retreat from the world
into a pure consciousness but to exhibit the fundamental relation between consciousness and the world
as the permanent, universal structure underlying all
particular experiences actual or possible. It suspends
all judgements about the world, or indeed about the
self, so as to concentrate on the structure which makes
any reference to a world or to a self possible at all,
that is the intentional self-world relation of compresence itself.

Secondly, there comes to the fore the notion of *intersubjectivity*, according to which the self's experience involves an 'experience of others', who, although
not presented directly to the self, are 'appresented'[5]
by virtue of the intertwining of conscious activities or
what Husserl calls 'intentional transgression'. That being so, I am, and know myself, as 'situated' and we
are brought back to the concrete existent, and reflection on the plane of a universal thinker or absolute
consciousness is excluded.

It is finally excluded with the clarification of the
even more fundamental concept of the *Lebenswelt* in
*Erfahrung und Urteil*, published in Prague in 1939.
This concept places the self firmly 'in the world', the
two constituting an indissoluble nexus and entertain-

---

[4] A. de Muralt, *L'Idée de la phénoménologie: l'Exemplar-
isme husserlien*, Presses Univ., 1958, p. 251. Cf. A. de Waelhens, *Existence et Signification*, Louvain and Paris, Nauwel-
aerts, 1958, p. 107; G. Berger, *Le Cogito dans la philosophie
de Husserl*, Aubier, 1941, pp. 49-50.

[5] *Méditations cartésiennes*, Vrin, 1947, pp. 126-7.

ing relations of complementarity rooted in 'la coexist-
ence première avec les choses et avec autrui'.[6]

Here is the field of 'l'expérience originaire', now
identified beyond doubt with the field of existence.[7]
And it is the structure of this experiential, existential
ground that phenomenology has to uncover and describe. The phenomenological reflection becomes a 'réflexion sur un irréfléchi':[8]

> C'est une philosophie transcendantale qui met en
> suspens pour les comprendre les affirmations de l'at-
> titude naturelle, mais c'est aussi une philosophie pour
> laquelle le monde est toujours 'déjà là' avant la réflex-
> ion, comme une présence inaliénable, et dont tout
> l'effort est de retrouver ce contact naïf avec le monde
> pour lui donner enfin un statut philosophique. C'est
> l'ambition d'une philosophie qui soit une 'science
> exacte', mais c'est aussi un compte rendu de l'espace,
> du temps, du monde 'vécus'.[9]

Husserl's philosophy may be viewed as an attack on
two dominant currents of thought: the Kantian and
the positivist. At the root of both of these is a similar
dualistic fiction. Both ask us to picture a world on the
one side duplicated by a mind on the other. The Kantian will explain their coming together in terms of synthetic acts of mind imposing its categories on sense-
experience. The positivist will claim that external
stimuli produce 'states' in the mind (psychological determinism); then, having got the object into the mind

---

[6] A. de Waelhens, *L'Idée phénoménologique d'intentionnalité,* in *Husserl et la pensée moderne,* p. 128.

[7] 'Der Rückgang auf die Welt der Erfahrung ist Rückgang
auf die "Lebenswelt", d.i. die Welt, in der wir immer schon
leben, und die den Boden für alle Erkenntnisleistung abgibt
und für alle wissenschaftliche Bestimmung' (*Erfahrung und
Urteil,* Hamburg, Claassen u. Goverts, 1948, p. 38).

[8] M. Merleau-Ponty, *Phénoménologie de la perception,* Gallimard, 1945, p. iv.

[9] Ibid., p. i.

in the form of sense-data, will account for the complexity and structuring of experience in terms of their combination (psychological atomism and associationism).

None of this, however, argues Husserl, corresponds to the reality of experience. We are encouraged in this dualistic fallacy by scientific psychology, taking its abstract concepts—states, sense-data, etc.—for concrete fact, and confirmed therein by linguistic usage, notably the subject-predicate form of grammatical discourse. What Husserl does is to direct attention back to concrete, 'antepredicative' experience and to attempt the faithful description of the phenomena of consciousness as these are displayed in its operations at the level prior to conceptual elaboration. Such is the force of Husserl's slogan: 'to the thing itself'.[10]

According to Husserl, consciousness, as so revealed in its fundamental structure, is intentional, directed towards the object as the *telos* of an inner impetus to self-transcendence. The *cogito* of Descartes must be replaced by a *cogito cogitatum*: 'consciousness is always consciousness of something'. The world is presented to it immediately by virtue of what Husserl calls the 'noematic' structure of experience. At the same time, the world is apprehended in and through the intentions of consciousness (by way of the 'noetic' structure of experience), which grasp it in a certain way, give it or rather allow it to appear with a certain pattern, a certain sense, meaning or value. These two structures (noematic and noetic) are correlated structures of a *same* intentional structure of experience, the one being its objective and the other its subjective side, the mode of 'being given' and the mode of 'sense-giving', the presentation and the presentative act.[11]

[10] The appeal from constructions to what is directly given is the emphasis in the second volume of the *Logische Untersuchungen*.

[11] '. . . Ces concepts de 'noèse et de noème ne renvoient pas à des *composantes* du vécu, mais à deux structures corrélatives du même vécu. La noèse est le vécu comme intentionnel,

There are various types of the basic intentional structure—perceptual, imaginative, mnemonic, emotive, cognitive.[12] These types are the Husserlian 'essences' revealed by the 'eidetic reduction' or 'intuition of essences'. Phenomenology is concerned with the description and clarification of those essences, the various modes of intentional sense-giving which are also the modes in which the world (Being) is apprehended and reveals its meanings.

All these structures or essences, however, refer back to, and are determinations of, the primary and 'most general formal structure' of experience 'designated by the schema *ego-cogito-cogitatum*',[13] that initial compresence of self and world which lies at the root of the 'objective sense', defined by Lauer as 'le mode de présence de l'objet dans la conscience'[14] and which guarantees that the intentional structures of consciousness embody revelations of Being and of its meanings.

It has to be noted that we are not here dealing with mere psychological phenomena, but with the permanent, universal structures of consciousness.[15] For that

---

l'accent portant sur ses composantes subjectives (noétiques). Le noème est la structure intentionnelle du vécu, regardé du côté objectif. . . .' (Q. Lauer, *Phénoménologie de Husserl: Essai sur la genèse de l'intentionnalité*, Presses Univ., 1955, p. 200).

[12] *Méditations cartésiennes*, p. 43.

[13] 'La structure la plus générale qui, en tant que forme, embrasse tous les cas particuliers, est désignée par notre schéma général *ego-cogito-cogitatum*' (ibid.).

[14] Lauer, op. cit., p. 217.

[15] 'Car la Wesenschau, en tant qu'elle est expérience, en tant que l'essence est à saisir à travers l'expérience vécue, sera une expérience concrète; mais d'un autre côté, en tant qu'à travers mes expériences concrètes je saisis plus qu'un fait contingent, une structure intelligible qui s'impose à moi chaque fois que je pense à l'objet intentionnel dont il s'agit, j'obtiens par elle une connaissance, je ne suis pas enfermé dans quelque particularité de ma vie individuelle, j'accède à un savoir qui est valable pour tous.' (Merleau-Ponty, *Les Sciences de*

very reason they are grasped as such, not by process of abstraction or comparison of instances, but as concrete operations directly visible to intuition.[16] And this in turn because the 'reduction' is a 'radical reflection' within the framework of existence, the object of which is to return to the root of thinking and which 'découvre finalement derrière elle l'irréfléchi comme sa condition de possibilité, sans laquelle cette réflexion n'aurait aucun sens'.[17]

Any treatment of phenomenology with reference to its developments in France must begin by emphasizing those realist implications so strongly urged by Husserl in the later stages of his thought, for it is they, in a country where the dominant currents have been either idealist or positivist, which have revolutionized its philosophical 'style'. Phenomenology, indeed, cuts beneath the predicative subject-object dualism by designating an antepredicative experience of the world as the ground and condition of the revelation and constitution of meaning:

> Sous toutes les acceptions du mot sens, nous retrouvons la même notion fondamentale d'un être orienté ou polarisé vers ce qu'il n'est pas, et nous sommes ainsi toujours amenés à une conception du sujet comme ek-stase et à un rapport de transcendance active entre le sujet et le monde. Le monde est inséparable du sujet, mais d'un sujet qui n'est rien que projet du monde, et le sujet est inséparable du monde, mais d'un monde qu'il projette lui-même.[18]

l'homme et la phénoménologie, Introd. et 1e partie, Le Problème des sciences de l'homme selon Husserl, Cours de Sorbonne, n.d., p. 14.)

[16] Berger, op. cit., p. 51.

[17] Merleau-Ponty, op. cit., p. 53. Cf. *Phénoménologie de la perception*, p. ix.

[18] Idem, *Phénoménologie de la perception*, p. 491.

This is Heidegger's 'ontic truth', described by Marcel as a 'confused and global experience of the world',[19] the field of compresence and intersubjectivity containing the self and, *in relation with it*, the world and other selves as, to quote Merleau-Ponty, 'l'horizon permanent de toutes mes *cogitationes* et comme une dimension par rapport à laquelle je ne cesse de me situer'.[20] Consciousness and the world are complementary, consciousness 'intending' the object, and the object being 'for' a consciousness. In experience, however, we may distinguish a subjective and an objective pole. Taking the first, phenomenology rejects the positivist, determinist explanation of conscious phenomena as the effects of external factors. These phenomena are less phenomena *in* consciousness than phenomena *of* consciousness. The subject is implicated therein since it is for and by my consciousness that the world appears in a certain perspective and with a certain sense, that from 'a' world it becomes 'the' world 'for me', 'my world'.

My consciousness is 'la source absolue', 'par laquelle d'abord un monde se dispose autour de moi et commence à exister pour moi'.[21] And this by virtue of my intention whereby I select certain rather than other possible senses that the world offers. A house in my immediate experience of it may be a fine piece of architecture, a subject of hope or fear: all these are one house, but its 'being' or 'meaning' is constituted on each occasion by the particular intention in which it is embodied. In visual perception itself the being or sense of the object is the result of an intention that makes *explicit* certain of its potential aspects. Similarly with emotional experience. If I am afraid to climb a precipice, it is not it that 'produces' my fear. It is I, says Sartre, who 'choose' to view it as terrifying,

[19] See *The Mystery of Being, I: Reflection and Mystery*, Harvill Press, 1950, pp. 51–2.
[20] Op. cit., pp. vii–viii.
[21] Ibid., p. iii.

that is to make explicit that particular meaning: it is in that particular way that it comes to 'ex-sist' 'for me'. But not only does my intention determine the being of the precipice, it also determines the being of my self. I am 'choosing myself' as terrified. The precipice is the occasion for me to be 'for myself' in a particular mode.[22] Thus Sartre, like Heidegger, can assert that consciousness is 'nothing', being without content.[23] It is wholly definable in terms of the self's sense-giving relationship with the world. Emotion is such a 'total act' of consciousness. So too is imagination. Sartre's two works on imagination are designed to show that the image, far from being a content of consciousness, is the result of an act of the whole of consciousness whereby an absent reality is evoked as present. In Merleau-Ponty's words, 'imaginer, c'est former un certain mode de relation avec l'objet absent'.[24]

Turning to the objective pole, the phenomenologist rejects the idealist account. Consciousness is a 'project towards the world': the latter is immediately present; it is 'there', as the primary situation which determines all senses.[25] We do not rejoin the world in the Kantian manner by some express act of synthesis. The mind-world unity is given. Hence the rejection of the traditional French 'reflexive analysis' which claims, as does the Cartesian *cogito*, to provide awareness of the thinking self independently of the world.

[22] F. Jeanson defines consciousness as 'un être dont l'être est en question pour lui-même, un être dont l'être n'est pas fait mais qui a à faire son être; un être, enfin, qui dépend de lui-même dans sa manière d'être'. (*La Phénoménologie*, Téqui, 1951, p. 70.)

[23] Sartre, *L'Être et Le Néant*, Gallimard, 1943, pp. 71-2.

[24] Merleau-Ponty, *Sciences de l'homme*, p. 20.

[25] 'Cette ceritude du monde général est toujours opération (ou accomplissement, *Verzug*) et elle précède tout, non pas comme énonciation et prémisse au sens propre, elle détermine le sens, elle fonctionne comme sol de dévaluation: étant signifie étant dans le monde.' (Husserl, quoted by Wahl, *La Krisis*, p. 123.)

Thus Sartre argues that 'toute conscience est positionnelle, en ce qu'elle se transcende pour atteindre
un objet', and that 'toute conscience positionnelle
d'objet est en même temps conscience non positionnelle d'ellemême'. From which he infers that the reflective consciousness, far from being primary, has for
condition a pre-reflexive *cogito*: 'il y a un cogito pré-
réflexif qui est la condition du cogito cartésien'.[26]
There is no consciousness of the self independent of
the intentional consciousness directed towards the object. Not that Sartre denies 'self-consciousness'; what
he argues is that there is no consciousness *of* the self
(the 'of' is dictated by syntactical requirements and he
proposes to bracket it). Self-consciousness is not another, additional consciousness, but one with the intentional consciousness, 'un avec la conscience dont
elle est conscience'; 'cette conscience (de) soi, nous
ne devons pas la considérer comme une nouvelle conscience, mais comme le seul mode d'existence qui soit
possible pour une conscience de quelque chose'.[27]

Marcel equally strongly rejects the Cartesian *cogito*
as secondary and refers it back to a pre-reflexive *ego
sum* or *j'existe* expressive of the antepredicative
unity: 'une philosophie qui part du *cogito*, c'est-à-dire
du noninséré, ou même de la non-insertion en tant
qu'acte, risque de ne pouvoir jamais rejoindre l'être'.[28]
The subject is given 'in relation' as a self-transcending
consciousness, intending a world which it renders
meaningful by its presentative and constitutive acts,
but never itself localizable, since it can never become
a simple object of contemplation for itself.

Experience thus presents a nexus wherein conscious-

[26] Op. cit., pp. 18–20.
[27] Ibid., p. 20. Cf. A. de Waelhens: 'La présence de soi à
soi n'est pas une possession de soi significative en elle-même,
mais une évidence *récupérée sur l'évidence de la présence à
l'autre.*' (*Existence et Signification*, p. 114.)
[28] *Du Refus à l'invocation*, Gallimard, 1940, p. 90. Cf.
*Etre et Avoir*, Aubier, 1935, p. 249.

ness and the world are mutually implicated, the latter as the 'permanent horizon of all my *cogitationes*'. In perception the conscious intention renders explicit some aspect or meaning of the object, so bringing it to be for consciousness. But the other possible aspects remain implicitly as the 'horizon' and are an integral part of the perception.[29] In my perception of a chair, I 'intend' the chair and may secure an explicit vision of the front, but I also have an implicit vision of the back and sides. They are the implicit themes of my actual perception. And these in turn are fringed by other elements drawn from the object's wider environment:

> Ainsi chaque objet est le miroir de tous les autres. Quand je regarde la lampe posée sur ma table, je lui attribue non seulement les qualités visibles de ma place, mais encore celles que la cheminée, que les murs, que la table peuvent 'voir', le dos de ma lampe n'est rien d'autre que la face qu'elle 'montre' à la cheminée. Je peux donc voir un objet en tant que les objets forment un système ou un monde et que chacun d'eux dispose des autres autour de lui comme spectateurs de ses aspects cachés et garantie de leur permanence. Toute vision d'un objet par moi se réitère instantanément entre tous les objets du monde qui sont saisis comme coexistants parce que chacun de'ux est tout ce que les autres 'voient' de lui.[30]

Temporally, too, as well as spatially, the object of perception is seen in its relatedness and is bordered by a fringe of retrospection and prospection:

> . . . Chaque présent fonde définitivement un point du temps qui sollicite la reconnaissance de tous les autres, l'objet est donc vu de tous temps comme il

---

[29] See Husserl, *Méditations cartésiennes*, pp. 38–9.

[30] Merleau-Ponty, *Phénoménologie de la perception*, pp. 82–3. Cf. Kuhn, *Concept of Horizon*, loc. cit.

est vu de toutes parts et par le même moyen, qui
est la structure d'horizon.[31]

The present contains the immediate past and the imminent future and, implicated and enveloped in them,
their immediate past and future.

All experience exhibits this seemingly limitless spatial and temporal *emboîtement*. And, as there is in addition an intersubjectivity of minds whereby my perceptual intentions are intertwined with those of others,
my perceptual field takes in the whole world. My experience appears as a single field for the display and
constitution of senses and values of the world, in
which all possible senses and values are involved:

> Le réel est un tissu solide, il n'attend pas nos juge-
> ments pour s'annexer les phénomènes les plus sur-
> prenants ni pour rejeter nos imaginations les plus
> vraisemblables. La perception n'est pas une science
> du monde, ce n'est pas même un acte, une prise de
> position délibérée, elle est le fond sur lequel tous
> les actes se détachent et elle est présupposée par
> eux.[32]

The real of my experience is not a mass of discrete
parts, but an organized whole of which the parts are
enveloped. We do not, as psychological atomism
would have it, build up the world out of isolated sense-
data, any more than, as Bergson says, in reading we
pass from the letter to the word. Being itself is a whole
already instinct with meanings, and consciousnesses
are in the world as the *media* through which those
meanings, by their embodiment in the intentional
structures of consciousness, are actualized and made

[31] Merleau-Ponty, ibid., p. 83. Cf. Kuhn: 'The present perception of the object before me is a link in a chain of successive
perceptions each of which either had or will have a presence
of its own.' (Op. cit., p. 113.)

[32] Merleau-Ponty, ibid., p. v.

explicit against the background of the whole, from
which they emerge but without ever losing their relatedness to it.

At the centre of the process is what Merleau-Ponty
calls 'le perspectivisme de mon expérience'. What is
given is a whole, but a whole seen in perspective, its
parts 'enveloped' in such a way that the moment or
object of experience contains, as it were telescoped
within each other, a limitless series of implicit 'horizons'. Pure objectivity—which is a conceptualisation
of concrete experience—comes about precisely by an
abstractive process whereby the enveloped, perspectival elements are disjoined and spread out as on a
map. Such is the abstract, scientific notion of a 'universe', 'c'est-à-dire d'une totalité achevée, explicite, où
les rapports soient de détermination réciproque', in
place of what is given in experience, namely a 'world',
'c'est-à-dire d'une multiplicité ouverte et indéfinie où
les rapports sont d'implication réciproque'.[33]

The relation then between self and world is one of
compresence, as between a consciousness which 'projects' towards the world and a world which seeks to
become 'for' a consciousness. This being so, the phenomenologist argues, conscious phenomena are not
susceptible of treatment by the scientific method of
'explanation'. Scientific or causal explanation works by
way of analysis of a situation, which is resolved into its
elements, one of the latter being then designated as
cause of the event. The scientific investigator will ana-
lyse a conscious event, such as my fear, into elements
(states of mind, bodily states, external conditions,
etc.), and will then designate one or other of these
elements, as required, as the cause of my fearing. But,
it is argued, this is simply to do away with the phenomenon, to dissolve the bond between the subject
and his world in terms of which alone his phenomena
have meaning. The causal explanation will have told

[33] Ibid., p. 85.

us nothing. At the most it will have correlated series of data, established a constant relation or law. That may well suffice for the sciences where, as causality is now used, all that is required is the establishing of a permanence or equivalence. But in studying conscious phenomena what is sought is meanings, not mere legal connections.

These phenomena do not offer material for problems, or are problems of a special sort, problems, as Marcel puts it, 'that encroach upon their own data'.[34] For the 'data' here are not objective in the sense of their being dissociable from the self-world intention. They are in fact incorporated in this intention as the embodiment of a meaning which the intention realises, of a mode of being of the self and of the world which it constitutes. My fear is myself fearing, 'signifying' and constituting both the world and myself in a certain way; it is the revealing through the medium of my fearing intention of a particular meaning that Being offers.

My fear is therefore a single, total event in which situation, states, behaviour, image and act are indissoluble moments. All are part of one sense-revealing intention, one 'phenomenon', which simply vanishes when subjected to analysis. Phenomenology therefore proposes a method not of causal explanation but of description and clarification, what Husserl calls 'noematic reflection', as opposed to analysis, in that it works within the subject-object unity. Its task is to describe the meanings or senses of Being as they are revealed and actualized in intentional experience: as they represent modes of comprehending the world on the one hand, and modes of being of the world and modes of being of the self on the other. The phenomenologist describes the *total* event, both the sort of world that is so constituted, the way it 'appears' for a particular intention in terms of sensations and images,

[34] *The Philosophy of Existence*, Harvill Press, 1948, p. 8. Cf. *Etre et Avoir*, p. 145.

and the sort of intention that lies behind it in terms of the subject's particular situation. Marcel defines the method as 'the clarification of two unknowns',[35] thus emphasizing both the descriptive and clarificatory nature of the method and the fact that what is described takes place at the antepredicative level of compresence, implication and obscure relatedness before conceptualisation, where alone analysis functions legitimately. Phenomenology, declares Merleau-Ponty, 'c'est l'essai d'une description directe de notre expérience telle qu'elle est, et sans aucun égard à sa genèse psychologique et aux explications causales que le savant, l'historien ou le sociologue peuvent en fournir'.[36]

It is at this point that the phenomenological concept of 'negativity' emerges. In traditional logic negation at the predicative level is a function of exclusion purely and simply. It is Hegel who first considers negation in its relation to consciousness, and not merely with reference to negative propositions. For him negativity is what conditions the dialectical structure of consciousness, which advances by constant affirmations and negations, no sooner positing an idea than it posits its contrary.

Phenomenology develops this view and in particular the implication that negativity is constitutive of consciousness.[37] Conscious experience is both a way of being and of not-being, there is both identification with the object and differentiation from it, amounting to a negation of what is. Sartre points to emotional experience: when one is conscious of being sad, one *is* one's sadness, but at the same time one *is not* one's sadness (or, as he says, one is 'playing at being sad').

[35] *The Mystery of Being*, I, p. 13.

[36] Merleau-Ponty, op. cit., p. i.

[37] Cf. J. Hyppolite, *Genèse et Structure de la Phénoménologie de l'Esprit de Hegel*, Aubier, 1946, p. 184; J. Wahl, *Le Malheur de la conscience dans la philosophie de Hegel*, Presses Univ., 1951, p. 2.

It is in this sense that it may be said that 'man is what
he is not, and is not what he is'.[38]

All experience, however, exhibits this negativity
within positivity characteristic of consciousness, whose
'structure d'être . . . consiste à être l'autre sur le mode
du non-être'.[39] Involved in all conscious activities is a
'distancing' with respect to what is given immediately.
Conscious appropriation of the object, it will be re-
called, consists in endowing it with a certain sense by
viewing it in a certain perspective. For the *en-soi* to
become a *pour-soi* there must be selection and determination and therefore a transcending of the brute
immediacy of fusion with the object, where all senses
and all perspectives exist, but as mere possibilities because undetermined and undifferentiated:

> Nous n'avons pas d'autre manière de savoir ce que
> c'est qu'un tableau ou une chose que de les regarder
> et leur *signification* ne se révèle que si nous les re-
> gardons d'un certain point de vue, d'une certaine
> distance et dans un certain *sens*. . . .
>
> Dans le monde en soi, toutes les directions comme
> tous les mouvements sont relatifs, ce qui revient à
> dire qu'il n'y en a pas.[40]

---

[38] Sartre goes on to an arbitrary hypostatization of 'le néant'
and argues that, since 'la conscience ne peut produire une
négation sinon sous forme de conscience de négation, . . . la
condition nécessaire pour qu'il soit possible de dire *non*, c'est
que le non-être soit une présence perpétuelle, en nous et en
dehors de nous, c'est que le néant *hante* l'être'. (Op. cit.,
pp. 46–7.) In short, in all experience giving rise to negative
judgements there is an intentional relationship with a 'néant'
as an entity. The assertion 'Pierre is not in the café' is grounded
in the *vision* of 'Pierre s'enlevant comme néant sur le fond de
néantisation du café.' (Ibid., p. 45.) For an interesting critique
of the 'négativisme philosophique' of Sartre and Heidegger,
see E. Morot-Sir, *La Pensée négative*, Aubier, 1947, pp. 294 ff.

[39] A. de Waelhens, op. cit., p. 117.

[40] Merleau-Ponty, op. cit., p. 491.

Negativity has its place in Marcel's phenomenology too. His 'participation' is not identification, but a reciprocal determining and constituting of subject and world that allows the terms of the relation to participate and yet preserve their distinctiveness. Experience itself, says Marcel, is no mere passive 'reception', but has active and 'dialectical aspects', all the more so the 'ontological reflection' that rises upon it. And Marcel stresses the importance of 'distance':

> What we are concerned with is a kind of borderland which thought must keep in existence between itself and its object; or, to express this more dynamically, we are concerned with the act through which thought is stiffened to resist the temptation to engulf itself in its own object and become merged with that object.[41]

At no point, however, is there radical disjunction between subject and world. This distance is purely 'internal': it is a sort of room which consciousness makes for itself within the world in order to bring the meanings of the world to light. But these views are only understandable when related to the phenomenological theory of truth which underlies its claim to be an ontology. Phenomenology returns to Greek, and primarily pre-Socratic sources by defining truth as a 'revelation of Being'; as 'the revealedness and revelation of what is', according to Heidegger, or as the 'sudden access to some reality's revelation of itself to us' according to Marcel.[42] The basis of true assertions lies in an 'antepredicative evidence' by virtue of the initial compresence. 'Nous sommes dans la vérité et l'évidence est "l'expérience de la vérité".'[43]

[41] Op. cit., p. 147.
[42] Heidegger, *On the Essence of Truth*, in *Existence and Being*, Vision Press, 1949, p. 334; Cf. *Being and Time*, SCM Press, 1926, p. 263. Marcel, op. cit., p. 53.
[43] Merleau-Ponty, op. cit., p. xi.

But this revelation of Being is possible only through
the sense-determining intentions of consciousness. If
truth is a property of Being (the property of revealing
itself as it is), it is also a quality 'conferred on the object by the mind that grasps it'.[44] And this determining of a particular sense or truth (out of the infinity
of potential senses or truths offered) is made possible
only by the negative structure of consciousness, which
allows it both to be and not to be the object presented
to it, since consciousness both possesses the object and,
by distancing itself from the object, constitutes it as
other than it is, as an object 'for itself', in short, as a
particular, limited determination of the object, corresponding to its own particular intention or project. So
that Being reveals its truth because it is appropriated
by a consciousness which, by an act of withdrawal and
limitation, determines a 'being' of Being, that is, a
manifestation of Being in one of its modes, in one of
the *particular*, *limited* senses or values implicit within
it.

This distance, which allows for the determination
and limitation that are the condition for Being to reveal itself, Heidegger calls 'openness'. It is the light
which allows us to see Being manifested, but always
within the limits of its determination in consciousness.[45] Moreover, paradoxically, it is this very dis-

---

[44] Marcel, op. cit., p. 64. Cf. Merleau-Ponty: 'Un rocher in-
franchissable, un rocher grand ou petit, vertical ou oblique,
cela n'a de sens que pour quelqu'un qui se propose de le
franchir, pour un sujet dont les projets découpent ces détermi-
nations dans la masse uniforme de l'ensoi et font surgir un
monde orienté, un sens des choses.' (Op. cit., p. 498.)

[45] 'L'Ouverture, lorsque nous y accédons (et nous y accédons par cela même que nous sommes homme) ne nous
dissout donc pas dans une totalité sans limites: elle établit, au
contraire, comme une sorte de champ clos, de lice, où l'étant
selon *ses* limites, va se manifester pour que nous le dévoilions,
pour que, selon ses diverses dimensions, nous le *disions*.' (A.
de Waelhens, *Phénoménologie et Vérité*, Presses Univ., 1953,
pp. 79–80). Cf. Marcel, op. cit., pp. 63–5.

tance, negativity and limitation which founds phenomenology as a positive ontology. For if I am, in so far as I intend it, one with Being, and at the same time distinct from it, since I grasp it as constituted by me, I hold it in its 'being-for-me', that is, I 'comprehend' it in the most fully positive mode of knowledge.[46] So that the negativity of consciousness that appeared to deny positive knowledge of Being is precisely what assures it:

> Car cette vie signifiante, cette certaine signification de la nature et de l'histoire que je suis, ne limite pas mon accès au monde, elle est au contraire mon moyen de communiquer avec lui.[47]

The notion of internal distance has other important implications. The self-world compresence is seen to possess a spatio-temporal volume. And the study of this qualitative structure leads to a reassessment of the classical concepts of space, time and the body.

Distinct from the *corps-objet*, the body as idea, is the body as experienced immediately at the ante-predicative level, the *corps-sujet*, 'ce corps que je suis sans pouvoir m'identifier logiquement à lui'.[48] 'Je ne suis pas devant mon corps, je suis dans mon corps, ou plutôt je suis mon corps.'[49] This experience of the body is a spatial experience. 'Le corps,' says Merleau-Ponty 'est éminemment un espace expressif.' But this 'spatialité du corps propre' differs from the abstract space of the physicist composed of points external to

[46] 'En effet, que je puisse être (pour les viser) les choses que je connais ou que je fais sans les être (puisque je ne me confonds pas effectivement avec elles), cela revient à admettre que je les saisis dans ce qu'elles sont sans pourtant m'identifier à elles comme étants, c'est-à-dire que je comprends leur être.' (A. de Waelhens, *Existence et Signification*, p. 117.)

[47] Merleau-Ponty, op. cit., p. 519.

[48] Marcel, *Du Refus à l'invocation*, p. 39. Cf. *Journal métaphysique*, Gallimard, 1935, p. 323.

[49] Merleau-Ponty, op. cit., p. 175.

one another, being structured not upon the point but upon 'le point horizon', that is the parts enveloped so as to form a perspective. It is a 'spatialité de situation' and not 'de position'.[50]

The particular perspectival system is constituted in terms of a particular sense-giving intention or way of acting in the world. 'Mon corps m'apparaît comme posture en vue d'une certaine tâche actuelle ou possible.' The *espace vécu* is an 'espace orienté'.[51] The body is at the centre as the organ whereby the subject constitutes a meaningful world for itself, giving it form in its dynamic schemas, which represent not so much objective spatial determinations as 'qualified situations', in that they are the qualitative expression of the subject's active relation to the world.[52]

Similarly, there is a temporal structure of the body, the *temps vécu* of concrete experience, it too characterized by the envelopment of its parts, as distinct from conceptual time with its past, present and future external to each other. The present of real time is a 'champs de présence' containing past and imminent future as indistinct horizons (Husserl's retentions and protensions), and exhibiting what Marcel calls a 'triangulation' or 'rapport entre l'immédiat, l'anticipé, et aussi le remémoré'.[53]

Together concrete space and time form what Marcel terms the category of 'depth',[54] the spatio-temporal dimension centred on the full, volume-laden spatio-temporal present of 'being-in-the-world'—l'épaisseur du présent pré-objectif, où nous trouvons notre cor-

[50] Ibid., pp. 171, 116–9.

[51] Ibid., pp. 116, 118.

[52] 'C'est seulement au prix d'une abstraction vicieuse que nous dissocions ce vivant, le fait qu'il vit, et les schèmes dynamiques par lesquels s'exprime sa situation.' (Marcel, *Du Refus à l'invocation,* p. 115. Cf. p. 117.)

[53] Marcel, *Homo Viator,* Aubier, 1944, p. 58. Cf. Merleau-Ponty, op. cit., pp. 475–6.

[54] Marcel, *The Mystery of Being,* I, pp. 192, 194.

poréité, notre socialité, la préexistence du monde'.[55]
For phenomenology space and time have to be understood neither as subjective categories nor as empirical
features of the world, but in terms of the ontological
relation between subject and world, that is of the
world-directed projects of the self:

> . . . Je ne suis pas dans l'espace et dans le temps,
> je ne pense pas l'espace et le temps; je suis à l'espace
> et au temps, mon corps s'applique à eux et les em-
> brasse.[56]

In this sense, space and time are 'objective', and are
found 'in the world'.[57]

If this is so, it is by virtue of the self-body-world
compresence, and this involves the attribution to the
body of a new status. The body acts as what Marcel
calls the 'médiateur absolu' and Merleau-Ponty the
'véhicule de l'être au monde'.[58] Experienced as 'une
masse gestuelle disponibole', 'mon corps est spatialisant et m'insère dans les choses'.[59] By it the self acts
in the world and constitutes the spatio-temporal *ek-
stases* which give it shape and meaning. On the one
hand, the body is continuous with the self, as the organ whereby the self selects its perspective and en-
dows the world with a particular sense. On the other,

[55] Merleau-Ponty, op. cit., p. 495.

[56] Ibid., p. 164.

[57] 'Le temps universel vient au monde par le Pour-soi. L'En-
soi ne dispose pas de temporalité précisément parce qu'il est
en-soi et que la temporalité est le mode d'être d'un être qui
est perpétuellement à distance de soi pour sli. Le Pour-soi, au
contraire, est temporalité, mais il n'est pas conscience *de* temporalité, sauf lorsqu'il se produit lui-même dans le rapport
"réflexif-refléchi". Sur le mode irréfléchi il découvre la temporalité *sur* l'être, c'est-à-dire dehors. La temporalité univer-
selles est *objective*." (Sartre, op. cit., p. 255.)

[58] Merleau-Ponty, op. cit., p. 97.

[59] G. Madimier, *Conscience et mouvement*, Alcan, 1938,
p. 448.

the body is continuous with the world, and this in two ways: first, it is through the body and its situation that the world offers a particular possibility of sense to the presentative and constitutive act of the subject; secondly, it is through the body that the particular sense offered and absorbed into the intentional act is expressed in significant behaviour—action, gesture, language. There is not a self, plus a body, plus a world, but a single sense-formulating event with three moments: the taking up into consciousness of a sense from the world, its organisation within the bodily mechanism, its projection back into the world in the form of behaviour—an event, in short, of which 'thinking' is the subjective and behaviour the objective side.[60]

Essential to this account is the view that bodily activity is already a form of reflection. 'Déjà la motricité, prise à l'état pur,' writes Grünbaum, 'possède le pouvoir élémentaire de donner un sens.'[61] There is a 'rationalité du corps propre' inasmuch as the latter in its dynamic schemas is a selective and organizing activity. The dualism established between 'thinking' and 'experience' is the corollary of the mind-body dualism and is refutable on similar grounds. Relations are not imposed by mind in the Kantian manner on an inert matter of experience, nor are they, in the empirical manner, derived inductively or inferentially from experience. They are given in experience and constitutive of it:

[60] One may note the close similarity between these views and those developed by Bergson in *Matière et Mémoire*. For a full analysis of the latter's theory of perception and its relationship with phenomenology, see my *Bergson, Philosopher of Reflection*, Bowes and Bowes, 1957, in particular chap. IV, *Mind as Act*, and chap. VI, *Meanings and Intentions*. Cf. also Merleau-Ponty, *Éloge de la philosophie*, Gallimard, 1953.

[61] Grünbaum, *Aphasie und Motorik*, Zeitschrift f. d. ges. Neurologie und Psychiatrie, 1930, quoted by Merleau-Ponty, *Phénoménologie de la perception*, p. 166.

La rationalité est exactement mesurée aux expériences dans lesquelles elle se révèle. Il y a de la rationalité, c'est-à-dire: les perspectives se recoupent, les perceptions se confirment, un sens apparaît. Mais il ne doit pas être posé à part, transformé en Esprit absolu ou en monde au sens réaliste. . . .

La rationalité n'est pas un problème, il n'y a pas derrière elle une inconnue que nous ayons à déterminer déductivement ou à prouver inductivement à partir d'elle: nous assistons à chaque instant à ce prodige de la connexion des expériences, et personne ne sait mieux que nous comment il se fait puisque nous sommes ce nœud de relations.[62]

The very generality that we associate with pattern, sense and meaning has its concrete source before ever conceptualisation proper develops, in experience, in the acquisition, that is, of motor habits. It is the body, says Merleau-Ponty, 'qui donne à notre vie la forme de la généralité et qui prolonge en dispositions stables nos actes personnels'. Such stable dispositions or habits are a form of understanding: 'on dit que le corps a compris et l'habitude est acquise lorsqu'il s'est laissé pénétrer par une signification nouvelle, lorsqu'il s'est assimilé un nouveau noyau significatif'.[63] For Marcel too experience is no mere passivity, but made up of acts constitutive of senses which come into being in and through the network of reciprocal relations of self and world. It is not a subjective but an intramundane and intersubjective event and, as such, contains the grounds of universality and generality, a generality that has its primary location in the body as the agent of 'permanence ontologique'.[64]

In short, sensations, images, all that is so often con-

[62] Merleau-Ponty, ibid., pp. xv–xvi.

[63] Ibid., p. 171.

[64] Marcel, op. cit., p. 83; *Etre et Avoir*, p. 138. One may compare Bergson's theory of the origin of the concept in action. Cf. my *Bergson*, pp. 79–80.

sidered mere material to be worked up into 'thought', are already thought, comprehension taken at their concrete cognitive root and 'in process'. But, if there is rationality at the antepredicative level, it is one that bears the mark of ambiguity, for it is the product of a fluid and variable relation between the self and the world, and it expresses itself only partially in the explicit act, image or word, which trail behind them an indeterminate and shifting background of implicit meanings and overtones—Being itself as the inexhaustible reservoir of sense, transcending all particular determinations of sense as their ultimate and ultimately undefinable ground and source. 'Le monde et la raison,' declares Merleau-Ponty, 'sont mystérieux, mais ce mystère les définite . . . la phénoménologie a pour tâche de révéler le mystère du monde et le mystère de la raison';[65] or, in short, to use Marcel's expression, 'le mystère de l'être.'

It would no doubt be hazardous to attempt any close parallel between contemporary French and British philosophical trends. Yet phenomenology, as it has evolved in France, is not without its bearing upon the most recent developments in analytical philosophy.

One will recall how the starting-point in Britain was the logical positivism associated with Russell, Carnap and the early Wittgenstein of the *Tractatus Logico-Philosophicus* and developed by Ayer and others. It led to the assertion that all meaningful statements fall into either of two classes: logical propositions, analytic, formal, tautological and irrelevant to factual experience; empirical, descriptive statements about matters of fact, susceptible of objective verification and therefore of being designated true or false. The application of this 'Occam's razor' excluded from meaningful utterance all statements not falling into those categories, such as moral, metaphysical and theological statements.

[65] Merleau-Ponty, op. cit., p. xvi.

Even at this stage it might be noted however that phenomenology and analysis met on one point: the clear cut distinction between logic and fact. Both reject the old-fashioned ontologizing which claims to account for the universe by *a priori* reasoning. Both assert the impossibility of proving assertions about existence from logical premises. Both agree that the real cannot be accounted for, only described. Hume's distinction between the 'is' and the 'ought', which looms so large in current ethical discussions in Britain—such as the distinction Nowell-Smith makes in his *Ethics* between the theoretical and the imperative—has its parallel in much phenomenological thinking.

Phenomenology, of course, particularly in its French enlargements, differed from the outset in envisaging a new type of ontology. It affirms that the world is given *as it is* and that the structures that 'appear' to consciousness are the very structures of Being. The Kantian distinction between phenomenon and noumenon and the conception of substance as a substratum underlying what appears fall to the ground.

> Relatif, le phénomène le demeure car le 'paraître' suppose par essence quelqu'un à qui paraître. Mais il n'a pas la double relativité de l'*Erscheinung* kantienne. Il n'indique pas, par-dessus son épaule, un être véritable qui serait, lui, l'absolu. Ce qu'il est, il l'est absolument, car il se dévoile *comme il est*. Le phénomène peut être étudié et décrit en tant que tel, car il est *absolument indicatif de lui-même*.[66]

Phenomenology thus envisages an experiential or positive ontology consisting of the description of the typical structures of Being (or patterns of meaning) as they appear directly to consciousness in its typical modes or structures of intentional experience—religious, moral, cognitive, emotive, etc.

[66] Sartre, op. cit., p. 12.

Returning to later developments in analysis, one may recall that doubts arose about the first statement of its position—about the verification principle (is it not metaphysical?)—above all, about the reasonableness of classing moral, metaphysical or religious statements as simply 'meaningless'. The result is seen in the recent work of Wisdom, Ryle, Nowell-Smith and the Wittgenstein of the *Philosophical Investigations*. The upshot has been to add a new class of statements, whose meaning is understood by the way the statement is used (the 'use principle').[67] Thus, according to Braithwaite, the use (i.e. the meaning) of moral and religious assertions is to express an intention to act in a particular way.[68]

But this is to recognize that such statements are relative to some way of acting in the world, some mode of sense-giving and of evaluating. To say 'I ought to be (or must be) courageous' has meaning only for one who seeks to 'choose himself' as courageous and to 'choose' the world as a place where courage may exist.[69] And it has meaning because he in-

[67] Cf. J. O. Urmson, *Philosophical Analysis*, Clarendon Press, 1956, p. 179: G. J. Warnock, *Analysis and Imagination*, in *The Revolution in Philosophy*, Macmillan, 1956, pp. 112–5: Wittgenstein, *Philosophical Investigations*. Blackwell, 1953, §109, 117, 340; cf. G. Ryle, *The Theory of Meaning*, in *British Philosophy in the Mid-Century*, Allen and Unwin, 1957, pp. 239 ff.

[68] 'Just as the meaning of a moral assertion is given by its use in expressing the asserter's intention to act, so far as in him lies, in accordance with the moral principle involved, so the meaning of a religious assertion is given by its use in expressing the asserter's intention to follow a specified policy of behaviour.' (R. B. Braithwaite, *An Empiricist's View of the Nature of Religious Belief*, Cambridge Univ. Press, pp. 15–6.)

[69] P. H. Nowell-Smith argues that 'I ought' is merely a special case of 'I shall' and expresses a decision purely and simply (*Ethics*, Penguin Books, 1954, pp. 267–8). Cf. Braithwaite: 'To say that it is belief in the dogmas of religion which is the cause of the believer's intending to behave as he does is to put

tends the world in this way and constitutes this particular sense which it contains.[70] Both phenomenology and recent analysis call back from abstract, generalized thinking to doing, and ultimately locate the source of thinking in 'being-in-the-world'.[71]

These new conceptions, moreover, have raised doubts about empirical statements themselves. A scientific theory does certainly more than translate a state of affairs: it is operational in intent, a policy for action, originating from activity in the world and implying an evaluation of the world.[72] The phenomenologist would go further and assert that even a simple

---

the cart before the horse: it is the intention to behave which constitutes what is known as religious conviction.' (Op. cit., p. 16.)

[70] Wittgenstein comes near to recognizing this in passages such as the following: 'You say to me: "You understand this expression, don't you? Well then—I am using it in the sense you are familiar with."—As if the sense were an atmosphere accompanying the word, which it carried with it into every kind of application. If, for example, someone says that the sentence "This is here" (saying which he points to an object in front of him) makes sense to him, then he should ask himself in what special circumstances this sentence is actually used. There it does make sense.' 'A main source of our failure to understand is that we do not *command a clear view* of the use of our words—our grammar is lacking in this sort of perspicuity. A perspicuous representation produces just that understanding which consists in "seeing connexions" . . . The concept of a perspicuous representation is of fundamental significance for us. It earmarks the form of account we give, the way we look at things. (Is this a "Weltanschauung"?).' (Op. cit., §117, 122.)

[71] Cf. H. H. Price's account of concepts as dispositions rather than entities (*Thinking and Experience,* Hutchinson, 1953, pp. 314–5). Cf. G. Ryle, *The Concept of Mind,* Hutchinson, 1949, chap. II, and my *Bergson,* chap. VI.

[72] For F. Waismann a scientific theory is a construction that reflects our own activity. (*Verifiability,* in *Essays on Logic and Language,* Blackwell, 1951, First Series, p. 140.)

empirical statement such as 'the table is round' is the expression of a particular sense-giving intention.[73]

Both phenomenology and analysis indeed represent a reaction against abstraction and a recall to the concrete, to the subject acting in the world and expressing itself in meaningful behaviour. If the phenomenologist might not accept all the implications of Ryle's definition of the self as 'the sum of its acts', he would agree that it is only in its acts and its behaviour policies and patterns, linguistic included, that the self can be studied, since for him consciousness is nothing but this sense-giving and expressive activity. And both currents belong to their age of philosophical 'insecurity'. Both reject the complacency of the system builder, seeing the starting-point of philosophy in a state of 'unease' ('I don't know my way about,' as Wittgenstein puts it), its procedure as tentative and clarificatory, and its function as in large part therapeutic.

To trace the influence of phenomenology in literature would be a major task. Perhaps the nature of its impact is best seen in literary criticism, particularly in the works of Gaston Bachelard, Georges Poulet and Jean-Pierre Richard.

These writers are concerned with describing essences, structures, patterns of meaning. Underlying their descriptions is a phenomenological postulate: that literary creation is a sense-giving and sense-revealing activity whereby the writer constitutes his self and a world for himself. It is a world of sensation and image before conceptualisation, what Bachelard calls 'la zone des rêveries matérielles qui précèdent la contemplation'.[74] But it is a meaningful world: indeed it is the world as the writer comprehends it di-

---

[73] Waismann describes a fact as 'What we notice . . . it is our work . . . something that emerges out from and takes shape against a background.' (Ibid.)

[74] *L'Eau et les rêves*, Corti, 1947, p. 6.

rectly in terms of his particular sense-giving intention.

To deal with it the critic must eschew analysis, disruptive of the texture of the whole, which *is* its meaning, and confine himself to description. He must submit himself to the text so as to allow the patterns of meaning embodied in its structure to disclose themselves. A sort of intuitive vision must come into play, if only because the meanings are not fully located in the express content, which carries overtones and undertones that constitute, as in perception, a carefully graduated implicit background. The critic's success will depend largely on his ability to bring to light relations and patterns not immediately discernible.

Above all, he must penetrate below the level of ideas to that pre-conceptual plane where the writer operates in his choice of image, symbol and sound, in Richard's words 'au cœur de la sensation, du désir ou de la rencontre'.[75] The critic will concern himself, says Bachelard, with the '*départ de l'image* dans une conscience individuelle', with the image as the union 'd'une subjectivité pure mais éphémère et d'une réalité qui ne va pas nécessairement jusqu'à sa complète constitution'.[76] For it is not a fully objectified world that the phenomenologist studies, but concrete modes of being or meanings of the world grasped within the dynamic process of their revelation and organization, at the moment when the writer 'anticipe la représentation du réel' just because he still remains 'lié au réel par la présence selon le corps'.[77]

At this level the work is seen to exist in its own space and time, structured in depth and volume. This structure the critic has to bring to light. He cannot follow out the mere chronological order of image or sensation, for the development of a poem is no causal sequence: he must be sensitive to relations that lie

[75] *Littérature et sensation,* Ed. du Seuil, 1954, p. 14.

[76] *La Poétique de l'espace,* Presses Univ., 1957, pp. 3, 4.

[77] M. Dufrenne, *Phénoménologie de l'expérience esthétique,* Presses Univ., 1953, vol. II, p. 658.

below the surface. Such a criticism discards the traditional techniques of sociological, biographical and
mere psychological criticism. It takes the work as a
fact, an existent, a 'world', that has no condition other
than itself. As such it cannot be accounted for nor explained, for its explanation is itself. It is the embodiment of a set of meanings, and the critic's sole task is
to uncover and describe them.

The significance of phenomenology lies in the return
to the 'expérience originaire du monde' as the root of
thinking. In France this involves something of a revolution, signifying a rupture with the Cartesian tradition of dualism on the one hand, of analysis on the
other. It is not, however, unrelated to French tradition—the tradition of Diderot and Rousseau, of Maine
de Biran and Valéry. Maine de Biran is particularly
significant, as witnessed by the renewed interest in
his thought since the 'thirties. Beneath his at first sight
dualistic psychology lies a subtle appreciation of the
organic link between consciousness and the body, and
his *Anthropologie* anticipates the method and views
of phenomenology in a remarkable way.[78]

[78] What Maine de Biran's reflexive analysis distinguishes as
'le fait intime' of consciousness is causal effort experienced
concretely as a relation between two terms, one the determination of the will, the other the bodily movement effected.
These two terms are given together and simultaneously as 'un
seul rapport à deux termes, dont l'un ne peut être isolé de
l'autre sans changer de nature ou sans passer du concret à
l'abstrait, du relatif à l'absolu'. (*Réponses à Stapfer*, in
*Œuvres choisies*, Aubier, 1942, p. 236. Cf. p. 239.) It is this
immediate relation, which through the body secures the inser-
tion of the self in the world, that is the source of positive
knowledge and the concrete origin of the concepts such as
cause, self and time. Each of the two terms of the relation 'entre
comme principe élémentaire dans toute connaissance réelle ou
de fait, sans constituer par lui-même cette connaissance'. (*Rapports des sciences naturelles avec la psychologie*, Ibid., p. 188.)
For it is only by their embodiment in the relation as inseparable

Of French phenomenologists Marcel and Merleau-Ponty come closest to its essential aim. Sartre, while asserting that the self exists only in its relation to the world, is led into a position which seems to empty the assertion of its fundamental import. His statement that 'je suis celui que je serai sur le mode de ne l'être pas' is phenomenologically valid in so far as it formulates the negative structure of consciousness as described above. But he goes on to hypostatize this negative factor: there is for him an actual entity—'le néant'—introduced by consciousness between itself and the given. Thus he argues that 'il n'y a jamais de motif *dans* la conscience: il n'en est que *pour* la conscience', and all phenomenologists would agree, since consciousness, taking the motive up into its intention, makes it other than it is. But Sartre goes on to assert that 'du fait même que le motif ne peut surgir que comme apparition, il se constitue lui-même comme inefficace' and that there is a '*rien* qui sépare le motif de la conscience', this *rien* being precisely man's freedom.[79]

Now Sartre can only make this inference because of its initial premise, namely that there is an absolute opposition between the *en-soi* and the *pour-soi*, as between what by definition is fully positive and fully coincident with itself, without any inherent possibility of discrimination, and what is characterized by nega-

and complementary terms that they together provide knowledge. Abstracted from it and considered as absolutes they are not the objects of positive knowledge but of 'indeterminate belief' (ibid.). Failure to see this leads to the rationalist and to the empiricist error respectively, the one starting from the subject, the other from the object as absolutes. And Biran observes in a manner that would be acceptable to any phenomenologist: 'Toutes les difficultés de la science viennent de ce que nous voulons toujours concevoir dans l'abstrait ce qui nous est donné primitivement et nécessairement en relation.' (Quoted by J. Wahl, *Tableau de la philosophie française*, Ed. Fontaine, 1946, p. 102.)

[79] Op. cit., pp. 69, 71, 72.

tivity, relation and difference.[80] From the very outset, in fact, Sartre places a sense-originating self *over against* a world which is devoid of meaning and incapable of any effective contribution to the emergence of meaning. The world, other selves, the self's own past, are a wholly indeterminate and passive ground for the projects of the self's unconditioned freedom and for its choice of values *'ex nihilo'*.[81]

For Marcel and Merleau-Ponty on the other hand the self is truly 'in the world'. The latter is already a reservoir of potential values and meanings: it is therefore already structured, although its structures are potentialities and await the sense-giving intention to be actualized.[82] Included in those potential values is all that is significant in the self's past; and although they do not determine, they constrain and solicit the self. So that its sense-giving activity is no mere unconditioned choice or negating of the past or of the world as given, but the product of 'call' and 'response', to employ Marcel's phrase. Self and world entertain a relation of complementarity and meanings emerge within this relation as between a sense-giving and a sense-revealing term. This is the process of *recueillement* described by Marcel whereby 'the reality, confronting which one ingathers oneself, itself becomes a factor in the ingathering' and where 'a man's given

---

[80] Sartre argues that the *Néant* being nothing cannot produce itself, nor can it come from the *en-soi*, which is wholly positive; it can therefore only come from consciousness (ibid., p. 129). But, if this is so, it is difficult to see how the *en-soi* can be even potentially structured or contain even a possibility of meaning.

[81] Op. cit., p. 70. Cf. p. 76.

[82] 'Le *Dasein* est lui-même spatial, ou, plus exactement, spatialisant, mais il n'exerce cette spatialisation que parce que lui-même lié à un monde qui implique l'espace, non point l'espace organisé et structuré de notre vie courante, mais la possibilité d'une telle organisation.' (A. de Waelhens, *La Philosophie de Martin Heidegger*, Louvain, Ed. de l'Instit. Sup. de Phil., 1947, p. 63.)

circumstances, when he becomes inwardly aware of them . . . become . . . *constitutive* of his new self'.[83] And it is in this light that Merleau-Ponty criticizes Sartre in his *Les Aventures de la dialectique*, attributing his political errors and his rejection of the humanist tradition to the failure to recognize historicity or the organic structure of experience which links the self in a relation of reciprocity with the world, other selves and the past.

These criticisms are to the point. All that has been gained by phenomenology would be lost by the return to what might prove to be a subjectivism and dualism in a new guise. Phenomenology defines experience as a project towards the world, initiated from the world and emerging again into the world in the form of meaningful action, and so securing the persistence and renewal of pattern in time and history. If it puts the self at the centre as the agent of change, it recognizes that the self is at every moment actively informed by the world on the one hand and actively

---

[83] *The Mystery of Being*, I, pp. 126, 134. For Marcel's detailed criticism of Sartre's views, see *Homo Viator*, pp. 233 ff. Cf. also M. Farber, *Aspects of Phenomenology and Existentialism from 1945–1948*, in *Philosophie*, XIV, *Psychologie, Phénoménologie et Existentialisme*, Hermann, 1950, pp. 145–8. It may be added that Sartre's recent *Critique de la raison dialectique* (Gallimard, 1960) would appear to mark an effort to resolve his dilemma. 'Le lieu de notre expérience critique n'est pas autre chose que l'identité fondamentale d'une vie singulière et de l'histoire humaine:' '. . . ma vie . . . doit se découvrir elle-même au fond de son libre développement comme rigoureuse nécessité du processus historique pour se retrouver plus profondément encore comme la liberté de cette nécessité et enfin comme nécessité de la liberté.' (Ibid., pp. 156, 157.) But the development of the *Critique*, which takes the form of a marxist logic of history—'une totalisation mouvante et dialectique qui n'est autre que l'histoire ou . . . que le "devenir-monde-de-la-philosophie"' (pp. 29–30)—seems to bear little relation to the phenomenologically inspired content of *L'Etre et le néant*.

committed to it on the other. The subjective is the pole of a relation, in itself nothing:

> Le pôle subjectif n'est *rien*: c'est-à-dire qu'il n''est' pas à la manière d'une chose, il n'est pas localisable, il n'est pas un être du monde. Il n''est' que dans la mesure où il *existe*, et il n'existe ('ek-siste') qu'en se projetant vers: il n'est qu'en étant ailleurs, *hors-de-soi-dans-le-monde*; il est, si l'on veut, cette impossibilité d'être soi.[84]

Experience is no mere subjectivity. The phenomenon of consciousness is the embodiment of a sense which comes from the world, is actualized in the sense-giving intention and is projected back into the world as action. Everything significant takes place 'out of' the self, in a closely woven nexus of space and time which commits the self directly to the world and to other selves. Participation, intersubjectivity, organism, these are the key words of phenomenology. If the self can be defined, it is as a 'relation agissante'.[85] It can, says Marcel, be assigned no precise frontiers. It is the focal point of a transcendence, the unlocalizable medium for the revelation of meaning:

> L'univers est un ensemble de significations que tisse et retisse incessamment l'expérience humaine. Ce ne sont pas des significations que nous créerions en constituant le monde; le monde est avant nous. Quand notre conscience s'éveille, il est déjà là et nous sommes en lui. Mais il est inachevé et ambigu; et dans une interaction réciproque nous constituons avec lui un ensemble de significations, qui est la réalité et la rationalité mêmes.[86]

[84] Jeanson, *La Phénoménologie*, p. 75. Cf. G. Gusdorf, *La Découverte de soi*, Presses Univ., 1948, p. 503.

[85] J. Wahl, *Traité de métaphysique*, Payot, 1953, p. 256.

[86] G. Madinier, *Conscience et signification*, Presses Univ., 1953, p. 34.

This is the key discovery of phenomenology. It requires us to go beyond the psychologism of traditional philosophy and to view the human product not as the product of the individual, solipsistic mind, but as an 'intramundane phenomenon', a 'manière d'être du monde', a mode of Being itself, brought into 'existence' through the self-world project.[87] It also asks us to view the product as a trans-subjective, preconceptual but already rational system of meanings which, by virtue of the play of intertwining intentions, the intersubjectivity of selves and the unitary ground, which is Being itself, contains generality and universality sufficient to establish valid and significant discourse. For the integration and embodiment of meanings offered by the world in the sense-giving intention is not only the typifying structure of all creative activity, it is the foundation of all comprehension or understanding, grasped at their cognitive root.[88]

Finally, phenomenology recognizes the fact of 'mystery'. Meanings and values are known only as embodied in the mediating intentions of selves and as modes of Being. Being itself, the source and ground, remains hidden. Yet this Being is present as the ultimate reference, the ultimate horizon of experience. Herein lies what Marcel calls 'the ontological mystery of knowledge'. Being is the 'opaque datum', what resists, in that it transcends all determinations of value and sense as their hidden but implicated source and ground. This is what renders the philosophy of values 'susceptible de se transcender elle-même et de pointer vers ce qui la dépasse infiniment'—towards the realm of 'silence' which lies beyond language in that 'la parole

[87] Cf. A. de Waelhens, *La Philosophie de Martin Heidegger,* p. 50.

[88] 'On comprend l'être des choses lorsque celles-ci sont intégrées et pro-jetées à l'intérieur de nos possibilités propres. Les choses acquièrent un sens—le seul dont elles soient capables —en tant que matière de nos possibilités.' (Ibid., p. 269.)

est issue de la plénitude du silence, et que celui-ci lui confère sa légitimation'.[89]

Hence phenomenology as ontology assumes the ambiguous form of both a descriptive science and a mystical search. A science in so far as it describes, without seeking to explain or justify, the structures of experience and the modes of Being therein embodied. A mystical search in that this science is never complete but points to an ultimate transcendence never possessed:

> Il s'agit de reconnaître la conscience elle-même comme projet du monde, destinée à un monde qu'elle n'embrasse ni ne possède, mais vers lequel elle ne cesse de se diriger.

> Que l'être soit toujours ce qui n'apparaît que par un étant et que nous ne puissions nous fixer directement sur lui, rend cet être exprimable seulement par un acte de visée capable lui-même de porter au-delà de ce qu'il désigne.[90]

There lie the limits of ontology as of language itself.[91]

Here again perhaps phenomenology comes close to certain contemporary analytical views inspired by Wittgenstein in recognizing that language comes up against certain opaque data.[92] Of such ultimates are

---

[89] Marcel, *Les Hommes contre l'humain*, La Colombe, 1951, pp. 129–30; Idem, Preface to M. Picard, *Le Monde du silence*, Presses Univ., 1954, p. xii.

[90] Merleau-Ponty, op. cit., pp. xii–xiii; A. de Waelhens, *Existence et Signification*, p. 120.

[91] Cf. J. Wahl, *Vers la fin de l'ontologie: étude sur l'Introduction dans la métaphysique par Heidegger*, S.E.D.E.S., 1956, p. 257. Cf. also G. Madinier, *Vers une philosophie réflexive*, La Baconnière, 1960, pp. 65 ff.; E. Lévinas, *De l'existence à l'existant*, Ed. Fontaine, 1947, pp. 170–2.

[92] M. B. Foster notes that the initial cause of collision between religious philosophy and earlier analysis lay in 'the assumption that all thinking is an answer to our questions'. (*Mystery and Philosophy*, SCM Press, 1957, p. 27.)

values, inseparable from our experience of things. They are neither entities existing in an autonomous realm and open to some special intuition, nor observable properties of things, nor arbitrary creations of the subject. In a sense they seem to be all these—both in fact and independent of fact, as E. W. Hall has said.[93] All that we can truthfully assert is that they are a function of the structures incorporating subject and object in experience where—in the modes in which they appear—they are open to description. In themselves they remain ultimates.

This recognition of the 'unsayable' coupled with the assertion that philosophy is concerned with what can be said defines the ambiguous status of reflection as understood by phenomenology. It inspires the tension which underlies philosophical writing in France, torn between the description of existence or 'being-for-me' and the 'nostalgie de l'être,' of Being as ultimate ground, that inhabits all thinking.[94] Nor may it be too much to attribute in part to the pervasive influence of phenomenology a similar tension apparent in contemporary French literature, the *nouveau roman* and drama being cases in point. At the centre of both philosophy and literature is the awareness of the self's antepredicative relationship with the world and of consciousness as an unending process of constituting meanings against a background from which they emerge and into which they retreat—like so many shifting presences, testifying to a reality that transcends language and discourse and yet legitimates them.

[93] *What is Value?*, Routledge and Kegan Paul, 1952, pp. 247–9.

[94] 'Tout langage apparaît comme indépassable (et c'est en ce sens qu'il y a pour nous primat de la connaissance sur l'Etre) et pourtant comme, en soi, dépassé (et c'est en ce sens qu'il y a primat de l'Etre sur la connaissance).' (F. Alquié, *La Nostalgie de l'Etre*, Presses Univ., 1950, p. 136.)

# IMAGINATION

## Hide Ishiguro

One of the key themes of Sartre's philosophy is the freedom of the human mind. Sartre asserts that the human mind escapes causal determinism and, like Kant, believes that we do not discover our freedom as agents by empirical observations. In order to demonstrate his position, Sartre has had to pay great attention to areas of the human mind which it was traditionally supposed could best be explained by the operation of causal laws, i.e. imagination and emotion. Imaginings, Sartre wants to say, are not happenings which we observe, no more than are emotions. For Spinoza, who attempted to fit in all activities of individual minds into a causal scheme, imagination represented the aspect of mind which was least related to correct understanding and which in a way was most passive, most directly determined by other things and by the disposition of one's body. But even Spinoza wrote that 'if the mind, when it imagines non-existent things to be present, could at the same time know that those things did not really exist, it would think its power of imagination to be a virtue of its nature, and not a defect, especially if this faculty of imagining depended upon its own nature alone, that is to say if this faculty of the mind were free'.[1] It only

Reprinted by permission of Routledge & Kegan Paul Ltd., London, and Humanities Press Inc., New York, from *British Analytical Philosophy*, edited by Bernard Williams and Alan Montefiore. (Routledge & Kegan Paul, "International Library of Philosophy and Scientific Method" series, 1966.)

[1] Spinoza, *Ethics* Part II, Prop. XVII. Note to Corollary. Mr. Gordon Blair reminded me of this passage during a discussion on Sartre.

happened that in Spinoza's universe, man's faculty of imagination could hardly ever be said to depend solely on its own nature. In contrast to this, Imagination for Sartre epitomises the nature of mind which escapes causal determination. It is this which enables us to think of possibilities and alternatives, and hence gives us the capacity of choosing and intending.

Although perhaps in not quite a radical way, imagination has been re-examined as an important part of the philosophy of mind by analytical philosophers. It is no longer treated as a faculty the understanding of which has little to do with our knowledge of other mental activities. We can therefore also use the results of their conceptual enquiry to assess the beliefs and theories of Sartre.

Several analytical philosophers, like Sartre, have rejected the view that images are mental objects. In fact, the study of imagination is one of the subjects where the problems raised by philosophers of the two isolated worlds of Europe and Britain most resemble each other. The difference between Sartre's *L'Imaginaire*[2] and the notes concerning imagination in Ludwig Wittgenstein's *Blue and Brown Books*[3] or the chapter on imagination in Gilbert Ryle's *Concept of Mind*[4] is much smaller than the difference between *L'Imaginaire* and the works of Sartre's French predecessors or that between Ryle's enquiry and those of the British empiricists of the Humean tradition.

It is amusing to observe philosophers who claim to use completely different methods and profess the greatest mistrust of each other's methods yet manage to arrive at similar deadlocks. For at first glance nothing seems more different than the treatment of the problem of imagination by Ryle and by the continental phenomenologists, notably Sartre. Sartre asserts that since Descartes, 'We know that a reflexive con-

[2] Paris, 1948.
[3] Oxford, 1958.
[4] London, 1949.

sciousness gives us absolutely certain data', and thus all we must accept is 'what reflection will tell us'. His 'simple method' consists of 'producing images in ourselves and then reflecting upon these images in order to describe them, in other words to determine and classify the characteristics distinguishing them'.[5] On the other hand, Ryle, with his seemingly behaviourist approach, denies the value of introspection as a method of finding out facts about our mind, and tries to show throughout his controversial book how people since Descartes have been misled into believing that by introspection we can have indubitable knowledge of what happens in our mind. Ryle not only denies the value of introspection, but seems to deny the existence of those inner mental processes which people have believed to be discernible by introspection.

> The radical objection to the theory that minds must know what they are about, because mental happenings are by definition conscious, is that there are no such happenings, there are no occurrences taking place in a second-status world, since there is no such status and no such world and consequently no need for special modes of acquainting ourselves with the denizens of such a world.[6]

One can sympathize with Ryle's scepticism about introspection. People who believe in the value of introspection have often described psychological facts which throw little light on the philosophical problem at issue. For example, Bertrand Russell wrote that the word 'or' corresponds to a state of hesitation and that hesitation arises when we feel two incompatible impulses neither of which is strong enough to overcome the other.[7] If this is the kind of thing that one discovers by introspection then one can justly deny that intro-

5 L'Imaginaire, p. 14.
6 The Concept of Mind, p. 161.
7 Russell, Inquiry into Meaning and Truth, 1940, p. 84.

spection has any *special* place in philosophy. The facts discovered are as contingent as any particular fact observed in the world.

In spite of their radically opposed principles the methods of Ryle and of the phenomenologists are not very dissimilar. The introspection or the 'reflection' of the phenomenologists does not aim at discovering psychological facts like the ones above. Indeed one of Husserl's enterprises was to denounce the infection of philosophy by empirical psychology. And in *L'Imaginaire* what Sartre discovers by 'reflecting on his mind' is not the content of the particular images he has, nor the various patterns of association of ideas. His work shows that what he means by reflecting is the asking of questions like 'Can I go on discovering new facts about the things I imagine as I do when I perceive things?' 'Does it make sense to say that one has found a new feature of an object one is imagining which one hadn't realized before?' 'Do I see or observe the objects which I imagine in the same way in which I see or observe things in the world?' 'When I picture something do I think that it belongs to the spatio-temporal world in which I find myself?'. This method of enquiry is not very far from that of Ryle.

We have already seen why the study of imagination was important for Sartre in his programme of demonstrating that the mind escapes causal determinism. But why is it important for Ryle? Imagination is important for Ryle in his attempt to demolish the Cartesian dualism of mind and body. In order to combat the view that there are mental events and physical events taking place side by side when human beings act, one has to give a satisfactory explanation of the activities of our mind when it is preoccupied with imaginary objects. For, as Ryle says, 'imaginary' is usually taken to be synonymous with 'mental'. An imaginary object is considered as the mental entity *par excellence* which exists in a universe independent of the physical world. Thus if anyone is—as I am—interested in rejecting Cartesian dualism, one is led to be interested

in the success or failure of a programme of Ryle's type.
The chapter on Imagination is consequently a section
of the *Concept of Mind* about which the greatest
amount of dissatisfaction has been expressed. People
usually consider the world of our imagination as being
private and internal, and accessible only to introspection. Even if one agrees with Ryle that mental terms
do not always simply refer to introspectible mental
entities or events (for example, Ryle seems to be right
to point out that a 'belief' refers not to any mental
occurrence or process but to a disposition to do certain things, etc.), one finds it difficult not to think that
one has a privileged access to one's own world of
imagination. Now Ryle thinks that when we do sums
on a piece of paper or when we read a book, we are
not doing two things, one of them private and the
other public, at the same time. We do not first do
sums mentally and then put them down on paper, nor
do we arouse in ourselves a purely inner process
called reading by moving our eyes across the page and
perceiving certain letters. The publicly observable behaviour of putting the sums down on paper *is* the mental act of doing sums, and perceiving groups of letters
in a certain way *is* reading. He says, '. . . when we
describe people as exercising qualities of mind we are
not referring to occult episodes of which their overt
acts and utterances are effects: we are referring to
those overt acts and utterances themselves'.[8] How
would Ryle's argument work in the case of imagination? When we imagine things we do not usually perform any publicly observable acts at the same time.
Would anything remain of imagination after being op-
erated on by Ryle's razor?

People might say that all mental activities are in
essence private and internal and, therefore, that there
is nothing specially occult and inaccessible about the
workings of our imagination. Why should our having a
pain, for example, be less private than our picturing

8 *Concept of Mind,* p. 25.

things? In the case of pain, however, there usually occur certain symptoms or natural behaviour which the person exhibits. And although there is no logically necessary connection between the statement that someone is in pain and the statement that someone is exhibiting certain symptoms or behaviour (since one can be true and the other false), yet there is a connection between the concept 'pain' and certain patterns of human behaviour. Imagination betrays no such symptoms and is accompanied by no natural gestures. As Ryle himself writes: 'If you do not divulge the contents of your silent soliloquies and other imaginings, I have no other sure way of finding out what you have been saying or picturing to yourself'.[9] Can he sensibly admit this and deny that the process of imagining is introspectible at the same time? The workings of the imagination seem to resist explanation in terms of publicly observable behaviour, even in terms of 'pretending', as Ryle does, so long as 'pretending' is given only a behaviouristic account. We can therefore see the point of Sartre's method of beginning from reflexion.

But if, as Sartre suggests, we adopt 'reflective' or introspective method in studying imagination, what do we reflect on? For, as I have already mentioned, it is not only Ryle, but Sartre also, who denies that images are objects in the mind. Sartre claims that our habit of thinking about objects in space in spatial terms has led people mistakenly to suppose that images are in the mind, and the objects of imagination are in the imagination. When I picture Julius Caesar to myself, the proud-looking Emperor that I am imagining is not in my mind in the same way in which the historical Julius Caesar was in Rome. The object of my imagination, both Sartre and Ryle are eager to tell us, is not a mental entity, an image which has the characteristic of being like the real Caesar but no other qualities, like a painting without a canvas. I imagine the histori-

[9] *Concept of Mind*, p. 61.

cal Caesar and not the image of him. In Ryle's words:
'Much as stage murders do not have victims and are
not murders, so seeing things in one's mind's eye does
not involve either the existence of things seen or the
occurrence of seeing them'.[10]

It is true that when I picture an object, the image of
the object is not located in my mind in the same way
as this painting I see or this piece of sculpture which
I touch is located in time and space. If one were to
say that mental images existed in the mind simply because the person alone can be aware of the objects he
imagines, then by the same kind of reasoning one
would be able to say that the objects of perception
exist in the mind (as many have indeed said). My
visual field can only be *my* visual field, and the things
I see are all in this field. One can properly talk of temporal and spatial location only after identifying and
establishing a public time and space. Even if one were
to talk of the location of objects in private time and
space, as in the case when I say that an event pre-
ceded another in my dream or that I saw an apparition in the centre of my visual field, the objects of my
imagination could still not be described as being located 'in my mind'.

But will this fact justify Sartre's claim that images
and perceptions, far from being psychic factors of
similar quality, exclude each other?[11] Are he and
Ryle right in their very similar argument against
Hume's assimilation of seeing and having mental images? Hume was never able to make a clear distinction between 'impressions' (sensations) and 'ideas'
(images in our terminology). Hume thought that one
could distinguish the two kinds by their vividness, i.e.
'ideas' or 'images' are according to Hume less lively.
But we do not have perceptions of a neutral kind,
scrutinize them and then decide by their vividness
whether we are perceiving things by our senses or

10 *Concept of Mind*, p. 245.
11 *L'Imaginaire*, p. 156.

imaging, where imaging does not mean having hallu-
cinations, but an activity which one engages oneself
in. We do not see mental images as we see things.
As a matter of fact, according to Ryle, we do not see
mental images at all, except in a metaphorical sense.
He points out that this can be brought out more
clearly by thinking of 'smelling'. When one smells the
smithy one visited as a child one is not smelling a
special smell. One is not smelling a faint smell nor
a copy of a smell. One fancies one smells: it is a
game of make-believe. Thus, Ryle claims that just as
mock-murder is not the committing of a mild or faint
murder, picturing is not seeing a faint object: 'imagining occurs but images are not seen', 'I have tunes
running in my head but no tunes are being heard'.

Some people may feel that this statement is pre-
posterous. When I picture my mother's face, what I
see need not be a faint replica as Hume suggests, nor
need there be any danger of confusing my act of picturing with my really seeing her. Nevertheless, it
seems true that I am seeing an image since I have an
experience such that I can describe what I am picturing to myself.

The point of denying that we see mental images
might be the following. When we see something we
are, of course, aware of the fact, i.e. we have a certain
kind of inner experience. Having this experience is,
however, not the only criterion by which we judge
that a person sees.[12] For example, if a person with his
eyes firmly shut were to say that he sees a table, we
would not be willing to grant him that he really sees
it, even if there happened to be a table before him.
Similarly, if someone were to say, 'I see a table but
there is none', our first reaction would be to say that
he was mistaken. And it has been claimed that the
person must either *think* that he sees a table when he
doesn't, or he sees something which looks like a table.

[12] I refer to the fact that one of the criteria by which other
people judge that I see is the report I give of my experiences.

One cannot claim, it has been argued, to see something which does not exist simply because we would not call this 'seeing'. It is not a question of idioms or ordinary language. The point is that the concept of seeing which we use is tied to many assumptions about public objects, visual organs, human behaviour, etc., and is not uniquely related to our having certain experiences. In order to discover these assumptions, and thus to understand the concept, it is never sufficient just to 'reflect on our consciousness'. It is necessary to examine the occasions when we would be prepared to say that we see and in what circumstances we do say so. Ryle's point is, put simply, that when I picture something, what I am doing does not satisfy the ordinary accepted concept of seeing, which is intimately linked with our ideas about visual sensations and about the existence of things seen. If I can picture something with my eyes closed, the act of picturing is compatible with having no sensations and nothing akin to them. It cannot be confused with my seeing a picture. But is this true?

I will picture the birth of Venus to myself. I see a female creature with long golden hair. She is looking at the waves round her with a slightly disdainful look, her lips are pouting, her arms are plump. Now what does Ryle deny that I am doing? If he is saying that he refuses to call it 'seeing mental images of Venus' merely because what I am doing differs, as we have seen, from standard cases of seeing, then it will be a quarrel over language. Anyone, including Hume, with all his confused terminology, would have realized that there was some difference between picturing and seeing. If, in spite of that, many philosophers called picturing 'seeing mental images', it was because they thought the similarity between the two processes more important than the difference. The boundaries of a concept or a meaning of a word are usually vague and elastic. It is for us to decide whether we should change the boundaries or not. One cannot stretch a concept at the expense of making it self-contradictory or too vague to be of any use, but at times one has to be willing to extend or narrow the boundaries fixed by ordinary usage, if one finds it more appropriate to do so. After all it is human beings who decide whether a concept is used metaphorically in a certain case or whether it is used literally. With this in mind I will show why I still agree with Sartre and Ryle that there are some interesting differences between my act of picturing Venus, and seeing a picture of Venus.

Naturally, when I picture something, I am not seeing anything in the world. But the believers in mental images, whom I will call Imagists for short, have never claimed that when I picture Venus, I see Venus. They merely said that it was *as if I were seeing a picture of Venus*. Imagists were quite aware of the fact that my optical organs were not receiving any external stimuli, but thought that in spite of this difference I was having a similar experience to that of seeing, i.e. to that of seeing a picture of Venus.

One can here consider another argument which Sartre uses against the Imagists. It is simply wrong to think that I have an experience very similar to that of seeing a picture when I visualize. When I look at a real picture, for example, when I look at Botticelli's 'Birth of Venus', I can see it and describe it without knowing what it is a painting of. I can describe its colours, I will see that it is a nude woman rising from the sea. I can scrutinize and discover more and more details about the painting. When I picture something in my mind, it is entirely different. I cannot have a mental image without knowing what it is an image of. A mental image does not have qualities by itself as a painting does. There is no mental image as such. I have an image of a red object, but I do not have a red image. I do not behold an image which I then discover looks like a Venus, since my mental image consists solely of the description I am willing to give to Venus. As Ryle says, when I fancy I hear a very loud noise, I am not really hearing either a faint or loud noise. It would be absurd to ask, 'Do you have a soft replica of

a loud noise in your mind?' Thus having mental images
is quite different from perceiving.

Sartre writes similarly that the expression 'mental
image' is misleading because it suggests an object of
some kind. When I picture Pierre I do not, he claims,
have an awareness of an image of Pierre, but rather a
special kind of awareness of Pierre himself; an awareness which could be better described as an 'awareness
of Pierre-in-image' or 'imaging awareness of Pierre'.
And Sartre describes this by saying that an image is
not a mental object, but a relation. Sartre also points
out how wrong it is to describe imaging as a kind of
perceiving, although in doing so he often lapses into
confused terminology. When we perceive an object,
we are perceiving it from one of its infinite aspects.
We can go on learning new things about the object.
In Husserlian terminology, 'The object always goes
beyond my awareness of it'. When we picture things,
it is quite different. We cannot learn new things about
what we picture. 'An Image', Sartre writes, 'is defined
by its intention'. We can never learn new things about
it because it only has the qualities that we have put
into it. Sartre expresses this somewhat misleadingly,
and says, 'The object of imaging is never anything
more than the awareness one has of it'.[13] This expression, with its ambiguous use of the word 'object',
would seem to contradict his view that an image is
not an object, but a relation. For when I picture
Pierre, the man Pierre is the object of my awareness,

---

[13] Some people might object and say no, we do learn new
things about our images. When we want to prove a geometrical theorem we often learn from our mental images. We sometimes put down our images as diagrams and discover facts
from them. This is, however, wrong. We never discover new
facts from the diagrams as we would about ordinary objects of
perception. We discover or see what is entailed by the ideas we
already had or postulated by the aid of diagrams. Even when
we draw a triangle badly, we can read into it that the three
angles form 180° and are not bothered by the shortcomings
of the figure we have in front of us.

and not, as Sartre himself says, the image of Pierre. And Pierre is certainly much 'more' than the awareness I have of him! We should perhaps rephrase this expression of Sartre and interpret it as meaning that in imaging there is nothing more in the person's awareness of the object than what the person puts in.

Although Sartre, like Ryle, correctly points out the important difference between picturing and seeing a picture, it seems that he does not give a satisfactory analysis of imaging. Sartre says that an image is not a mental object, but a relation. What then is it a relation to? According to Sartre, whether I perceive him or imagine him, it is the man Pierre who is the object of my awareness.[14] It is easy to establish at least that there is a relation (in a Humean sense) between Pierre and my awareness when I perceive him in front of me,[15] but how is my awareness related to him when I picture Pierre who is absent? And when I picture the birth of Venus, what is the object of my awareness? In this case, to say that the object of imagination and perception is the same is to give no explanation at all, since there is no Venus either present or past to be perceived. There is another difficulty. When I picture Venus to myself and when I picture Brigitte Bardot, I seem to be doing the same kind of thing, although the objects of my awareness are radically different; one being a mythological fiction and the other a

[14] Thus the question 'Where do things exist which people imagine?' is not a spurious question for Sartre as it is for Ryle. In many cases, e.g. when I imagine my friend Pierre or picture Mont Blanc, the answer is 'In the world' or 'In Paris', 'On the Swiss-French border', etc. 'Things imagined' does not have to mean any mental entities, and I am sure that if the question is taken in Sartre's sense, Ryle will also consider it as being meaningful.

[15] A relation between Pierre in front of me and my awareness can be established by others (in a Humean sense) by correlating their observations of Pierre and the reports I give of my awareness.

woman in the flesh. Could this be explained without
positing mental objects?

Can we then say that when I picture $x$ the object of
my awareness is not $x$, but the description of $x$? This
seems to be obviously false. When we are picturing
Bardot or Pegasus, we are thinking of a person or an
animal and not of descriptions of them. What we con-
template is an instantiation of the description—a thing
which has certain properties rather than the properties
themselves. Yet, we can think of instantiations of certain descriptions, even if the world does not contain
such instantiations—in other words, even if such instantiations do not exist. We can therefore understand
why picturing Bardot and picturing Venus are not
such different kinds of activities although one is a live
human being and the other is a mythological fiction
which does not exist. For, to think of an instantiation
of descriptions which happen to be true of Bardot,
and an instantiation of descriptions traditionally
ascribed to Venus are not very different activities.

We also are made to see what is unsatisfactory
about Sartre's claim that an image is a relation rather
than a mental object. For if I claim that there is a relation, and in this case a two-term relation, then I
seem to be committed to claiming that there are two
entities of some sort which stand in a certain relation
to each other. Thus if my having an image of an object means, according to Sartre, that I stand in a special relation to that object, then, it would follow that
I and that object exist and that a particular relation
holds between the two. But as we have seen, one can
think of an instantiation of a property, without there
being such an instantiation in the world. I can picture
something with features which nothing in the universe
has. But I cannot be said to stand in any relation to
something which does not exist.

One might attempt to defend Sartre by suggesting
that even if an image cannot be considered as a relation between a person and another thing, it could be
taken as a relation between a person and a thought.

When I imagine Pierre why can I not be said to stand in a special relation to the thought of Pierre? But with such a theory, the whole point of explaining an image as a relation rather than a mental object seems to get lost. There would be a point of saying that I have a special relation to a thought—if the particular thought I have could also have an existence independent of me. But every thought is someone's thought. Since different individuals can have the same thought in the sense of the same kind of thought, one can always specify the identity of a thought as a universal independent of any particular person who has it. This fact does not still make it helpful or necessary to talk of 'relations' between the person and a thought. Having the thought could be considered a property of the person just as having a particular height or having a particular colour of hair could be.

It therefore seems better to not treat images and other mental phenomena as having thoughts, having fear and so on, as relations. We should rather say, as Brentano did, that they are 'relatively determined', i.e. that they are properties of a person which can be described only by grammatically relational propositions, although they are not relations proper.[16] We should not, according to Brentano, be taken in by surface grammar, for the words which give the objects of thought (or objects imagined) do not properly refer. The object of thought is given 'in modo obliquo' or opaquely.

The various features of consciousness which Sartre has correctly asserted, and which are based on views acquired from Brentano and the phenomenologists, i.e. that consciousness is transparent, that it is intentional and is about something, leads to the peculiarity of its having to be specified by reference to other objects or state-of-affairs and hence by relational propositions. But it does not lead to the view that the mind

[16] E. G. Brentano; 'Letter to L. Hillebrand', 21 May 1916.

is always related to some other thing or state-of-affairs
of which it is aware.

Having to be described with reference to something
else is not a feature peculiar to images, but according
to Sartre (following Brentano) it is a feature which
follows from the nature of consciousness in general.
Different states or acts of thoughts can be distinguished only by what they are about and not by some
mark of the consciousness itself. G. E. Moore had
written with reference to perception, 'The moment we
try to fix our attention upon consciousness and see
what, distinctly, it is, it seems to vanish; it seems as
if we had before us a mere emptiness. When we try
to introspect the sensation of blue, all we can see is
the blue; the other element is as if it were diapha-
nous'.[17] As we have seen, Sartre wants to point out
that this peculiar feature is shared by images as well.
(That is why he is led via his introspective method
to the relation view of images.) At the end of the first
section of *L'Imaginaire* he describes the deadlock
which confronts him in the 'terrain sûr' (!) of phenomenological description. 'We Know', he writes, '. . .
that in mental images there is a psychic datum which
functions as representation (analogon), but the moment we want to determine the nature and components of this we are reduced to making conjectures'
(which is empirical science and not phenomenology).
'We can describe what the image is an image of and
discover by reflection the qualities of the imagined
object', but 'we cannot hope to grasp the content of
our picturing mind through introspection'.

But if *all* mental phenomena are only 'relatively determined' or describable in terms of objects other than
themselves, and if the content of the picturing mind
cannot be grasped by introspection, how can one distinguish picturing or imagining from other modes of
thinking? Sartre explicitly says that images are neither

[17] G. E. Moore, 'Refutations of Idealism', *Philosophical Studies*, p. 25.

things which accompany thoughts nor interfere with thoughts, but constitute a subclass of thoughts themselves (*L'Imaginaire,* p. 158). Yet when it comes to the positive characterisation of images or what he calls 'imagining awareness' which distinguishes them from other thoughts, Sartre, like Ryle, is unsatisfactory. To say that we do not observe and learn new things from our images does not seem to be enough since we can have momentary perceptions of ephemeral events such as lightning which we cannot scrutinize and learn from, and yet they remain perception of events. External characterisation such as the existence or absence of external stimuli was available for Ryle in fixing the concept of imaging, but it isn't for Sartre with his phenomenological method. Moreover, for Sartre, people can picture and have 'imaging awareness' even when there are external stimuli of the relevant kind, so Ryle's conditions will not help. For example, people can have an image of the Infanta as they look at a canvas painted by Goya, or they can have an image of the Hamlet as they look at an actor performing now in Europe.

According to Sartre, when people exercise their imagination, the objects of their thoughts are imbued with the features of unreality: they are aware that these objects are not perceived, that they are not there and that they escape the laws of the perceived 'real' world. Perceiving and imaging are, he claims, two irreducible and mutually exclusive attitudes of the mind. But is this dichotomy of the real and unreal or of the perceived and imagined as evident as Sartre suggests? Sartre says, for example, that when I look at an actor mimicking a person X, so long as I am aware of the actor and his movements, I am perceiving him and thus the object of my awareness is 'real'. When I no longer see him as the actor himself, but as the person X whom he is mimicking, and when his gestures become for me the gestures of X, the object of my awareness is no longer the actor, but X who is not there. I cannot be said to be perceiving X, but,

according to Sartre, I have an image of X: an awareness of X, who is not there to be perceived as a real
object. We can in a way make sense of Sartre's assertion that the object of perception is real whereas that
of the image is not. If I perceive the actor, then given
the same conditions, other people should be able to
perceive him as well. Everyone who comes into the
theatre will see this man on the stage. Whereas if I
see the actor as X, it does not follow that all people
do or would have to see him as X. X is not a public
object which is there in the way in which the actor is
there. Thus, it might follow that if I see something as
X, I could not be perceiving the real X at the same
time.

Sartre's claim is, however, a stronger one than this.
He thinks that when I see the actor as the person he is
mimicking, I cannot be really perceiving the actor.
Similarly, if I see a painting as a portrait of X, according to Sartre I am no longer perceiving the painting (*Ibid.*, p. 156). And this seems to me to be evidently wrong. If I see Laurence Olivier as Hamlet,
I must on the contrary also be perceiving Laurence
Olivier. One cannot see X as Y without seeing X. It is
probably this fact which led philosophers to assume
that when I picture Y in my mind, there must be a
mental object which I see as Y; or that I must be
perceiving a mental image of Y. Although this latter
view is mistaken and, as we have seen, the fact that
I picture something does not entail that I see a mental
picture of the thing, it is not right to claim, as Sartre
does, that whenever we have an 'imaging awareness'
of something we could not at the same time be perceiving anything at all. On the contrary, it seems that
we will arrive at a better understanding of what it is
to image and to do things in our minds, if we examine
more closely the intricate relationship that holds between imaging and perceiving or between seeing as
and seeing.

In pointing out that imaging and seeing as is a species of thinking, Sartre, like Ryle, has concentrated

too much on the aspect of imaging which is voluntary.
As Wittgenstein says, there is a sense in which 'seeing
an aspect and imagining is subject to the will'.[18] Ordered to picture Venus, I would try to draw up a picture of her in my mind similar to what I would draw
on paper. It does not at all follow from this, however,
that visualizing is a pure *doing* or that it has nothing
akin to seeing. Suppose I try to visualize Venus but
am unable to do so. I try; I think of various Greek
myths concerning Venus, but I see nothing in my
mind's eye. In this case I will surely not say that I am
picturing Venus unsuccessfully or poorly. I will con-
fess that I do not picture her. Just as one cannot win
every time one wishes to win, one cannot picture
every time one wants to. Picturing is not a pure *doing;* it is a *happening* and an achievement as well.
There is a quality of picturing which can best be described as analogous to seeing, and in general, contrary to what Sartre implies, a quality of imaging
which can be best described as analogous to perceiving (in spite of differences which should be remembered), and which perhaps can only be described in
this way. Even Sartre acknowledges that when one
pictures something, the thing comes to the mind 'en
bloc', like a particular object of perception, and that
this distinguishes it from a concept.[19]

A person who pictures is not simply a fanciful man
who can entertain complicated hypotheses or build
up sophisticated suppositions. Picturing seems to be a
distinctly visual capacity as well, just as hearing tunes
in one's head is an auditory capacity. What I mean
can be brought out by the following example. If someone orders me now to follow the tune of the 'Goldberg
Variations' in my head, I am unable to do so, although
I know the piece in the sense that I will recognise it
if it is played, and even though I can give a description which will uniquely identify it. Try as I may I

[18] *Philosophical Investigations*, p. 213.
[19] *Ibid.*, p. 21.

cannot succeed in running through the tune in my
head. The best way to describe my failure seems to
me to say that I do not hear it. Ryle correctly said
that imaging is not a function of pure sentience. Sartre
rightly shows that imaging is not a pure happening.
But it is wrong to ignore the fact that there is an element of 'given' in it which is beyond our control, and
that this 'given' is best described by perception words.
Picturing in our mind is not merely a mental analogue
of the physical act of drawing on paper or canvas. It
also involves the analogue of our seeing what we have
drawn as we draw. And the word 'what' here seems
to refer not to the lines and shades we draw, but the
object depicted, i.e. what our drawing is a drawing
of. As I have argued elsewhere, I can claim to *see*
something in my mind in the same sense in which I
can claim to *see* Venus or the Infanta in a painting.[20]

What is it that makes us see an object as one thing
or another? We cannot choose to see an object as *anything* or picture whatever we like. The many questions
Wittgenstein asks in his *Blue and Brown Books* and
in his *Philosophical Investigations* about 'seeing as',
and the related problems raised by Merleau-Ponty in
*The Phenomenology of Perception* indicate the complexity of the problem. Personal and institutionalised
knowledge, conventions and inherited traditions, and
even skills that a man can acquire, affect and limit
what images we can have, and what we can see as
well. Until we have made it clear to ourselves whether
this is not a causal influence and limitation, we cannot
easily use imagination, as Sartre does, to epitomize
the freedom of the human mind.

[20] 'Imagination', *Proceedings of the Aristotelian Society,* Sup-
lementary Volume, 1967.

# AUTHENTICITY AND OBLIGATION

## Frederick A. Olafson

Discussions of the ethical aspects of existentialism tend to concentrate on the evaluative activities of individual human beings and on the nature of the freedom in which those evaluations are made. Typically, little is said about the moral relations in which such autonomous individuals stand to one another, or about the compatibility of an ethical theory based on the concept of autonomy with a recognition of some kind of moral obligation toward other human beings. This lack of attention to the social aspect of morality, it must be admitted, reflects a corresponding neglect on the part of most of the existentialist writers; and this neglect has led many critics to conclude that the concepts used by the existentialists in the analysis of evaluation are radically incapable of dealing with the phenomenon of moral community and the complex moral relationships to other human beings which such community comports. This charge has at least a *prima*

Reprinted, with alterations by the author for this edition, by permission of The Johns Hopkins Press from chapter 8 of *Principles and Persons: An Ethical Interpretation of Existentialism,* Frederick A. Olafson, The Johns Hopkins Press, Baltimore, 1967. Copyright © 1967 by The Johns Hopkins Press. The "existentialists" to whom I refer in this chapter are, in the first instance, Jean-Paul Sartre and, secondarily, Martin Heidegger and Maurice Merleau-Ponty. Since the completion of my book, the first major study of moral obligation from a generally existentialist point of view, J. Henriot's *Existence et obligation* (Paris: Presses Universitaires de France, 1967) has been published. While it is of considerable interest, it quite fails to recognize the limitation on individual freedom that is the essence of obligation; and it thus remains within the radically individualistic perspective which I criticize in this chapter.

*facie* plausibility about it which makes it all the more necessary to explore in detail the implications of the existentialist position for the whole topic of moral relationships among human beings. In this essay, I will attempt to show that, while the existentialists do not have a fully developed theory of obligation, they have presented in embryo at least a conception of what the basis of moral relations between human beings should be.

This apparent lack of interest on the part of the existentialists in the social dimension of morality is in striking contrast to the current orientation of much moral philosophy in the English-speaking world.[1] On the whole, the latter may be said to assume the existence of a more or less stable and harmonious society with a developed moral code and a highly articulated set of concepts defining the different role-relationships in which human beings may stand to one another, as well as the rights and duties associated with these roles. Under these circumstances, the job of moral philosophy is typically conceived to be the making explicit of the principles and rules with which, in such a state as this, we are assumed to be familiar, even if we may be unable to state them very clearly. Usually the acceptance of such rules is taken for granted and is not itself the subject of inquiry, but when a justification of the whole corpus of moral principles is called for, it is characteristically provided by arguments showing that an acceptance of these principles is in some sense definitive of human nature.[2] Since the human nature such writers have in mind is, in fact,

---

[1] For a somewhat different characterization of the contrasting approaches to ethical questions of existentialists and most English-speaking philosophers, see I. Murdoch's contribution to the symposium on "Vision and Choice in Morality," *Proceedings of the Aristotelian Society,* Sup. Vol. 30 (1956), pp. 32–58.

[2] See, for example, R. S. Peters, "Nature and Convention in Morality," *Proceedings of the Aristotelian Society,* Vol. 51 (1950–51), pp. 223–53.

the fully moralized human nature of a stable and relatively harmonious society, there is a sense in which in spite of its circularity this argument can claim a certain rough truth. In any case, one main result of approaching the subject matter of morality from this angle is that purely individual decisions, i.e., decisions for which a determinate moral context is lacking, are treated either as external to the whole province of morality, or are assigned to the interstices of the moral life in which the moral rules we do accept leave us free either to act or not to act in a certain way.

If we consider the examples used by the existentialists from this point of view, sharply different presuppositions immediately become evident. These examples almost uniformly concern individuals who are forced to act under circumstances in which the support given by established moral institutions is for one reason or another unavailable. Even when the background of choice *is* a functioning society to which the moral agent belongs, it is usually described in such a way as to undermine any assumption that a moral consensus or any genuine moral reciprocity exists. The paradigm situation from which a general characterization of morality is to be derived is thus one in which the individual moral agent is compelled to choose and to act in isolation from, or in the absence of, any collectively accepted and reciprocally applied body of moral rules. Correspondingly, the "normal" situation in which such guidance and support are available receives relatively little attention from the existentialists. Since action in such circumstances is, as we shall see, permanently threatened with "inauthenticity," it qualifies at best as a borderline example of the "moral." The latter is thus made coextensive with the whole province of human action, and no special importance is attached to the distinction between broader questions of individual self-determination and the kinds of question that are usually thought of as being answered by reference not to an individual ideal but to a rule that is common to at least some group of human beings. Instead of excluding the former—as often happens—from the moral sphere because they do not clearly involve the application of shared rules, the existentialists tend to feel that rule-governed situations can be included within it only to the extent that they can be shown to involve individual choice. Or, to put the same point another way, morality as a whole is the province of individual self-determination, and the social dimension of morality and relationships with others come in simply as one element in the design of an individual life.

It would be unprofitable here to debate the advantages and disadvantages of a conception of morality that takes individual choice in its purest form as its paradigm case, and sees in shared moral rules only a special case of individual self-determination.[3] The more important issue is to determine just how adequate an account of the moral relationships among human beings can be given by a theory that sets out from these root assumptions. As I have already indicated this inquiry carries one well beyond the limits of any moral theory that has so far been provided by the leading figures in the existentialist movement. In fact, it assumes the character of an effort to expand the few hints and suggestions that have been thrown out into a positive account of moral obligation. The possibility of such an extension of existentialist ethical theory is precisely what I want to establish in this paper. Before undertaking this task, it will be useful to examine a little more closely some of the reasons that have made the existentialists so reluctant to develop any account of obligation at all.

[3] An interesting discussion of the place of "rules" and "ideals" within morality as a whole can be found in P. Strawson, "Social Morality and Individual Ideals," *Philosophy*, Vol. 36 (1961), pp. 1–17.

# I

It is not difficult to locate the sources of the antipathy which the concept of obligation typically evokes in existentialist philosophers. The root notion in that concept is one of being bound in the sense of being subject to an effective restriction on the permissible range of human choice. Traditionally, this restriction itself has been thought of as independent of, and unremovable by, human volition. Indeed, many moralists have argued that it *must* be independent of choice if we are to be able to talk—as we all do—of what we ought to do even when we do not do it.[4] If morality were, at bottom, a matter of will and choice as the existentialists believe, then all obligations would be self-imposed. An obligation I have created, however, is one from which I can release myself; and the latter, so the argument goes, is no obligation at all. Particularly in cases in which our practice is at variance with our declared principles, the decision to act in a way that violates a recognized obligation might appear to be tantamount to such a release; and the sense in which, barring special circumstances, one could still be said to believe sincerely that acting otherwise would really have been right becomes very unclear. Moreover, beyond this special difficulty, there is the general problem of how the will can bind itself at all if it is not confronted with objective moral relationships *in re*, and, as Hume said, "has no object to which

---

[4] The view that moral obligation must be independent of human volition should not be confused—although it often is —with the quite different requirement that it be of such a nature that there *can* be conflicts between what we *want* to do and what it is our obligation to do. Sartre, as his theory of obligation shows, is certainly prepared to recognize that conflicts of the latter type occur but at the same time he holds that obligation as such is constituted by joint acts of choice.

it could tend but must return to itself *in infinitum.*"[5]
A will-created obligation would thus turn out to be
simply an indefinitely prolonged series of acts of will
which could never produce an uncancellable change
in the "relation of objects" by which it would then be
bound. By contrast, a truly binding obligation must
have its basis outside the will, and would impose a
restriction upon the will in much the same way as the
antecedent determinacy of fact is supposed to define
the goal of theoretical inquiry. Once the meta-ethical
stamp of intellectualism is thus set upon the concept
of obligation at the very outset, it becomes automatically unincorporable into any ethical theory based on
the idea of moral autonomy; and it is to this fact that
the existentialists' avoidance of the concept of obligation can most obviously be traced.[6]

There are, however, other sources of this negative
attitude toward the concept of obligation that are internal to the existentialist analysis of human being
itself. For the existentialist, and for Sartre in particular, the primordial relationship in which every human
being stands to every other tends to be one of conflict.[7] This is not to deny that agreement and coopera-

[5] See his *Treatise of Human Nature,* ed. Selby-Bigge (Oxford: Clarendon Press, 1888), Bk. 3, Pt. 2, sec. 5, "On the
Obligation of Promises," especially the footnote on pp. 517–18.

[6] Thus, I would interpret Sartre's very strong denial that
anything can oblige me to adopt any course of action (*L'Être
et le néant,* p. 69) not as a denial of the possibility of obligation
as such but rather of there being obligations which simply
confront the moral agent without his having in any way helped
create them. It should be noted, also, that Sartre speaks of the
unavoidability of choice as "une obligation perpetuelle," but
this use of the term is so different both from traditional conceptions of obligation and from Sartre's own conception of
self-created obligations that I have not given it any special
attention.

[7] "Le conflit est le sens originel de l'être-pour-autrui"
(*L'Être et le néant,* p. 431). In Pt. 3, ch. 3, of *L'Être et le
néant,* Sartre seeks to establish this thesis by detailed analyses

tion among human beings ever occur, nor is it to attribute a disposition to hostile and aggressive behavior to all human beings. Like Hegel in his famous analysis of the dialectic of the master and the slave, Sartre has in mind a type of conflict that is rooted in the very structure of the reciprocal relationship in which two human consciousnesses stand to one another.[8] The basis of this conflict is moral, and it lies in the fact that there can be no guarantee that the choices made by the "other" as an autonomous moral being will coincide with, or even be compatible with, my own. The appearance of another being enjoying the same moral freedom as I do is thus a challenge to, and a potential disruption of, "my" moral world which the other may well perceive simply as a

---

of "les relations concrètes avec autrui," among them love, hate, and sexual desire; and in each case he argues that we are caught between the alternatives of sadism and masochism, of treating the other as an object for one's self, or oneself as an object for the other. While neither of these strategies can succeed in suppressing our awareness of subjectivity and freedom —whether our own or the other's—Sartre insists that the disjunction they form is exhaustive. "C'est . . . en vain que la réalité-humaine chercherait à sortir de ce dilemme: transcender l'autre ou se laisser transcender par lui. L'essence des rapports entre consciences n'est pas le *Mitsein*, c'est le conflit." (p. 502) Although this inevitable conflict is said to be the origin of the "guilt" of each human being in relation to every other, this guilt can evidently not be expiated and even if I were to act in accordance with Kant's categorical imperative and make the moral freedom of the other my end, "cette liberté deviendrait transcendance-transcendée du seul fait que j'en fais mon but" (p. 479). It seems quite clear that this denial of the possibility of mutuality among human beings is in conflict with Sartre's later views as expressed not just in *Critique de la raison dialectique*, but in *L'existentialisme est un humanisme*, and was in fact abandoned by him.

[8] Sartre's most powerful description of this antagonistic relationship of human consciousnesses to one another can be found in the section entitled "Le regard," Pt. 3, ch. 1, of *L'Être et le néant*. Sartre's play, *Huis Clos*, has the same theme.

set of facts or objects cut off from the context of possibility and first-personal choice with which I endow them. Since another human being cannot *be* the effort of transcendence that I am, and within which I experience and give meaning to my world, he can only *know* me and my world in the objective mode and this knowing collapses the properly evaluative dimension of my acts and leaves them stranded as so many natural events awaiting another evaluative interpretation which may or may not coincide with mine. Because this "collapsing-cognitive" apprehension of my values as "mere facts" is conceived by Sartre to be primary and inescapable in my relationship to other human beings, the advent of the "other" is a harbinger of conflict and not of concord. Even if the other moral consciousness proved to be in harmony with my own evaluations, there could be no guarantee of the indefinite continuation of that harmony in which the possibility of conflict is therefore always latent. Thus, either by anticipation or in actual fact, the presence of another autonomous moral being like myself imposes upon me the ordeal of having my actions "devaluated" in the medium of another consciousness. In its most radical form, this devaluation may extend not just to the evaluative ordering of my world which I effect through my actions and choices, but to my very status as a moral personality. That is to say, another moral consciousness can do more than simply evaluate a situation differently from the way I do and thereby reduce my evaluations to the status of "facts." It can also deny me the status of a moral agent altogether and treat me merely as an instrument to—or an obstacle in the way of—the realization of its own values. It can, in short, treat me as a thing rather than as a person, and repudiate or never recognize at all those principles of reciprocity that hold between human persons who mutually recognize one another as such. The appearance of an alien moral consciousness involves not just the threat of a conflict with my "values," but the threat of my being absorbed into the moral world of the other through being denied recognition as an autonomous moral being.

When views such as these of other human beings as primarily sources of ultimate moral conflict dominate a theory of human relationships, it is not surprising that there should be little place within the latter for a doctrine of moral obligation. Sartre has, in fact, sometimes written as though there were no possibility of any genuine mutuality among human beings—only the alternatives of an aggressive imposition of one's own moral perspective upon others, or a kind of masochistic submission to their aggression.[9] But this is not the whole story. Sartre is at least as emphatic in his assertion that the refusal of recognition to alien moral personalities, like the refusal to recognize one's own autonomy, can "succeed" only through what he calls "bad faith." That is, in order to seal off my world from the intrusions of an independent moral consciousness, I must first locate and identify the latter, much in the way in which the hypnotic subject must "know" where a given object is in order *not* to be able to find it. Sartre's point is that there is an internal contradiction in such denials of moral personality to which there corresponds a very special duplicity or dishonesty in our relation to ourselves. More generally, in spite of his very sharp distinction between the evaluative sense that my actions have for me and the moral appreciation that may be made of them by others, Sartre recognizes that we cannot simply dismiss or disallow the image others form of us. In one dimension of our being—the public and the social dimension—we *are*, so he says, what we are for others; we cannot invoke our own conflicting sense of ourselves to invalidate that public assessment of what we are.[10] Sartre does not,

---

[9] *L'Être et le néant*, p. 502.

[10] For Sartre, the experience of shame is "une *reconnaissance* de ce que je *suis* bien cet objet qu'autrui regarde et juge." (*L'Être et le néant*, p. 319.) As one would expect, Merleau-Ponty's conception of the relationship among human

it is true, develop this doctrine of publicity and of the authority of an external view of our actions as the basis for a theory of obligation; and he sometimes seems to be saying merely that we must accept the fact that we are for others something quite different from what we are for ourselves. But elsewhere in his writings he does appear to be defending—and even pressing to the limits of paradox—the view that it is the public signification of my actions that is controlling in moral contexts, and that to the degree that the moral consciousness issues into the world and creates or accepts definite relationships to others, it cannot by itself control, in the sense of modifying by its own individual fiat, its situation vis-à-vis those persons.[11] In this sense at least, "being bound" is an inescapable feature of any moral experience that is more than a private reverie.

In the work of Maurice Merleau-Ponty, a recognition of the central importance of this element of publicity receives a specifically moral interpretation, and some suggestive hints are given as to the way in which a theory of moral community might be developed in a manner compatible with the fundamental existentialist doctrine that all morality rests ultimately on choice. Where Sartre is willing to recognize only the self-defining activity of human consciousness, set over against the moral opacity of the *en-soi*, Merleau-Ponty introduces a third, intermediate level—that of collective, funded meanings—which constitutes precisely the

consciousnesses differs significantly from Sartre's. For Merleau-Ponty, the consciousness of the other as an object is exceptional and marks a withdrawal from a shared understanding that human beings have of themselves and of others as active, purposive beings. See *Phénoménologie de la perception*, pp. 412 ff.

[11] It does not, of course, follow that we are the prisoners of the other in the sense of having to accept our identity for the other as our own sense of ourselves. As Sartre says, "je m'échappe d'autrui en lui laissant mon Moi aliené entre les mains." ( *L'Être et le néant*, p. 345.)

impersonal moral milieu in which most of our experience is situated. Not to reject the evaluations that are proposed to us by the community in which we live, is not *ipso facto* to *choose* them unless, Merleau-Ponty argues, we are prepared to suppress the distinction between our ordinary mode of consciousness and the specially cultivated mode in which all choice situations are antecedently marked out as such.[12] Merleau-Ponty is even willing to go so far as to say that, if negation is the basic attribute of subjectivity, it is possible only by virtue of the tissue of collective meanings upon which it supervenes.[13] No one of these has for Merleau-Ponty, any more than for Sartre, a compulsory hold upon the individual moral agent; but if he can opt out of any one of them, he can do so only in favor of another publicly defined mode of construing a certain type of situation, which may be recognized already, or which may have yet to establish its credentials.

Merleau-Ponty is here emphasizing, against Sartre and Heidegger, the essential place of the *"On"* or *"Das Man"* in any adequate account of the moral life. These writers condemn the anonymity of all "values" that are not, in the first instance, one's own first-personal choices, and see in any reliance upon collectively held

[12] *Phénoménologie de la perception*, p. 516. The central difference between Sartre and Merleau-Ponty on this point is not that the latter recognizes the *"sollicitation"* of the social milieu —Sartre recognizes that just as clearly—but rather that Merleau-Ponty attributes a "privileged" status to long-established policies and does not feel that *"la généralité du rôle"* must be consciously assumed in a purely individual choice as Sartre appears to do. (See *L'Être et le néant*, pp. 602–03.)

[13] "Si c'est par la subjectivité que le néant apparait dans le monde, on peut dire aussi que c'est par le monde que le néant vient à l'être. Je suis un refus général d'être quoi que ce soit accompagnée en sous-main d'une acceptation continuelle de telle forme d'être qualifiée (*Phénoménologie de la perception*, p. 516).

standards of evaluation and action the antithesis of the fully self-conscious autonomy which they call authenticity. By contrast, Merleau-Ponty views the mediating function of public "meanings" as an indispensable element in the dialectic between the individual and the moral community to which he belongs. It would be a great mistake, however, to suppose that he assigns to these impersonal significations any kind of objectivity in the sense of ultimate independence of choice that is denied them by Sartre or Heidegger.[14] His point is simply that individual choice exercises itself, not in the first instance upon all the logically possible options associated with a given situation, but rather upon the standing, socially established ways of interpreting those situations. He is also recognizing the fact that these evaluations present themselves with a certain impersonality, and that when we simply "go along" with them as most of us do most of the time, we are doing something that is subtly different from what we do when we explicitly adopt or reject them. The dialectic of moral self-definition is thus a confrontation of individual choice and established moral codes and not, except in extreme cases, one between individual choice and an *en-soi* that has been stripped of all the accretions that an established moral tradition in a historically continuous society imposes upon it.

It has been widely recognized among existentialists that the true locus of these collective evaluations is the language we use. This is true of the writers who like Heidegger and Sartre are most insistently hostile to all supra-individual tendencies in morality, and also of those who like Merleau-Ponty recognize the interdependence of individual choice and cumulative or "funded" evaluations.[15] In Merleau-Ponty's own

14 See for example his *Phénoménologie de la perception,* pp. 518–19.

15 Thus Sartre can say that "(la totalité du langage) ne peut rein être si ce n'est la *praxis* elle-même en tant qu'elle se

words, the function of language is to make us see ourselves as another "other," that is, to establish an intersubjective milieu within which the privileged position of the self is suppressed in favor of a standpointless and neutral mode of reference to all selves.[16] Similarly, when our choices receive expression in language, they are cast into a medium over which no individual has complete control, and which can therefore serve to express the joint evaluative attitudes of many. This is preeminently not a language in which a sharp distinction is made between our characterization of "situations" and our evaluative construals of them. When we use the words of this language to convey our own individual attitudes and choices, the latter are thereby subtly modified because the public language in which they are expressed lends them certain implications and subjects them to certain criteria of reasonableness that may run counter to the actual sense of our choice and may even cause our own judgments to appear "alien" to us. This phenomenon of the alienation of moral attitudes when they come to be expressed in a public and objective language has generated a counter-demand for the no doubt impossible elimination of all dependence upon an established moral consensus in our language and our personal moral choices.

---

manifeste directement à autrui; le langage est *praxis* comme relation pratique d'un homme à un autre et la *praxis* est toujours langage par ce qu'elle ne peut se faire sans signifier. . . . En fait les 'relations humaines' sont des structures interindividuelles dont le langage est le lieu commun." (*Critique de la raison dialectique,* p. 181.) In spite of the Marxist overtones of this passage, its meaning is not really very different from Heidegger's characterization of speech as "das 'bedeutende' Gliedern der Verständlichdeit des In-der-Welt-seins, dem das Mitsein zugehört, und das sich je in einer bestimmten Weise des besorgenden Miteinanderseins hält." (*Sein und Zeit,* p. 161.)

[16] See his "Sur la phénoménologie du langage," *Signes* (Paris: 1960) pp. 105–122, especially p. 121.

The real point of the existentialist argument on this issue, as it emerges from Merleau-Ponty's critique of Sartre, is not that we are, or should ideally be, entirely free of all dependence upon an *inter-monde* of public moral meanings; but rather that, whatever our degree of commitment to the latter, we can never be finally locked into any set of evaluations by the logic of our language. Certainly the very impersonality of the moral concepts we use, coming down to us as they do from a nameless past, conceals their origins in choice. When this happens, the rationality and order that are the achievement of a progressive systematization of individual choices come to be regarded as transcriptions of a rationality that is somehow implicit in the very situations with which our moral codes and concepts are designed to deal. In these circumstances, the inhibitions against revisionary individual choices are no longer just the practical difficulties that are inevitable whenever a system of commitments is called into question, but the kind of logical and metaphysical difficulty that prevents an individual from even thinking of himself as a potential critic of the code he has inherited. What the existentialists have done is precisely to resist the sorcery of language by which the objectivity of an established social consensus as reflected in the articulation of our moral concepts becomes confused with another kind of objectivity that choice is powerless to modify.

Nevertheless, important as all these observations on the role of publicity in the moral life undoubtedly are, they remain undeveloped in the writings of the existentialists. Their most serious attempt to provide a constructive theory of moral relationships among human beings is to be sought instead in their elaboration of the notion of authenticity, and in their effort to show that the very autonomy which as we have seen defines the moral condition of man, can also yield a principle of reciprocity on which a human community can be founded. I turn now to an examination of this doctrine of authenticity with a view to determining whether or not the existentialists are right in thinking that a positive ethic can be founded on the concept of moral autonomy.[17]

[17] While both Heidegger and Sartre disclaim any intention of drawing directly normative conclusions from their "ontologies" of human existence, and deny indeed that any such can be drawn, there can be no doubt that both of them in fact make a normative use of the concept of autonomy. In Heidegger's case, it is quite clear that the denial of normative intentions has to do with the possibility of using his theory of *Dasein* to generate answers to specific questions about what is right and wrong. (See *Sein und Zeit*, pp. 294, 298, 312). Heidegger himself states that "der durchgeführten ontologischen Interpretation der Existenz des Daseins liegt . . . . eine bestimmte ontische Auffassung vom eigentlicher Existenz, ein faktisches Ideal des Daseins zugrunde" (p. 310). He goes on to say that while "existentiale" or, as one might say, "second-level" analysis can never authoritatively settle "existentielle" or "first-level" questions about possible courses of action and obligations, it nevertheless has a certain "first-level" content.

> "Wenn das Sein des Daseins wesenhaft Seinkönnen ist und Freisein für seine eigensten Möglichkeiten, und wenn es je nur in der Freiheit bzw. Unfreiheit gegen sie existiert, vermag dann die ontologische Interpretation Anderes als ontische Möglichkeiten (Weisen des Seinkönnens) zugrundezulegen und diese auf ihre ontologische Möglichkeit zu entwerfen? Wenn die Analytik als existentiell eigentliches Seinkönnen die vorlaufende Entschlossenheit zugrundelegt, ist diese Möglichkeit dann eine beliebige?" (*Sein und Zeit*, pp. 312–13.)

To this last question Heidegger's answer is plainly "No"; and he develops a theory of conscience according to which *Dasein* constantly calls itself back from its absorption in the world to a recognition and acceptance of itself as a free and responsible being. In spite of the metaphorical character of this treatment of conscience as a "call," Heidegger makes it quite clear that it has no mystical implications and that to hear the "call" is simply "sich in das faktische Handeln zu bringen," i.e., to *act* in the full sense of that term. Once again, conscience does not

## II

Up to this point, moral autonomy has been described simply as a state in which human beings find themselves. Unavoidably, they see their situation in terms of possible alternatives among which they must choose; but they do not choose to see the world in this way.[18] So conceived, moral autonomy is not itself the

tell us for what we are responsible or what we ought to do. "Die Antwort vermag nur der Entschluss selbst zu geben . . . ihrer selbst sicher ist die Entschlossenheit nur als Entschluss," (*Ibid.*, p. 298). Very significantly, a "public conscience" that does gives answers to questions about conduct is identified as the voice of *Das Man* (p. 278); and "morality" is described as emerging from a conscience that is wholly individual (p. 286). For Heidegger's discussion of conscience and guilt, see *Sein und Zeit*, pp. 267–301.

Sartre's denial that ontology has normative implications can be found in *L'Être et le néant*, p. 720. Especially in *L'Existentialisme est un humanisme* he defends a view that is very similar to Heidegger's with respect to the use of autonomy as a goal, namely that it can yield a certain style of moral existence that excludes conduct based on "bad faith" but does not give answers to specific moral questions. Like Heidegger, Sartre rests his case for a normative use of autonomy on the fact that "l'homme est un être libre qui ne peut, dans les circonstances diverses, que vouloir sa liberté"; but he does not develop a theory of conscience and appears to hold simply that freedom, as the "nature" of man, implies a "volonté de liberté" without showing any concern about possible charges of circularity against which Heidegger defends himself at length. (*Sein und Zeit*, pp. 314–16.) At the same time as he shares this general position with Heidegger, however, Sartre also associates the Kantian notion of reciprocity with this "volonté de liberté," as Heidegger does not, and argues that while the content of morality is variable, its form is universal and this "form" includes not just the individual autonomy on which Heidegger insists but a respect for the autonomy of others. See *L'Existentialisme est un humanisme*, pp. 84–86.

[18] See *Sein und Zeit*, pp. 284–85 and *L'Être et le néant*, pp. 558–59.

source of any directives for human conduct; it is, instead, the relationship to ourselves and to the world that is presupposed by any such search for specific principles of action. Quite obviously it would be pointless to urge human beings to achieve moral autonomy when it is their inescapable state of being. On the other hand, if the existentialists wish to say (as they clearly do) that we can, and also that we should, choose to be free and autonomous beings, and that the achievement of this autonomy is the proper objective of a truly human life, the autonomy that is thus to be achieved cannot be the same as the autonomy that is a datum of human life.

A way out of this difficulty is suggested by Merleau-Ponty's "dispositional" interpretation of moral freedom. If the latter is conceived as a capacity for envisaging one's situation in terms of alternative possibilities of action, then it is certainly possible to distinguish between having such a capacity and activating it, and also between exercising it only within a very restricted area of one's life and seeking to extend it to all aspects of life. Whether one has such a capacity at all is presumably very much like the question whether a given type of being has the capacity for learning a language. One either has it or one has not—it is not chosen or achieved. But if autonomy is understood not just as a latent capacity but as the progressive development and exercise of that capacity, then it is, at the very least, not senseless to make this development itself a goal of moral effort. Interpreted now as identifying an object of choice and purposeful effort, the concept of autonomy would generate a directive to realize in ourselves an intensified moral self-consciousness, and to subject wider and wider tracts of our experience to analysis in terms of alternatives of voluntary action. It would presumably also direct that in relation to others one should do whatever one can to encourage and facilitate the development by them of a similarly heightened moral self-awareness. It is of course not at all easy to say just what steps would be required to this end but it seems highly probable that they would involve far-reaching and radical changes in our method of moral education.[19] In any case, the mode of life in which this distinction between choice and non-choice is rigorously enforced, and in which every choice is individual in character, is what the existentialists mean by an authentic human existence. Authenticity (or *Entschlossenheit*) may indeed be regarded as the prime existentialist virtue. It consists in the avoidance of that false relation to oneself and to others that is set up when choices are represented as something other than what they are—something for which the individual is not responsible. Inauthenticity, by contrast, is the arch-principle of mystification in the relationship between human beings and in the relationship of an individual human being to himself. As Sartre's writings make very clear, it is the main obstacle in the way of any truly human relationship based on a reciprocal recognition of one another as fully responsible moral agents. The authentic human being is one who has so thoroughly defined his relationship to the moral attitudes characteristic of the community to which he belongs—either by assimilating or by modifying or by wholly rejecting them—that he is able to make moral judgments in his own name and not just in the ventriloquistic and impersonal manner of a communal morality.

It still remains to ask whether the progressive development of this way of looking at the world—this profound moralization of the self—is a good thing and also, more importantly, whether the recognition of oneself as an autonomous moral being can provide

[19] The relationship between moral education and an ethical theory based on the concept of autonomy is discussed in A. Montefiore "Moral Philosophy and the Teaching of Morality," *Harvard Educational Review*, Vol. 35 (1965), pp. 435–449. Of fundamental importance for any consideration of this question is J. Piaget, *The Moral Judgment of the Child*, trans. M. Gabain (New York: Free Press of Glencoe, 1932).

a logically sufficient and necessary condition upon which moral relationships among human beings could be founded. It is this latter claim that is unmistakably suggested in the writings of the existentialists—particularly Sartre—but which has never been *argued* by any of them.[20] Some critics who have noted both this claim and the failure to support it by argument, have treated it as simply a hasty borrowing from Kant of a principle that does not emerge from the existentialist analysis of human nature at all but that is needed if the latter is not to issue in an unacceptable moral solipsism.[21] This way of treating the existentialists as simply inconsistent plagiarists in their constructive ethics, in its own way begs the same question to which Sartre and others have yet to give a reasoned answer: is the recognition of oneself as an autonomous moral being uniquely fitted to provide a principle of respect for and cooperation with other like beings? At this point, the interpreter of existentialism must make the effort alluded to at the beginning of this chapter, the effort to determine whether or not a constructive argument in support of the existentialists' affirmative answer to this question—the argument that the existentialists have failed to provide—can in fact be found.

It is always tempting to seek to justify the designation of some goal of human effort as a universally valid moral ideal by claiming that the human capability by which this goal is achieved represents the essence of

[20] Sartre does give at least a sketch of such an argument in *L'Existentialisme est un humanisme,* pp. 81–82, when he tries to show that "la mauvaise foi est . . . un mensonge" and that "l'attitude de stricte coherence est l'attitude de bonne foi." What he is getting at here is the fact that the person who claims to be confronted by moral "données" cannot present what are really his claims and preferences in a form that makes a reciprocal understanding with others possible. The latter must either take or leave his "intuitions" of moral truth, and in any case there is no basis for true mutuality.

[21] See for example, O. Bollnow, "Existentialismus und Ethik," pp. 995 f.

man. Thus, we might be led to argue that a capacity for autonomous choice is the quintessentially human function and not simply one capacity among many, whose relationship to and priority (if any) over other traits and powers of human beings has yet to be determined. It may indeed be the case, as the existentialists seem often to assume, that there is a certain progression in our ways of conceiving our own natures, and that this progression converges upon a definition in terms of capacity for autonomous choice.[22] Thus, we begin with the "natural" attitude in which we virtually coalesce with "what we are," i.e., with the attributes of physique, race, nationality, and culture that distinguish us from other human beings. At this stage, the capacity for self-objectification and self-choice may play virtually no part at all in our image of ourselves. This is also the stage at which the cleavages between the various natural communities into which human beings organize themselves are most absolute and unbridgeable. But when these characteristics that separate one human group from another lose their importance and their criterial status, as they tend to do with increasing communication and cooperation among these groups, the capacity for autonomous self-determination very likely will assume a prominence it did not previously have, although even then (as Sartre's analysis of bourgeois personality shows) an os-

---

[22] Such a development seems to be postulated by S. de Beauvoir, *Pour une morale de l'ambiguité*, p. 51 ff. where she speaks of adolescence as the period in which "l'individu doit enfin assumer sa subjectivité." A similar progression toward a stage of moral autonomy is described in detail in Piaget, *The Moral Judgment of the Child*, especially ch. 4. Piaget describes autonomy in a way that is strikingly similar to the conception of reciprocity outlined in this chapter. "The morality of autonomous conscience does not tend to subject each personality to rules that have a common content: it simply obliges individuals to place themselves in a reciprocal relationship with each other without letting the laws of perspective resultant upon that reciprocity destroy their individual points of view." (p. 397)

tensibly distinterested and "objective" attitude may in fact conceal highly restrictive criteria of equality.[23]

Even if it could be shown, however, that our various and partial conceptions of human nature converge on one in which the capacity for self-objectification and self-determination is separated out from all the irrelevancies of race and nationality and economic class, the properly normative question would still remain unanswered. What claim after all has *this* special capacity to be treated as the cornerstone of morality, whatever its place in some hypothetical schedule of human development may be? Unless the existentialist can show persuasively that the human capacity for interpreting experience *sub specie possibilitatis* generates distinctively moral relationships to other beings sharing this capacity, how can he defend himself against the charge—often made by critics—that he is simply proposing another form of moral essentialism and that what he puts forward as the essence of human nature reflects no more than his own arbitrary preference for one human capacity over others? I am assuming here that however large a place a writer like Sartre wishes to make for autonomous choice *within* his account of moral personality, he is not prepared to present that account itself as no more than his own choice.[24] I am also assuming that the only satisfactory answer to this challenge would be a moral one, i.e., a demonstration that autonomy provides the basis for moral community as other "essences" do not; and that "ontological" assumptions about what really constitutes human nature merely conceal the need for this kind of supporting moral argument.

[23] See, for example, Sartre's acrid reflections on "bourgeois universalism" in its relation to colonial populations in his Preface to Frantz Fanon, *Les damnés de la terre* (Paris: F. Maspero, 1961).

[24] This seems clear from Sartre's statement that "le choix est fondement de l'être-choisi mais non pas fondement du choisir." (*L'Être et le néant*, p. 561.)

While an argument must be made along these lines in behalf of the existentialist position, it is important not to pitch one's expectations too high. Even if it proves to be possible to show that the achievement of authenticity has a special relevance to some conception of obligation that is consistent with other stands taken by the existentialists on issues of ethical theory, it would by no means follow that this is the only goal to which our actions and choices must ultimately be directed. At times, some of the existentialists seem to espouse this latter view and have gone so far as to suggest that from the ultimate goal of moral freedom all other subordinate goals can somehow be extracted.[25] Clearly, however, such an extreme downgrading of "empirical" desires and goals to the status of mere symbolizations of an ultimate and exclusive goal of freedom would prove as implausible as Hegel's quite similar treatment of finite conation, and would seriously underestimate the independence and—in another sense of the term—the "autonomy" of the quite ordinary needs and desires that we all share. It may well be, as I will suggest later on, that authenticity is not just one more goal with no particular relationship to any others we may have; and that instead, it interpenetrates the whole corpus of our antecedently established aspirations in a peculiarly intimate way. But even if this proves to be the case, there can be no justification for simply assuming that this relationship is of the means-ends type or that all goals other than self-conscious moral freedom have a purely derivative and instrumental function.

There is a still more important *caveat* to be entered

[25] See, for example, S. de Beauvoir, *Pour une morale d'ambiguïté*, p. 34, where freedom is described as "la source d'où surgissent toutes les significations et toutes les valeurs." While Mme. de Beauvoir also speaks of freedom as "la condition originelle de toute justification de l'existence," she too often speaks of freedom as though it stood in a end-means relationship to other subordinate goals.

at this point. It is one thing to argue, as I propose to do, that certain distinctively human capabilities have a special importance in connection with the establishment of relationships among human beings that can effectively bind them to the performance of certain actions. It is quite another matter to argue that the possession of these capabilities by itself constitutes a *sufficient* condition for its being true that we have a moral obligation to respect the moral freedom of other human beings. If certain existentialists, like Simone de Beauvoir, hold, as they appear to, that the fact that we are autonomous beings provides a sufficient condition of our being under such an obligation to all human beings, I can only say that I think this is a mistake.[26] There are a number of familiar difficulties in the way of any effort to prove that man ought to be a moral being at all, i.e., that he has a duty to constitute communities with other beings like himself—whatever trait or capability is taken to provide the basis of that likeness—within which everyone is recognized as having a right to equal consideration. Many attempts have been made in the course of the history of moral philosophy to show that there is such an unconditional duty, but it is difficult not to feel that they have succeeded only by being circular and by inserting among the fundamental attributes of moral personality the very disposition to communal life that then duly emerges in the conclusion. If we agree with Aristotle's view that a wholly non-social being would have to be a beast or a God, as I think we must, and if, as can be plausibly argued, living in the society of other human

---

[26] See her *Pour une morale de l'ambiguïté*, pp. 95–103. Sartre is more cautious and admits that "la liberté comme définition de l'homme, ne dépend pas d'autrui"; but he argues that "dès qu'il y a engagement, je suis obligé de vouloir en même temps que ma liberté la liberté des autres." *L'Existentialisme est un humanisme*, p. 83. Whether "obligé" here refers to the obligation of logical consistency or of practical necessity is not altogether clear.

beings necessarily involves an implicit assent to the validity of some general rules governing relations between members of the group, then the interesting and important question for the philosopher is to determine how and on what basis this relationship among human beings is to be constituted, and not to prove that it ought to be set up at all. If a person were really disposed to challenge this assumption that human beings must, one way or another, live together on the basis of some shared understanding, and to reject root and branch the discipline and the restrictions that such a mode of life inevitably requires, it is not clear how one could even seek to persuade him to do otherwise, although one might well predict that he would be unable to carry out consistently his plan of living without any dependence on others. On the other hand, if as can normally be assumed to be the case, there is an initial disposition to find some basis for moral community, then it can be shown that certain capabilities which we "naturally" possess assume a special importance. By themselves, however, these capabilities, whether they be the ability to reckon consequences or to choose between alternative courses of action, do not declare that they must be used for the purpose of establishing a moral community among human beings.

## III

It is time now to turn to the concept of obligation itself, and to take note of certain of its features before going on to ask what the special relationship between authenticity and obligation may be. We may begin by considering the way in which claims that human beings have certain general duties can be established in the face of possible challenge. As has already been pointed out, such challenges are often met by arguments intended to show that the mode of conduct that is being called for is somehow part and parcel of our human nature, and thus cannot rationally be rejected by us. Since all conceptions of what constitutes our nature are themselves open to challenge, many philosophers have come to feel that the nature to which appeal is made must be one that has somehow been recognized as such by the person to whom the argument seeking to establish the reality of the obligation is being made. In the history of political philosophy, this perception has led to the elaboration of contractarian theories of obligation like Rousseau's, which justify all limitations on what may permissibly be willed by reference to certain postulated acts of assent by the very persons who are thus subject to what are really self-imposed obligations. The effect of such theories is to base all obligations on the obligation to keep a promise, and while some of the proponents of this view have associated it with excessively literalistic conceptions of the form assumed by these contractual undertakings to which they appeal, the notion of — promises as the basis of obligation generally can be separated from these irrelevancies. When this distinction has been made, the conception of promises as self-engaging acts proves to have great power and suggestiveness as a model for understanding moral relationships among human beings. I will argue that, when suitably interpreted, it can provide the elements of a theory of obligation and of moral community that can be accepted by the existentialists consistently with their commitment to the doctrine of moral autonomy.[27]

Promising is, of course, merely the clearest and most dramatic example drawn from the larger class of what might be called self-created obligations. What distinguishes obligations of this kind is the fact that the obligation is explicitly assumed by a given person at a more or less definite point in time. This assumption is often, as in the case of promising, a linguistic perform-

---

[27] In the outline I give here of a theory of obligation I have drawn at various points on the views of John Rawls as stated in "Justice as Fairness," *Philosophical Review*, Vol. 67 (1958), pp. 164–94, and in other articles.

ance of a certain kind, and involves the public use of a form of words that has the effect of placing the person who uses them under an obligation to the person to whom the promise is made. The effect of the use of the promise-formula is to license an expectation on the part of the person to whom the promise is made. What may not be so obvious but is of great importance for our purposes is that in so licensing another's expectations I must implicitly disallow in advance an appeal to any justifications for a failure to do what I have promised to do, other than those that fall within a certain more or less precisely defined range of excuses. One "reason" for non-performance that is disallowed by this formula would certainly be any such statement as "I don't want to" or "I have changed my mind." A person who tried to justify non-performance in this way would merely show that he did not understand the promise-making formula he had used. It is thus an intrinsic feature of the latter that it does effectively "change the situation" between two or more persons in a way that cannot be canceled by just any subsequent decision *not* to do what one decided to do in making the promise. The change thus made is not some magical modification of the relationships in which "objects" stand to us, but rather a linguistically effected change in the relationship between the person who makes the promise and the person to whom it is made. Given normal circumstances, once a person has put himself "on the hook" by engaging in the promise-making practice, he has bound himself in a way that carries with it all the externality and rigor that any deontologist could require.

It has sometimes been alleged that even self-created obligations require as a condition of their effectiveness that there be moral principles such as "Promises are to be kept," the truth of which is certified by an act of intellection that is logically prior to all particular acts of promise-making. In this way, the authority of special obligations is assimilated to what is assumed to be the standard case in which rational necessity is the basis of moral authority. It is perfectly possible, however, to agree with the cognitivist that "Promises are to be kept" is necessarily true; and yet, to hold at the same time that this is an analytic truth which generates an actual obligation only if we decide to engage in the promise-making activity. Thus, we come to be obliged only because we choose to use the promise formula, and if we chose never to use it, we would not be under an obligation. It would not make sense to argue that *Pacta sunt servanda* means that we *ought* to engage in promise-making practices; and therefore the obligation is one that we put ourselves under when we do so engage. It is of course true that most people do not think of themselves as deciding to take part in, or not to take part in, the promise-making activity which is a going social concern into which we are in some sense "born." The established social character of this practice does not, however, imply or require that there is any corresponding "natural" obligation with respect to promises at all; and it seems much more plausible to treat the whole logically structured activity of promise-making as a human contrivance, as Hume thought, and as one which does not have to be thought of in cognitivist terms at all.

To be sure, self-created obligations are usually held to be only one type of obligation. There are many others such as the obligation to deal justly with other human beings, or the obligation to prevent unnecessary suffering, which do not seem to lend themselves so readily to an analysis along these lines, and certainly do not involve any express acts of self-commitment as promise-making does. But the case of special obligations still provides a useful clue, because it is quite possible that even where such explicit verbal performances are absent, there may be other less obvious means by which, in effect, we authorize an interpretation of what we do or say, which becomes an implicit element in our relationship with other persons and has much the same force as an obligation. For example, it can be argued that simply by speaking a language we authorize others to assume that we are saying what we believe to be true, so that when we lie, we violate an obligation accepted implicitly through our use of language. So too, when we accept what has been determined by some principles of justice as our fair share in some distribution, the other participants are justified in assuming that we accept these principles and will abide by them in like cases even when it may be more advantageous to us not to do so. In this case, we have again and by our own action (though not by any explicit linguistic performance) accepted a rule of action—in this case, a rule of justice —and have, in effect, disallowed "I don't choose to" as a defense in the case of non-performance.

These examples suggest that the notion of a self-created obligation may be susceptible of generalization. While Hume was perhaps the first to propose a conception of rule-governed reciprocity as the basis of moral obligation generally, it is Kant's vision of the human community as a kingdom of ends that most clearly suggests the form this conception might take if pressed to the limit.[28] In place of Hume's rather skimpy list of the possible forms of reciprocity, Kant makes the principle of reciprocity the governing norm for all relationships among human beings. If I must never, as Kant says, treat any other human beings merely as a means (i.e. as a thing), then I must judge only those actions to be morally permissible which I can justify to those affected by them, by appealing to considerations which I would be prepared to accept if the situation were reversed. What is important here is not so much the actual content of these jointly acceptable rules of conduct, nor Kant's claim that this con-

[28] In his *Grundlegung einer Metaphysik der Sitten,* ed. E. Cassirer (Berlin: B. Cassirer, 1913) Vol. 4, pp. 291 ff. Kant's notion of a kingdom of ends is frequently referred to by Sartre, and while his comments are often critical, there can be no mistaking the influence of Kant's ethical theory on his treatment of moral questions.

tent can be uniquely determined by purely logical tests, but rather the mode of human relationship within which this consensus emerges. Each human being recognizes all other human beings as being, like himself, morally free and as endowed with the capacity for understanding, accepting, and carrying-out jointly acceptable policies; and this recognition becomes a principle of respect for the moral freedom of others through each person's disallowing an appeal to mere disinclination or subjective preference as a ground for non-performance of obligations deriving from those policies. A "kingdom of ends" as Kant calls it, or a "moral community" is simply a human society in which the fundamental relationship in which all the members stand to one another is that of persons to whom a rational justification by reference to considerations they can freely accept is due for all actions that significantly affect them.

There are, to be sure, features of Kant's conception of a moral community that pose difficulties for any radically voluntaristic ethical theory that seeks to appropriate it. It has already been pointed out that Kant did not for one moment suppose that the obligations connected with this mode of human relationship were self-created in any sense that implies choice. Furthermore, while he recognized that we can and too often do *choose* not to comply with the requirements of the moral law, he did believe that all of us unavoidably recognize the controlling normative status and validity of the mode of human relationship on which the kingdom of ends rests.[29] In other words, with every *Willkür* there is associated a rational will; and the presence in each of us of the latter insures that, whatever our professions, we will all be aware at some level of the true moral quality of our actions. What these assumptions seem to support is a belief that a moral community is always and necessarily realized among rational beings, even when it remains "invisible" by

[29] See Olafson, *Principles and Persons*, p. 40, fn. 6.

virtue of their failure to act in the manner required by the principles whose validity, on this account, they nevertheless recognize. But when we consider the actual state of most, if not all, human societies, it becomes highly problematic not only whether any of them would qualify as a moral community in the sense of one that effectively realizes a rational and just ordering of human relationships, but also whether there is the kind of universal though tacit recognition of the authority of this ideal. At the very least, the evidence is ambiguous. If we sometimes seem to give a paradoxical recognition to the ideal of true mutuality by seeking to *justify* inherently unjust arrangements to the very persons who suffer most from them, there are also large and unrecognized lacunae in our moral consciousness that are hard to reconcile with the view that we always envisage and judge our own actions from the standpoint of a member of a community of rational and moral beings. In any case, doubts about the degree of acceptance that the ideal of a moral community finds at any level make it necessary to go more deeply into the questions that were taken care of for Kant by his assumptions about the rational will present in each of us.

These are questions about the institution and acceptance of moral community among human beings. They are rendered more difficult by other weaknesses in the Kantian scheme, and by the unavailability to us of a number of alternative rationales of obligation which Kant, to be sure, repudiated, but which other moral philosophers have used extensively. If passing Kant's test of the validity of moral maxims is at most a necessary condition of the rightness of an action, and not a sufficient condition as he seems to have supposed it to be, then we will still be confronted by a number of formally valid but incompatible policies of action in any given situation. It becomes evident that if such conflicts are to be resolved and jointly acceptable policies are to emerge, a detailed consideration of specific empirical claims and needs will be necessary. Moreover, if we cannot simply assume, as Kant does, that there is a natural and unconditional obligation to submit one's claims to a rational adjudication, neither can we argue that treating other human beings as ends is the only rational policy for the conduct of life when prudence and self interest are the standard of rationality. Here again the evidence is far from clear and may even be generally favorable to this thesis. Even so, there is a notable disproportion between the strictness of the obligation to respect other human beings, as most of us would interpret it, and the incomplete, and in many respects ambiguous state of the evidence showing that to do so will always be in our interest. But if we drop, or in one way or another qualify, these assumptions which Kant associated with his conception of a moral community, the effort to realize this community will inevitably come to seem more like one possible policy, among others, which we might adopt in our relations with other human beings, and one which we must think of ourselves as *choosing*, and as choosing for reasons that themselves reflect certain evaluative preferences on our part.

If we were to allow this last point to stand without any further elaboration, however, we would in effect have given up all prospect of establishing *any* special connection between authenticity and obligation; and this essay is intended to show precisely that such a connection exists. In fact, the assertion that adherence to the ideal of a moral community is an arbitrary choice needs to be qualified in two important respects. First, it needs to be pointed out that while adoption of the principle of moral reciprocity and mutual respect does involve a choice, repudiating that policy in a really consistent way would be extremely difficult. All of us are reared in societies in which the notions of reciprocity and of justification play some role, however ambiguous and precarious that role may be; and while every individual is, in principle, free to assume in his own case, or reject, the "choices" made by others that are reflected in the moral code of the society in

which he is reared, there is, in practice, an obvious
limit to the degree to which he can consistently reject
these principles while continuing to be a member of
that or any society. Since we have been formed by
these practices, we cannot repudiate them *in toto* and
continue to be the social beings they have made us.
Even when we ostensibly reject only some portion of
these rules, there is a great likelihood that we will go
on tacitly appealing to and counting on the rejected
principle, at least in cases in which it is advantageous
to us to do so. If we do, we could hardly refuse to accept the authority of the principle in those cases in
which it would require the sacrifice of some short-run
interest of our own. In this sense, the authority of
moral principles might be said to be just the reverse
side of the practical difficulty of rejecting more than
a sharply limited segment of prevailing moral practices *without* committing inconsistencies of this kind.
There is no portion of that corpus of rules that is in
principle immune to revision, but the abandonment of
the whole would be tantamount to the dissolution of
all social relationships based on reciprocity with other
human beings. In this sense, principles *are* authoritative and independent of our wills; and their authority
would be simply that of the standing presumption that
we do wish to continue to benefit from existing forms
of mutuality, as well as of the practical difficulty of
consistently doing anything else. Of course, this presumption may be shown to be false in particular cases,
but it could still be used to account for the general
authority that is claimed for the whole range of forms
of social cooperation.

In some sense, then, moral communities do exist,
and in some measure all of us have been formed by
them, and as a practical matter would find it very difficult to "opt out" of the obligations they entail, even if
we were so minded. The further point that needs making is that if we are dissatisfied with the various "natural" communities to which we belong, and are dissatisfied not because these associations involve the

acceptance of obligations to other human beings, but because these obligations seem arbitrary and irrational and irrelevant to our real needs and desires, then only a purified conception of obligation as joint self-commitment based on mutual respect for one another's status as autonomous moral agents affords much prospect of a stronger and more satisfactory mode of human relationship.[30] More specifically, if what we want is more community and not less, then only self-initiated obligations will prove to be effectively binding when the supporting assumptions on which other conceptions of obligation rest have been abandoned. To be sure, when I signify to others a desire to work out with them understandings that will then be jointly accepted as norms governing my actions and theirs, I do not thereby surrender the right to criticize or to seek to revise the policies we progressively elaborate. I do, however, place myself in a position in which, barring quite exceptional circumstances, I must regard a refusal by me to do what these understandings require of me as unjustifiable, and therefore as wrong in the only sense of that term for which any common authority can be claimed. Even if I invoke my inalienable power to re-open the questions that were resolved by our joint understandings, and proceed to answer them differently and thus cancel that understanding, I cannot by the fiat of my will alter the fact that this was a shared, a public understanding, in which one crucial element was the surrender of unrestricted discretionary powers by all parties. I could consistently repudiate the publicly understood content of that understanding only by retreating into a kind of solipsism of the present mo-

---

[30] This is the sense in which I would understand Merleau-Ponty's somewhat cryptic statement that "la moralité est à faire." Merleau-Ponty himself explains this statement as meaning that "apart from a pure heteronomy accepted by both sides. . . . there is no given universality; there is only a presumptive universality." (*The Primacy of Perception*, pp. 30–31.)

ment, in which I deny that anything that I may have permitted myself to be understood as accepting at some moment in the past has any relevance to, or authority over, what I now judge to be my right. Certainly these understandings, like all policies that have a temporal stretch to them, are effectuated by a whole series of choices that we make over a period of time; but here, the initial choice has a quite special function which is both to create a locus of moral objectivity and to place it beyond our own sole control. That locus of objectivity is the "other"—the moral community that is constituted by these joint understandings; and if one major attribute of autonomous moral personality is the ability to reopen and to decompose into their elements of "fact" and "value" all policies of action that are proposed to it, then another equally important power is this ability to alter our situation vis-à-vis other human beings in a way that gives rise to a sense of right and wrong that we cannot repudiate.

Inevitably, a theory of obligation constructed on these lines will have a narrower range of application than our ordinary concept of obligation is thought to have; and to many, there will quite understandably seem to be as little continuity between the one and the other as there is, according to some critics, between our ordinary understanding of what is involved in choice and the existentialist version of that concept. The existence of these discontinuities may be freely conceded; as may the fact that there are great practical difficulties in the way of a review, in the light of this sharpened concept of obligation, of what are ordinarily thought of as being our duties to one another. Nevertheless, even in the absence of such a review, we are not entirely without means of giving effect to the ideas presented above. We can, after all, ask ourselves whether a given policy or principle is one that others *could* accept consistently with what we know about their needs and aspirations. While nothing, finally, can take the place of participation by those affected in the formulation or review of such policies, raising questions in this hypothetical form may at least enable us to eliminate many alternative courses of action on the ground that others can have no rational motive for assenting to them. Thus, it may be that many of the social arrangements and practices in the design and institution of which most people have had no share whatever, can be defended at least as interim expedients on instrumental or utilitarian grounds, and thus as presumptively acceptable to those affected by them, even though *ex hypothesi* they cannot claim any degree of "obligatoriness" in the special sense now attaching to that notion. If we seek, wherever possible, to transform that presumptive consensus into a real one by the widest kind of consultation and discussion, it is hard to see what justification there could be for dismissing this revised conception of obligation simply on the ground that it involves a break with more familiar and current ideas on the subject.

## IV

Now that an account has been given of both authenticity and obligation, the question of whether there is some special relationship between them must be faced. Does recognition by human beings of one another as morally autonomous beings, together with a disposition to intensify and extend wherever possible the kind of self-awareness on which this recognition rests, supply a uniquely suitable basis for a moral community characterized by binding relationships among its members?[31] There are reasons for

[31] The notion of authentic existence or *Entschlossenheit* as developed by Heidegger seems to be wholly lacking in social or other-regarding implications; and it is not even clear whether there is, in his view, an authentic mode of relationship to other human beings, although the passage from his book on Kant noted in ch. 7, n. 39, makes this seem likely. A hint of such an aspect of authenticity is contained in Heidegger's brief discussion of *Fürsorge* in *Sein und Zeit*, p. 122. In one of its forms, "die *Fürsorge*, die wesentlich die eigentliche Sorge—das heisst

thinking that it does, assuming always that there is a disposition to communal living based on something other than force or fear. It must also be assumed that the human beings who are so disposed have needs and desires that are not so hopelessly disparate as to be incapable of joint satisfaction, and that the powers with which these persons are endowed are not so incommensurate as to cancel out any motive that the stronger party might have for cooperation with the weaker. These material conditions seem to be roughly satisfied by human beings as we know them; and so, too (although here, no very great assurance is appropriate) is the further condition that the kind of choice of which the persons entering into these relationships to one another must be capable is not just momentary preference, but long-term commitments to joint policies, with all the implications for disciplinary controls over the actions of individuals that such policies involve.[32] Even though from the existentialist point of view there can be no once-and-for-all commitment to such policies that eliminates any subsequent reconsideration of the issues they pose, no long-range commitment at all can be made by persons who are constitutionally unable to resist impulses which may run counter to a line of conduct they have adopted. Unless these conditions are met, no stable human community is likely to be founded on whatever basis. When they are, however, the special kind of self-consciousness associated with authenticity has a contribution to make which must now be described.

Let us consider first the implications that a recogni-

---

die Existenz des anderen betrifft, und nicht ein *Was*, das er besorgt—verhilft dem Anderen dazu, *in* seiner Sorge sich durchsichtig und *für sie frei* zu werden."

[32] The notion that choice has a temporal stretch to it is common to all the existentialists, but it must be conceded that until Sartre developed his theory of obligation in *Critique de la raison dialectique* there had been little emphasis on any element of discipline associated with choice.

tion of oneself as a morally autonomous being might have for the way one presents oneself as a candidate for moral relationships to other human beings. The most salient of these implications can be very simply stated. If a man thinks of himself as a morally autonomous being, the very nature of this character that he imputes to himself is such as to absorb any other feature of his nature which he might designate as the basis for his relationships with other human beings, and on the strength of which he might demand respect and acceptance from them. Let us suppose, for example, that a man proposes to make the fact that he is a proletarian—or a white man—or a Buddhist—the primary basis of his association with other human beings. Since he is at the same time, as I am assuming, committed to the doctrine of moral autonomy, he will be forced to admit that his being a proletarian, or a white man, assumes the criterial function he assigns to it only as the result of a choice on his part. In fact, *being* a proletarian or a Buddhist or even a white man in any sense which implies the imposition of priorities by which, e.g., being a white man takes precedence for purposes of action over being something else, inescapably turns out to involve an exercise of the same autonomy that presides over the whole moral life. If this is so, then to demand that one be respected in one's capacity as a white man or as a proletarian is to demand respect as one who "chooses himself" as a proletarian, and could have "chosen himself" as something else. This, in turn, is indistinguishable from demanding recognition as a free moral agent—with this reservation, that it is not explained why respect is to be confined to those moral agents who freely choose themselves in this one way. The relevant point here, however, is that once the agent adopts the autonomist view of his own moral activity, every subsequent role he espouses must be understood as a mode of self-determination for which he bears final responsibility. For this reason, if he is prepared at all to enter into an association based on reciprocity and mutual recognition with other human beings, he can do so only in his capacity as a free moral agent. If he is an autonomous moral being, then in every subordinate goal he sets himself, and in every principle he adopts, he is also bringing into play that fundamental capacity for self-determination. He cannot repudiate or remain indifferent to the latter without, at the same time, withdrawing the claim he makes for the subordinate goals that are its expression.

This line of reasoning can quite obviously be extended so as to yield conclusions that cast light not just on the role in which I can present myself as a candidate for moral relationships with other human beings, but also on the terms of cooperation which I can offer to my prospective partners in a moral community. If they, too, are autonomous moral agents, and if they, too, can have obligations only by placing themselves under obligations, then what *could* I offer them except respect for this freedom of self-definition and self-engagement which they, like me, enjoy? Even if they were not to share my conception of moral personality, which, as I am assuming, is based on the doctrine of autonomy, and were to give priority to other attributes they possess, it seems clear that from my standpoint their establishment of these priorities would have to be regarded as itself an exercise of that same autonomy. In this context, it is important to emphasize once again a point that has already been made. This is that while self-conscious autonomy absorbs our other desires, wants, and aspirations by transforming them into so many forms of self-determining choice, it does not follow that these wants must be somehow derivable or deducible from the fact that we are autonomous beings. Quite obviously, many of them will pre-date the recognition of one's autonomy as a moral being; and in any case, they are absorbed into this autonomous condition not by some process of logical derivation, but by passing through a critical review as a result of which they are put forward, if at all, as claims with which others have to reckon as *my* choices, whatever their previous history and no matter how initially passive in relation to them I may have been.[33] They must, in other words, be *assumed.* The point that I am making here is simply that if we accept the doctrine of autonomy at all, we cannot avoid thinking of other human beings, for the purposes of possible moral relationships with them, as standing in this relationship to their own desires and wants.

This point has implications which make clearer how the aspiration to authenticity may facilitate the formation of moral relationships that can be truly binding. From what has already been said, it follows that the moral community that the existentialists project is one in which the only condition of membership is the very capacity for choice and self-commitment itself, and in which the members reciprocally recognize one another as "choosers." The force of this identification resides in the fact that it requires that each individual who is a member of such a community must regard himself, and be regarded by his fellows, as the sole and responsible arbiter of his own interests, and as controlling what may be called his "input" of claims into the public adjudicatory forum in which a common policy that resolves conflicts among claims must be formulated.[34] Thus the *données* of every moral

---

[33] Sartre's views with respect to the logical relationship of "original" and "secondary" choices to one another are stated in *L'Être et le néant,* pp. 548–50. While he makes quite clear that this relationship is not one of deductibility but a looser one in which particular choices may contribute to a larger thematic unity from which they cannot be strictly derived, it would be too much to claim that he endorses the interpretation I have offered of total choice as a "resultant." Thus, Sartre argues that I can make errors about the nature of my own original choice and this inevitably suggests that it has a more "categorical" or "occurrent" character than I have suggested it does.

[34] See S. de Beauvoir's statement, *Pour une morale de l'ambiguïté,* p. 198, that while "le bien d'un individu ou d'un groupe d'individus mérite d'être pris comme but absolu de

problem are provided by the expressed preferences of human beings, each of whom speaks for himself and whose "vote" must be allowed to register as it stands, and not be interpreted out of existence or tacitly overridden by some theory of human nature that by-passes or disallows the explicitly declared preferences of the individual. Nothing is more alien to the general ethos of existentialism than the kind of moral paternalism that "knows better" than the individual moral agent what is good for the latter, or worse still, what the latter "really" wants. As often as not, this is done by appealing to some view of what is involved in moral personality as such; and when, as frequently happens, this view turns out to have substantive moral implications, these are established as antecedent premises on which subsequent joint deliberation must proceed, and which it is powerless to revise. By contrast, the existentialist insists that every element entering into the consideration of a moral problem must be "sponsored" i.e., must come in as the declared preference of one of the parties to such a deliberation; and his declaration is to be authoritative for the other participants in the sense that none of them has the right to look behind or interpret this preference in any way that is not authorized by the person whose preference it is.

Perhaps the most important feature of the relationship between authenticity and obligation remains to be described; and in order to grasp its significance, one must understand how precarious and conditional such moral community as exists at any given time appears to the existentialists. As I have already indicated, there are writers on ethical theory who seem to assume the existence of a moral community as a presupposition of any distinctively moral activity on the part of individual human beings who belong to it. On this view, it does not make any sense to speak

---

notre action . . . nous ne sommes pas autorisés de décider à priori de ce bien."

of the defining principles of such a community as reflecting any kind of choice on the part of its members; they constitute instead a datum of the moral life antecedent to, and presupposed by, the choices of individual moral agents. I have indicated too that existentialist writers, by contrast, are typically much more strongly impressed by the fraudulence of what passes for moral consensus, and by the fragility and the partiality of such genuine consensus as does exist. Because they see so clearly the insecurity and the ambiguity of our actual moral practices as judged by the standard of true mutuality, the existentialists conceive the relation of each individual to the moral community in the volitional mode and that community itself as a *realisandum* or as an "endless task" in the Kantian sense. This view in turn is inspired by the perception that our moral failures are as often due to our not recognizing certain classes of human beings as candidates for moral relationships at all, as they are to non-performance of duties within the sphere in which we do recognize the authority of moral principles. Precisely because the concept of autonomy is formal in the sense of abstracting from substantive rules of conduct, it makes possible a clearer focus upon the moral relationship between persons which is the precondition for a successful resolution of questions of conduct, as well as upon the problematic and vulnerable character of such moral community as exists.

If we now consider these views in the context of the theory of obligation and of the moral community sketched out in the preceding section, it is difficult not to conclude that the existentialists have made a valid and important point. It may well be the case that natural communities like the family can continue to exist and even thrive although their members simply fulfill the duties assigned to them by their roles within these communities, and no one explicitly formulates the nature of his role to himself in such a way that it incorporates a statement of the basic relationships between human beings on which that community rests. It seems impossible, however, that a moral community such as I have described should ever exist except as it is sustained by an awareness on the part of its members of the mode of relationship to others that it involves and by a conscious determination to persevere in it. For the moment we lose the sense of ourselves and of others as "choosers" or lose our belief in the importance of this mode of identifying one another, our capability for actions and decisions that are truly shared will be affected. In a moral community, the whole corpus of rules and policies must remain in principle permanently open for reconsideration and possible revision if that community is to be completely sovereign in the sense of being able to raise and to resolve in a manner binding on all whatever issues it may face. But in order to be sovereign in this sense, the members of a human group must recognize one another as endowed with the capacities of choice and self-commitment which make it possible for them to be participants in such collective choices.[35] To the extent that that recognition is effectively denied or is restricted by unilaterally imposed limits on the scope of choice, a moral community ceases to exist, and with it, relationships of obligation lapse. Those who might otherwise be subject to obligations will not have been permitted to act jointly with us to change our relations to one another in a way that would be binding; or perhaps not even they themselves will have fully grasped their capacity for so altering their own situation. In any case, in the absence of reciprocal recognition of one another as capable of this special kind of choice, a certain mode of human relationship becomes an un-

[35] This notion of a collective or joint choice, which has been developed so extensively in the *Critique de la raison dialectique*, is not a recent addition to Sartre's ethical theory and can be found as early as *L'Existentialisme est un humanisme* where Sartre says that "(la) liberté se veut dans le concert." (p. 83.)

available option; and it is this mode of relationship that alone renders obligation intelligible.

Here then, we touch on the deep underlying motive for associating authenticity with obligation in the way the existentialists do. Because the various natural communities into which we are born only very imperfectly embody the ideal of human mutuality, we, as individuals, must continuously define for ourselves the moral community in which we effectively live. By so doing, we contribute in differing degrees to the expansion or contraction of such genuine mutuality as in fact exists; and if it is true, as I have argued, that mutuality is a condition of obligation, then we can properly speak of choosing to be obliged by choosing the mode of human relationship that makes obligation possible. Moreover, like all policies, the policy of living together with other human beings on the basis of a reciprocal recognition of one another's autonomy becomes effective *only* through corresponding choices made by individual human beings. When human beings single out their capacity for choice and self-commitment and place a value on it by seeking to extend and intensify their awareness of the choices that are open to them, and when they are able to describe these choices to themselves in such a way as to make evident the full burden of moral implication they carry, the making of such choices bearing on the constitution of a moral community will at the very least be facilitated. If, at the same time, they understand that only a similar recognition and prizing of the autonomy of other human beings can provide the framework within which the claims they may wish to make on others will have a place, they will surely perceive in the existentialists' positive evaluation of our capacity for autonomous moral choice, not just a facilitating but a necessary condition of the form of life they seek.

## V

There has been one major exception to the existentialists' lack of interest in the social and institutional aspect of morality. At least since the end of World War II, the French existentialists have evinced a strong and continuing interest in Marxism, and have indicated—sometimes defiantly and sometimes rather wistfully—their awareness that its mode of dealing with moral questions represents a direct antithesis to the moral individualism of their own position.[36] This confrontation of existentialism and Marxism has led to a number of exchanges which have contributed in some measure to our understanding of the existentialist approach to questions of social morality; but these have been largely polemical exercises rather than attempts to build a general theory of human relationships on the foundation of the doctrine of autonomy. This last is what Sartre had promised to do "in a coming work" at the end of *L'Être et le néant*, but that work has never appeared.[37] In its place, Sartre published in 1960 the first volume of *Critique de la raison dialectique*, a major effort to reconcile the principal theses of existentialism with those of Marxism through a reinterpretation of the dialectical structure of human action or praxis.[38] In this book, Sartre goes so far as to speak of existentialism as an "enclave within Marxism"; but, while a final judgment on the rela-

[36] See, for example, Merleau-Ponty's *Humanisme et Terreur*, which marks the first major attempt by an existentialist to do justice to some of the insights of Marxism without accepting either its materialism or its determinism. Merleau-Ponty's political philosophy was to undergo considerable revision in his later *Les aventures de la dialectique* (Paris: Gallimard, 1955).

[37] *L'Être et le néant*, p. 722.

[38] A very useful summary outline of the argument of this book can be found in R. D. Laing and D. G. Cooper, *Reason and Violence: A Decade of Sartre's Philosophy—1950–1960* (New York: Humanities Press, 1964).

tionship between the two as Sartre now understands them must await the completion of the *Critique,* a number of critics have already expressed doubts about the absorption of Sartre's earlier views by his more recently adopted Marxism and have suggested that on a number of points of crucial importance it is the latter that has had to accommodate itself to existentialism rather than the other way around.

By itself, the first volume of *Critique de la raison dialectique* is an enormous and—by reason of its formidably complex style and vocabulary alone—an extremely difficult book to understand. Many of the topics it takes up have little or nothing to do with ethical theory; and its central concern is rather with the philosophy of the social sciences. Its principal thesis is that our mode of understanding of social institutions and of social change is never wholly independent of our practical attitudes and commitments with respect to them, and that both take the form of certain conceptual syntheses or "totalizations" by which our social environment is organized with a view to action. In essence, this amounts to a new version of Hegelianism, qualified by a recognition of the underlying contingency of all human actions, individual or collective, and also by Sartre's express endorsement of a thoroughgoing ontological individualism according to which individual human beings are ultimately the only dialectical agents and any collective praxis must be understood as a complex function of an indefinitely large number of individual dialectics. In any case, a large place within Sartre's statement of this theory of society is assigned to the emergence of what he calls "groups"—human communities based on reciprocity—out of "serial" aggregates in which human beings cooperate with one another as they do in a queue, but without any recognition or acceptance of an effective identity binding them together. The paradigms which Sartre uses for his analysis of the emergence of groups are drawn from revolutionary situations in which a crowd suddenly

acquires a conscious unity of purpose and acts as a
single body. While much of what he has to say about
such formations and the circumstances of scarcity and
class antagonism which they presuppose, is very interesting, it would seem to fall more into the province
of social psychology (insofar as the latter deals with
the phenomena of self-identification among members
of an emergent social group) than into that of ethics.
Embedded in this theory of groups, however, there
is a long discussion devoted to the "pledge" by which,
a "group-in-fusion" is transformed into a permanent
unit of social cooperation. In the course of this section,
Sartre gives an account of human relationships based
on self-created obligations which in its essentials runs
parallel to the conception outlined earlier in this chapter.[39] While some of the special assumptions attached
to this theory as well as the forbidding terminology
in which it is couched make it unsuitable for use as a
general statement of an existentialist theory of obligation, its main points must be briefly noted here as a
means of substantiating the general thesis of a compatibility between autonomy and obligation which I
have been defending.

The most noteworthy feature of Sartre's theory of
the pledge is its recognition that through a promise
or its equivalent, human beings can change their situation vis-à-vis one another in such a way as to bring
into existence reciprocal rights and obligations which
then constitute effective limits on the exercise of each
individual's autonomy. In language that often recalls
—rather strangely—that of Hume's discussion of obligation, Sartre repeatedly calls the human group based
on reciprocity an "invention" by which individual
human beings produce a new form of relationship to
one another by binding themselves (i.e. by restricting
their own liberty of choice) on the condition that
others do likewise.[40] This performance requires that

---

[39] *Critique de la raison dialectique*, pp. 381–460.

[40] On the other hand, Sartre asserts against Hume that a

each participant become what Sartre rather awkwardly calls a "third"—a kind of ideal, and in some sense at least, impartial agent who shares certain goals with others and identifies *their* actions in pursuit of these goals with his own. This new identity typically emerges in the course of some spontaneous joint action such as the taking of the Bastille. The pledge is essentially a formalization of the relationships so formed and is designed as a guarantee of the permanence of the newly-formed group against dissolution when the external dangers that were the occasion for its formation temporarily recede. Eventually, the permanent group takes on institutional form through the increasing differentiation of social functions and roles within the group and the consequent elaboration of codes of practice; and since the institutionalized group is always in danger of relapse into a purely external or "serial" mode of relationship among its members, the pledge has to be constantly renewed. Here it is important to note that Sartre recognizes that this renewal occurs not through explicit acts of swearing faith to one another but through any act of reciprocity such as aiding another who is in need. Indeed, as Sartre says, "it is always a case—except in emergencies—of *renewing* the pledge."[41]

A number of passages are of particular interest because they express so clearly both Sartre's recognition of the possibility of a self-imposed limit on what an autonomous being may do, and his conception of the reciprocal understanding on which this self-limitation by each individual rests.[42] Thus we are told both that my belonging to the group is my free project and that this project by its nature makes a claim on each mem-

---

pledge or promise *can* effect an irreversible change in one's situation: "Le serment n'est ni une détermination subjective ni une simple détermination du discours, c'est une modification réelle du groupe par mon action regulatric" (p. 441).

[41] *Ibid.,* p. 493. Emphasis added.

[42] *Ibid.,* pp. 439 ff.

ber of the group. It amounts, in fact, to an undertaking by me to satisfy the claims made on me in my capacity as a "third"; and this free undertaking is explicitly declared to involve a limitation of my liberty. In order that I may be able to count on other members of the group, each of them must be able to count on me; and they can be expected to respect limitations on what they may legitimately do, only if I honor their claim to a similar limitation on me. The pledge thus creates a "transcendence" of the group over its members which Sartre describes as an absolute right, and which he also speaks of as a "positing of man as an absolute power of man over man under conditions of reciprocity." In this way, through my own choice, obligation becomes a feature of my condition as it never was before; and it cannot simply be negated by my consciousness without thereby authorizing the use of violence by others to insure compliance. Finally, because the basis of human relationships within this newly created body is, for the first time, mutual recognition of self-imposed obligations toward one another, the pledge that brings the group into being is in fact, as Sartre says, "the beginning of humanity."

This beginning takes on an imperatival character by virtue of its being permanent in a way that makes it indefeasible for all future time; it thus refers the recognition of one human being by another back to the reciprocal affirmation of two common traits: we are one because we issued from the primeval slime at the same time and because each one enabled the other to do so with the concurrence of all the others. Thus we are if you please a unique species that made its appearance by a sudden mutation at a given point in time; but our specific nature unites us *qua* freedom. In other words, our common being is not an identical nature in each one of us, but rather a reciprocity that presupposes the setting of conditions on both sides; in approaching a "third" I do not recognize my own inert essence as it is manifested in another example. I recognize instead my indispensable accomplice in the act that will tear us loose from the soil, the brother whose existence is not distinct from mine and comes to me as my existence, but nevertheless depends on mine as mine does on his (with the concurrence of all the others) in the irreversibility of a free assent. . . . We are brothers in the sense that after the creative act of the pledge we are our own sons, our own joint invention. Moreover, just as in real families, this fraternity expresses itself in the group through a set of reciprocal and unique obligations which are laid down by the group on the basis of its situation and its goals (i.e., general obligations to render mutual assistance and obligations to perform particular actions or tasks in specific and rigorously defined situations.) But as we have just seen these obligations simply express the shared character of the underlying exigency and of the act of self-creation which has taken place and which constitutes the irreversible mortgage of our commitment with respect to future action.[43]

[43] "Ce commencement devenant pour chacun nature impérative (par son caractère de permanence indépassable *dans l'avenir*) renvoie donc la reconnaissance à l'affirmation réciproque de ces deux caractères *communs:* nous sommes *les mêmes* parce que nous sommes sortis du limon à la même date, l'un par l'autre à travers tous les autres; donc nous sommes, si l'on veut une espèce singulière, apparue par mutation brusque à tel moment; mais notre nature spécifique nous unit en tant qu'elle est liberté. Autrement dit notre *être commun* n'est pas en chacun *une nature identique;* c'est au contraire la réciprocité médiée des conditionnements: en m'approchant d'un tiers, je ne reconnais pas mon essence inerte en tant qu'elle est manifestée dans un autre exemple: je reconnais le complice nécessaire de l'acte qui *nous* arrache à la glèbe, le frère dont l'existence *n'est pas autre que la mienne,* vient à moi comme la mienne et pourtant dépend de la mienne comme la mienne dépend de la sienne (à travers tous) dans l'irréversibilité d'un libre consentement. . . . Nous sommes frères en tant qu'-

While these and other passages clearly establish a close correspondence between Sartre's conception of obligation and the theory of the moral community outlined in earlier portions of this paper, other features of his position raise certain questions. To take one example, there is in Sartre's account a very strong emphasis on the violence to which I expose myself from other members of the group by virtue of the pledge I have given as a member. There would seem to be some danger that this emphasis will obscure the very important distinction between the motive I have for keeping faith, and the valid basis for my obligation to do so. My motive may well be fear of the consequences of violating my pledge; but I would be under an obligation even if for some special reason I did not need to fear reprisals. In one place, however, Sartre goes so far as to say that the "indépassibilité" of the commitment assumed through the pledge may vary in degree from individual to individual, and that the prospect of violence in the event of infidelity serves to raise the level of this "indépassibilité," and thus to make it less probable that I will fail in my duty.[44] This is no doubt true in one sense, but it misses what is surely the distinctive force of the pledge which is to make non-performance and default *unjustifiable*, no matter what our tendency to keep or to break faith may be in the face of a certain level of

---

après l'acte créateur du serment nous sommes *nos propres fils*, notre invention commune. Et la fraternité, comme dans les familles réelles, se traduit dans le groupe par un ensemble d'obligations réciproques et singulières, c'est-à-dire définies par le groupe entier à partir des circonstances et de ses objectifs (obligations de s'entraider en général, ou dans le cas précis et rigoureusement déterminé d'une action ou d'un travail particulier). Mais ces obligations—nous l'avons vu à l'instant—ne traduisent à leur tour que la communauté de l'exigence fondamentale et tout aussi bien de l'auto-création passée comme hypothèque irréversible de la temporalisation pratique." (*Ibid.*, p. 453.)

[44] *Ibid.*, p. 459.

prospective violence. That prospect may after all confront us whether or not we have pledged ourselves. What the pledge does is to disallow in advance any right we might claim either to do as we please or to resist such reprisals as our failure to comply may call forth from the group. On the other hand, as I have shown earlier, Sartre seems to recognize quite clearly that the core notion in obligation is that of a logical self-binding, and not that of a threat; and if at other times he argues that what effectively produces social cohesion is the prospect of violence, this may be explained by his evident feeling that too strong an emphasis on the internal logical structure of the pledge would tend to suggest that the latter is no more than a "reciprocal determination of discourse . . . a mere game of signs and meanings."[45] Nevertheless, these apparent inconsistencies do create some doubt as to whether Sartre would give the weight to the notion of logical self-binding within his conception of obligation which it seems to deserve, and as long as this doubt subsists, it cannot be said, with complete confidence, that his views tally perfectly with those advanced earlier in this paper.

A question arises also about the limited character of the groups within which, on Sartre's view, rights and duties come into being. The context of discussion makes amply clear that these groups stand in antagonistic relationships to other groups or social classes, and that the formation of a group typically takes the form of a response, through internalization, to a previous identification of it *as a group* by an antagonistic social class. It follows that the community thus formed and the obligations it comports are in no sense universal and include only those who, by their actions, demonstrate their affiliation. It may be that in his promised discussion of the way dialectical relationships among groups generate the movement of "History" Sartre will develop a theory along Marxist lines

[45] *Ibid.*, p. 447.

of the eventual emergence, through conflicts among restricted groups, of truly universal human community—an authentic "cité de l'homme." If so, it may well turn out that in such a society obligation will rest solely on the common human capacities of autonomy and rationality, and no longer on the special interests of restricted groups; but Sartre has also told us that we can know nothing of the freedom that will characterize that eventual society and presumably, therefore, nothing of the form that obligation will assume in it either.[46] Nevertheless, it does seem clear that in Sartre's view the momentum behind the movement toward such a state will be provided not by the internal logic of the idea of reciprocity but by the progressive resolution of the deepseated conflicts between material interests which, until they are overcome, render impossible the emergence of a common interest and the sense of a common human identity.

One may agree with Sartre that moral communities have material presuppositions, and still feel that he has underestimated the logical if not the causal power of the notions of reciprocity and justification. Even if it turns out that genuine social cooperation among different interest groups must await the emergence of new relationships of production and distribution of goods, the most general features of such a new economic system itself must, one would think, be derived from, or at least pass the test of, some conception of the social arrangements that could justly be accepted by all elements in a society. This in turn presupposes a use of the notion of reciprocity beyond the limits of any restricted group. It is clear, too, that no restricted group can ever employ its moral vocabulary beyond the limits of its internal affairs for the purpose of justifying a *refusal* to seek larger and more comprehensive forms of social accommodation. It would, after all, be rather incongruous to claim a

---

[46] *Questions de méthode* (Paris: 1960), p. 32. This study is bound in the same volume as *Critique de la raison dialectique*.

right to disregard systematically the interests of the very groups from whom a recognition of that right is then solicited. Insofar as such extra-mural use of the moral notions operative within a restricted group is contemplated at all, its legitimacy would be dependent on its taking the form of an appeal for a wider recognition and realization of the idea of reciprocity; and this is what Sartre with his rather fanatical emphasis on the limited character of groups has thus far failed to make sufficiently clear.

It is at just this point, of course, that the need will be most keenly felt for a truly and unconditionally universal form of obligation—one that goes beyond both the Sartrian conception of obligation as effective only inside restricted pledge-groups and the wider, "no right not to . . ." conception of obligation presented earlier in this essay. This would have to be a type of obligation that would permit us to assert that it is our positive duty, in all historical circumstances and in all social classes, to do what we can to bring into existence a truly universal human community. Sometimes the demand for such a conception of obligation is deprecated on the ground that the only relevant weakness of the available theories of obligation is that they provide us with nothing to say to individual human beings or restricted moral communities (if there are such) that in actual fact neither seek nor propose a wider sphere of moral relationships. This, it may be claimed, is not a very serious deficiency, since the stance of such an individual or community, in the unlikely event of its being consistently maintained, could only be defined as a repudiation of the assumptions under which alone a wider moral community can even be sought. One may concede the force of this rebuttal and still feel that a conception of obligation as reciprocal self-binding cannot provide an adequate basis for certain moral attitudes to which, if we have them at all, we are likely to attach great importance. Specifically, we do feel that we have moral obligations of various kinds toward many human beings who are either temporarily or permanently incapable of true participation in a moral community because they cannot "bind themselves." Children, for example, are unable, before a certain age, to grasp the notion of justification and to make long-range commitments; and feeble-minded or deranged persons are permanently incapacitated in this respect. Then too, there are persons who have reached maturity in cultures quite different from our own in which the idea of basing moral relationships on voluntary reciprocal understandings is quite unfamiliar. Even at certain levels of our own society there are persons whose experience has been such that they are unable to attach much, if any, meaning to such ideas. Nevertheless, many people feel that moral restraints on what may permissibly be done are operative in these cases, in spite of the absence of any relationship based on mutual recognition of one another as autonomous moral beings. The question therefore arises of how such an extension of the notion of obligation beyond the range of effective moral community can be justified.

This is not a question that can be answered in a way that is likely to satisfy those who raise it. It is perhaps just possible that a deeper analysis of the principle of reciprocity and of the cognate notion of justification might show that even within restricted moral communities based on a common economic interest or shared racial characteristics there is nevertheless a tacit recognition given to the primacy of the human capacity for rational choice.[47] If so, it could be argued

[47] Sartre may be implying something of this kind when he says that "le malaise secret du maître, c'est qu'il est perpétuellement contraint de prendre en consideration la *réalité humaine* en ses esclaves (soit qu'il compte sur leur addresse ou sur leur compréhension synthétique des situations, soit qu'il prenne ses précautions contre la possibilité permanente d'une revolte ou d'une évasion), tout en leur refusant le statut economique et politique qui definit *en ce temps* les êtres humains." *Ibid.*, pp. 190–91.

that moral relationships within such groups reflect a recognition that equal consideration is due to their members by virtue of their possession of this attribute of human nature, and not by virtue of the other (e.g., racial) characteristics which may, nevertheless, for other reasons be subjoined to it as criteria of membership in this group. Obviously, such an analysis would present grave difficulties, but if any progress could be made in this direction, the basis would be laid for an even stronger charge of inconsistency against any group that refused like consideration to members of other groups in the event that circumstances were sufficiently favorable to permit them to extend that consideration without undue risk to themselves. Perhaps, too, other parallel lines of argument might be constructed to deal with the case of those who are incapable, whether temporarily or permanently, of sustaining moral relationships of the type proposed. After all, all of us are children before we are adults and any one of us may become mentally incapacitated, so we do have a stake in seeing to it that such persons are treated as having, within the limits of feasibility and prudence, the same rights and duties as they would have if they could speak for themselves, since in choosing for them we may well be choosing for ourselves. More than this it would probably be unfair to ask an ethical theory to establish. No ethical theory is likely to be able to show that loving concern for other human beings and perhaps for animate creation as such is a duty; and to this rule existentialism forms no exception.

# PESSIMISM AND OPTIMISM
# IN SARTRE'S THOUGHT

*Francis Jeanson*

I have quite recently had the good fortune to join a company of actors who performed *In Camera*[1] in various French towns. My part, I must add, consisted only in being chairman after each performance of a public debate, in which the producer and the actors themselves took part. Now it may not be superfluous to recount the surprises this experience afforded me.

The reactions of the audience were with a few exceptions clearly divided into two categories: on the one hand there were those who, while attracted by the qualities of the play deemed it depressing (desperate, black, entirely negative); on the other those who, wishing to redeem it, contrived to discover some positive outcome or seek an authenticity—which is barely there—in the behavior of the characters. What is more, this division appeared most clearly at the one performance when the audience was exclusively composed of Catholics. So that I had to fight on two fronts, showing that this play was no vehicle for a nihilistic philosophy, a philosophy of despair and the absurd, and yet that it was a serious misunderstanding of the play to presume that the author is putting forward some positive attitude. The philosopher's concern for a *moral order*, a preoccupation throughout the play, remains implicit from beginning to end and is never expressed directly. From the opening ex-

A translation of an article "Pessimisme et optimisme dans la pensée de Sartre," from a collection "Les écrivains devant Dieu," reprinted by permission of Desclée de Brouwer, Paris.

[1] This play is Sartre's *Huis-clos;* Americans will recognize it more easily, perhaps, as *No Exit* [ed.].

changes, Sartre deliberately creates a dead-end situation for the three "damned" characters: it is therefore useless to indulge in any comparisons between their respective chances of salvation. What was then the purpose of those spectators who persisted in detecting an invitation to hope when the door opens unexpectedly toward the end of the play or in establishing a sort of moral hierarchy among the attitudes of Inès, Garcin, or Estelle?

Apart from the rare and hopeless cases of devotees who were exercising their charity, it seems to me that hope was the only way for the spectators to react to the extraordinary human demand of the play (or rather, and more broadly, to the very obvious integrity which characterized both Sartre's work and the life he has indeed been living before our eyes for more than twenty years). As their interpretation seems to proceed from a very positive concern, I should like to attempt here to "demystify" it, while conceding that it gave me the opportunity to understand more fully one of the essential aspects of the play.

*In Camera* is a black play; to try to paint it pink will not help us to see what is valuable in it. Sartre's dramatic works, as the author himself has taken pains to make clear, aim at staging "situations so general that they are within the range of everyone's experience." Kean, the actor; Nekrassov, the crook; or Frank, the prisoner are, in Sartre's eyes mere projections of our human condition. The hell of *In Camera* concerns us equally, even if you and I are neither militant pacifists suspected of having betrayed our cause and convicted of cruelty toward our wives, nor aggressive lesbians, nor empty-headed criminals dedicated to seducing men and becoming mere objects in their eyes; nor are we, properly speaking in hell—no more than the characters themselves; Sartre does not believe in God or the Devil, nor consequently does he believe in "final damnation" or in "a life after death." We must conclude that it is life on earth (our lives now, on this earth) that he meant to describe, and one may ask

why he chose such an overtly mythical dress for his
description. It must be because he is anxious to suggest that all happens *as if we were already dead,* in
as far as each one of us reaches the point of a self-
imposed paralysis, in the name of an elusive gaze from
others, in trying to escape from the comparative judgments of such and such real consciousness. In point
of fact these three supposedly "dead" characters are
restless, they struggle, torture each other, set problems
for themselves, which, with slight variations, could
very well torment us also. How far then are our lives
different from theirs?

1) *First answer:* In *no* way at all. We all are the
victims of this infernal cycle, of the negative circularity
of human relationships; we are all caught, perverted,
corrupted in the very core of our volition, by this perpetual "final judgment" which every one of us weighs
heavily on all, for fear of feeling it weighing upon
himself.

2) *Second answer:* In every way. *We* retain the
possibility of transcending our acts into other ones;
thus specifying, altering, rectifying their significance,
while the three characters in the play are hypotheti-
cally cut off from the real world, forever deprived of
any hold over it.

Not only does *In Camera* waver between these two
answers but so also does the whole movement of Sartre's thought permeated as it is with reflection upon
the problem of morality, upon the praxis of existence,
upon a potential humanization of mankind. Through
the discussions I have had with the many audiences of
the play, I came to see that it is vain to pretend to
eliminate the first interpretation if one only substitutes the second one instead.

Yet at first a few fairly strong arguments. Whether
or not one altogether sympathises with its concrete
manifestations, Sartre's behavior never betrays any
sign of fatalism or resignation. ("In every circum-
stance," he says readily, *"there is something to be
done."*) His philosophy offers from the outset the con-

cept of a *free* and *responsible* consciousness, i.e. a consciousness condemned by its very lack of being constantly to go beyond its own states, to give them new meaning, transform them, to assume responsibility for them within *the future it chooses to project.* Finally, Sartre himself has firmly insisted on the fundamental role of this outlook in his very conception of the theatre.

> If it is true that man is free within a given situation and that he chooses himself in and by that situation, the playwright must create simple and human situations and characters who choose their freedom in these given situations. . . . The most moving experience the theatre can explore is a character in the making, the moment of his choosing, the free decision which involves a moral attitude as well as a whole life.

And the temptation to assert the triumph of the optimistic thesis over the pessimistic one is all the stronger since these few arguments seem to prove the pessimists wrong, pointing out to the causes of their misunderstanding.

For it is obvious that in offering a "dead-end" situation (one might call it an anti-situation), *In Camera* only presents the *very converse of freedom,* that is what freedom becomes when it turns upon itself (*se renie*) or rather what it has become from having too long done so. Hence one could show that the play is really constructed on two levels, one of which, although the most fundamental, only shows in transparency: the relationship the play describes between existence on earth and "life" in hell might indeed symbolize a sort of *extreme passage* (*passage à la limite*) when the drastic misuse of our freedom (its turning upon itself) would irreversibly change it into an object, and turn our respective situations into abstractions in which nothing could be *done.* It is evident that Sartre would not have cared to offer this symbol had

the hell of *In Camera* been the ineluctable conclusion
of our real existence. This is true no doubt, but it does
not follow that the opposite thesis is lacking in some
elements of truth. Take, for instance, *Being and Nothingness* which belongs to the same period as *In Camera:* you will find in turn corroboration for both theses.
If you intend to call pessimistic the thought expressed
in the work, one might object that, no matter how stark
the descriptions of human reality (that is to say of the
consciousness in relation to itself, to the flesh, to objects as well as to other people's consciousness), the
author has nonetheless observed for instance: "These
considerations do not exclude the possibility of a morality of deliverance and salvation, but this can only be
achieved as the outcome of a radical conversion which
it is inopportune to consider now."

—And he has stated explicitly in another passage:
"This does not mean that there is no absolute escape
from bad faith. But it implies a recovery, a correction
of man corrupted at his own hands, which we shall
call 'authenticity' but which we cannot consider here."
—And finally he has repeated in his conclusion that
while the ontology which offers these descriptions cannot formulate of itself moral prescriptions, it suggests
a potential ethics which will assume its responsibilities
before a human reality—*en situation.* If on the other
hand you refer to these texts or to a few others, as an
authority in order to justify optimism, you might very
well be reminded that in the same *Being and Nothingness* one reads: *"All human reality is a passion".* *"Man
is a useless passion,"* and that furthermore Sartre has
still to publish this famous "ethics" whose prescriptions were to help us transcend bad faith to live our
liberty authentically.

To return to our three characters, we shall no doubt
verify that Sartre has in no way wanted to question
or compare the contents of their acts from a moral
viewpoint: he underlines, not what each one has done,
but the fact that all three led *villainous* lives. The mistake Estelle made in choosing to be "woman-object"

was to consider others in their turn only as obstacles to or instruments for the realization of her desires; the mistake Inès made was to answer the reproval of society which she felt was threatening her "as a damned woman" with unmitigated aggressiveness. However, if we now turn to Garcin, we shall have to admit that his situation is identical in so far as he has used all his cunning in persecuting his wife, but that it also differs considerably: he has committed himself to a collective struggle and the question of the meaning of his life is put on a different level from the one they all three of them share. . . . In his case, we are confronted with a freedom which has attempted to find expression in sharing in a communal enterprise, in serving a human cause. While it is comparatively easy in the first case to imagine what *positive* attitude each of the characters might have adopted toward himself and the others, how are we to decide in the second alternative if Garcin should have allowed himself to be arrested or on the contrary striven to go and pursue his pacifist action somewhere else in order to "testify"? His accidental "cowardice" is of a different order from his "wickedness" and from that of his other companions. It is only circumstance which has called his attitude into question and which leaves its meaning forever open.

One might remark that their three situations are eventually similar. It is true that *from their point of view* (or rather from this absence of any point of view and grasp of reality to which they have been henceforth condemned) the difference is nonexistent; but *in our eyes,* I doubt if it is so. As long as we have some moral exigency, it seems likely to me that we shall refuse to equate these two types of accidents which Inès treats more or less as equivalent in a short and striking formula: "One always dies too soon or too late". This formula does not only illustrate the *moralisme* (righteousness?) of popular wisdom, in its comparative optimism: "Better late than never"—"It is

never too late to mend," or comparative pessimism:
"Procrastination is the thief of time," "One can't make
up for lost time," "It's always later than you think."
It suggests that all of us, insofar as our self-awareness
has not yet been infected by vanity or guilt, always
intend to make use of whatever time is left to us to
remedy our past errors, assume greater responsibility
for our lives, and strengthen our relationship with
others. Whether this intention is "meant" or merely a
velleity, whether we actually take steps to make our
daily lives conform to it is another matter; I only want
to point to this conviction of ours: we generally believe
that whatever evil we diagnose in our behavior *could*
be eradicated *if we exercised self-control*.

Such is the principle of a *"radical change"* put forward by Sartre in different chapters of *Being and
Nothingness*. And the lengthy analysis of *In Camera*
which I have just inflicted upon the reader has perhaps given us the opportunity of describing the very
rich complexity which colors Sartre's attitude toward
moral problems from the start. At least we discern
that it is not so easy to define Sartre's pessimism.

When the philosopher shows us the case of Garcin,
untowardly checked in an attempt which might have
served his cause, he is describing an *absolute failure*,
in all events our failure since we cannot pretend to
order our lives with the hope we might die at the
"right moment," i.e. that of our glory. When he talks
of Estelle and Inès (or of Garcin, the tormenter of
his wife) possibly he is then describing a *relative failure*, meaning that it is up to us to avert it, if needs
be almost instantaneously. Is Sartre absolutely pessimistic in the first case, and only partially in the second? If all moral conversion implies, as he has stated
repeatedly, some concrete commitment to a human
struggle, are we not to consider both cases equally
desperate, since the failure only appears relative to
the second case insofar as one imagines that one can
substitute the first one for the second.

This is a natural conclusion with Sartre, a real penchant; but the opposite penchant is also present, and Sartre wants us to bear this in mind in a much later text than *In Camera*.

> A great number of people in the world are in hell because they depend too much upon the judgments of others. That does not mean this is the only relationship with others. What I wished to show was precisely that many people are prisoners of a whole series of habits, of customs, that they pass judgments upon themselves which hurt them but which they do not even try to alter, that these people are as if dead in the sense that they cannot break out of the prison of their cares, worries, habits and thus remain the victims of the judgments passed on them. This is the reason for their being dead. Anybody walled in by the judgments and actions which they do not wish to change are more dead than alive. . . .

If one confines oneself to these observations a complete reversal of outlook emerges. Sartre does not probe into death: for him the existing consciousness is totally responsible for the choices it makes for itself. Are we going to find ourselves steeped in optimism yet again? Not quite! for I have deliberately left out the part of the quotation which contained what is to me *a crucial contradiction*, as it throws the best possible light on the genesis of Sartre's thought on our own moral statute. Here is the rest of the quotation:

> I mean to say . . . that others are, after all, our best means of achieving self-knowledge. When we reflect upon ourselves, when we try to know ourselves, we in fact use the knowledge others have acquired about us. The means we have to judge ourselves are the means others have and gave us.

Hence one is forced to conclude that freedom is not as responsible and sovereign as one might have thought, neither for that imprisoned consciousness which was described to us as not wanting to escape the judgments weighing upon it, nor for any consciousness whatsoever: *"The determining influence others have on each one of us"* seems to condemn any one of us to adopt only a negative attitude of abstention and diffidence to avoid the weight of his judgments upon them, or of their judgments upon him. For a philosophy which aims at being practical, entirely directed by a demand for concrete universalization of mankind, for the effective recognition of man by man, we seem to have here a *rather pessimistic* conception of the relationships between different types of consciousness. And yet this conclusion would appear insignificant compared with many other illustrations offered by Sartre himself: these give us some flashes of insight into what one might very well call an obsessional attitude. The double obsession it reveals, the fear of being *robbed* or *violated* is only an apparent contradiction: if the consciousness is constantly afraid of being stripped of its sovereignty, robbed, it is because others have stealthily taken hold of it from the start and are increasingly speaking in its place.

Already in "Erostrate" (one of the tales collected under the title *The Wall*) the hero, Paul Hilbert loathes "men" because they have taken possession of the meaning of life. He cannot formulate, simply for himself, what he would like to think independently from them, and what he formulates escapes him and becomes *theirs:*

> The thoughts which I did not mean for them, I could not divorce myself from them; they remained within me like vague organic movements. The very tools I used, I felt were theirs; words, for example: I would have liked words of my own; but those I have at my disposal have been hanging around in so many other people's consciousness. They organize themselves within me, independently, according to those habits they acquired in other people's consciousness.

And when this radical rebel who likes "black heroes" and dreams of becoming one of them, eventually goes down one evening into the street, planning to shoot the first human specimen he comes across, his first reaction at the sight of the passers-by in the street is not unlike the situations in *In Camera* and echoes the remark Sartre made previously: "Why kill all these people who are already dead?" Paul Hilbert rejects the humanism most of his fellow men seem to think so highly of; he sees it only as the token of satisfaction men are stupid enough to confer upon themselves: they avail themselves of it so as not to have to reconsider the being they have *become,* "this living dead man" others have made of him either by "dispossessing" or "possessing" him—whichever you please.

Such is, doubtless, the first of the major illusions which Sartre wished to dispel, the illusion that mankind has already attained self-realization, man's *illusory recognition of man,* this wretched complicity which everyday life establishes between types of consciousness which are created, recreated, and finally "uncreated," types of consciousness which are "too human" and which have given up *inventing man as a whole.*"

# SARTRE AS CRITIC

## *Harold Wardman*

What will be discussed here above all is Sartre's response to individual works of art and literature.[1] 'La psychanalyse existentielle' is, for Sartre, 'moral description' which tends to treat a work of art not as an end in itself. It treats it as an integral part of the artist's life and creative processes. It will therefore not be considered here except insofar as in his studies of Baudelaire and Genet, for example, Sartre does respond to their writings as literature.

It is doubtful, however, whether theory ought to be left out of account altogether. One will therefore begin by a brief statement of Sartre's theory of literature without expounding *engagement*. This is well enough known, but there is one aspect of Sartre's attitude to literature which may be less so. For him, a work of literature should be 'gratuitous' because, for example, it should not try to influence the reader's feelings but appeal to his freedom. Further, it should be 'gratuitous,' because it is not a means to an end or utilitarian, which is how, according to him, the bourgeois regard it, when they do not look on it as a mere pastime.[2] 'Gratuitousness', for Sartre, makes the literary work an 'image of freedom'; it must be 'une fin absolue' and have the value of a categorical imperative if it is to help bring into being the city of ends

---

This essay written especially for this edition by Dr. Wardman.

[1] Cf. also on this topic, G. H. Bauer, *Sartre and the Artist*, Chicago, 1969, where Sartre's views on certain poets, notably Baudelaire and Mallarmé, differ in important respects from the account of them given here.

[2] *Qu'est-ce que la littérature?*, Gallimard, Collection Idées, 1948, p. 168.

of the future envisaged in *Qu'est-ce que la littérature?* Neither is a literary work a product, though its
function is to represent 'la libre conscience d'une société de production' and to 'contester l'aliénation' du
travail.[3] In this sense it becomes more and more
closely connected with the idea of a literature of
*praxis* without ever being considered as a means to an
end.

Now this emphasis on 'gratuitousness' makes Sartre
relatively well-disposed toward writers who scarcely
fit into the pattern of *engagement*. After criticizing
Flaubert, Maupassant, and later writers for using 'internal narrators' and for lacking a sense of history, he
goes on to praise their work because of its 'gratuitousness' and because it does appeal to the reader's freedom. Moreover:

> Elle a poussé la contestation jusqu'à l'extrême, jusqu'à
> se contester elle-même; elle nous a fait entrevoir un
> silence noir par-delà le massacre des mots, et, par-
> delà l'esprit de sérieux, le ciel vide et nu des équival-
> ences; elle nous invite à émerger dans le néant par
> destruction de tous les mythes et de toutes les tables
> de valeur, elle nous découvre en l'homme, en place
> du rapport intime avec la transcendance divine, une
> relation étroite et secrète avec le Rien.[4]

Such literature is also seen, in quasi-sociological terms,
as an expression of 'la fête', as defined by Roger Cail-
lois:

> Si l'on se rappelle que la fête est . . . un de ces mo-
> ments négatifs où la collectivité conseum les bien
> qu'elle a amassés . . . depense pour le plaisir de
> dépenser . . . on verra que la littérature, au XIXe
> siècle, fut, en marge d'une société laborieuse qui
> avait la mystique de l'épargne, une grande fête

[3] Op. cit. *Situations* II p. 261–2.
[4] *Qu'est-ce que la littérature?*, p. 180.

> somptueuse et funèbre, une invitation à brûler dans
> une immoralité splendide, dans le feu des passions,
> jusqu'à mourir.[5]

In short, such literature was a safety valve, which
suggests that it was politically harmless. On the other
hand, Sartre maintains, it culminated in Trotskyist
surrealism and contrived to fulfill a political function
because 'de la fête perpétuelle à la Révolution permanente il n'y a pas si loin'.[6] Finally, although it
'betrayed' literature, it discovered the importance of
'la somptuosité des moyens d'expression'.[7] This is to
admit the importance of style and one hopes that it is
meant to apply to Baudelaire, who gets little credit
for his own 'gratuitousness' elsewhere. But admitting
the importance of style does not save Flaubert
from censure or Sartre from a remarkable error of
judgment:

> Flaubert écrit pour se débarrasser des hommes et
> des choses. Sa phrase cerne l'objet, l'attrape, l'im-
> mobilise et lui casse les reins, se referme sur lui, se
> change en pierre et le pétrifie avec elle.[8]

How could this possibly be true of 'la promenade en
forêt' and many another episode in *Madame Bovary*?
   We have seen how 'la fête' can stand for 'conspic-
uous consumption' and can call literature in question
by 'le massacre des mots' through which we see 'le
ciel vide et nu des équivalences'. 'La fête' is therefore opposed to 'l'esprit de sérieux'. Twenty years after
symbolism, Sartre affirms, the French writer had not
lost 'la conscience de la gratuité absolue de l'art . . .'
but was divided between 'l'esprit de sérieux . . . et

[5] Ibid., p. 180–87.
[6] Ibid., p. 181.
[7] Ibid., p. 182.
[8] Ibid., pp. 162–63.

l'esprit de contestation et de fête qu'il retrouve devant une page blanche. . . .'[9]

The reference to Mallarmé here is unmistakable.

As a form of destructiveness 'la fête' can be connected, especially through surrealism, with what Jean Paulhan, in *Les Fleurs de Tarbes*, calls 'le terrorisme'. For Sartre this consists in preferring acts to words, poetry to prose, or 'spontaneous disorder to composition'. It is an attempt to make literature an expression of life instead of sacrificing life to literature. He himself never practices it, but, like surrealism, it influences him, especially when he is trying to distinguish between poetry and prose.

This distinction must now be briefly considered. According to him, poetry, sculpture, and music do not lend themselves to *engagement*: words, colors and sounds found in these arts are not signs because they refer to nothing outside themselves. Colors in painting are things, not a language; they do not express emotions but are 'impregnated' with them:

> Cette déchirure jaune du ciel au-dessus du Golgotha, le Tintoret ne l'a pas choisie pour *signifier* l'angoisse ni non plus pour *la provoquer*; elle est angoisse et ciel jaune en même temps. Non pas ciel d'angoisse ni ciel angoissé; c'est une angoisse faite chose, une angoisse . . . empâtée par les qualités propres des choses, par leur imperméabilité . . . leur permanence aveugle . . . c'est-à-dire qu'elle n'est plus du tout lisible, c'est comme un effort immense et vain, toujours arrêté à mi-chemin du ciel et de la terre, pour exprimer ce que leur nature leur défend d'exprimer.[10]

Now this is a passage in which the manner is at least as important as the matter. The main idea expressed in it, helped by a touch of anthropomorphism,

[9] *Qu'est-ce que la littérature?*, *Situations* II, p. 209.
[10] Op. cit. Collection Idées, p. 14.

is that of incarnation, as is made quite plain by another
passage from the same context:

> Les longs Arlequins de Picasso, ambigus et éternels,
> hantés par un sens indéchiffrable, inséparable de
> leur maigreur voûtée et des losanges délavés de leurs
> maillots, ils ont une émotion qui s'est faite chair et
> que la chair a bue comme le buvard boit l'encre.[11]

Now one of Sartre's difficulties is deciding just how
far art can become material or suffer incarnation in
matter. As can be seen from *L'Imaginaire*, his position in this respect is similar to Collingwood's: a work
of art is not to be identified with the material object
which gives it form, whether this is the sound of music
or the matter of a statue. This is why he can say, of
passion expressed in music, that it undergoes a 'tran-
substantiation' and a 'degradation'. This does not prevent him from writing an enthusiastically perceptive
passage on the realism of Vermeer, even though what
concerns him here is not so much incarnation as aesthetic finalism:

> Le réalisme de Vermeer est si poussé qu'on pourrait
> croire d'abord qu'il est photographique. Mais si l'on
> vient à considérer la splendeur de sa matière, la
> gloire rose et veloutée de ses petits murs de brique,
> l'épaisseur bleue d'une branche de chèvrefeuille, l'ob-
> scurité vernie de ses vestibules, la chair orangée de
> ses visages polis comme la pierre des bénitiers, on
> sent tout à coup au plaisir qu'on éprouve, que la
> finalité n'est pas tant dans les formes ou dans les
> couleurs que dans son imagination matérielle; c'est
> la substance même et la pâte des choses qui est ici
> la raison d'être de leurs formes; avec ce réaliste . . .
> c'est dans la passivité même de la maitière que nous
> rencontrons l'insondable liberté de l'homme.[12]

[11] Ibid., p. 16.
[12] Ibid., pp. 71–72.

Sartre's point is simply that whether we are talking about matter in Vermeer or words in poetry, the artist cannot be said to use either. For the poet, according to Sartre, language is a 'structure' of the external world. 'Outside' language, it is as though he first had a silent contact with things instead of first knowing them by name, and then came into contact with words through his senses, discovering in them 'une petite luminosité propre et des affinités particulières avec le ciel et la terre et toutes les choses créées'.[13] The physical aspect of a word is said in some sense to be reflected in the word itself, in the meaning it has and without which words in poetry would be mere sounds or signs on paper. 'Coulée dans le mot, absorbée par sa sonorité ou par son aspect visuel, épaissie, dégradée, elle est chose. . . .'[14] In all its physical aspects it is said to mirror an aspect of the world; as part of a language these aspects have meaning; this meaning, however, does not designate objects; the word which is the 'verbal image' of the willow is not necessarily the word 'willow'. So it must be regarded as having a physical aspect which at the same time reveals its meaning. This theory is doubtless open to criticism, but, right or wrong, it lies behind Sartre's sensitivity to words as poetic objects of a surrealist kind:

> Florence est ville et fleur et femme, elle est ville-fleur et ville-femme et fille-fleur tout à la fois. Et l'étrange objet qui paraît ainsi possède la liquidité du fleuve, la douce ardeur jaune de l'*or* et, pour finir, s'abandonne avec *décence* et prolonge indéfiniment par l'affaiblissement continu de l'*e* muet son épanouissement plein de réserves.[15]

This is to set up a train of association in the mind by letting the imagination play freely round a word. It

[13] Ibid.
[14] Ibid., p. 19.
[15] Ibid., p. 21.

is also by association that the words of a poem are related to each other, but cease to be words:

> Les mots-choses se groupent par associations magiques de convenance et de disconvenance, comme les couleurs et les sons, ils s'attirent, ils se repoussent, ils se *brûlent* et leur association compose la véritable unité poétique qui est la *phrase-objet*.[16]

Francis Ponge, Sartre maintains, in 'L'Homme et les choses'[17], attempts to see things before they become tools. A poem is a thing—'une synthèse perpétuellement évanescente de l'unité vivante et de la dispersion inorganique . . . une statue ensorcelée; nous avons affaire à des marbres hantés par la vie . . . (à) un effort avorté de la pierre vers l'existence organisée.'[18] Ponge's aim is to describe not 'l'ondoiement des apparences' but 'la substance interne de l'objet'[19] and so express our desire to effect symbolically the fusion of existence and being, that is, the modes of being of consciousness and things. While we cannot, according to Sartre, in reality be both conscious and thing-like, we do find ourselves, phenomenologically speaking, in things, outside ourselves in such a way that '. . . l'homme . . . se perd pour que le galet existe'.[20]

But even a prose work of literature, however utilitarian he may say prose is, is not 'given' in language; on the contrary, it is 'silence et contestation de la parole' in so far as it has about it an inexpressible quality.

Now in an attempt to explain what lies behind this difference between poetry and prose, Sartre puts forward an existentialist interpretation of poetry and of a poetic attitude to the world. According to this theory,

16 Ibid., p. 22.
17 *Situations* I, pp. 245 ff.
18 Ibid., p. 275.
19 Ibid., pp. 275–76.
20 Ibid., p. 291.

poetry 'originally' created the 'myth of man', while prose 'portrayed' him. In reality, actions are means to ends and subordinate to their result; thus, even in picking up a pen, man is 'aliéné par ses fins'.[21] In poetry, this relation is reversed, action becomes an end in itself and the world becomes a 'pretext' to action, in the sense that, poetically viewed, the Trojan war was a pretext for the fight between Achilles and Hector. Action, cut off from its ends, turns into prowess or dance; the poet, apparently, becomes indifferent to the success or failure of action. The only end to which he is not indifferent is the fate of man himself, who becomes 'la fin absolue'.

This brings in then the question of the success or failure of the human enterprise or history, as Sartre calls it. Poetry becomes identified with a failure which throws man back on himself but which is also a form of 'contestation' because it brings out man's superiority to the world which threatens him. The problem for poetry, apparently, is to express this 'contestation' without becoming *engagée*. How it might be said to do so will be seen later in connection with Sartre's approach to Mallarmé.

As to the distinction between poetry and prose, Sartre admits that it is not absolute. Rather oddly, but following from the above, prose is apparently to be associated with success in communication, poetry with failure or the incommunicable. Now we have already seen Sartre admitting that there is an incommunicable or inexplicable element even in prose, which means that *engagement*, for him, is not a communication theory of art. Moreover, there is obviously good sense in recognizing that the distinction in question is not absolute, in saying about all prose being to some extent 'poetic', '. . . nous ne sommes plus sur le plan de la communication concertée mais sur celui de la grâce et du hasard; les silences de la prose sont poétiques parce

---

[21] *Qu'est-ce que la littérature?*, Collection Idées, p. 45, n. 4.

qu'ils marquent ses limites. . . .'[22] The fact remains that success or failure are now restricted in meaning to success or failure in communication, a shift of meaning of which Sartre himself does not seem aware.

Now we have noted his recognition of the poetic prose of Francis Ponge. As to the 'coefficient d'adversité' of the world apprehended by poetic vision, there are some interesting examples of this in some of the novels reviewed in *Situations* I. It is true that in writing on Faulkner and Dos Passos, he seems mainly concerned with time, but time, for him, in the true novel must have 'irreversibility': '. . . le roman exige une durée continue, un devenir, la présence manifeste de l'irréversibilité du temps'.[23] The novelist, he says, in his article on Mauriac, must make us feel the 'resistance' of time by telling his narrative from several points of view and so working on our sense of expectancy and impatience.[24] (Like Hemingway in *A Farewell to Arms*), he must also make us aware of the resistance of things, of words and consequently of dialogue and character:

> Dostoïevski eût entouré Thérèse de figures denses et secrètes dont le sens a chaque page eût été sur le point de se livrer, m'eût échappé, mais M. Mauriac m'installe d'emblée au plus profond des coeurs.[25]

According to one of the best pieces of critical writing in the book, it is precisely this quality which is lacking in Camus' *L'Étranger*. What he finds instead in it is 'cette succession de présents inertes qui laisse entrevoir par en-dessous l'économie mécanique d'une pièce montée.'[26] Sartre appears to allow that Meursault's indifference does give his character a certain

---

[22] Ibid., p. 48, n. 5.
[23] *Situations*, I, p. 121.
[24] Ibid., p. 46.
[25] Ibid., p. 51.
[26] Ibid., p. 121.

density. At the same time, he appears to doubt whether the 'absurd' is adequately expressed in a work where every detail is made use of to constitute an ordered sequence working toward the hero's downfall, in short —'une oeuvre classique, une oeuvre d'ordre, composée à propos de l'absurde et contre l'absurde.'[27] Classical and satirical—this is perceptive of *L'Étranger*, but it is curious that he should give more weight to its form than to its fundamental seriousness.

The density and resistance of people and things, the irreversibility of time, even mystery and suspense, these are the artistic values which Sartre looks for in the novel. They have their importance, but it is to be noticed that they are largely technical in nature, that Sartre as a critic seems to be interested in what interests him as a novelist. This is understandable but limits the value of his criticism. It is curious, too, that he should show relatively little interest in the moral aspect of the novel. He is also somewhat inconsistent in expecting from prose fiction what poetry, according to him, should by its nature provide. What he does find in poetry can be seen from his introduction to *Orphée noir*.[28] Here he sets out to explain why the black man's self-awareness had to be poetic and why his poetry is the only great revolutionary poetry.

The European working class has not produced poetry, he maintains, for two reasons: its experience of nature is technical: '. . . la Nature c'est pour lui la Matière, cette résistance passive, cette adversité sournoise et inerte qu'il laboure de ses outils. . . .'[29] Secondly, the language which it uses in the class struggle takes it out of itself into the sphere of the objective. Now the black man's experiences in relation to the French language 'le sentiment d'échec devant le langage considéré comme moyen d'expression directe', which, he contends, lies behind all poetic experience.

27 Ibid.
28 *Situations* III, pp. 229 ff.
29 Ibid., p. 234.

The 'échec' in question is that of prose, when we discover, like Roquentin, that words no longer succeed
in naming the world, so that language looks like a
broken-down machine and there takes place what
Georges Bataille calls 'l'holocauste des mots'. By a
process of reasoning not wholly convincing, Sartre
concludes, with Mallarmé, that the world can now
only be apprehended through silence—'évoquer, dans
une ombre exprès, l'objet tu par des mots allusifs, jamais directs, se réduisant à du silence égal'.[30]

Sartre then tries to equate Mallarmé's conception of
poetry with the 'autodestruction of language' of the
surrealists.

> Personne n'a mieux dit [i.e. than Mallarmé] que la
> poésie est une tentative incontatoire pour suggérer
> l'être dans et par la disparition vibratoire du mot: en
> renchérissant sur son impuissance verbale, en rendant
> les mots fous, le poète nous fait soupçonner par delà
> ce tohu-bohu qui s'annule de lui-même d'énormes
> densités silencieusses. . . .[31]

While there seems to be more of surrealism than
Mallarmé here, it is in the light of this so-called 'holo-
caust' that Sartre interprets the reaction of the black
races against the French language of their masters.
Their aim, he says, is to 'destroy' it, meaning simply,
to break up the usual associations of words, like Aimé
Césaire in *Les armes miraculeuses*. French has to become un-French and lose its whiteness, while black
becomes a color or a light—'(le) noir pays où dorment
les anciens n'est pas un enfer ténébreux: c'est une
terre de soleil et de feu'.[32]

But the black poet cannot, apparently, free himself
entirely from the ambiguity of the word 'black', implicit in a solar and racial hierarchy. The result, Sar-

[30] Ibid., p. 246.
[31] Ibid., pp. 246–47.
[32] Ibid., p. 249.

tre argues, is a poetical exploitation of paradox like the
'autodestructive' objects of the surrealists, '. . . Il y a
une noirceur secrète du blanc, une blancheur secrète
du noir, un papillottement figé d'être et de non-être
. . .' which finds expression in Césaire's 'ma grande
chair de nuit à grain de jour. . . .'[33] Thus black is no
longer a privation of light but a refusal or destruction of 'cette clarté d'emprunt qui tombe du soleil
blanc. . . .'

Following the logic of this Hegelian negation, the
black man must rediscover his own origins in folklore
or in that state, where, in Mallarmé's words, 'la parole
crée les dieux'. There are, according to Sartre, two
ways back to this 'primal simplicity', one objective,
through African songs and dances, the other subjective, with Césaire and his surrealist methods which
involve getting beneath the superficial surface of
reality to awaken,

> . . . les puissances immémoriales du désir . . . du
> désir qui, par sa folle énergie cosmique, replonge
> l'homme au sein bouillonnant de la Nature et l'élève
> en même temps au-dessus de la Nature par l'affirma-
> tion de son droit à l'insatisfaction.[34]

But whereas surrealism, he argues, was not revolutionary insofar as it aimed at a reconciliation of opposites, a poem by Césaire, by contrast, 'éclate et tourne
sur lui-même comme une fusée . . . c'est un perpétuel dépassement'.[35] Nevertheless, he sees Césaire's
poetry as the fulfillment of surrealism turned against
white culture, creating, not describing, 'la négritude—
objet'. Such poetry he regards as essentially 'pure' or
free from any taint of prose. It is the vehicle of negritude, but this makes for poetry, not prose, because it
is a living rapport with nature.

[33] Ibid., pp. 250–51.
[34] Ibid., p. 253.
[35] Ibid.

. . . le noir reste le grand mâle de la terre, le sperme
du monde. Son existence, c'est la grande patience
végétale; son travail, c'est la répétition d'année en
année du coit sacré.[36]

This negritude is not Bergson's 'intuition chaste et
asexuée' but a pan-sexuality which is fundamentally
androgynous.[37]

The unity of organic and sexual symbolism, this sexuality of men and women metamorphosed into plants
and animals is for Sartre the greatest originality of
African poetry. The other great theme of negritude
which impresses him is the theme of 'l'authenticité
recueillie de sa souffrance'. Because of its sufferings,
the black race is a chosen race, so that insofar as it
takes on itself the sufferings of all men, negritude is
a passion, except that there is nothing resigned about
it. Dionysian, in the Nietzschean sense, negritude
searches for 'la souffrance inexpiable qui est l'essence
universelle de l'homme' and which unites with the fertility of the natural world.

Finally, this experience of suffering is said to be ambiguous. Behind it we are to see an historical experience—the black man's experience of the Fall in the
form of slavery. But as this is caused by the white
man, the suffering becomes anti-Christian and turns
into revolt. A kind of philosophy of history intervenes
now to support the immediacy of Sartre's response to
negritude. The memory of slavery and the abolition of
slavery turn into the future god of liberation.

Etrange et décisif virage: la race s'est transumée en
historicité, le Présent noir explore et se temporalise,
la Négritude s'insère avec son passé et son avenir
dans l'Histoire Universelle, ce n'est plus un état . . .
c'est un devenir . . . c'est une entreprise, une pa-
tiente construction, un futur.[38]

[36] Ibid., p. 266.
[37] Ibid., p. 268.
[38] Ibid., p. 277.

But Sartre concludes that negritude is after all only a phase, destined to give way to new and universal values. Negritude finds itself in self-renunciation, since only the black man can be asked to renounce pride in his color.

Whether this is in fact the case is a matter of opinion. On matters of fact one does more than once want to disagree with Sartre. One feels that in characterizing the black man as 'le sperme du monde' he is being absurdly unrealistic; that he is romantic about the black man's relation to nature which is probably no more organic than that of the white peasant. And questions of fact are important since it is no use to the black man to pretend that he is other than he is. Sartre does, of course, see him through the poetry of negritude and as an interpreter of this poetry he is difficult to equal, because of the intense rhetorical sympathy with which he responds to it. This, for a European— and a Cartesian—is no mean achievement.

The nature of his response to African poetry makes all the more intelligible his much more critical attitude to Baudelaire's. Now Baudelaire has a feeling for the gratuitousness of art which is not unlike Sartre's. For Sartre, however, what is wrong with Baudelaire, apparently, is his frigidity, his dandyism, his cult of sterility and his conception of the writing of poetry as a self-discipline instead of an expression of 'la spontanéité créatrice'.[39] It is difficult not to feel, however, that Sartre's case against Baudelaire suffers from a reluctance to consider the latter's poetry independently of the man himself. This point is too obvious for it to be necessary to develop it.

It is not to deny that Sartre does, in a sense, consider Baudelaire's poetry as poetry. He contends, in the first place, that all poets attempt to bring about fusion of existence and being or mind and matter, as previously considered. This fusion is, apparently, im-

[39] Sartre, *Baudelaire*, Gallimard, p. 129.

possible,[40] though Baudelaire seems to some extent
to achieve it. Poets are said to create

> . . . de certaines natures ambiguës, chatoiement d'ex-
> istence et d'etre qui les satisfont doublement—à la
> fin parce qu'elles sont des essences objectives et
> qu'ils peuvent les contempler et parce qu'elles pro-
> cèdent d'eux et qu'ils peuvent s'y retrouver.[41]

What Sartre calls 'le spirituel' is 'le fait poétique
baudelairien'. His definition of this seems to imply
that Baudelaire has succeeded in writing poems which
fuse the two orders of being and existence:

> Le spirituel . . . n'est pas tout à fait, une discrétion
> profonde l'empêche . . . de s'affirmer à la manière
> d'une table ou d'un caillou; il se caractérise par une
> manière d'absence, il n'est jamais tout à fait là, ni
> tout à fait visible, il reste en suspens entre le néant
> et l'être par une discrétion poussée jusqu'à l'ex-
> trême.[42]

Evidence for this in Baudelaire is provided by 'les
admirable vers du *Guignon*', where the scent of flow-
ers exists 'à regret'. Sartre excels at the kind of subtlety of language required to characterize an impalpa-
bility which is yet incarnate in words. It explains, he
thinks, Baudelaire's love of scents and smells—a smell
being 'ce corps désincarné, vaporisé, resté, certes, tout
entier lui-même, mais devenu esprit volatil'.[43] Other
instances cited are Baudelaire's preference for twilight,
the overcast skies of Holland—in fact, '. . . tous les
êtres, choses et gens, qui semblent meurtris, brisés ou
qui glissent vers leur fin: les "petites vieilles" et, tout

[40] Ibid., p. 199.
[41] Ibid., p. 200.
[42] Ibid.
[43] Ibid., p. 201.

aussi bien, la lumière d'une lampe que le petit jour pâlit et qui semble vaciller dans son être'.[44]

While there is much to be said for this, 'les petites vieilles' are surely more than 'embodied thoughts' ('des pensees corporifiées'). Before one can be satisfied that this expression does contain the essence of Baudelaire, is it not necessary, for example, to take into consideration, not only 'les petites vieilles' as human beings, but the entire poem of that title? What he responds to finally in Baudelaire is an ambiguous mode of being, as can be seen from this characterisation of the suggestiveness of beauty: '. . . ce type étrange et forgé de réalité, où l'être, et l'existence se confondent, où l'existence est objective et solidifiée par l'être, où l'être est allégé par l'existence. . . .'[45]

Such ambiguity is typical of his philosophy in *L'Être et le néant*, where one so often finds in his phenomenological descriptions neither being nor existence in a pure state but a subtle interpenetration of the two.

For him, consciousness, freedom, or again, existence, to use another cognate term, enters into all our states of mind so that we are never 'thinglike'. 'Perpétuellement absents à mon corps, à mes actes, je suis en dépit de moi-même, cette "divine absence" dont parle Valéry.'[46] Or, as he says in his study of Genet: 'C'est le vertige, le manque, le néant, la négation qui marquent l'émotion poétique.'[47] When this is considered together with his awareness of 'absence', it is clearly no accident that he should have felt sufficiently drawn to Mallarmé to write a preface to a selection of his poems.[48] Unfortunately, this preface is anything but a coherent piece of writing.

What is clear about it is that Sartre responds to the

[44] Ibid., p. 202.

[45] Ibid., p. 208.

[46] Sartre, *L'Être et le néant*, p. 100.

[47] Sartre, *Saint-Genet, comédien et martyr*, p. 277.

[48] Mallarmé, *Poésies*, préface de J. P. Sartre, Gallimard, 1966.

process of 'negation', comparable to his own 'néantisation', which is characteristic of much of Mallarmé's
poetry, as in, 'Une dentelle s'abolit/Dans le doute du
Jeu suprême/A n'entr'ouvrir comme un blasphème/
Qu'absence éternelle de lit'. Or, again, in 'Le vierge,
le vivace et le bel aujourd'hui . . .', what is no more
than an imaginary movement dies away, according to
Sartre, leaving behind an infinite and undifferentiated
surface. On the other hand, he asserts, this 'negative
logic' discloses 'un symbole sensible qui nous renvoie
à la tragédie humaine et celle-ci se dissout dans le
néant'.

The 'human tragedy' in question is the 'impossibility
of being a man' (that is, of being satisfied with being
mortal) which Mallarmé discovered because he lived
through 'la mort de Dieu'.[49] From this there results, in
Sartre's view, a poetry conceived as an act of destruction, its language evoking 'l'absence de tout' and so
calling itself in question.

As so often with Sartre, it is when he sees Mallarmé's
poems in the context of his life that they move him
most. What is most poignant about them, for him,
comes from the fact that they arouse our enthusiasm
whereas Mallarmé himself held them to be of no account. Mallarmé dying before his work was finished,
conscious both of its vanity and of its necessity, is, for
Sartré, comparable with mankind dying of atomic
destruction or the cooling of the sun. This is a case of
the poet identifying his 'failure' with that of the human
race, as mentioned earlier. Yet Mallarmé's art is said
to be an 'imposture' and his poems are called 'des ob-
jets truqués', for the rather curious reason that these
'sonnets nuls' embody what Sartre, following Mallarmé
and Valéry, calls 'absence' or constitute poetry conceived as 'self-negating', an apt vehicle, consequently,
for Sartrian ontology, where the self, by its nature, negates itself and its world.

The tendency in poetry to unify, as Sartre sees it,

[49] Cf. *Saint-Genet,* p. 324.

the diversity of the world by an 'expansive' movement, is represented for him by Rimbaud, to whose
poems he applies Breton's term, 'une explosante—
fixe'.[50] 'Voir en l'aube un peuple de colombes, c'est
faire sauter le matin comme une poudrière.'[51] At the
opposite pole is the 'stable, theological universe' of
Baudelaire and Mallarmé where unity is imposed on
the discontinuous by a movement described as 'retrac-
tile'.[52] This is the universe, relatively 'passive and fem-
inine', which, in Sartre's view, was chosen by Genet.

He also finds in Genet 'les Jeux de l'être et du non-
être de Mallarmé', which reflect the ambiguity of the
human condition, as does Rimbaud's 'salon au fond
d'un lac', because it paradoxically brings together a
pair of opposites like a surrealist composition.[53] A
striking feature of what he also calls 'l'exténuante vo-
lupté de l'absence et du rien' in Genet[54] are the
'tourniquets' or the circular, dialectical process of negation which is as much part of his own ontology as it
is of his subject. Thus, Sartre's reconstruction of Genet's life, the latter's progress towards emancipation
through art, takes the form of a vertiginous delight in
the play of appearance and reality. The degree of detail in passages of analysis of what sometimes seems
relatively unimportant gives the work an air of almost
wilful extravagance. Consider, for example, Sartre's
analysis of Genet's first attempt at poetry: the expression, 'moissonneur des souffles coupés'. This turns out
to be yet another of those self-negating expressions
which is said to mean literally 'nothing'.[55] All this as-

---

[50] Ibid., p. 438. Cf. Sartre's analysis of Genet's, 'Surgit,
toute raide et noire, d'un vase, une branche de cerisier que
les fleurs roses en plein vol soutiennent', ibid., pp. 43–47.

[51] Ibid.

[52] Ibid., p. 429.

[53] Ibid., p. 256.

[54] Ibid., p. 262.

[55] Ibid., p. 287. For an almost 'precious' elaboration of detail, cf. the analysis of the line, 'Le jardinier est la plus belle
rose de son jardin', ibid., pp. 469–71.

pect of Genet, molded to some extent in Sartre's own
image, is well summed up by the latter's characterization of *Les Bonnes:* 'Cet extraordinaire truquage, ce
fal enchevêtrement d'apparences, cette superposition
de tourniquets qui renvoient sans relâche du vrai au
faux et du faux au vrai. . . .'[56]

For Genet's art, as one might by now expect, involves imposture; his prose and his novels are 'false'.
This need mean no more than that they are not what
they seem, as in Genet's theatre. But where Genet's
novels are concerned, Sartre means more than that.
He argues that the result of the 'truquage' is to trap
the self-righteous reader into being contaminated by
what one might call the 'coprophilia' to be found in
Genet. This seems to suppose a rather unlikely degree
of naïveté and credulity on the part of such a reader.
Moreover, we are asked to believe that, by infecting
others, Genet frees himself from the evil which they
had projected on to him. His works then have for him
the therapeutical importance of psychodrama, which
suggests that they are little more than a kind of phan-
tasmagoria. Sartre tends to confirm this impression by
such statements as '. . . la poésie de Genet c'est la
fuite vertiginéese des significations vers le néant'. But
for poetry to be like this is, for Sartre, perfectly legitimate. It ceases to be true poetry when, as in 'Con-
damné à mort', which does indeed seem unremark-
able, it tends to turn into prose.[57] On the other hand,
he will affirm that in Genet, moral experience is at bottom only verbal,[58] or that his characters are so many
'fantasies' whom he ironically impersonates.

Nevertheless, there is, according to Sartre, a moral
seriousness in *Pompes funèbres:*

> . . . (il) poursuit le 'travail du deuil' justqu'à en
> transformer la douleur vécue en Eidos de la sen-

---

[56] Ibid., p. 572.
[57] Ibid., p. 477.
[58] Ibid., p. 520.

sibilité et jusqu'à prendre la conscience la plus ample
et la plus claire. Puisqu'ils étaient au bout du monde,
au sommet de ce roc porté à la pointe extrême de
*Finis Francae* ils pouvaient regarder sans souci, se
donner tout entiers à l'execution parfaite de cet acte
. . . Il fallait le rendre aussi intense que possible.
. . . Que leurs moments soient brefs mais chargés de
conscience.[59]

However, it is difficult to see this in the context of the
work as evidence of a moral preoccupation.

Secondly, the 'verbal experience' is not necessarily
confined to the surface of Genet's prose. It is the structure of his works that Sartre finds particularly original.
It is, he maintains:

. . . la composition métaphysique du monde médié-
val: un univers d'analogies; des images ordonnées
suivant les hiérarchies d'une société noire et dont
chace symbolise tout. . . .[60]

Each character is thus a different modulation of the
original theme. The beauty of *Pompes funèbres* then
derives from its rigorous unity and 'contrepoint somptueux'.

Sartre is not altogether consistent on Genet, and he
seems to make excessive claims for his works when he
ranks them with Joyce's *Ulysses*, Baudelaire, and
Mallarmé.[61] Fundamentally, what he admires in Genet
is a characteristic which he responds to in other
works: 'dematerialisation of words and vertiginous
metamorphosis'—'ces extraordinaires métamorphoses
qui nous faisaient plonger dans un monde vénéneux.'[62]

In sculpture, Sartre has written on Giacometti and

[59] Ibid., p. 484.
[60] Ibid., p. 499.
[61] On *Ulysses*, ibid., p. 441.
[62] Ibid., p. 502.

Calder.[63] His main point in his article on the former is a relatively technical one: representational sculpture varies with the position of the spectator and his distance from it; he has thus to reconstruct it from several viewpoints and it is relative to each of these. The sculptors of such work have been tempted by the 'superabundance' of space and so led into creating figures with heavy gestures and limbs. Giacometti by contrast, recoiling from 'l'infini de la divisibilité' wants to 'dégraissir l'espace . . . le comprimer pour lui faire égoutter toute son extériorité'.[64] He sculpts a statue 'as he sees him'. Thus it has imaginary space, the point being that for Sartre a work of art is not to be identified with the material of which it is made. Giacometti's statues have to be seen at a distance, in the sense that one sees no more of them by getting close to them. Yet everything is there except matter: . . . à vingt pas, on ne voit pas le fastidieux désert des tissus adipeux, il est suggéré, esquissé, signifié, mais non donné. . . .[65]

It is not altogether clear why these figures, sculptured 'in relativity', none the less attain an 'absolute'. Sartre, however, is very successful in evoking the ambiguity of these strange, elongated forms with their rugged surfaces. Giacometti has avoided what Sartre calls 'l'éternel affaissement de la matière'. He has solved the sculptor's problem: 'comment faire un homme sans le pétrifier?' by creating '(des)esquisses mouvantes, toujours à mi-chemin entre le néant et l'être, toujours modifiées, améliorées, détruites et recommencées,'[66] by choosing to work in plaster, '. . . une matière sans poids, la plus ductile, la plus périssable, la plus spirituelle . . . Jamais matière ne fut moins éternelle, plus fragile, plus près d'être humain'.[67] Sartre excels, we have seen, in evoking tran-

[63] *Situations* III, pp. 289 ff.
[64] Ibid., p. 295.
[65] Ibid., p. 299.
[66] Ibid., p. 293.
[67] Ibid., p. 294.

sitoriness, evanescence, and mobility in art, partly natural and partly spiritual.

Similarly, Calder's *Mobiles*[68], for him, avoid the immobility of bronze or gold. Made of 'des matières
inconsistantes et viles', they do not suggest movement,
they capture it: '. . . passe un frisson errant, il s'y em-
pêtre, les anime et le canalisent en leur donnant une
forme fugitive. . . .'[69] A mobile is thus 'une petite
fête locale . . . un jeu pur de mouvement. . . .'[70]
Neither suggestive, nor imitative, they are the least
'mendacious' art-form. Again they occupy that ambiguous halfway position to which Sartre is strongly drawn
—'à mi-chemin entre la servilité de la statue et l'indé-
pendance des événements naturels . . .',[71] or as he
says again later '. . . à mi-chemin entre la matière et
la vie. . . .'[72] As such, Sartre argues, they may only
refer to themselves; they are lyrical inventions, technical combinations and symbols of Nature's fertility—
'cette grande Nature vague, qui gaspille le pollen
et produit brusquement l'envol de mille papil-
lons. . . .'[73]

Where painting is concerned, Sartre's unfinished
study of Tintoretto contains disappointingly little response to his art. For that one has to go to a short
article published in the review *L'Arc*.[74] Now Tintoretto's picture of Saint George and the Dragon (in the
National Gallery, London), seems to show the saint
saving the princess by killing the dragon. Divine intervention helps him in this, in the form of an angel,
from whom falls a radiance which touches the saint
as it reaches the earth. In the background are the walls
of a city. This is not how Sartre interprets the picture.

[68] Ibid., pp. 307 ff.
[69] Ibid., p. 307.
[70] Ibid., p. 307.
[71] Ibid., pp. 308–9.
[72] Ibid., pp. 310–11.
[73] Ibid., p. 311.
[74] 'Saint Georges et le Dragon', *L'Arc*, no. 30, 1966, pp. 35 ff.

He sees 'two privileged shapes' representing 'notre impuissance absolue': there is the city in the distance, with its 'inconsistance' giving it the pallor of fear; its vertical walls express its abandonment of the princess, the meaning of the 'inconsistante rigidité' of these walls is that the issue between the saint and the dragon will be decided without help from men. Heaven and earth are also separated by the horizontal plane on the right. Now Tintoretto often depicts the rarefied quality of the light in Venice. Its quality is such that it dissolves the materiality of all it touches. This is what Sartre himself has successfully described in words.[75] There is good reason why Sartre should be sensitive to the evanescence of light. In this picture, 'Jacopo ramasse et dilue sa ville dans un cône de translucidité',[76] so that we see 'la métamorphose de la lumière en ville et de la ville en lumière',[77] but Heaven, Sartre argues, is excluded. Tintoretto paints 'cette volatile lumière' but puts it out of reach, so that the saint and the dragon fight it out under a leaden sky with the light of the supernatural on the horizon. Thus l'homme doit gagner ou perdre son procès sous les bitumes d'un ciel fermé'.[78] This is a typically existentialist view and arresting enough, but difficult to reconcile with what one sees on the painting and continues to see no matter how often one looks at it.

Secondly, and this too is a characteristically Sartrian preoccupation: there is, for Sartre, an element of 'truquage' in the picture. Tintoretto, he insists, has concealed the saint's right hand holding the spear and part of the spear itself, so that his action becomes 'secret' and as 'absent' as the city ramparts. This detracts from the saint's exploit; it is as though he were leaning on his horse rather than on the dragon and this emphasizes the 'powerlessness of man'. There is no

[75] Cf. 'Venise, de ma fenêtre', *Situations*, IV, pp. 444 ff.
[76] *L'Arc*, pp. 42–43.
[77] Ibid., p. 80.
[78] Ibid., p. 81.

doubt that the saint's right hand is hidden and this may be an artistic defect, but it is difficult not to feel that Sartre may be reading too much into this detail, just as it is difficult to see what he claims to see—the saint relying on the momentum of his horse to kill the dragon.

In writing on Giacometti as a painter[79] Sartre wonders how a painter can avoid outline in portraiture, so as to overcome the inertia and passivity of line. With Giacometti's striated forms each trait is a centrifugal force, there is no contour round things and only 'le plein' in transition between 'l'être' et 'le néant' is conceivable. Thus the outline of an arm or a hip is lost in 'un miroitement de lumières qui l'escamote.'[80] We watch 'une brusque dématérialisation' as the outline of legs disappears 'en brume lumineuse', so impossible it is to say where the void begins and body ends. This is not disintegration:

> Nous sommes en face du réel pur, invisible tension du papier blanc . . . Giacometti refuse également l'inertie de la matière et l'inertie du pur néant; le vide, c'est du plein détendu étalé; le plein, c'est du vide orienté. Le réel fulgure.[81]

The same problem is encountered in painting the 'fullness' of an object. Here the white streaks of Giacometti's paintings serve as pointers or guides to the eye. Sartre is then led to consider the problem of depicting the one and the many. A chestnut tree can look like 'une grosse boule unanime et foisonnante' or a collection of leaves painted singly. In fact, Sartre argues, what one sees is both: 'une cohésion fourmillante, un éparpillement reployé'.[82] Giacometti conveys this impression because he wants his figures to move

[79] *Situations*, IV, pp. 347 ff.
[80] Ibid., p. 355.
[81] Ibid., pp. 356–57.
[82] Ibid., p. 358.

from '(le) continu au discontinu'; he suggests 'la parfaite précision de l'être sous l'imprécision du con-
naître'.[83] This is why it is difficult to describe the facial
expression of Giacometti's figures. We see, 'un visage
fantôme qui se forme, se déforme et se reforme', as in
Genet:

> . . . (le) jeu du paraître et du disparaître, de la fuite
> et de la provocation . . . Coquettes, oui, et gracieus-
> es, puisqu'elles sont tout en actes, et sinistres à cause
> du vide qui les entoure, ces créatures de néant at-
> teignent . . . à la plénitude d'existence parce qu'-
> elles se dérobent et nous mystifient.[84]

From this, Sartre draws the disappointing conclusion that Giacometti is like a conjuror, and that those
who look at his pictures are his dupes and accom-
plices. This is the view, all too familiar in Sartre, that
works of art are 'fakes' because artists work in the
realm of the imaginary and create only 'trompe-l'oeil'.
One feels that Giacometti deserved more insight from
existentialism than this.

In writing on Masson[85] Sartre shows once again his
capacity for entering into the spirit of a 'Dionysian' art
coming within the category of 'explosante—fixe'. In this
kind of art, '. . . être c'est panteler dans un écartèle-
ment infini et participer . . . à la furieuse marée terres-
tre qui conquiert à chaque instant sur le néant de
nouvelles régions d'être'.[86]

But Masson, he argues, is concerned with line; he
wants to reveal the potential movement of immobility or to 'fixer ce bouleversement perpétuel, ces ex-
plosions protoplasmiques en série, qui lui paraissent
former la contexture intime des choses. . . .'[87] He

[83] Ibid., p. 359.
[84] Ibid., p. 361.
[85] Ibid., pp. 387 ff.
[86] Ibid., p. 391.
[87] Ibid., p. 392.

makes line into a pointer by making it a 'vector' which forces the eye to move along it in a particular direction. It thus has, incidentally, that 'irreversibility' which Sartre wanted to see in the novel.

Now what gives a line this quality, he reasons, is its human significance, as with objects in general. Thus a mountain can be seen existentially, as a climb or a heap, according to whether I see it as 'une insolente escalade' or as an image of social forces 'qui m'écrasent et de mon effondrement secret.'[88] Similarly, a vector must reflect human transcendence. Man must, therefore, be the magnet pole which draws all points toward him and through whom all nature is seen. A Dionysian painter, showing nature impregnated with human energies, Masson replaces circles by whirling movements and vertical lines, by rising and falling movements. But his aim, in painting these 'dancing contours', 'this universal sabbath', is to paint time.

At their most typical, Masson's paintings depict metamorphosis:

> . . . puisque l'homme seul anime la nature, c'est la forme humaine qu'il va inscrire partout, qu'il fera briller un instant à la crête des choses et qui se defera en gerbes végétales, en éclaboussements minéraux.[89]

In hills there are thighs, calves and sexual organs; roots are hands without ceasing to be roots. This is not a 'pansexualism', which would make his art too literary. Legs and calves change hilltops into vectors, the female sexual organs evoke neither fecundity nor rut but discord and openness, 'la dislocation explosive d'un corps.'[90]

This is not a symbol but 'un schème moteur': 'ce déséquilibre équilibré traduira seul cette transcend-

88 Ibid., p. 395.
89 Ibid., p. 398.
90 Ibid., p. 399.

ance humaine qu'il veut peindre sur les choses. . . .'[91]

Thus line represents not limit or finitude but 'explosion'—'une certaine manière d'être tout ce que l'on n'est pas et de n'être jamais tout à fait ce qu'on est. . . .'[92] In short, what we are shown is an ambiguous reality, eminently phenomenological. Metamorphoses are what strike us in Masson but all the apparent savagery and sexual violence of his art is subordinated to the graphic representation of movement.

Masson's next step was to abandon line and put a greater emphasis on living substance. It is this, finally, which breaks its bonds and spreads across the picture, thus revealing Masson's Dionysian myth at its purest:

> Les jambes, les cuisses, les seins, dans ses dernières toiles, tombent dans le ciel, dans l'air, toute l'eau, tout le ciel, les murs, le plafond, deviennent seins ou cuisses . . . tout est dans tout, la jambe dans la montagne et la montagne dans la jambe.[93]

Thus Sartre finds in Masson an ambiguity and a play of appearances and metamorphoses animated by Dionysian energies which are, however, subjected to the discipline of formal properties. This is an art comparable with French African poetry but striking more of a balance between the instinctive and the cerebral.

Sartre's article on Wols or Wolfgang Schülze,[94] is a difficult introduction to a difficult but rewarding artist who invites literary and philosophical interpretation. This is a temptation which Sartre does not altogether resist. As he says, Wols was influenced by surrealism, though his art is less literary, and one could add, by Cubism, to judge by some of the wonderful shapes in the series, 'Cités et Navires'. Sartre

---

[91] Ibid.
[92] Ibid., p. 400.
[93] Ibid., p. 406.
[94] Ibid., pp. 408 ff.

treats him, understandably, in relation to Klee, but whereas 'l'un crée ou recrée les merveilles de ce monde, l'autre en éprouve la merveilleuse horreur'. Both reveal in their art a religious attitude to the world. With Wols, this is fashioned by the Bhagavad Gita and Taoism and, as Sartre sees it, it is a pessimistic one. Coming from such sources, however, it clearly need not be.

At bottom, according to Sartre, Wols sees in the world and paints his own alienation—hence the curious title of the article—especially in such self-portraits as *La Pagode* and *Le Pantin*— '. . . Manchot . . . actionné par un étrange appareil compliqué, vieillot qui règle par-derrière ses mouvements. . . .'[95] Such painting, apparently, expresses a hallucinatory experience of being haunted by 'cloportes', an experience not unknown to Sartre himself. Similarly, *Janus bifrons portant l'aquarium* (1940) depicts '(un) univers arachnéen, trouée de transparences suspectes . . .'[96] which is not the world of Klee. Again, in the early gouaches which intend to depict a cosmic upward movement, this is pulled downward by a terrestrial inertia or dominated by repellent swarms of insects:

> . . . les mouches pullelent et les puces et les punaises volantes, pustules flottantes . . . cet affreus essaim turne en dérision l'effort des plantes humaines pour se deraciner.[97]

Both Klee and Wols are, as artists, 'totalitaires et cosmiques' and so both are 'revealers of being' without seeing in the same way 'la préhistoire du visible'.

Thus Wols paints objects which inspire fear, express hallucinatory experiences or render the fascinating

95 Ibid., pp. 411–12.
96 Ibid., p. 415.
97 Ibid., pp. 416–17.

ambiguity of the relation between the part and the whole, the one and the many:

> . . . le mirotement fixe de l'insaisissable manifeste et cache dans l'incertain rapport de la partie ou tout et du tout à la partie, dans l'inachèvement double de l'Un et de la multiplicité.[98]

It is an art of metamorphosis: '. . . chaque chose se change immuable en son contraire, chacun s'affirme et se nie simultanément, composition qui s'épuise et se défaille en cours de route, décomposition inter-rompue'.[99] It is a world of coming into being and passing away in which the different parts perpetually 'contest' one another.

It is not easy to see what this might mean. That this is so, Sartre thinks, and here one is unfortunately on familiar ground, makes Wols yet another 'virtuose de la prestidigitation', painting 'faux semblants' and 'analogies trompeuses'. It is as difficult here as before to believe that a good painter produces 'fakes'.

However, after 1940 a change came over his art. The otherness of being, Sartre claims, can be shown by two methods:

(1) 'révéler dans un doigt la présence cancéreuse de Tout', like Dubuffet or

(2) by deliberately painting 'non-doigts' or em-bodying the world in objects not found in it. Wols's paintings thus manifest:

> . . . la rigoureuse équivalence de la fauve marti-enne . . . ce ne sont plus des hommes qui s'étirent, mais des substances innommables . . . qui ne sym-bolisent rien ni personne et semblent appartenir si-multanément aux trois règnes de la nature. . . .[100]

98 Ibid., p. 422.
99 Ibid., pp. 422–23.
100 Ibid., p. 426.

They are said to manifest 'naked being' seen from outside which is impossible to look at 'sans vertige'.

But how is it possible to show things 'other than themselves'? Sartre takes as an example the painting called, though not by Wols, 'La Grande Barrière qui brûle'. He takes us right up to the picture:

> . . . 'indéniable unité de la forme nous impose de *voir* l'unité de la substance savamment tirée de l'intérieur; un seul être se compose et se décompose simultanément sous le regard, un immobile vacillement de lammatière partout suspecte . . . Tout arbre mort est falaise, toute falaise est jambe, toute mambe est reptile, toute vie, médusée, n'est qu'un processus instantanée de pétrification. . . .[101]

Metamorphosis, mirage, fascination, these are the existentialist characteristics which stand out here as elsewhere.

'Permanent transsubstantiation' is the first law, according to Sartre, of this method of composition. The second consists in creating—

> (Un) jeu savant de transparences . . . finit par brouiller les plans . . . Par des transformations imperceptibles de l'être . . . Au centre flamboyant de la gouache, l'altérité se renforce, c'est le carrefour des incertitudes: enjambements, jaillissements inertes, transparentes opacités, métamorphoses . . . tout s'arrache à un enracinement qui n'existe que par le multiple effort dépoyé pour s'y soustraire . . . Ce que je vois, moi, prisonnier du monde, c'est du dehors, le monde même où je suis resté, c'est moi; je suis l'envers brûlant et saignant de cette chose qui rougeoie . . . Dedans et dehors, ange et fou, objet autre, autre sujet: cette ambiguité me concerne . . . et . . . ne cesse de m'inquiéter.[102]

[101] Ibid., p. 428.
[102] Ibid., pp. 429–32.

Sartre thus reaches the point where he experiences his own alienation. There is little doubt of the similarity between the world of *La Nausée*, for example, and that of Wols. If he sees more than may be 'there', he does so imaginatively and with commendable attention to detail and beauty of form as well as to a philosophical meaning which he may project into it:

> . . . il n'est pas une de ses gouaches qui ne soit belle
> . . . l'intégration rigoureuse des formes et leurs merveilleuses couleurs tendres ont pour office de manifester notre damnation.[103]

Both Masson and Wols, in different ways, depict discord and torment. So also, in yet another way, does Lapoujade,[104] who wanted to paint torture and massacre and remain abstract, the problem arising, not from politics, but from the 'exigencies of his art'.

Previously, Sartre argues, there had been two solutions to this problem: either by 'la troublante imitation de la réalité' or by making paint into what he calls a procession or ballet, like Titian, to whom he is incapable of being just, and so by making 'des terreurs tranquilles'. Of the two exceptions to this, Goya, Sartre argues, tended to paint his own vision (a statement not meant to apply, presumably, to the 'Disasters of War'), and Picasso in painting destruction in 'Guernica' benefited from the artistic trend toward the break-up of figurative form. This kind of painting also comes into the category of 'explosante—fixe' and so painting destruction is not detrimental to beauty. (This could arguably be a matter of taste. 'Guernica' is a masterpiece but difficult to view with detachment.)

Now the beauty of a painting, Sartre wisely asserts, is not apparent at a glance. The process of unification effected by the brush is continued by the eye. This is

[103] Ibid., p. 434.
[104] Ibid., pp. 364 ff.

entirely consistent with Sartre's conception of the active role played by the reader or spectator:

> . . . à nous d'accoler ces brusques expansion de couleurs, ces condensés de matière; à nous d'éveiller des échos, des rythmes . . . pour construire, il suffira d'établir des rapports visibles . . . pour garantir cette construction, pour la sauver d'une absurdité totale, l'unité transcendante est nécessaire. Par elle, le mouvement du regard est assuré de ne s'arrêter jamais; c'est ce tourniquet des yeux qui produisent la permanence de l'unité invisible: donc nous tournerons, si nous nous arrêtions, tout éclaterait.[105]

Vertigo is clearly an important, though constructive, aspect of aesthetic experience for Sartre. When this doctrine is applied to painting of the 'explosante—fixe' variety, multiplicity in unity is to be sought by the eye looking for 'l'unification de cet éparpillement somptueux'. This involves giving to an indefinitely divisible surface the indivisible unity of a whole. Lapoujade chose in particular the problem of painting a crowd as seen by itself—'telle qu'elle se subit et qu'elle se fait ici et partout. . . .' How can an artist paint a crowd 'sans privilèges' or merely one anonymous individual among many?

> Lapoujade donnera aux foules une matière mouvante mais rigoureusement unie. Au sein de la dispersion l'unification des particules désintégrées réalise un au-delà; l'unité explosive des masses . . . Le peintre nous conduit . . . L'essential est dans la singularité des chemins que trace le pinceau . . . la matière ne prétend pas faire voir l'invisible . . . Elle *suggère* par sa texture et ses itinéraires. Rigoureuse déter-termination plastique, indétermination relative de l'épreuve: ce contraste sert le peintre; les taches serrées semblent s'écarter les unes des autres; un

nouveau chemin, brusquement découvert, oblige les couleurs à pâlir en installant de nouveaux rapports entre elles . . . nous saisirons, a travers ces métamorphoses, la présence sans partie de la manifestation s'incarnant avec toutes ses densités à la fois.[106]

This is the existentialist way of 'reading' a painting, discovering the painter's 'chemins' which are as much ventures into the unknown as 'les chemins de la liberté'. Such a pictorial incarnation meets the Sartrian requirement of solidarity, the nearest he comes to reconciling painting and *engagement*. The more technical part of Sartre's analysis might well apply to one of the two of Lapoujade's canvases in the Musée d'Art Moderne, 'La Barricade', with its marvelously explosive riot of colors. But it is not at all apparent that it conveys the experience of crowdlike anonymity.

Finally, the theme of music and engagement is considered in his introduction to a work by René Leibowitz, 'L'Artiste et sa conscience'.[107] Music, for Sartre, is, of course, an art without meaning. While opposing mythmakers, such as the signatories of the Prague manifesto, who use music to create 'une émotion sacrée', since Leibowitz has shown that music has freed itself from alienation, would it not be possible for it to contribute to history by holding before the workers an image of 'total man'? But if music is to be defined as 'une révolution permanente', it clearly risks carrying this freedom into other spheres. Moreover, defined as 'une révolution permanente', it clearly risks carrying this freedom into other spheres. Moreover, if that is what music stands for, a bourgeois public will hear 'evolution and progress'. The fact remains that music is autonomous and needs an audience of specialists, so how can it express 'les hautes idées progressistes des masses populaires?' Yet 'engagement musical', if it exists, must be in the sound itself.

[106] Ibid., pp. 382–83.
[107] Ibid., pp. 17 ff.

Implied in a Brandenburg concerto, Sartre maintains, is a relationship to its time, as the Renaissance is to the Gioconda smile—'la présence silencieuse, en tout objet sonore, de l'époque entière et de sa conception du monde'. Perhaps this is 'engagement musical'. The Prague manifesto was right in one respect in implying that 'reality is never inert'. Thus the artist must, to create a truthful image of our time, consider it from the point of view of the future because the future will decide what today's truth will be.

The work of art is both an individual production and a social fact. In Beethoven, rather surprisingly, one can find:

> . . . une image musicale des Assemblées révolutionnaires . . . Il n'a pas bouleversé les règles de son art . . . et pourtant on dirait qu'il est au delà des triomphes de la Révolution, au-delà même de son échec.[108]

Musical 'engagement' is perhaps possible if the artist lives out the contradictions of his time, like the writer in *Qu'est-ce que la littérature?*, sincerely and passionately enough, without any literary intention, for the world, with all its violence and conflict, to be transformed by him into music. In that case, he contends, the claims of freedom and *engagement* would be reconciled.

Most of the arts considered here, according to Sartre, are not figurative or representational. In theory, spirit is, so to say, incarnate in matter, but, preferably, for him, in such a way as to be ambiguously intermediate between the two extremes, as in Baudelaire, Calder, and Giacometti's sculpture. The work of art is imaginary and not thing-like, matter being a degradation or an 'affaissement'. Nevertheless the 'coefficient of adversity' of things is necessary to poetic failure and poetic vision, as it is, in the form of re-

[108] Ibid., p. 35.

sistance and 'irreversibility', to the novel. Again, some art—Rimbaud, Masson, the French African poets, Lapoujade—is Dionysian, embodies violence and merits the description, 'explosante—fixe'. Here, as before, art is ambiguous or contradictory. Sartre seems particularly sensitive in art to metamorphosis, as in the French African poets Masson and Wols. The contradiction is such as to mirror the human condition, however true it is that non-figurative art is incompatible with *engagement*. Thus even in Mallarmé, Sartre discerns 'la mort de Dieu' and the tragedy of the human condition, a poetry as pure as 'la poésie noire' can be revolutionary, an abstract painter like Lapoujade can paint violence in crowds and the dramatic art of Wols shows us our own alienation.

# SARTRE'S LITERARY CRITICISM

## *Otto Hahn*

Sartre's aim is to understand, but what does he seek
to understand and how does he go about it? In describing the progression of his thought and method
from his first literary criticism to appear in the *Nouvelle Revue Française,* up to his work on "Flaubert" which is still in preparation, we shall seek out
the answers he has given and the techniques he has
employed. Thenceforth we shall follow the different
directions his interest has taken and the different
attempts he made to elaborate a study of the mode
of being of the consciousness of which he gives an
account in the *Critique de la Raison Dialectique.*

To simplify, his works of literary criticism may be
divided in two parts, separated by the Korean War
of 1951: on the one hand, the study of consciousness,
and on the other, the study of history.

The whole of the first part has as its basis a question
which Heidegger had asked: how is thought at all
possible? But the German philosopher poses the problem in very abstract and general terms: how did
thought arise and how did Man one day become conscious of himself? Sartre poses the problem in more
reliable terms: in what way does consciousness function? Up to and including "Baudelaire", the study of
the mode of being of the consciousness is, as it were,
the gold-standard which dominates his whole undertaking.

A translation of "L'oeuvre Critique de Sartre," by Otto Hahn
which originally appeared in *Modern Language Notes,* Vol. 80,
No. 3 (1965), pp. 347–63. Reprinted by permission of the editors and Johns Hopkins Press, Baltimore. Copyright © Johns
Hopkins Press, 1965.

Sartre's literary criticism takes as a starting-point his article entitled "Une idée fondamentale de Husserl". Here Sartre describes the mode of being of the consciousness and puts forward a phenomenological and anti-subjectivist interpretation of it.

Referring back to Husserl, he empties the consciousness of its "contents" and taking the opposite point of view to psychological approach he puts forward an idea of consciousness which projects itself "on the road, the town, the midst of the crowd". That is Proust out of the way, he says. The *inner life* at the same time too. At that time the young Sartre wished to go beyond subjective attitudes. To this end, he casts aside modes of behaviour, attempts only to group the intelligibility of phenomenological structures and makes it his aim to establish a new "traite des passions" which would study the "properties of things and beings". This objectivist realism which allows him to escape from the idealism which dominated his studies is the easier for him to come by in that, benefiting from a privileged childhood, his mind is not encumbered by the unhealthy world of childhood attachments: he simply does not believe in them. It is with optimism then that he organized universal ideas with a view to a future phenomenological encyclopaedia. Thenceforth, as if this imaginary statute of reality were already realised, he considers singularities such as childhood fixations, contradictions and fears as evading responsibility for reality, as attitudes lacking in authenticity. This position should divert him from that which constitutes the very stuff of fiction.

He does, however, like some novels, he even admires them, but does not believe in them. How can there be love without belief? Sartre feels that his co-operation is being taken for granted; beguiled by outward appearance, he feels cheated. He wishes then to find the secret of the charm in order to unmask it and he examines novels to discover the trick, the cheat or the artifice. His first article, devoted to *Sartoris* attempts to catch Faulkner in the act. Going back to the description of consciousness (consciousness, according to Sartre, is always consciousness of something), he analyses the characters: finding nothing in the old Bayard Sartoris's consciousness, Sartre has the impression that Faulkner is concealing a secret which, in fact, does not exist: "Is he the dupe of his own art? Is he lying to us?" asks Sartre. Using a bad novel as example, he thinks he has laid the hoax bare: but studying other novels from the view-point of the mode of being of the consciousness, he finds himself once again faced with the same problem which he attempts to solve by an appeal to the vague notion of beauty: "The world of Dos Passos is impossible—as is that of Faulkner, Kafka, Stendhal—because it is contradictory. But it is for that very reason that it is beautiful, for beauty is a veiled contradiction." (*Nouvelle Revue Française*, 1938)

Soon afterwards in *Mauriac*, Sartre develops the implication of his theory. The merit of a novelist bears no relation to his errors: inauthenticity and the partiality of a point of view are of small importance if the author preserves the structures of consciousness and its temporal opening into a free future.

Sartre, who in the beginning seems implicitly to be asking the question: how is it that, since there is only *one* objective reality, there are also novels, goes beyond the notion of veiled contradiction and writes, "Art depends on appearances alone". And in the conclusion to *Mauriac* he specifies: "There is no room for a privileged observer". In accepting only a partial view, Sartre is led to the notion of "situation" which he tackles for the first time in his review of Nabokov's novel *La Méprise* (*The Mistake*). For the first time in Sartre's thought the understanding of a book is accompanied by an understanding of its author. Linking the situation of the subject of the novel, the particular stylistic devices and the quirks of writing, Sartre demonstrates their organic unity. The author's interpretation resides in the uncovering of this unity.

In "Faulkner's Sense of Time" written at the same

period, Sartre defines the critic's job. First of all to
define the "Metaphysic" and then to appreciate the
technique. By "appreciate" Sartre means to compare
the construction of the novel with the particular mode
of being of the consciousness, a mode of being relative to the author's metaphysical conception. Then to
conclude, Sartre gives his opinion on the metaphysics
implicit in Faulkner which makes him rediscover the
contradiction which he had found in the majority of
writers: "I like his art but I do not believe in his metaphysics".

Three years later, in 1943, Sartre tackles the notion
of the absurd and of existence concerning the position of man in the world and his relationship with
others. . . . Camus's *Outsider* gives him the opportunity of developing his own theories. His method
remains the same: taking the *Myth of Sisyphus*, he
defines Camus's metaphysics, then appreciates the
technique of the *Outsider*; the way the author uses
grammar and the thread of the story.

The relationship between Being and Existence leads
him on to the study of Bataille. Sartre still believed
in those days in the transcendence of existential structures, and Bataille is precisely a man searching for
a transcendence. But for Sartre, transcendence is the
abstract framework of our existence, the "fundamental
absurdity, the *artificiality*, that is the irreducible contingency of our being-there, of our existence devoid
of aim and reason". For Bataille, transcendence would
mean to make Being and Existence coincide, which
is an impossible wish. Perhaps Sartre in studying
Bataille, wanted to discover how a man launches
himself into a metaphysically impossible undertaking,
which he doggedly persists in. Sartre here for the
first time enters the intimate world of one of the authors he is studying. He does so by limiting himself
to behaviour and to the nature of inner experience
but stops on the threshold of psychoanalysis. The
article "A New Mystic" marks the end of the first
evolution of Sartre's thought. Then he widens his field

to embrace the problems of language. In both *Aller-Retour* (*To and Fro*) and *L'Homme et Les Choses* (*Man and Things*) devoted to Ponge, he reaffirms his belief in the possibility of an objective knowledge which can be reduced to existential terms. But his method as well as the direction which motivates his criticism remain identical: it is a general problem which preoccupies Sartre: when he meets this problem in some author, he then defines the particular dialectics of the author and compares it to the dialectical structure of this problem. For example, he will compare the idea which Camus has of the absurd in relation to the phenomenology of the Absurd, or he will compare Bataille's idea of Being and Existence with the real dialectics of Being and Existence. This manner of proceeding projects only a relative understanding on the author studied. Sartre analyses the salient point, the forms and the structures of the Project but neglects the causes which gave birth to the Project. Why does Ponge divert his attention from History in order to concentrate on Things only? Why did Bataille pursue his impossible dream of transcendence? Sartre is preoccupied rather in imparting a phenomenological description to the project as if expecting that a phenomenological description would bring him to positive knowledge, and men to authentic behaviour.

His study of Bataille ends with the words: "The rest is the concern of psychoanalysis"; his study of Descartes poses the question of freedom. In *Baudelaire* he takes up the question of freedom once again and also that of psychoanalysis which was left hanging in the air at the end of the study on Bataille. This synthesis makes Sartre's method progress towards a vaster totalization. Sartre in his study of Baudelaire proposes to recall the story of a consciousness at grips with freedom; the aim is to re-live a man's life from the inside. It is from this point of view that the notion of "Original Choice" makes its appearance in Sartre's works of criticism. The study is divided into five parts.

| Choice 1 | Baudelaire described objectively with reference to his choice (en soi). |
| Choice 2 | Baudelaire as he felt himself (pour soi). |
| Behaviour 3 | The imaginary world or the mind of Baudelaire with reference to his modes of behaviour. |
| Behaviour 4 | Relationships with others. |
| Conclusion 5 | The poetical phenomenon. |

Four times Sartre describes Baudelaire on four different levels, the first two levels concern Baudelaire's *choices* and the next two his *modes of behaviour*.

1. Starting from the original choice, from the breaking point, Sartre questions Baudelaire's objective significance; he describes his character as well as the way in which he exhibits his singularity. In his description, Sartre resituates Baudelaire in the general context of his childhood. It is in connexion with a phenomenology of childhood and with a "transcendence of existential Structures" that Sartre sees both Baudelaire's situation and objective significance. The study progresses on two levels, the particular and the general. Moving from the one to the other Sartre proceeds by means of differential notations. In passing, Sartre touches upon general topics: Action, the Creative Act, the Revolutionary and the Rebel . . . when he speaks of Baudelaire's attitude towards them. The study progresses by *means of comparisons.* As in his previous studies Sartre imposes a particular dialectic on a more general phenomenological system.

2. On page 60, Sartre returns to Baudelaire's childhood and starts on the objective description of it: the way Baudelaire understands himself, understands the notions of Good and Evil, the impression which he wants to make on others and the faces others turn to him. To highlight Baudelaire's subjective attitude, Sartre recreates the atmosphere, the "insignificant" mother, "good old Ancelle" and gives his opinion on the judges and torturers whom Baudelaire chose for

himself. It is possible to understand Baudelaire's inner world only if reality is described for us at the same time or at least given a value judgement by the critic.

3. The portrait he gives of Baudelaire comes to an end on page 114, and Sartre examines the features of his character, linking them with the structures which rule the *constitution* of the imaginary world, his loathing of nature, his coldness etc. Sartre places the constitution of the imaginary world in the anti-naturalist current of the nineteenth century. In addition, he studies the existential qualities of the Reality which Baudelaire constructed:

a) Baudelaire's idea of Nature, the plant world, fertility, captive water

b) the body and woman for Baudelaire, the longing for artifice, theatrical costumes, the cult of frigidity and of whiteness.

In linking these features and in synthesizing them, Sartre sums up the general movement and defines the farthest limit of the Baudelarian mind.

4. Sartre examines dandyism on page 153, that is Baudelaire's social behaviour. First of all, he describes the places and attitudes of artists in the nineteenth century, in relation to the aristocracy, the bourgeoisie and the proletariat. Sartre then asserts the singularity of Baudelaire's behaviour and defines his singularity in relation to that of Flaubert, Gautier and Mérimée. Next Sartre takes up again the features studied before, fastidiousness in dress, disguise, his love of mystification, and analyses them in their relationship to Others: finally he outlines the significance of Time and Progress for Baudelaire.

5. Sartre examines on page 199 the *poetic phenomenon*, connecting it with Baudelaire's relation to the past. He describes how Baudelaire pursues the synthesis of Being and Existence, then at which level he wishes to gain possession of things and obtain fusion with them, and lastly how Baudelaire uses meanings. The last ten pages of the book deal with a *living* por-

trait of Baudelaire. Before sketching the final portrait, Sartre has carried out four cross sections all arranged on the same schema: the features of his character appear and succeed one another and whilst still developing, they are confronted with reality and value judgements. It is this same rhythm of dispersion and reassembling which characterizes Sartre's literary criticism, and which runs through his works. However the four parts overlap and in each one the same elements are taken up:

—Masochism, which is Baudelaire's objective means for recovering Being (First part—en soi),
—becomes in the second part the search for judges, the "conscience face to face with Evil", self-punishment;
—in the third part (The Imaginary World), masochism appears through the emphasis on the idea of sin, power and coldness searched for in women since "the cold woman is the sexual incarnation of the Judge";
—in the fourth part, masochism is transformed into a search for punishment through defiance and sinking into Evil.

The *gaze* is examined in turn as a reflexive gaze, the seeking after the gaze of others, as the gaze of the cold woman, the pleasure of looking at Others, and as the gaze by which Others possess you. The desire to be repulsive (second part) overlaps the desire to scandalize (fourth part). The "White-Frigidity-Lunar" sequence is absorbed into the lucidity of the gaze which overlaps the relationship with Others and these relationships allow Sartre to begin the chapter on Eroticism. This treatment in depth displays Sartre's wish to reassemble the character whose mechanism he has taken to pieces. He insists several times, moreover, on this idea of a mechanism taken to pieces, because for Sartre neither the "en-soi" nor the "pour soi" nor the "Imaginary World" exist independently from the other levels: "The description which we have attempted is inferior to the portrait in that the former is successively built up whilst the latter is simultaneous", he wrote, and "the features mentioned here one after the other are in fact connected together in an indissoluble synthesis in which each one is the expression of itself and of all the others simultaneously". He then talks of the interdependence of all modes of behaviour. . . .

For Sartre, at this stage of his evolution, to understand Baudelaire's character is to understand Baudelaire's mode of being, his relationship to himself and to the world, it is to understand a situation transformed by an original force. Sartre thus singles out Baudelaire's possible choices and indicates the reason which led the poet to choose one path rather than another. In addition, to understand a work is to rediscover the significance Baudelaire gave to language; or in other words, to reconsider language as the means for Baudelaire is to recover Being.

So far, Sartre always had one aim in his study of artistic works, to describe the consciousness' mode of being, to define contingency and the Absurd. In writing *Baudelaire,* Sartre's aim is not to demonstrate why the *Fleurs du Mal* have an artistic value or release an aesthetic emotion, but to show that although a consciousness is hampered by a childhood fixation it is not necessarily deprived thereby of its freedom, and that "the free choice which a man makes by himself completely coincides with what is called his destiny". Despite this specification, Sartre was very much criticized by such eminent critics as Bataille, Blanchot, Georges Blin who reproached him for having made an indictment on Baudelaire's inauthentic conduct without taking into consideration the authentic success of the *Fleurs du Mal.*

Art, indeed, occupies an imaginary plane which is not a carbon copy of life. The imaginary is made up from lived experience and in the same way description of lived experience helps in the understanding of the imaginary but the one does not totally account

for the other. Therefore the inauthentic behaviour
of an author does not automatically vitiate the authenticity or the bearing of his work.

Thus it is that Sartre starts his *Saint-Genet, Actor
and Martyr* published five years after *Baudelaire,*
intending to give the complete understanding of a man
and his work. By this time, Sartre has already defi-
nitely abandoned his belief in the existence of "artificially isolated essence and types": having psycho-
analyzed metaphysics in Baudelaire, he believes in
them no longer. It is at this moment in the evolution
of his criticism, simultaneous with the Korean War
and the failure of Liberation that he introduces historical preoccupations into his work. It is true that
the study on Genet takes on an amplitude which the
previous book had not possessed. The childhood fixation is not only a shock, a breaking point, but a fact
which occurs within the framework of a social phenomenon. It is as if the social milieu itself is returning
the blow. In addition, the social milieu is seen in
historical perspective and as an alienating process.

At the beginning of the work Sartre outlines his
method: "If we wish to understand this man and
his world, there is no way of doing it other than to
reconstitute the original occurrence, by means of the
mythical representations which he gives us of it. The
method is obvious: to re-establish facts in their true
significance through the analysis of the myths". In order to follow Sartre's approach to understanding we
shall give the schematic structure of his *Genet.* To be
clearer, we shall leave aside Sartre's judgements, being understood that when he talks of Good, Evil,
Beauty, Crime or Masochism he gives a new definition
of these notions, gives a value judgement of them in
their relationship to Genet. Let us emphasize however that these value judgements are not given in
addition but as an integral part of the general process
of understanding. One can only grasp Genet's venture by these judgements of general bearing.

Like Sartre's preceding work, *Saint Genet* is divided

into five parts, but this time Sartre follows a chronological order.

## I. CHILDHOOD. At seven

<table>
<tr>
<td>Catégorie<br>en Soi et<br>pour soi</td>
<td>1)</td>
<td>The melodious child. Sartre describes how the first "deviation" took place. He first studies Genet en soi and situates him in society: the motherless child, the bastard, an "porte-à-faux", i.e. insecure in the peasant community which clings to the land and property (l'Avoir et l'Etre). Then Sartre tackles the pour soi; he describes the ecstatic experiences of the bastard who disputes his bastardy by identifying himself with saintliness (l'Etre) and who in addition identifies himself with property through Theft (l'Avoir).</td>
</tr>
<tr>
<td>Pour Autrui<br>(for Others)<br>and relation-<br>ship of the<br>pour soi and<br>Pour Autrui</td>
<td>2)</td>
<td>A vertiginous word. Sartre studies the child-thief from the view-point of the pour autrui; the bastard hemmed in by distrust, suddenly caught red-handed; a word, reflecting the social order, gives the young thief, unconscious of the nature of his actions a place apart in society. Sartre next studies the relationship between the pour soi and the pour autrui: the child when stealing behaves like a dreamer. Caught in the act, categorised by one single word he finds himself and suffers his pour autrui. From that moment on, he is changed by Others into an Object.</td>
</tr>
</table>

## II. THE THIEF: from ages 10 to 15, 18 to 22 and from 20 to 22.

<table>
<tr>
<td>En soi</td>
<td>1)</td>
<td>I shall be—changed by others into an object (his childhood is evoked for</td>
</tr>
</table>

the second time) Genet recognises
himself as such and decides on theft
as an activity "I shall be a thief". Sartre studies the objective significance
of Genet's definitive decision, as well
as its objective implications. He goes
on to show how by taking upon himself a *fait accompli,* Genet is at once
a Realist and an Idealist.

*Pour soi*   2) *I have decided to be.* This chapter
means to explore Genet's inner expe-
rience. Sartre studies the subjective
significance of Genet's decision, i.e.
his own awareness of it as well as its
objective implications. So Genet assumes himself as an object fixed for
all time by Others. "I have decided to
be what crime has made of me". Sartre analyses the conflicting postula-
tions implied in the decision of Being
Evil: the domain of Being is that of
Fate, Genet encroaches on innocence. He is therefore led to Doing
Evil, for Doing implies a free decision. So Genet resorts to two systems
of values, which leads Sartre to study
the categories of Being and Doing.
Then he throws some light on his
method: "Logically we should pursue
our study from both points of view
simultaneously, but the result would
be inevitable confusion. So we shall
examine separately the intention of
being and that of doing. We shall
trace Genet's conversion from its origin, attempting through a cross-
section to examine these intentions in
the instantaneous nature of their
manifestation: this will be what one
might call a static description. But

one must not forget that these intentions coexist. . . . We shall indicate in a third paragraph the immediate and vague relationship which connects them". Thus, still on the level of the *pour soi,* Sartre gives a static description of

a) the Intention of Being a Thief, guilty, the Incarnation of Evil
b) the intention of becoming a Thief, guilty, the incarnation of Evil
c) Sartre studies the relationships between the intention of Being and of Doing. To Do in order to Be. In this last paragraph Sartre resumes the dialectic of Being and Doing from childhood (evoked for the third time) and comes to a double postulation in Genet's case (POUR SOI) formulated as follows: If Evil is Fate (fatal), I am a Martyr, a Victim, a Saint; if I choose Evil of my own free will I am the Prince of Crime, the Black Archangel.

Relationship between *pour soi* and *pour autrui*

3) *The Saint-Criminal-Couple:* 15 to 18 years old. So far Sartre has described the character. Now he looks at it again in a historical perspective. The double postulation of Being and Doing (of the Saint and the Criminal) says Sartre, does not remain inert; upon which he adds, "It lives, changes, grows richer with the years; it is transformed by the contact with experience and the dialectic of each one of its components: we shall have to trace it through its evolution." Sartre studies the evolution of the Intention of Being a Saint, then the Intention of Becoming a Criminal

through his relationship with Others.
Sartre chooses the domain of sexuality to elucidate the relationship between the *pour soi* and the *pour
autrui*, because in this activity and
through Others man asserts himself
as Desire, as desire to be; this individual adventure moreover is easily
describable. Sartre resumes the outline, the pattern of the Intention of
Being in order to study the child violated by the gaze of others and who
decides to turn his *pour autrui* inwards, make his *pour soi* coincide
with his *pour autrui*. Sartre studies
pederasty and crime in terms of the
intention of Being and Doing. This
double postulation appears in the
desire to be loved and the desire to
become the torturer of others, masochism and acknowledging abjection.
The chapter ends with the failure
of the attempt at pederasty which
Genet had expected would justify the
Being. Once again he finds himself
alone.

Dialectic    4) *Je est un autre* (I is other) from 18
of Being      to 20. Sartre describes Genet as a
"conscience non thétique de Soi". He
describes the consciousness Genet
has of his Being reflected in Others
and the direction he takes in his
search for the accomplishment of the
Being through the mediation of
Others. He then describes the circular movement of the Genet who cannot find himself as other, and the adventure of the consciousness which
apprehends itself only as liberty, is
as Nothingness, void.

Dialectic
of Doing

5) *A work.* Sartre returns to the moment when the "child has simultaneously decided to *be* bad and to *do* Evil", he maps the path which leads from Being to Existence, i.e. the problems before Genet when he chooses to do Evil. This chapter is divided into two parts: Genet's formal determinations and his material determinations—in other words, the dialectic of the possible on the levels of the consciousness and of society.

a) Formal determinations: Genet invests the world with a statute, he gives it rules; but first of all what is Evil? Sartre indicates Genet's position in the dialectic of Good and Evil and his relationship between Being and Non-Being; Evil for Others, from Genet's point of view is the relationship between the conscience and Good and Evil; Sartre shows that to decide to do Evil is to pay homage to Good; only an unconscious brute can do Evil whilst being ignorant of Good. For Genet the question would be how to reach lucidly the abject stage of the unconscious brute.

b) Material determinations: "which is the most criminal act?" Evil in Society, Evil for religion, with regard to other men, with regard to the original crisis? Sartre comes to the conclusion that absolute Evil is impossible. He then describes the causes which brought Genet to choose treachery and includes treachery in the dialectic of Good and Evil for Genet.

Relationship between *pour soi* and *en soi*— Relationship between *pour soi* and *pour autrui* —Relationship with *autrui*

6) *To Succeed in Being.* Sartre returns to childhood and to the intention of Being. He establishes the formal and the subjective determination of saintliness.

a) formal determinations: saintliness as a social phenomenon, its objective function in a consumer society.

b) subjective determinations: saintliness as a direction of inner-life: Jouhandeau, St. Theresa of Avila. To be a Saint, to become a Saint. The use Genet makes of saintliness.

Concrete totality of inner experience

7) *Cain*—18 years old. Sartre proposes to give a syncretic portrait of Genet "such as he sees himself at about 18". This chapter resumes all the preceding analyses and synthesises them. It is divided into five paragraphs.

a) the affective climate. What Genet likes, his desires, his introvert nature: masochism and reflexive sensual enjoyment. How the universe appears to him, what figure he means to represent in the world. How he experiences his Being.

b) Genet faced with the outside world and the significance of Genet's world. His attitude towards the world: this paragraph is divided into three parts—

Genet and his tools
Genet and nature
Genet and miracles (i.e. events in which Genet recognises his fate).

Sartre resumes here his analysis of the sacred and comes to the aesthetic consideration.

c) Genet and language: 20 to 22 years old. After a brief sketching of the function of language, Sartre describes the attitude of Ponge, Leiris, Bataille, Parain before this question. He then describes that of Genet and the same patterns already studied re-occur: guilt, silence and theft. Genet uses language to fake the meanings; treachery and unnatural love are linked to the unnatural use of the language; thus Sartre shows how a situation manifests itself in language. He then studies language as self-expression, as the desire to be. Finally, Sartre analyses one image of Genet, extracts its meaning and natural quality.

d) the denial of history: Sartre studies the way Genet lives an event. He resumes the analysis of the "becoming-object". Since Genet is a repetition, a reaffirmation of his own past, he consequently has no history.

e) the denial of reason: the vicious circle. Sartre dismantles Genet's circular sophistics. Unnatural thinking meets the study of unnatural love. Sartre again reconsiders his analysis on the (female) Saint, pederasty, the criminal and treachery. *Last paragraph*: dream and reality. Having traced the course of the vicious circle—of the circular prison—Sartre connects it with the delirium of double-faced images, delirium of lucidity, the dream of contestation, the fairy-play without an audience encircles the steps of the unpun-

ished thief and the comedy of the
thief caught red-handed. At that
stage Sartre comes to poetry.

### III. THE AESTHETE from 20 to 26 years old.

1) *The strange hell of beauty.* This
chapter is divided into three parts:
The image (*en soi*), the gesture
(*pour soi*) and finally, the unity of
the *en soi* in the praxis: the word.

*En soi*    a) the image: how, by claiming Evil for
himself, Genet transforms an act into
an image and protest. Sartre resumes the analysis of Evil on the
level of the imaginary, the dream,
the desire to be: he is forced to return to sexuality, the privileged
ground of the imaginary: onanism.

*Pour soi*    b) The gesture: the dream transforms
the Act into gesture. Sartre describes
how an image is taken up again and
transformed into a manifestation.
Relationship between Evil and
beauty. How Genet uses beauty to
make gesture unreal.

c) Sartre explains why Genet realizes the unity of image and gesture
through words. The words perform
a kind of magnification in the domain of the imaginary, "Magnification and irrealisation".

2) *Towards a liberation:* 26 years old.
Sartre describes the contradictions
brought about by ageing. The evolution of sexuality. Theft as a way of
asserting and freeing the self. How
Genet is led to realize the imaginary
situations through writing.

IV. THE WRITER: 30 years old.

*Pour soi and relationships with autrui*

1) *A mechanism:* From the word to the work. The metamorphosis of the aesthete into a writer joins up with the main lines of conduct Sartre read into the Child-Adult relationship, e.g. oppression, exclusion from society, search for solitude, defiance, exhibitionism. Then Sartre analyses the creation of the first poems. He sees a link between poetic creation and passive sexuality which is but one step in Genet's evolution towards prose writing and active sexuality.

2) *And me.* Sartre analyses the awakening of the consciousness taking place through the process of creation. This chapter is divided into three paragraphs:

*Pour soi*

a) The creatures (characters?). Sartre describes the process which determines the choice of the characters and defines the significance of this choice: the creatures harbour Genet's onanistic dreams: they are thus organised on the same lines as his dreams and reconstruct his desires. The analysis of the characters overlaps the analysis of sexuality.

Relationships with *autrui*

b) The words: Sartre analyses the relationships Genet establishes with the words, and through the words tries to establish with his reader. This analysis is the same as the analysis of the relationship with others.

c) The images: the affective schema of the image and its latent choice of being: with the image Genet reconstructs the shapes of his desires. Sartre therefore is describing the conception of the world reflected by the reconstruction of the universe which Genet effected. The interrelations between the creatures echoes back to a desire for a certain social order.

3) *As a murder:* Sartre studies the sort of communication this art proposes and the artifice Genet uses to achieve it. Sartre resumes the analysis of Genet turned into an Object by the gaze of others and removes this attempt (which had ended in failure) to a higher plane: through the book Genet transforms himself into an object and can apprehend himself as an object abandoned to the gaze of others. Eventually by analysing the composition and inner structure of Genet's work, Sartre describes the path along which Genet seeks to take his reader.

4) *My victory:* This last chapter describes Genet going beyond his situation by objectively realising the imaginary schema of his infantile crisis. Sartre sums up: moral content of Genet's work and its effect on the reader.

## V. PLEA FOR USING GENET WELL.

Sartre goes back to the significance of Genet's work in our society. Effect on the reader. The perspective the reader ought to adopt. The awakening of consciousness one finds in Genet's work.

In *Saint Genet,* Sartre's method is more or less perfected. His regressive-progressive method analyses the past in the light of later events (his sexuality at 15 is explained by his sexuality at 25 or 35), the synthesis is made from the childhood crisis. Sartre's aim is to rediscover the "multidimensional unity of the act". To reach his aim he proceeds schematically in the following manner:

*Analysis* 1) to decipher the significance of a work, by studying it objectively as an act.

2) to replace this act and its significance in relation to the childhood choice.

*Synthesis* 3) to reconstruct the act subjectively from the childhood choice, in the context of formal determinations.

4) to replace this subjective reconstruction in the context of the material determinations of society. As the interaction of these elements cannot be dissociated, each section overlaps the other and every time he has the opportunity of doing so, Sartre reiterates that for the sake of understanding, he is compelled to solidify the elements artificially and to leave out the totalisation process in order to examine static ensembles.

By describing man from the inside, Sartre does not come to the description of a subjectivity, because to describe from the inside is in fact to describe the movement by which the outside is turned inwards and the inside outwards. There is therefore a continuous movement between the outside and the inside, man and society, subjective and objective meaning, and each level enriches and elucidates the others with the descriptions of this double movement. What is more, the analyses are differential (events are always considered in relation to a general judgement). Evil for Genet is studied in relation to the objective structures of Evil.

Sartre's technique is thus a phenomenological and differential analysis, followed by a spiral "totalisation", which always touches the same points; and each progression joins the totalisation at a higher level

which opens new perspectives, so that the totalisation could develop *ad infinitum*. What Sartre wants
to understand is the peculiar character of a work
which in its turn refers to the peculiar character of
man. And man's peculiar character is "his totality in
its process of objectivation".

To understand a work, then, for Sartre is to re-
produce in a self-translucid way, the activity of the
writer in the domain of human activity. By repro-
ducing the totality in its processes of objectivation,
one revivifies the author's aggressiveness, his frustration, his protest, the meaning he attributed to language and one discovers thus the significance of the
work.

Sartre's technique, whilst offering men a certain
approach to self-awareness, aims at unifying the present state of human knowledge (sociology, psychoanalysis, history, linguistics, anthropology).

Conjointly, Sartre's way of understanding, which
aims at giving an account of the depth of experience,
is unlimited investigation. His "Flaubert" such as it
appears in the *Critique de la Raison Dialectique*
covers an even vaster scope than his *Genet*. The conception of the childhood crisis, for example, which
was but a crack in the surface of *Baudelaire* becomes
a rift in *Genet* and widens to include in "Flaubert"
both the notion of class apprehended as a reality and
a pathological study of family. ("Flaubert's father,
who thought himself wronged by his 'boss' Dupuytre,
terrorised everyone in his family with his talent, his
fame, his irony. . . .") This pathological study refers
to the irreligiousness of the father—the "little intellectual bourgeois, son of the French revolution . . . ,
whilst the notion of class refers to a moment in History, to the stifled growth of family capitalism, the
return of the landed gentry, contradictions within the
regime, poverty in the still as yet insufficiently educated working-classes"—the historical moment finds its
place in the movement of history.

Understanding for Sartre does not aim at constituting a final "knowledge". Sartre does not believe in it, any more than he believes in absolute truths existing outside time. For him, there can only be a consciousness which is constantly posing itself questions and which develops *ad infinitum*.

# SARTRE AS A PLAYWRIGHT:
## *THE FLIES* AND *DIRTY HANDS*

## *Walter Kaufmann*

It is customary to underestimate Sartre as a playwright, and *The Flies* is often discounted as if it were merely another of those all too numerous modern plays that involve adaptations of Greek tragedies. While most such dramas do not brook comparison with their ancient models, the mere fact that a dramatist has chosen a theme previously handled by great tragic poets does not necessarily reduce his work to a mere pastiche. Euripides did this time and again, and so did Sophocles and even Aeschylus. In some such cases, the plot and the characters assume the added significance of deliberate innovations and eloquent disagreements.

In *The Flies,* Sartre resembles Euripides in leaving his characters no mythical stature and also in his interest in psychology. Like Euripides, he is a social critic, *engagé,* and, according to some critics, an irrationalist, according to others a rationalist.[1] (Surely,

"Sartre as a Playwright: *The Flies* and *Dirty Hands*" is here reprinted, with the author's and publisher's permission, from Walter Kaufmann, *Tragedy and Philosophy,* Doubleday 1968, Doubleday Anchor Books 1969, Copyright © 1968 by Walter Kaufmann, sections 51 and 52. The author first presented his evidence for Nietzsche's influence on *The Flies* in "Nietzsche Between Homer and Sartre: Five Treatments of the Orestes Story," in *Revue Internationale de Philosophie* (1964), but [he feels that] the book supersedes that article. The version printed here contains one major addition: the paragraph that includes note 7.

[1] The usual view is that existentialism is a form of irrational-

such labels are as unhelpful as optimism and pessimism.) Sartre is infinitely more irreverent than Euripides, and humorous throughout. While he shares Aeschylus' and Euripides' strong philosophic interest, he agrees with Sophocles that the double slaying of the mother and Aegisthus was clearly justified, that Orestes brought back freedom, and that he (though not Electra, who repents in the end) was a hero.

Like Euripides, Sartre attacks religion—but unlike Euripides, he finds it on the side of tyranny. Sartre brings Zeus upon the stage and attacks Christianity and the doctrine of original sin.

Everybody has all-too-human motives, which are of interest; only Orestes is all but unmotivated: his two murders are almost what André Gide called *actes gratuits.* Tired of detachment, Orestes seeks a commitment, and accepts one that will, at least for a moment, restore the freedom and dignity of his people, though we have every reason to doubt that they will make the most of these gifts.

We have come close to the central difference between *The Flies* and all the Greek versions of the story, from Homer to Euripides. Sartre's Orestes is not motivated by the desire or duty to avenge his father. If we want to understand this crucial innovation, we find less help in Sartre's philosophy than—in Nietzsche's. Indeed, Nietzsche's influence on *The Flies* was immense. A few passages from Sartre's play may show this. Near the end of Act ɪɪ, picture 1 scene 4, Orestes says:

"There is another way—*my* way. . . . I must

---

ism, but Iris Murdoch entitled an early study of Sartre, which is very perceptive: *Sartre: Romantic Rationalist* (1953).

As for Euripides, Nietzsche pictured him as a rationalist in *The Birth of Tragedy* (1872), while E. R. Dodds has entitled a paper in *Classical Review* (1929), "Euripides the Irrationalist." See Walter Kaufmann, *Tragedy and Philosophy* (1968), section 50: "Was Euripides an 'irrationalist'?"

descend—do you understand?—descend among you. . . ."

"Suppose I took upon myself all their crimes. Suppose I wanted to earn the name of 'guilt-stealer,' and heap on myself all their remorse. . . ."[2]

Here we find echoes of three different passages from Nietzsche:[3]

"'This is *my* way; where is yours?'—thus I answered those who asked me 'the way.' For *the* way —that does not exist."

"I must descend to the depths, as you do in the evening when you go behind the sea and still bring light to the underworld, you overrich star. Like you I must go *under*—go down, as is said by man, to whom I want to descend."

"Were a god to come down upon earth, he should do nothing but wrong: to take upon oneself *guilt* and not punishment, that alone would be godlike."

The last quotation, from *Ecce Homo*, is nothing less than the quintessence of Sartre's *Flies*. The dig at Christianity is expanded in the play, and Orestes becomes a great anti-Christian savior figure—a truly Nietzschean hero. Even "the buzzing of the poisonous flies" is to be found in *Zarathustra*, Part I, in the chapter "On the Flies of the Market Place."

Next consider a passage from Act II, picture 2, scene 5. Zeus is speaking to Aegisthus:

[2] In Stuart Gilbert's English version, *Tableau I* becomes scene 1, and the *Scène* numbers are omitted. The above translations are mine.

[3] All Nietzsche translations are from *The Portable Nietzsche*, tr. Walter Kaufmann. Italics in the original. The first two come from *Zarathustra*, Part III, ch. 11, and Prologue, sec. 1; the last from *Ecce Homo*, ch. I, 5. Interesting parallels to the final quotation may be found in the chapter "On the Adder's Bite" in *Zarathustra* I.

"Do you know what would have happened to Agamemnon if you had not killed him? Three months later he'd have died of apoplexy on the breast of a pretty slave-girl. But your crime served my ends. . . . You have looked back on your deed with horror and disowned it. Yet what a profit I have made on it! For one dead man, twenty thousand others plunged into repentance."

Compare Nietzsche's *Twilight of the Idol,* chapter I, 10: "Not to perpetuate cowardice against one's own acts! Not to leave them in the lurch afterward! The bite of conscience is indecent." And *The Will to Power* [234]: *"The bite of conscience:* a sign that the character is no match for the deed." But no two epigrams can give any adequate idea of Nietzsche's influence at this point. Both Sartre's deliberately shocking attitude toward death as essentially natural and his attitude toward guilt feelings are deeply anti-Christian and Nietzschean.

Nor is the matter of leaving one's act "in the lurch afterward" a passing point in the play: This is what Electra does in the end, while Orestes stubbornly resists this temptation and thereby rises to heroic stature.

Our third passage from *The Flies* comes from the next scene [6]. Aegisthus, struck, asks Orestes: "Is it true you feel no remorse?" And Orestes replies: "Remorse? Why? I am doing what is right." Superficially, it might seem that Sartre simply sides with Sophocles against Aeschylus and Euripides—but in fact the opposition to remorse, not only in this specific case in which Orestes believes that he is "doing what is right" but quite generally, is almost as central in Sartre's play as the idea that it is far nobler to take guilt upon oneself than only to accept punishment. Indeed, the two ideas belong together and are not Sophoclean but Nietzschean. Orestes is a redeemer figure because he removes the people's guilt feelings. In *Zarathustra* one leitmotif of Nietzsche's philosophy is once summed up succinctly in these words: *"That man be delivered from revenge, that is for me the bridge to the highest hope . . ."* [II.7]. The bite of conscience is understood by Nietzsche (and Freud)[4] as a form of revenge—against oneself. But in *The Flies* the opposition to revenge in the obvious and ordinary sense is even more obvious than the polemic against guilt feelings.

Let us now turn to Orestes' dialogue with Zeus near the end of Act III, scene 2. Orestes describes his sudden realization of his freedom: ". . . Nothing was left in heaven, neither Good nor Evil, nor anyone to give me orders." Zeus urges him: "Come back among us. Come back. See how alone you are; even your sister has abandoned you." We are immediately reminded of Nietzsche's "beyond good and evil," of his insistence that man gives himself his right and wrong, and of his emphasis on the loneliness that descends on those who leave the herd and its allegedly God-given values. Compare, for example, *Zarathustra,* "On the Way of the Creator":

> "'All loneliness is guilt'—thus speaks the herd . . . and when you will say, 'I no longer have a common conscience with you,' it will be a lament and an agony. . . . But do you want to go the way of your affliction, which is the way to yourself? . . . You call yourself free? . . . Free *from* what? As if that mattered . . . free *for* what? Can you give yourself your own evil and your own good . . . ? . . . Thus is a star thrown out into the void and into the icy breath of solitude. . . . The time will come when solitude will make you weary. . . . There are feelings that want to kill the lonely; and if they do not succeed, well, then they themselves must die. But are you capable of this—to be a murderer?"

[4] *Genealogy of Morals,* II, sec. 16; *Das Unbehagen in der Kultur* (1931, *Civilization and Its Discontents*), sec. 7.

In Part III, "Upon the Mount of Olives," Nietzsche mocks those who warn him against loneliness, moaning: "the ice of knowledge will yet freeze him to death!" "Loneliness," he says, "can be the escape of the sick; loneliness can also be escape *from* the sick."

When Zeus entreats Orestes to "come back," Orestes replied in Nietzsche's spirit:

> "I shall not come back under your law; I am condemned to have no other law but mine . . . for I am a man, Zeus, and every man must invent his own way."

When Electra repents, Orestes remains "faithful to the earth" [*Zarathustra*, Prologue 3] and recalls to our minds *Ecce Homo* [II, sec. 10], "My formula for greatness in a human being is *amor fati:* that one wants nothing to be different, not forward, not backward, not in all eternity"; and *Twilight of the Idols* [IX, sec. 49]; "Such a spirit who has *become free* [a phrase that superbly fits Orestes] stands amid the cosmos with a joyous and trusting fatalism . . . *he does not negate any more.*"

Thus Orestes says to Zeus: "I do not hate you. What are you to me?" And finally: "Man's life begins on the other side of despair." This last phrase may remind us of the final three sections in *Nietzsche contra Wagner*—above all, of the beautiful "Epilogue," which is among the finest things Nietzsche ever wrote.[5] Indeed, the final metaphor of *The Flies* that of the pied piper, was also repeatedly used by Nietzsche in connection with the ideal man, with Socrates, and with himself.[6]

In the first chapter of *Ecce Homo* (section 7) Nietzsche says: "My practice of war can be summed

[5] *Portable Nietzsche*, 680 ff.

[6] *The Gay Science*, sec. 340; *Beyond Good and Evil*, sec. 295; *Twilight of the Idols*, Preface; and *Ecce Homo* III, sec. 6.

up in four propositions. First: I only attack causes
that are victorious. . . . Second: I only attack causes
against which I would not find allies, so that I stand
alone. . . . Third: I never attack persons. . . . Fourth:
I only attack things when every personal quarrel is
excluded, when any background of bad experiences
is lacking. . . ."[7] It is interesting to note how these
four propositions fit Orestes but not Electra. She did
not attack alone but waited for Orestes, and unlike
her brother she did attack persons. The fourth proposition spells out their difference most clearly. She is full
of resentment; he is not. And afterwards she repents
and he does not.

Because Sartre is himself a philosopher, everybody
seems to have assumed that his plays, including *The
Flies*, must embody his own philosophy. But *The Flies*
is at variance not only with the Marxist philosophy
of Sartre in his fifties, less than twenty years after he
wrote this play, but also with the philosophy of the
famous lecture "Existentialism is a Humanism," delivered in 1946, only three years after *The Flies*. Then
Sartre argued that "Nothing can be better for us unless it is better for all," and that "If . . . I decide to
marry and have children, even though this decision
proceeds simply from my situation, from my passion
or my desire, I am thereby committing not only myself, but humanity as a whole, to the practice of
monogamy."[8] Surely the ethic of *The Flies* is far more
individualistic, less Kantian, and, in one word,
Nietzschean. Nor do we find the ethic of *The Flies* in
*Being and Nothingness* (*L'être et le néant*) or *No
Exit* (*Huis Clos*), which were finished the same year.

[7] *Basic Writings of Nietzsche, Translated and Edited, with
Commentaries,* by Walter Kaufmann, The Modern Library,
Random House, New York 1968, p. 688. The applicability of
this passage to *The Flies* was pointed out to me by Christopher
Fermanis in a paper he wrote for me in the fall of 1969.

[8] *Existentialism from Dostoevsky to Sartre,* ed. Walter Kaufmann, 292.

We find it only in *The Flies* and in the writings of Nietzsche.

The play represents a great oddity. Written by a philosopher, it embodies the ethic of another philosopher—to be sure the first man mentioned in *Being and Nothingness,* and a man whose decisive influence on existentialism has long been recognized.

In keeping with Socrates' ancient charge against the poets, Sartre, when he wrote *The Flies,* perhaps did not fully know what he was doing; his inspiration may have been partly unconscious, as he projected images and impressions received when reading Nietzsche. "Hell is—other men"—the most famous line in *No Exit,* perhaps in all of Sartre—is surely an unconscious echo of Nietzsche's "no longer knows any other nausea than other men."[9]

Nietzsche, whose books have such a striking artistic quality, also had an immense influence on Stefan George and Rilke, on Christian Morgenstern and Gottfried Benn, Thomas Mann and Hermann Hesse, Gide, Malraux, and Camus.

Indeed, Camus' last major work, *The Fall,* is close to *The Flies*—and to Nietzsche—insofar as it represents an impassioned attack on guilt feelings and specifically on the Christian doctrine of "the fall." Most critics failed to understand it because, unlike Camus, they were not steeped in Nietzsche. But the book may be read as a case history of the will to power of the sick who find the Christian teaching that all men are guilty and sinful tailored to their needs because it allows them to feel superior to their betters: while protesting their own unworthiness, the weak look down on those who refuse to admit how guilty they are. Indeed, the anti-hero of *The Fall* cannot be understood apart from the concept of the will to power, which is constantly alluded to. The book is even more Nietzschean than *The Flies.*

[9] *Beyond Good and Evil,* end of sec. 203.

*The Flies* is a prosy play and much more didactic than the ancient treatments of the same theme; but it could be argued that, being entirely in prose, the play is more of one piece than Euripides' *Electra* in which the many didactic passages are more disturbing. Of course, Sartre as a dramatist is not in the same class with Euripides, any more than Sartre as a philosopher is to be ranked with Plato. Nevertheless he invites comparison with both. The point would be more obvious if Sartre had given up philosophy to write plays, instead of forsaking both careers much of the time for the sake of journalism. Even so, nobody else has ever written such highly technical and academic philosophic treatises and also plays as good as Sartre's. In the story of tragedy and philosophy he occupies a unique place.

It is ironical that the philosophy in *The Flies* is not Sartre's own; but *No Exit* and *Dirty Hands* (*Les mains sales*) are even more philosophical, and most of the philosophical themes in these plays *are* his own. Partly on that account, we are not tempted to call either of these plays a tragedy. *No Exit* is set in hell, deals with eternal damnation, and might be said not to be much more static than *Prometheus; Dirty Hands* deals with a tragic situation, reminiscent of *Julius Caesar:* a man considers killing for the public good a statesman whom he comes to see as a truly great man who commands profound admiration. Yet the treatment is not tragic but largely cerebral. This is clearly deliberate: like Bertolt Brecht, Sartre has no wish to evoke ruth and terror or a great deal of emotion; he prefers to offer fare for thought. At this level, however, he is vastly superior to Brecht.

Although it was Brecht's avowed intention to make the audience think, it was also his purpose to persuade; and trying to do both, he succeeded in doing neither. Partly because he was so bent on persuasion, partly because he lacked any great gift for handling ideas, the "thoughts" expressed in his plays are usually simplistic and exceedingly unsubtle.[10] Sartre, on the other hand, especially in *Dirty Hands,* which deals with themes that Brecht had treated too,[11] is subtle to a fault.

Of course, Brecht meant to reach the masses, but he never did. Sartre's plays are read far more widely than Brecht's. Indeed, vast numbers of students read them on their own.

Let it not be said that Sartre lacks the ability to create fascinating characters. To invite the reader to be critical, reflective, and unemotional, to dispense with poetry and pathos, and yet to convince the reader that one of the characters in a play is an authentically great man, outstanding both in his perception of political realities and as a human being, is no mean feat. Hoederer in *Dirty Hands* is a magnificent creation. We *see* his brilliance as we never see that of Brecht's Galileo. Yet Hoederer's death is not felt to be tragic; it is part of a highly successful attempt to show how difficult it is to say why we do the most important things we do, and how it is legitimate to give our actions meaning ex post facto.

Again the central inspiration comes from Nietzsche: "*In honor of Shakespeare.*—The most beautiful thing I could say in honor of Shakespeare *as a human being* is this: he believed in Brutus and did not cast one grain of suspicion on this kind of virtue. He devoted his best tragedy to him—it is still called by the wrong name—to him and to the most terrible quintessence of high morality. Independence of the soul—that is at stake here! No sacrifice can then be too great: even one's dearest friend one must be able to sacrifice for

---

[10] *The Caucasian Chalk Circle* with its collective-farm frame story is merely one example.

[11] Above all in *The Measures Taken* (*Die Massnahme,* 1930). Brecht himself called it a didactic play. Whatever its virtues are, subtlety is not among them.

it, though he be the most glorious human being, the embellishment of the world, the genius without peer. . . . The height at which he places Caesar is the most delicate honor he could show Brutus: only in this way is his inmost problem raised to a prodigious height, no less than the strength of soul that could cut *such a knot.* . . . Twice in this tragedy he brought a poet on the stage, and twice he poured such impatient and ultimate contempt upon him that it sounds like a cry —the cry of self-contempt. . . . One should translate this back into the soul of the poet who wrote it."

This passage in *The Gay Science* [sec. 98] does not stand alone. In *The Case of Wagner* [sec. 2] Nietzsche quotes "Don José's last cry, which concludes the work:

> *Yes. I have killed her,*
> *I—my adored Carmen!*

Such a conception of love (the only one worthy of a philosopher) is rare: it raises a work of art above thousands."

In the final scene of *Dirty Hands*, Hugo, who has killed Hoederer, says: "I loved Hoederer, Olga. I loved him more than I ever loved anyone in the world." But in this play Sartre's attitude toward Nietzsche is not what it is in *The Flies*; it comes closer to Euripides' attitude toward the old myths. Sartre tries to imagine in detail what people really feel and think when they do the deeds that later are so easily romanticized. What kind of man must demonstrate his strength of soul by killing? When Nietzsche wrote of *Julius Caesar*, he was thinking of his break with Wagner, as has long been recognized. Sartre, at first glance, does not seem to read personal experiences into an ancient tragic situation; he seems to follow the example of Euripides in taking a close look at a modern Brutus.

This Brutus figure, however, puts us in mind of the

poet on whom Shakespeare poured such contempt "that it sounds like a cry—the cry of self-contempt."

> HUGO: I have no gift for anything.
> HOEDERER: You have a gift for writing.
> HUGO: For writing! Words! Always words! [VI.2]

*Des mots! Toujours des mots!* The title of Sartre's autobiography, *Les Mots,* sounds like a wounded cry, and more than once Sartre has voiced his feeling that writing philosophy and plays while others are starving strikes him as frivolity. He could have invested Hugo with great pathos, making us feel that Hugo's death at the end of the play is tragic. There might have been a parallel to Goethe's Werther, a sort of caricature of the author: Werther and Hugo must die to permit Goethe and Sartre to go on living. But while *The Suffering of the Young Werther* inspired a wave of suicides, *Dirty Hands* arouses no comparable emotion. Why?

Self-consciousness and irony are carried so far in this play that we are closer to *Hamlet* than to *Julius Caesar;* but Hamlet, whom Hugo resembles in repeatedly delaying a murder he is instructed to commit, *is* a tragic figure, even when he laments that he "Must (like a whore) unpack my heart with words."[12] Although many passages in *Hamlet* cross the line into black comedy and almost farce—for example, the scene[13] in which Polonius asks, "What do you read, my lord?" and Hamlet replies: "Words, words, words" —much of the time Hamlet speaks in glorious verse, and in spite of his melancholy we are made to *feel* that the events and deaths we witness are enterprises of great moment. It would have been a relatively easy

[12] II.2, beginning. Not only *Les Mots* puts me in mind of *Hamlet;* the title of *L'être et le néant* alludes to "To be or not to be." Voltaire, for example, in his famous essay "Sur la tragédie" in *Lettres Philosophiques* (sometimes translated as *Letters Concerning the English Nation*) renders these words "de l'être au néant."

[13] II.2, near the end.

matter to persuade us that the action in *Dirty Hands* is of great importance, but precisely that we are not allowed to feel.

Sartre, like Brecht and Shaw and Ibsen, works in Euripides' succession rather than in Shakespeare's. Few of Samuel Johnson's errors are as widely credited as his curious notion that tragedy and comedy are "so little allied" that there was not "among the Greeks or Romans a single writer who attempted both."[14] All of the great Athenian tragic poets wrote satyr plays, and Euripides not only wrote comedies (*Helen*) but even what Johnson on the same page calls "the mingled drama" (notably, *Alcestis* and *Ion*). Most interpreters agree that Athene's speech at the end of the *Ion* is utterly at variance with Euripides' own feelings and almost farcical. The poet no longer feels the need to be explicit; if we have not grasped his view of the proceedings by this time, we won't now. The impression we get is that he is too bitter for accusations and laments and prefers irony. This is sufficiently in keeping with the whole tone of the play to work, and yet it provides a powerful and unexpected climax.

Aeschylus and Sophocles had never pushed irony that far, nor did Shakespeare, except for *Troilus and Cressida*, which has something of the flavor of Euripides. In many ways, however, Euripides is more modern than even Shakespeare. He is more mistrustful of grandiloquence, tradition, and alleged nobility; he keeps looking critically upon the plots he uses, dissociates himself from them by means of prologues and explicit comments in which characters within his plays question the ancient stories; and his irony suggests the loss of hope and faith.

Consider Euripides' *Iphigenia in Aulis*. We can hardly marvel sufficiently at its modernity. The structure of Heinrich von Kleist's *Prinz von Homburg* [1810], one of the most celebrated German plays, closely resembles Euripides' plot. The prince, like Iph-

14 Preface to Shakespeare, 321.

igenia, is doomed to die, lives through the most intense dread of death, finally resolves to die coura-
geously, but at the very last moment the catastrophe
is averted. Still, Euripides is infinitely more modern,
not only because *Iphigenia* is a "mingled drama." Unlike Kleist, he remains ironically detached from the
final heroic resolve, suggesting clearly that the glorious
vision of his heroine is a delusion. We may wonder
whether the poet could possibly believe what he lets
her believe; but no doubt remains when in the end
she asks her mother, Clytemnestra, to make sure that
Orestes grows up and becomes a strong man, and
when she entreats her not to hate Agamemnon. We
are made to feel that nothing will turn out the way
the bold young martyr thinks it will. We are reminded
of the all-too-feminine enthusiasm of the Chorus, at
the beginning of the play, for the great warships and
all those supposedly so valiant men.

Such a high degree of self-consciousness and irony,
such a relentless probing of what passes for nobility,
and such extreme disillusionment put one in mind of
Goethe's Mephistopheles in *Faust;* there is not much
else that brooks comparison with it before the twentieth century.

Even more than Goethe, however, not to speak of
Ibsen, Euripides presents immense suffering on the
stage—in *Iphigenia* and *Ion,* too—and does not shrink
from writing passages of profound pathos. Sartre does
not permit himself any such emotional indulgence. In
the last act of *Dirty Hands,* Hugo says, "I had been
living for so long in tragedy," and "What if it were
all a comedy?" and "Oh, this is a farce." All along we
feel that Sartre refuses to turn his play into a tragedy
and asks with Hugo whether it is not perhaps a comedy or farce—whether life is not best seen as a farce.
Yet he will not grant us the catharsis of laughter. He
is intent on exploring problems and making us think.

Is *The Flies* a tragedy? Most readers would probably say that it is not because the end is not tragic.

Yet we call the *Oresteia* and Sophocles' *Electra* tragedies although their endings are not tragic—and the
end of *The Flies* is far more tragic than the end of
Aeschylus' and Sophocles' versions of the story. But
the necessary condition of a play's being a tragedy is
not that it ends badly but that it represents on the
stage suffering so intense and immense that no conclusion can eradicate this impression from our minds.
Since it has become unfashionable to present on the
stage agonies like those of Cassandra and Prometheus,
Ajax and Philoctetes, Heracles and Electra, an un-
tragic conclusion is rarely compatible with tragedy;
more and more, it is the end that has to bear the
burden of tragedy.

In *The Flies* the total impression is more one of
irreverent reflection than of "the *sublime* as the artistic
conquest of the horrible." While Aeschylus and Sophocles "looked boldly right into the terrible destructiveness of so-called world history as well as the cruelty
of nature,"[15] Sartre tells us that "life begins on the
other side of despair." The despair is taken for
granted, along with the fact that it is amply warranted; what we are shown on the stage is not the
staggering suffering that leads to despair but the
young man who triumphs over despair. *That* is why
the play is not a tragedy. And while the spirit of the
play is Nietzschean, the poetry of suffering, of which
Nietzsche himself was a master, is lacking. One may
feel like saying to Sartre, as Nietzsche once said to
himself: "It should have *sung*, this 'new soul'—and not
spoken!"[16] Though Sartre, unlike Nietzsche, has written plays, Nietzsche, unlike Sartre, was a poet.

Nietzsche noted that it was of the very essence of
Greek tragedy that it is a response to "the absurdity
of being" and a triumph over nausea [*Ekel*].[17] Suf-

[15] *The Birth of Tragedy*, sec. 7.

[16] Preface to the 2d ed. of *The Birth of Tragedy*, sec. 3; p. 20
in my translation.

[17] *The Birth of Tragedy*, sec. 7. Anyone interested in the

fering becomes beautiful, and "only as an *aesthetic phenomenon* are existence and the world eternally *justified*." This dictum, one of the leitmotifs of *The Birth of Tragedy* [introduced in sec. 5], is characteristic of the early, romantic Nietzsche, and Sartre, far more than the later Nietzsche, is post-romantic. Yet as a description of Greek—and Shakespearean—tragedy, the point of the young Nietzsche is well taken: the sufferings of Sophocles' Electra and Antigone, Ajax and Oedipus are voiced in such superb poetry that readers and spectators feel emotionally liberated as they discover words for their own mute grief; and the experience of so much beauty, though it certainly does not "justify" suffering, reconciles us, at least temporarily.

Sartre has no wish to reconcile us to the world. He would sooner accept the counsel of Karl Marx and change the world, but as a playwright—unlike Brecht —he does not seem to have much hope of that. *The Flies* may have been a summons to action. When first performed under the Nazi occupation, it certainly involved a challenge to stop wallowing in guilt feelings, reproaching oneself, and feeling that one's miserable fate was deserved; but the deliverer, Orestes, is a Nietzschean individualist who owes nothing to Marx. In *No Exit* and *Dirty Hands,* Sartre holds a mirror up to men—or rather he places men in a hall of mirrors, seeing every act, motive, and feeling in so many different perspectives that the effect approaches comedy. But we are never allowed to relax and resolve unbearable tensions in laughter. We are constantly forced to question. Sartre is the most Socratic playwright.

---

genesis of French existentialism should reread this section. The theme of nausea, prominent here, recurs even more prominently in *Zarathustra.*

# SARTRE AS DRAMATIST

## David Bradby

---

The fashionable view of Sartre in this country is to think of him as primarily a philosopher and essayist who uses the theatre merely to propagate his philosophy. *The Oxford Companion to French Literature* accurately reflects the approach of most critics when it says: 'His plays, like his novels, are usually a means of conveying his philosophical ideas, but they are also very good theatre and have been successful when performed.'[1] The method is to take a number of the ideas expressed in the philosophical works and then to trace them through the plays. This is certainly a legitimate and fruitful approach, but by no means the only appropriate one, since it considers only one aspect of the plays, their ideas, and fails to take account of their value as works of the theatre. When Sartre is characterised as 'a philosopher, in whose hands the theatre is but a tool skilfully used',[2] one must point out that in the work of such a writer the means of expression can seldom be totally separated from the content.

Francis Jeanson is the only major exception to this trend. He devotes the first half of his general study of Sartre not to the philosophy, nor the prose works, but to the theatre. He talks of its dramatic qualities, stresses the importance of drama for Sartre, and points out that all the most important Sartrian themes find

This article, which first appeared in *The Philosophical Journal*, is reprinted by permission of the Editor.

[1] Oxford, 1959, p. 662.

[2] GROSSVOGEL, DAVID I., *Twentieth Century French Drama*, New York, 1961, p. 133. (Columbia paperback no. 22.)

expression in his theatre.[3] Since this is so, it seems that for Sartre the theatre is as complete and valid a form of expression as the philosophical essay. In fact an examination of the way in which, in his philosophical writings, he expresses some of his favourite ideas to do with Being reveals that he has constant recourse to metaphors drawn from the vocabulary of play-acting. This is shown clearly by the well-known example of the waiter in his major early philosophical work *L'Être et le Néant* (*Being and Nothingness*):

> Considérons ce garçon de café. Il a le geste vif et appuyé, un peu trop précis, un peu trop rapide, il vient vers les consommateurs d'un pas un peu trop vif, il s'incline avec un peu trop d'empressement, sa voix, ses yeux expriment un intérêt un peu trop plein de sollicitude pour la commande du client . . . Il joue, il s'amuse. Mais à quoi donc joue-t-il? Il ne faut pas l'observer longtemps pour s'en rendre compte: il joue *à être* garçon de café.[4]

> Let us consider this waiter in the café. His movement is quick and forward, a little too precise, a little too rapid. He comes towards the patrons with a step a little too quick. He bends forward a little too eagerly; his voice, his eyes express an interest a little too solicitous for the order of the customer . . . He is playing, he is amusing himself. But what is he playing? We need not watch for long before we can explain it: he is playing *at being* a waiter in a café.

In order to describe his behaviour, Sartre suggests that the waiter is acting a part which offers him a guide to behaviour in any given situation and enables

[3] JEANSON, FRANCIS, *Sartre par Lui-Même*, Paris, 1955, p. 11.

[4] *L'Être et le Néant*, Paris, 1943, pp. 98–99; translated by Hazel E. Barnes as *Being and Nothingness*, London, 1957. The translation given is on p. 59. N.B. The English verb 'to play' does not contain quite so obviously as the French 'jouer' the second meaning which is important here: 'to act'.

him to escape the more difficult but more authentic course of reacting freely to each new situation that presents itself. In his lengthy description of all the waiter's gestures, we can see what delight he takes in building up his metaphor of the play-actor in order to present as vividly as possible precisely what is inauthentic in the waiter's mode of Being.

Not the least interesting thing about this examination of Being in terms of acting a role is that it shows how Sartre joins the long tradition of French 'moralistes' in his approach to Man. Like all of them, from Molière to Gide, he gives a central place to sincerity, authenticity; and like them, in separating the sincere from the hypocritical, he concentrates on showing up the hypocritical. In his novels as well as his plays, it is frequently a character guilty of escapism who occupies the central position. The logical culmination of this approach to the problem of Being is, naturally, to be found on the stage: it can be seen in the shape of the actor, the man who assumes a role and then admits only those parts of reality that fit with his role. The fullest discussion of the problem in these terms is found in *Kean* where the central character is the original *hypocritēs*, the actor. Kean is presented as the eternal actor who can never stop acting, even in his private life, and reminds us that the fundamental idea of Sartre's ethic, that Man is free to create his own values by exercising his free choice within the limitations of a given situation, is only an application in a larger context of what the actor calls improvisation.

It is clear that for Sartre what men are can only be approached through what they do, and in order to examine what they do, he has to place them in situations whose limitations he can control. The idea of the 'situation' is of central importance to his thought. Mary Warnock sums it up in these words:

The possibility of acting must always be realised in the context of the world, and this includes for each of us his situation and the people with whom he is. The question, then, becomes one of trying to discover how far a free agent can escape from his particular situation in his choices.[5]

Through an insistence that ethics can be usefully discussed only when taken in the context of a given situation whose controlling factors are known, he is led to devise situations, as a dramatist devises situations, even in his non-dramatic works. Not only is Sartre naturally given to devising dramatic examples in his philosophic writings, but the dramatic urge can be found in the very structure of his ideas: the process of building up a situation towards a dénouement seems fundamental to his thought.

This can be seen if we look at another example from *L'Être et le Néant* which shows how Sartre has to devise a dramatic situation to express one of the most fundamental points in his theory of Being: the power of another person's view of us in determining our own essence. To illustrate this, he uses the example of shame, but he does not discuss the emotion in the abstract. Instead, he describes himself listening at a keyhole. He imagines that he is eavesdropping out of jealousy, interest or vice, and concentrating solely on what he sees through the keyhole. His awareness of himself is almost non-existent. But just then he hears steps in the corridor and realises someone is watching him. At this point he feels shame because the other person's look makes him aware of himself once more and he accepts the judgment implied in the look. His example is clearly dramatic, in the way a situation is carefully built up, with alternative motives supplied

[5] *The Philosophy of Sartre*, London, 1965, p. 133. For a philosophical explanation of the terms 'situation', 'en situation', and 'dépassement' see *L'Être et le Néant*, Part IV, Chapter 1, particularly p. 591 and pp. 633–38.

for the eavesdropping, and then moved on to a dénouement.[6]

Thus when Sartre began to write plays he was
clearly not using the theatrical form perfunctorily;
through it he was expressing a philosophy which has
a fundamentally dramatic structure and which finds
natural expression in dramatic form. As if to illustrate
this point, the situations he devised in his plays were
always intensely dramatic. Thody points out that Sartre's dramatic world 'has a . . . surprising affinity with
that of Greek Tragedy' in that it depicts 'boundary
situations': murder, adultery, incest, torture, and his
plays always contain violence and passion.[7] Sartre is
well acquainted with Greek tragedy; he gave a course
in it to Dullin's actors and has frequently referred to
it in his pronouncements on the theatre. An interesting
elaboration of his theory of freedom in the situation,
which demonstrates his theatrical approach to this
idea and the way he links it with classical tragedy, can
be found in an early text on the theatre, a lecture
given in the United States in 1946 and printed in *Theatre Arts* as 'Forgers of Myths'. He starts by defending
Anouilh's *Antigone* from accusations of lifelessness
by the American critics who had claimed that Antigone herself had no character. In a splendidly po-

[6] See *L'Être et le Néant*, pp. 317–18. It is interesting that
his early life as recounted in *Les Mots* (*Words*), was dominated
by play-acting. He was a very precocious child and could not
for a long time escape from the sensation that he was merely
acting a part for the benefit of the adults. His grandfather encouraged this and there are frequent references to the theatrical
quality of life in their home. For example: 'I adored surprises.
They were always happening at home. Mysteries, sometimes
amusing, sometimes full of virtue, unexpected presents, dramatic revelations. . . . In short, melodrama was my staple diet.'
(*Les Mots*, Paris, 1964, p. 84; translated by Irene Clephane as
*Words*, London, 1964, pp. 71–72).

[7] THODY, PHILIP, in his introduction to *Les Séquestrés
d'Altona* for the 'Textes Français Classiques et Modernes'
series, London, 1965.

lemical passage, Sartre says that Antigone is indeed not a character in the traditional sense:

> She represents a naked will, a pure free choice; in her there is no distinguishing between passion and action. The young playwrights of France do not believe that men share a ready-made 'human nature'. (What men share) is not nature, but the situation in which man finds himself. (Man is a) free being, entirely indeterminate, who must choose his own being when confronted with certain necessities. A man who is free within the circle of his own situations, who chooses, whether he wishes to or not, for everyone else when he chooses for himself—that is the subject-matter of our plays.

He defined this as a theatre of situation, saying that people would be distinguished:

> not by character, but rather as actions are divergent or clashing, as right may conflict with right. . . . In this we return to the concept of tragedy as the Greeks saw it. . . . We do not reject psychology, that would be absurd: we integrate life.[8]

It can be seen that Sartre had a clear and very ambitious idea of what he wanted to express through theatre. He was equally emphatic about how it should be expressed. The theatre had to speak through 'myths which anyone can understand and feel deeply'. It had to depict a point of climax: 'one does not reach death by degrees, one is suddenly confronted with it'. And yet a certain austerity was necessary. He was looking for a style which combined simplicity with dignity. He said that in *Morts sans sépulture* (*Men Without Shadows*) he had aimed for conciseness, 'elipses,

[8] 'Forgers of Myths, The Young Playwrights of France', in *Theatre Arts*, Vol. XXX, No. 6, 1946, pp. 324–35.

brusque interruptions, a sort of inner tension in the phrases'.[9]

Of course, the theatre has always been for him an art form which demands its own style. He has commented on the fact that when writing for the stage, he expresses himself differently. He says that what attracts him about the theatre is that a play must succeed immediately, or it disappears. His very means of expressing this idea is dramatic:

> ce coup de force et cette voix forte et le risque de tout perdre en une nuit. Cela m'oblige à parler *autrement*, cela varie.[10]

> the feat of strength and the loud voice that are necessary and the risk of losing all in one night. That forces me to speak *differently*, changes things.

Here we see how Sartre dramatises the very act of writing a drama. He likes placing himself in a situation involving risk so that, like Goetz, he has the sensation of staking all on a 'coup de force'.

We have seen that Sartre demanded a theatre of situation and we shall see that a dangerous or restricted situation is vital in all his plays. It would be possible to refer back at this point to the ideas of 'situation' and 'dépassement' as expounded in *L'Être et le Néant*, but it is also possible to refer back to *Les Mouches* (*The Flies*) and see the idea of freedom in situation developing through the drama. The importance of the situation as it evolves in the plays is not only that it presents an obstacle which must be 'dépassé', but also that it provides a necessary framework for action if the idea of liberty is to have any meaning, since liberty in a vacuum is meaningless. In *Les*

---

[9] Ibid., pp. 330–32.

[10] *L'Express*, 17th September 1959, p. 35. (The translation given here is mine, as are all the others, with the exception of the two extracts from *Being and Nothingness* and the extract from *Words* in note 6.)

*Mouches*, Orestes arrives at Argos theoretically free, but it is an unrealised freedom. The Tutor sums it up:

> sans famille, sans patrie, sans religion, sans métier, libre pour tous les engagements et sachant qu'il ne faut jamais s'engager.[11]

> without family, country, religion or job; free to commit yourself to anything, yet knowing that you should never become committed.

But Orestes is not satisfied. He feels lighter than a cobweb floating ten feet from the ground and longs to become involved in the situation, to become 'a man who belongs somewhere, a man among his fellow men'. He only experiences true freedom after he has accepted that he does belong in the situation and has committed himself to act by acknowledging his duty to murder in defiance of the gods. Another example of the sort of framework which Sartre thinks necessary for freedom can be seen in his statement that Frenchmen had never been so free as during the German occupation, since every thought of their own was an affirmation of refusal to accept German propaganda and therefore an affirmation of liberty. The presence of an oppressive German power, by providing a severely limited situation, gave the opportunity for freedom to be more frequently exercised.[12]

Sartre no longer holds quite such a straightforward belief in the freedom of Man,[13] but this was his belief

[11] *Théâtre I*, Paris, 1947, p. 26; translated by Stuart Gilbert as *The Flies*, Penguin Plays, 1962.

[12] *Situations III*, Paris, 1949, p. 11.

[13] 'The other day I reread a prefatory note of mine to a collection of these plays—*Les Mouches, Huis Clos* and others—and was truly scandalised. I had written: "Whatever the circumstances and wherever the site, a man is always free to choose to be a traitor or not. . . ." When I read this, I said to myself: it's incredible, I actually believed that!' Sartre speaking in 'Itinerary of a thought', *New Left Review*, No. 58, November–December 1969, p. 44.

during the period from 1943 to 1955 when his first eight plays were written.[14] And since the deliberate contrivance of a dramatic situation was so important to Sartre in his expression of freedom and commitment, it is logical to suggest that these ideas can be expressed more satisfactorily in the language of drama than they can in the language of philosophy. Mary Warnock, in her book *Existentialist Ethics*, expresses just this idea from the point of view of the philosopher:

the demands of philosophy, exactness, objectivity, and the attempt to say what is true, are the very demands which Existentialism is committed, on principle, to rejecting. Perhaps we must conclude that Existentialism, as a way of thinking, is more naturally suited to express itself in novels, plays, films, and other un-argued statements of how the world is.[15]

Another philosopher, Anthony Manser, concludes his book on Sartre on much the same note, suggesting that, our moral experience being unsystematic, our moral senses can perhaps benefit more by reading works of fiction than by the abstract study of ethics. He quotes D. H. Lawrence, 'It seems to me it was the greatest pity in the world when philosophy and fiction got split'.[16]

Sartre has achieved a reintegration of just these two elements, fiction and philosophy, in his plays. But because he has also written pure philosophy, his success in achieving the reintegration has often been over-

[14] I have concentrated mainly on these plays. There is not space to consider in any detail the changes in Sartre's thought and approach to the theatre which culminated in *Les Séquestrés d'Altona*. On this subject, see J. Palmer's article in *French Studies*, April 1970, pp. 150–62.

[15] London, 1967, p. 57.

[16] MANSER, ANTHONY, *Sartre, A Philosophic Study*, London, 1966, p. 264.

looked. He has frequently claimed descent from Greek tragedy, emphasising its paradoxical clash of right with right. Like the Greeks, he found the dramatic form the right one for expressing certain fundamental ideas about Being. An examination of the essentially theatrical elements of the plays in their own right, instead of the usual approach of interpretation according to the philosophy, will show how this is achieved.

The stage settings, a basic element of all theatre, provide a good starting point for this examination. As one would expect from a writer who lays such emphasis on the situation, these are never mere accessories to the action, but have their part in conveying the total meaning of the play. The first production of *Les Mouches* was in fact criticised because Dullin's décors had emphasised so strongly the repulsiveness of the cult of the dead. An essential part of the horror of *Morts sans sépulturt* derives from the way the décor conveys a house which is being used as prison and torture chamber. We are constantly aware of the helplessness of the characters because they cannot escape, they are trapped in their setting.

This use of a restricted setting to provide a concrete manifestation of his characters' metaphysical situation is especially clear in *Huis Clos* (*In Camera*, or, *No Exit*), whose very title emphasises this quality by its suggestion which is not only of the law-courts, trials, judgments, but also of the mysteriously sealed doors, the chamber where the course of justice can be witnessed only by the participants. Sartre's stage direction indicates simply, 'a Second Empire drawing-room with a bronze on the chimney-piece'. A later stage direction says that Garcin picks up a paper-knife. In the course of the dialogue, a bell, an electric light and three sofas are mentioned, there is nothing else. Garcin comments that there are no windows or mirrors and the design for the original production in 1944 expressed this very effectively by showing a bricked-up window-frame, and some torn plaster over the fire-place where a mirror should have been. The 'sealed-in' impression was completed by the fire-place also being bricked up.

This décor is extremely important for the play for two reasons. First because half the effectiveness of the opening scenes depends on the characters' astonishment at finding themselves together in a Second Empire drawing-room. Second because this is the traditional setting for the bourgeois French boulevard comedy, so the audience also has a trick played on it, since it does not get the boulevard comedy it expects. But it is also important because, through the very falseness and theatricality of the setting, Sartre is saying something about the kind of hell the characters make for themselves. It is one of false attitudes and theatrical gestures, like Estelle's insistence, the moment she enters the room, that she must have a different sofa which will match her dress better. Garcin recognises this element in the décor:

> Après tout, je vivais toujours dans des meubles que je n'aimais pas et des situations fausses; j'adorais ça.[17]

> After all, I always lived with furniture I disliked and in equivocal situations; I adored that.

At the end of the play, when he finally realises his need to escape from hypocrisy, he is unable to leave the room. Having chosen to live inauthentically in a 'situation fausse' he only discovers its horror when he is trapped by it.

*Les Mains Sales* (*Crime Passionnel*), though it moves between different locations, also depends on the restrictions of the settings, built up not only by the sets themselves, but also by imaginative means. The first is the framework of the play within the play. The fact that everything is being re-enacted after some four years' interval, confers on it the hermetic

[17] *Théâtre I*, p. 127; translated by Stuart Gilbert as *In Camera*, Penguin Plays, 1958.

quality of past experiences which was achieved in *Huis Clos* by the play being set after the characters' deaths. Secondly, the setting for the play is one of violent restriction, since we know there are four armed men posted round Olga's house and Hugo has only until midnight to accept the party's dictates or be murdered. Finally, inside the play within the play itself, we find a couple of strong-arm men with machine-guns, and the whole atmosphere of a heavily guarded, walled house.

Although a more fluid type of presentation was necessary for *Le Diable et le Bon Dieu* (*Lucifer and the Lord*) and *Nekrassov*, it is to be noted that much of both plays takes place in situations which are restricted in the sense that armed invasion or capture by the police are threatened. But the restrictiveness of the stage setting only reaches its apogee with Sartre's last play, *Les Séquestrés d'Altona* (*Altona*) whose very title contains the idea of imprisonment, and which is dominated by the figure of Franz, who refuses to leave his self-imposed prison until the end of the play, when he only comes out in order to commit suicide.

The décor for this play is totally crushing. The house, like Hoederer's, is isolated, the furniture is heavy and ugly, the room of the 'ségnestré' dominates the set as it dominates the lives of the play's characters. The whole house is so densely surrounded by trees that only a ghastly green light can penetrate. The set creates the impression of a hideous trap, a monstrous edifice with built-in powers of survival, compelling the Gerlath family to remain living in it although their reasons for doing so may have vanished.

One of the basic functions of such restricted settings is to show up all forms of 'bad faith', escapism, pretence, irresponsibility, superstition. The most dramatic way of achieving this is to place a man guilty of one of these failings in a situation where he shows himself up; and the effectiveness of this technique is partly a

result of the laughter it provokes. Sartre's very important use of humour in this way was hardly discussed by contemporary reviewers although one or
two perceptive writers did realise its significance, like
Marguerite Duras in her review of *Les Mains Sales*.

The humour is nearly always ironic and involves
setting up a situation in which one outcome is expected, but which then leads to something different
and surprising. Sartre's own description of irony may
help to define this type of procedure:

> Dans l'ironie, l'homme anéantit, dans l'unité d'un
> même acte, ce qu'il pose, il donne à croire pour n'être
> pas cru, il affirme pour nier et nie pour affirmer, il
> crée un objet positif mais qui n'a d'autre être que
> son néant.[18]

> In irony a man annihilates what he posits within one
> and the same act; he leads us to believe in order not
> to be believed; he affirms to deny and denies to
> affirm; he creates a positive object but it has no being
> other than its nothingness.

Thus irony is closely connected with the power to
negate which Sartre finds at the very basis of Man's
conscious Being, and it is therefore not surprising that
he uses it frequently and to great effect. This effect is
usually achieved by the affirmation of something
pleasant or seductive which disguises an unpleasant
truth. A good example is in the opening scenes of
*Huis Clos*.

In this play a situation is provided which seems to
prepare the audience for a traditional boulevard comedy, but turns out to be quite different. Again, to the
characters the situation at first seems harmless but
turns out to be quite the opposite. It must be stressed
that Sartre deliberately arouses laughter to reinforce
the ironic effect. This is done by brutally contrasting
the instruments of torture the characters had ex-

[18] *L'Être et le Néant*, p. 85; *Being and Nothingness*, p. 47.

pected to find in Hell with the drawing-room in which
they actually find themselves. The incongruity of the
setting is increased by the fact that one element of
the traditional Hell is included in the room—its heat.
The horrifying situation which is developed out of
these humorous beginnings is all the more effective
for having started in this way. Moreover, the play
ends on a note of laughter, hysterical laughter as the
characters realise the full incongruity of their situation, the sheer absurdity of the eternity before them.
The irony of Hoederer's death in *Les Mains Sales*,
arising from nothing more than a stupid mistake, and
coming after all the self-doubt of Hugo and the brave
confidence of Hoederer, reveals the same ability to
use the derisory to dramatic effect.

But although these two plays provide impressive
examples of irony derived from an incongruous situation, gradually built up to contribute to the play's
total meaning, irony can also be used to achieve minor results. It is used as a means of establishing character. In *Huis Clos*, Estelle is constantly revealing her
vanity and frivolity which seem so completely incongruous in the context of eternal Hell. It is because of
the seriousness of her situation that it seems so ridicu-
lous when she refuses to sit on one of the sofas because
its colour does not match her dress nicely and when
she refuses to allow Garcin to take off his jacket. Sartre
cruelly raises laughter at her expense with her reaction
of incredulous horror to Garcin's suggestion that they
should all keep quiet, 'Do you expect me to be silent?'[19] and he builds up an equally cruel portrait of
the superficially seductive Jessica in *Les Mains Sales*.
But this kind of humour, is best used in the frankly
satirical portraits of the newspaper director or the society hostess in *Nekrassov*. Tableau II scene 4, where
the director is trying desperately to find a striking
headline has been rightly quoted by Thody as one of

[19] *Théâtre I*, p. 147.

Sartre's funniest scenes.[20] Again, it contains the element of incongruity: he is more concerned with the shock effect of his headline than with the news it communicates, so he ends up inventing the news that will give him the best headline.

The ironic situation can also be used in an almost didactic way as in *Le Diable et le Bon Dieu* where Goetz finds that a leper is not interested in his gesture of love, but prefers to receive an indulgence, thus demonstrating the power of church-sanctioned superstition.[21]

But frequently these aims are all combined to a greater or lesser extent in the same passage. In *Les Mains Sales* tableau III scene 1, the ironic situation helps to build up the characters, to make a point about the need for authenticity in human relationships, and in addition, to show how the situation could be overcome and why it is not. The following extract comes at the end of this long and very amusing scene. Hugo has been showing his unwillingness to face facts by lapsing into melodramatic fiction, telling Jessica that Hoederer has 'a huge scar, a wig and a glass eye'. At first this is simply amusing, but it soon becomes apparent that they cannot break out of the game. Jessica discovers that Hugo is on a secret mission to kill Hoederer, but neither is capable of authentic emotion and they find they cannot discuss the matter seriously. It is interesting to see how Sartre introduces an element of despair into the dialogue without changing the circular movement which had made it amusing earlier in the scene:

JESSICA. Eh bien, nous allons le chloroformer et l'attacher à la gueule d'un canon.

HUGO. Jessica! Je suis sérieux.

[20] THODY, PHILIP, *Jean-Paul Sartre, A Literary and Political Study*, London, 1960, p. 119.

[21] *Le Diable et le Bon Dieu*, Paris, 1951, p. 157; translated by Kitty Black as *Lucifer and the Lord*, Penguin Plays, 1965.

JESSICA.   Moi aussi.

HUGO.   Toi, tu joues à être sérieuse. Tu me l'as dit.

JESSICA.   Non, c'est toi.

HUGO.   Il faut me croire, je t'en supplie.

JESSICA.   Je te croirai si tu crois que je suis sérieuse.

HUGO.   Bon. Eh bien, je te crois.

JESSICA.   Non. Tu joues à me croire.

HUGO.   Nous n'en sortirons pas.[22]


JESSICA.   Well then, we'll chloroform him and tie
   him to the mouth of a cannon.

HUGO.   Jessica! I'm being serious.

JESSICA.   Me too.

HUGO.   No, you're just playing at being serious. You
   told me so.

JESSICA.   No, that's what you're doing.

HUGO.   Please, I beg you, you must believe me.

JESSICA.   I'll believe you if you believe I'm being
   serious.

HUGO.   Alright then. I believe you.

JESSICA.   No, you're playing at believing me.

HUGO.   There's no way out.


There is powerful irony in the fact that what started
as a game of pretence or play-acting has taken over
as the only possible reality. Through this play-acting
they have avoided the necessity for authentic reactions for so long that they are no longer capable of
them. This short extract demonstrates not only the
tension and economy with which Sartre uses dialogue
to show up two inauthentic attitudes, but also provides an example of his wit and humour.

Many examples could be quoted to show that in
Sartre the urge to entertain is never totally separated
from the urge to philosophise or to teach. Simone de
Beauvoir relates how, as a young man, his gifts as an
entertainer impressed everyone at the Ecole Normale

[22] *Les Mains Sales,* Paris, 1948, p. 75; translated by Kitty
Black as *Crime Passionnel,* Methuen, 1961.

Supérieure,[23] and *Les Mots* (*Words*) reveals that his
urge to surprise and entertain goes back to a very early
age. The wish to entertain is perhaps particularly evident in another element of his dramatic writings:
their use of suspense. We have seen the essentially
dramatic nature of his philosophy arising from an emphasis on the situation and the continual possibility
of transforming this situation by a free human will (as
Orestes does) or of evading the task (as Electra does
in *Les Mouches*). This gives to the plays a dramatic
progression which holds the audience in suspense because the situation is constantly being shown as open
to develop in not one, but a variety of different ways.
This is clearly the case in a play like *Morts sans Sépulture* in which there is continual uncertainty about
whether torture will force the 'maquisards' to talk, or
in a play like *Nekrassov* in which the whole story is
built around a criminal's flight from the police and his
deliberate imposture which seems about to be shown
up at any moment. But it is also true of *Huis Clos*, a
play whose situation is hermetically impervious to
change, and for this reason it is worth looking not only
at the ideas of the play, but also at the way in which
Sartre constructs a suspenseful plot and exciting dialogue. In *Huis Clos* he does this by putting false con-
fessions in the mouths of both Garcin and Estelle, then
gradually revealing the truth. The progression from
falsehood to truth is strewn with semi-confessions and
false attitudes which build up our interest in discovering the real facts in the same way that a thriller, by
judicious uncovering of false scents, keeps its audience
guessing. The climax of this process occurs when the
door of the room finally opens and it seems for a moment that they will be able to leave. But at the same
time, they all finally realise their dependence on one
another and so decide to close the door. This is rather

[23] Beauvoir, Simone de, *Mémoires d'une Jeune Fille
Rangée*, Paris, 1964, p. 335; translated by James Kirkup as
*Memoirs of a Dutiful Daughter*, Penguin, 1963.

an artificial 'last chance' but it provides a dramatic picture of how the characters have chosen their own hell, while the suspense of the play is brought to a climax.

This movement of revelation advancing the play from situation to situation is essential to all Sartre's theatre and is particularly characteristic of *Le Diable et le Bon Dieu*, which shows Goetz moving from one inauthentic situation to another in his search for an authentic response to reality. Sartre plays on the audience's emotions, first encouraging emotional identity with one character or attitude, then showing its drawbacks, in a dramatic movement which generates suspense as it moves from one reversal of situation to another. This can be seen throughout the play; the most extreme example is perhaps the end of tableau III. Here there is a sudden reversal of the whole direction the plot has been taking up to this point, when Goetz decides to accept Heinrich's challenge that he cannot devote himself to doing nothing but good.

The text seems to come close to the Brechtian idea that for every choice that takes place on stage, an alternative choice should be shown to have been possible. This technique is most movingly and excitingly used to portray Catherine's absolute but frustrated love. Despairing of Goetz ever allowing her to stay with him, she hides a discontented officer in the tent, who is willing to kill Goetz if she gives him a pre-arranged signal. The suspense is built up as she gives Goetz a last chance, but immediately after being forced by his cruel attitude to give the signal, she cannot bear to let it happen, changes her mind, and shouts a warning to him at the last moment.[24] The emotions of both Catherine and Goetz are portrayed with the maximum of suspense and both are given ample chance to change their minds.

The deliberate contrivance of suspense in a dramatic situation which undergoes perpetual transforma-

[24] *Le Diable et le Bon Dieu,* p. 94.

tion naturally puts great emphasis on the art of the dialogue, and an example of Sartre's skill in this respect has already been given in the brilliant scene between Hugo and Jessica from *Les Mains Sales*. Although his theatre is, in his own definition, a theatre of situation rather than a theatre of psychology,[25] he has enriched it with well-defined characters whose internal movements and external conflicts advance the plot from one situation to another. All the plays present psychological conflicts of varying intensity, a fact which has led critics to see this as their most important element.[26] The name of Strindberg has been invoked, particularly in connection with *Huis Clos*, where the very action depends on the shifting relationships between the three characters as each member of the trio in turn is dominated by another while the third tries to escape, or watches, planning revenge.[27] But the importance of Sartre's characterisation lies not so much in its intensity as in its dramatic nature. What interests him is to see how a given character will react in a given situation. He builds up his characters, not through the use of monologue but through dialogue and through contrast with other characters. Thus for example, while Hugo wonders, Hamlet-like, about whether he should kill Hoederer, his state of mind is investigated in a series of confrontations with Slick and Georges, Jessica, Olga, Hoederer himself. Above all, Sartre loves to present character through action: to show the reasons leading up to someone's choice, the choice itself being made and then the consequences of that choice. This is exactly the pattern followed in *La Putain Respectueuse* (*The Respectful Prostitute*).

Yet another means of presenting character dramatically which Sartre uses a great deal has already been

[25] See note 8.

[26] E.g. see Manser's remarks on *Les Mains Sales* in op. cit., p. 233.

[27] BENTLEY, ERIC, *The Playwright as Thinker*, New York, 1946, pp. 233–37.

mentioned: the portrayal of character by means of role-playing. This has become a favourite device since Pirandello used it to contrast illusion with reality, or illusion with illusion. But Sartre uses the idea of the role to contrast authentic and inauthentic behaviour. Goetz, in *Le Diable et le Bon Dieu,* attempting to play the role of a good man, is forced to behave hypocritically, to pretend he has received the stigmata. Only when he abandons the idea of acting a precise role can he achieve authentic behaviour.[28]

Examples of Sartre's skill with dialogue and character can be found in every one of his plays and it is interesting to see that the most compelling dramatic dialogue often depends for much of its effect on the use of imagery. We have seen how Sartre places his characters 'en situation' by creating concrete situations through the plays' settings. Imagery is often exploited in what amounts to a similarly concrete fashion in order to convey a character's mental state. The use of similar imagery in the novels and essays should not disguise the fact that it is often highly dramatic or even borrowed from the language of play-acting. In the passage quoted from *Les Mains Sales* the image is precisely one of play-acting: 'le jeu'. Similarly the contrasting images of the density of authentic Being and the formlessness of contingency are well exploited in the dramatic opposition of the solidity of Hoederer and the indecisiveness of Hugo in the same play. Hugo cannot, until the end, feel as if he has any weight: 'Bon Dieu, quand on va tuer un homme, on devrait se sentir lourd comme une pierre.' (God, when you are going to kill a man, you should feel stony-solid.) He contrasts himself with Hoederer: 'As-tu vu comme il est dense? Comme il est vivant?'[29] (Have you seen

[28] Since this article first went to press, a study of Sartre's theatre has appeared which investigates his use of role-playing in some detail: Dorothy McCall, *The Theatre of Jean-Paul Sartre,* New York, 1969.

[29] *Les Mains Sales,* p. 120.

how solid he is, how full of life?) And he handles the coffee-pot saying that it looks real when Hoederer touches it. Just as Garcin said he had always lived in 'des situations fausses', so Hugo exclaims 'je vis dans un décor',[30] (I live in a stage set) and both constantly feel the need of a mirror to ensure them of their own objective existence.

Sartre thus emerges as a skilful and very entertaining master of the stage who has found the theatre particularly suitable for the elaboration of a philosophy which is itself profoundly theatrical. This is a very different perspective from the one often taken of his plays as mere illustrations of a predetermined philosophic theory. In fact this latter approach probably arose from the difficulty contemporary reviewers found in knowing how to interpret Sartre's plays. The most unfairly judged of all was *Les Mouches* whose first production seems to have been obscured by political considerations and which was too new for its audience, who did not know how to approach it. R. J. North quotes Marcel's comment that 'the members of the audience were unable to relate Sartre's concept of liberty to their own experience'.[31] Maybe this was because Sartre, so far from illustrating theory, was in fact elaborating it as he wrote the play. Victor Brombert quotes Sartre as saying that he evolved the concept of liberty in *Les Mouches while* writing the play.[32] By the late 'forties, *L'Être et le Néant* was becoming more widely known, *L'Existentialisme est un Humanisme* (*Existentialism and Humanism*) had been published in 1946 and the reading public, which was becoming more aware of Sartre's general outlook, naturally began to interpret the plays in the light of

[30] Ibid., p. 132.

[31] NORTH, ROBERT J., Introduction to *Les Mouches*, London, 1963, p. 49.

[32] BROMBERT, VICTOR, 'Sartre and the Drama of Ensnarement', in *Ideas in the Drama*, ed. John Gassner, New York, 1964, p. 170.

the philosophy. Armed with this guide, they flocked to his long-running productions in a spirit of great seriousness. They were conscious of following the latest developments of the Existentialist movement and the papers brought this out by derisively likening the movement to a religion, calling Sartre the Pope of Existentialism.

When Press reaction to Sartre's plays was not hostile because of incomprehension, it was often hostile for political reasons. For example, the first production of *Les Mains Sales* was disappointing to Sartre since the Press chose to see it as anti-communist. He had tried to forestall partisan political reactions in the interviews he gave before the opening. In one of these he said:

> Je pose le problème de la fin et des moyens . . . je ne prends pas parti. Une bonne pièce de théâtre doit poser les problèmes et non les résoudre. Dans la tragédie grecque, tous les personnages ont raison et tous ont tort: c'est pour cela qu'ils se massacrent et que leur mort atteint à la grandeur tragique.[33]

> I raise the problem of ends and means . . . I do not take sides. A good play should raise problems, not solve them. In Greek tragedy all the characters are right and yet all are wrong, which is why they massacre each other and their deaths reach the proportions of tragic greatness.

But despite this, more ink was spilled on deciding whether it was pro- or anti-communist than on the question of its value as a play.

In this sort of way the topical aspects of the plays were seized on and their dramatic value ignored. But it is interesting to see that most of them were not produced as intellectual pieces with a restricted appeal. Rather, they were put on as commercial ventures in the normal way, and in most cases paid off hand-

---

[33] *Combat,* 31st March 1948.

somely. *Morts sans Sépulture*, *La Putain Respectueuse*, *Les Mains Sales*, *Le Diable et le Bon Dieu* and *Nekras-sov* were all produced at the Théâtre Antoine, some-thing of a stronghold of boulevard comedy, and were often performed by actors who had made their names in boulevard theatre. André Luguet and François Périer were well known for this kind of acting when they took part in the first production of *Les Mains Sales*.

Thanks to Sartre's use of humour, sex, murder, in-trigue, suspense, and his integration of these elements of popular entertainment into a serious discussion of ideas, the plays were successful.[34] And this success is a pointer to the fact that, so far from being a mere illustration of ideas properly belonging to philosophy, the plays show a rich handling of the dramatic vocabu-lary; so much so that the wrong treatment can plunge them into melodrama. According to Simone de Beau-voir's amusing account, this is exactly what happened to the New York production of *Les Mains Sales* (under the title of *Red Gloves*).[35]

Fourteen years after 'Forgers of Myths', Sartre made the following statement, which shows his unequivo-cable belief in the impossibility of separating philos-ophy and drama:

Today, I think that philosophy is dramatic. It is no longer a question of contemplating the immobility of

[34] Sartre's interest in popular forms of entertainment can be seen from the accounts of his visits to the cinema in *Les Mots* and from Simone de Beauvoir's remark that while he was do-ing national service, 'Sartre was continually asking me for "funny third-rate novels".' (*La Force de l'Age*, Paris, 1960, p. 51; translated by Peter Green as *The Prime of Life*, Penguin, 1965.) And also: 'we devoured large numbers of detective stories which were becoming popular at that time'. (Ibid., p. 53.)

[35] BEAUVOIR, SIMONE DE, *La Force des Choses*, Paris, 1963, p. 186; translated by Richard Howard as *Force of Circum-stance*, Penguin, 1968.

substances which are what they are, nor of finding rules for a succession of phenomena. It is a question of man—who is both an *agent* and an *actor*—who creates and plays his drama, living the contradiction of his situation to the point of breaking himself apart or solving his conflicts. A play (whether epic, like the work of Brecht, or dramatic) is today the most appropriate form to show man in *action*—that is, simply, man.[36]

[36] Quoted by D. McCall, op. cit., p. viii.

# THE EXISTENTIALIST REDISCOVERY
# OF HEGEL AND MARX

## George L. Kline

I

### Introduction

The relation between phenomenology of the Brentano-Husserl type and existential philosophy of the Kierkegaard-Heidegger type is often held to be intimate and fruitful. Jean-Paul Sartre and Maurice Merleau-Ponty attempted to combine, and sometimes claimed to have succeeded in combining, the two tendencies. But the union was never perfect: Sartre remained a "phenomenologizing existentialist,"[1] Merleau-Ponty an "existentializing phenomenologist."

George L. Kline's essay from *Phenomenology and Existentialism*, E. N. Lee and M. Mandelbaum (eds.), The Johns Hopkins Press, Baltimore; reprinted by permission of the author and The Johns Hopkins Press. Copyright © by The Johns Hopkins Press.

[1] From the beginning—in his essay "The Transcendence of the Ego," written in 1934 and published in 1936—Sartre was a "revisionist" Husserlian, rejecting the substantial self of Husserl's "egology" and the semi-Platonic essences of his *Wesensschau*. But Natanson overstates the contrast between Sartre and Husserl when he insists that Sartre's method "deserves the name 'phenomenological' only in so far as Hegel's phenomenology is intended, . . . it is quasi-phenomenological if we are referring to Husserl's variety of phenomenology" (Maurice Natanson, *A Critique of Jean-Paul Sartre's Ontology* [Lincoln, Neb.: 1951], p. 74; compare also p. 99). Mrs. Warnock seems to me to put the matter more equably, if more vaguely, when she says simply that "Sartre owes far more to Hegel than to Husserl" (Mary Warnock, *The Philosophy of Sartre* [London: 1965], p. 70).

From a sufficiently Olympian perspective, phenomenology and existential philosophy at mid-twentieth century often appear to support each other—in Peirce's earthy phrase—"like two drunken sailors," i.e., sincerely and warmly, but ineffectively.

The relationship between the two remains delicate and controversial. I shall not attempt to throw fresh light on it, except incidentally. My concern is mainly with existential philosophy of the Sartrean type. I shall refer less often to "phenomenology" than to "*the* Phenomenology," meaning, of course, Hegel's *Phänomenologie des Geistes—Phenomenology of Mind* or *Spirit*—of 1807. I focus upon Sartre rather than upon Heidegger or Jaspers, because it was Sartre (and to a lesser extent Merleau-Ponty) who brought Hegel and early Marx into the mainstream of twentieth-century existentialism.

## II

### Hegel Rediscovered

The "rediscovery" of Hegel and Marx to which my title refers took place in Paris during the 1930's and 1940's. The French existentialists were highly selective in their appropriation of Hegelian and Marxist thought; indeed, their rediscovery verged on "intellectual re-creation," if not *creatio ex nihilo intellectualis!* In Sartre, for example, stress fell on specific themes drawn from specific works of specific periods in both Hegel and Marx. Sartre took over not only ideas that were there to be taken, but also at least a few ideas that were *not* there, or at least were not intended by their authors to be taken in the way that Sartre took them.

With minor exceptions, Hegel, for Sartre, meant *early* Hegel (through 1807) and above all the *Phenomenology*. The *Phenomenology* in turn meant two major themes: (a) the struggle for recognition among selves, and the master-slave dialectic; (b) alienation, including self-alienation; and two minor themes: (c) the "unhappy consciousness" and (d) "the death of God."

I shall sketch the historical background of (1) the rediscovery of Hegel, (2) the rediscovery of the *Phenomenology*, and (3) the rediscovery of the two major and two minor themes.

1. Until early in the twentieth century, Hegel's thought was doubly eclipsed: in the middle of the nineteenth century by French positivism and toward the end of that century by neo-Kantianism and, to a lesser extent, the half-positivist, half-Kantian "empiriocriticism" of Mach and Avenarius. The movement "back to Kant" of the 1880's and 1890's was intended as a short-circuiting of Hegel himself as well as of post- and anti-Hegelian positivism.

The "rediscovery" of Hegel coincided with the discovery and publication of the long-lost early works. These works were quoted and discussed at length in Dilthey's commentary of 1905,[2] and mentioned in Croce's more general and critical commentary of 1906 (published on the seventy-fifth anniversary of Hegel's death).[3] The works themselves were published by Nohl in 1907 under the title *Theologische Jugendschriften* (Early Theological Writings). The title is misleading because many of the early works are nontheological, and some of them are antitheological.

However, this Hegel revival was not yet a rediscov-

[2] Wilhelm Dilthey, *Die Jugendgeschichte Hegels* (Berlin: 1905); reprinted in Dilthey, *Gesammelte Schriften,* Vol. IV (Leipzig and Berlin: 1921). Dilthey does not discuss the *Phenomenology*.

[3] Benedetto Croce, *Ciò che è vivo e ciò che è morto della filosofia di Hegel: Studio critico seguito da un saggio di bibliografia hegeliana* (Bari: 1906). German translation by K. Büchler: *Lebendiges und Totes in Hegels Philosophie* (Heidelberg: 1909). Croce makes only brief and perfunctory references to the *Phenomenology*.

ery of the *Phenomenology*, even though the early works pointed toward it.

2. In both the mid-nineteenth century and the early twentieth century, the *Phenomenology* was generally eclipsed by Hegel's later works—especially the *Science of Logic* and the *Encyclopedia of Philosophical Sciences*. The *Phenomenology* was scarcely mentioned by serious commentators. (It had been taken very seriously indeed by the young Marx and by such neo-Hegelians as Cieszkowski,[4] but Marx's early works remained unpublished, and Cieszkowski was virtually unknown.) A partial exception was provided by the Russians, and this—curiously enough—may have a bearing on the French existentialist rediscovery of the *Phenomenology*. Alexander Herzen, in 1842, wrote of it (in a private letter not published until much later):

> Toward the end of the book it is as though you were plunging into the sea: profundity, transparency, the breath of *Geist* bears you along . . . *lasciate ogni speranza*—the shores disappear; salvation resides only in your own breast. And then a voice is heard: *Quid timeas? Caesarem vehis.* Fear dissolves, the shore appears; the fair leaves of fantasy are stripped away, but the sap-filled fruits of reality [*deistvitelnost = Wirklichkeit*] remain. The mermaids have vanished, but a full-breasted maiden waits for you. . . . Such was my impression. I read to the end with heart pounding, with a kind of solemnity. Hegel is Homer and Shakespeare together, and that is why respectable people find his Anglo-Greek dialect incomprehensible.[5]

[4] August von Cieszkowski, *Prolegomena zur Historiosophie* (Berlin: 1838).

[5] Letter to A. A. Krayevski, written in Novgorod, February 3, 1842. In A. I. Herzen (Gertsen), *Sobraniye sochinenii* (Collected Works), XX (Moscow: 1961), 128.

Similarly appreciative if less lyrical comments were made by the Russian Slavophiles, especially Ivan Kireyevsky and Alexis Khomyakov, during the late 1840's and early 1850's. By the 1850's Herzen himself was calling the Hegelian dialectic (as exhibited in the *Phenomenology*) an "algebra of revolution."[6] In 1892, in a substantial and sympathetic article on Hegel in the standard Russian encyclopedia of the period, Vladimir Solovyov referred to the *Phenomenology* as Hegel's "best work."[7] One of the first translations of the *Phenomenology* into a foreign language was the Russian version edited by Radlov in 1913. (Baillie's English translation had appeared in 1910.) Another and much better Russian version, by Gustav Shpet, was published posthumously in Moscow in 1959 as Volume IV of Hegel's *Sochineniya*. It is one of the best translations to date in *any* language.

The first serious twentieth-century European study devoted mainly to Hegel's *Phenomenology* was Jean Wahl's *Le Malheur de la conscience dans la philosophie de Hegel* (Paris, 1929). Here again there appears to be an underground link with non-French sources. Josiah Royce's posthumous *Lectures on Modern Idealism* (edited by his student, Jacob Loewenberg) had appeared in 1919 and included three chapters—over seventy-five pages—on the *Phenomenology* (pp. 136–212). Wahl, unlike most French philosophers of the interwar period, knew English well, had studied Royce, and had published a book on English and American philosophy in 1920.[8] Wahl's 1929 study of the "unhappy consciousness" lists Royce's *Lectures on*

[6] A. I. Herzen, "Byloye i dumy," Part IV, chap. xxv, *op. cit.* (Moscow: 1956), IX, 23. Compare *My Past and Thoughts: The Memoirs of Alexander Herzen*, trans. Constance Garnett, II (London: 1924), 121.

[7] V. S. Solovyov, "Gegel," *Entsiklopedicheskii Slovar Brokgaus-Yefron*, Vol. VIII (i.e., XV), 1892, p. 218.

[8] *Les Philosophies pluralistes d'Angleterre et d'Amérique* (Paris: 1920).

*Modern Idealism* in the bibliography (p. 202), quotes Royce twice, and refers to Roycean interpretations of Hegel several times.[9]

Of course by 1929 Wahl had also read Heidegger's *Sein und Zeit* (1927). But it should be emphasized that Hegel's *Phenomenology* is scarcely mentioned in Heidegger's long book. To be precise, it is cited twice; both references are to the final chapter, on "Absolute Knowledge," and have to do with Hegel's views of time. And these references are overshadowed in Heidegger's work by numerous references to Hegel's *Logic* and *Encyclopedia*.

Another stimulus to interest in Hegel generally and the *Phenomenology* in particular, for Sartre and Merleau-Ponty as well as for Kojève himself, was the special Hegel centennial issue of the *Revue de Métaphysique et de Morale* published in 1931. It was a large issue (233 pages) and an impressive one, with contributions by Croce, Nicolai Hartmann, and Charles Andler, among others.[10] Andler's article, which is devoted to the *Phenomenology*, discusses the impor-

[9] The quotations appear on pp. 34, n. 1, and 73, the references on pp. 74, n. 2; 96, n. 2; 113, n. 2; 152, n. 1. Royce's *Spirit of Modern Philosophy* (1892), pp. 190–227 of which are devoted to Hegel, is also listed in Wahl's bibliography.

[10] The contents of this issue are as follows: Benedetto Croce, "Un cercle vicieux dans la critique de la philosophie hégélienne," pp. 277–84; Nicolai Hartmann, "Hegel et le problème de la dialectique du réel," pp. 285–316; Charles Andler, "Le fondement du savoir dans la 'Phénoménologie de l'esprit' de Hegel," pp. 317–40; Victor Basch, "Des origines et des fondements de l'esthétique de Hegel," p. 341–66; René Berthelot, "Goethe et Hegel," pp. 367–412; M. Gueroult, "Le jugement de Hegel sur l'antithétique de la raison pure," pp. 413–39; Edmond Vermeil, "La pensée politique de Hegel," pp. 441–510. The possible significance of this special issue of the leading French philosophical journal of the period for Sartre's rediscovery of Hegel is noted by Klaus Hartmann in his *Grundzüge der Ontologie Sartres in ihrem Verhältnis zu Hegels Logik* (Berlin: 1963), p. 3.

tance of "the negative"[11] but makes no reference to alienation, the master-slave dialectic, or the unhappy consciousness.

However, Nicolai Hartmann's article,[12] although it refers to the *Phenomenology* only in passing, makes two significant points about it and a further relevant point about the *Logic*. First, Hartmann calls the *Phenomenology* Hegel's "first masterpiece" and says that it remains "a fundamental work";[13] second, he speaks of the "famous dialectic of master and servant" and devotes an extended passage to explicating it.[14] Presumably he called this dialectic "famous" or "well-known" in 1931—before the publication of Marx's Paris Manuscripts of 1844—on the basis of three serious earlier discussions: (a) that of Jean Wahl (1929), not referred to by Hartmann himself; (b) that of Richard Kroner, in Volume II of *Von Kant bis Hegel* (1924), which Hartmann refers to in the Preface to (c) Volume II of his own book, *Die Philosophie des deutschen Idealismus*, 1929, a long section of which (ch. 2: pp. 295–362) is devoted to the *Phenomenology*. This chapter includes several pages on the struggle for recognition among selves and the master-slave dialectic (pp. 332–35). The exposition is lucid and sympathetic; there are many quotations from Hegel's text. Hartmann makes clear his admiration for the master-

[11] Charles Andler, "Le fondement du savoir . . . ," *Revue de Métaphysique et de Morale*, XXXVIII (1931), 319f.

[12] The article was written in German and translated into French by R.-L. Klee. The German original, entitled "Hegel und das Problem der Realdialektik," was subsequently published in *Blätter für deutsche Philosophie*, 1935, and reprinted in Vol. II of Hartmann's *Kleinere Schriften* (Berlin: 1957), pp. 323–46.

[13] Nicolai Hartmann, "Hegel et le problème . . . ," *Revue de Métaphysique et de Morale*, p. 288.

[14] *Ibid.*, pp. 308f. The French phrase—"la dialectique fameuse du maître et du serviteur"—is stronger than the original, which speaks only of "die bekannte Dialektik von 'Herr und Knecht'" (cf. *Kleinere Schriften*, II, 340).

slave dialectic, calling it "one of the finest things in the *Phenomenology*," concise and "plastic" in form, highly significant in content. He finds it the best example in Hegel of a dialectic that inheres in the subject matter itself.[15] Hartmann in 1929 also anticipated Kojève's lectures of 1933–39—and Marx's rediscovered Paris Manuscripts to be published in 1932—when he noted the "revolutionizing principle" in the master-slave relation, pointing out that the slave's work affects not only the *thing* worked on but the *man* who does the working, that the slave cannot shape (*bilden*) things without shaping himself. "This," Hartmann concludes, "may be regarded as the universal foundation for a philosophy of work."[16]

Finally, to round out the possible contribution that Nicolai Hartmann may have made to the existentialist rediscovery of Hegel, we note that he—or rather his French translator—uses the exact phrase that Sartre was to adopt as the title of his major philosophical work: he refers to the dialectic of "L'Être et le Néant" at the beginning of Hegel's *Logic*.[17]

Alexandre Kojève was not only Russian-born; he had written a dissertation on Solovyov, stressing the latter's philosophy of history, a study which would surely have brought him into contact with Hegel in general and the *Phenomenology* in particular. Kojève was the first scholar in France to comment on the *Phenomenology* in detail—in a suggestive, often brilliant, sometimes eccentric, even perverse, study that has not yet found an equal in any language. This commentary was given to the public in lectures at the École des Hautes Études in Paris annually between 1933 and 1939 and distributed in mimeographed form

---

[15] Nicolai Hartmann, *Die Philosophie des deutschen Idealismus*, II, 1929; cited from the 1960 Berlin edition, two volumes in one, p. 333.

[16] *Ibid.*, p. 335.

[17] *Revue de Métaphysique et de Morale*, XXXVIII (1931), 311.

during those years, although not published until 1947.
Sartre and Merleau-Ponty attended some of Kojève's
lectures[18] and doubtless read the mimeographed versions of those that they did not attend. It seems safe
to assume that these lectures were the main direct
source for the impact of Hegel's *Phenomenology* upon
French existentialist thinkers during the 1930's. Kojève, in turn, was stimulated by Russian, German, and
French sources. The Russian sources were his study of
Solovyov and perhaps the Russian translation of the
*Phenomenology;*[19] the German sources were doubtless those mentioned above—the commentaries of Nicolai Hartmann and, perhaps, Richard Kroner; the
French sources included Jean Wahl's 1929 study of the
unhappy consciousness and perhaps also Andler's 1931
article on the *Phenomenology* in the *Revue de Métaphysique et de Morale.*

During the late 1930's Jean Hyppolite, under Kojève's influence, began to publish articles on Hegel
and the *Phenomenology.* His translation of the latter
appeared in two volumes in 1939 and 1941; his detailed commentary followed in 1946.[20] Hyppolite's com-

[18] See Wilfrid Desan, *The Marxism of Jean-Paul Sartre* (Anchor Book edition; New York: 1966), p. 24. According to Desan,
Hyppolite also attended Kojève's lectures. Desan erroneously
dates the first lecture series in 1936; it was given in 1933.

[19] Another possible Russian stimulus to Kojève's interest in
Hegel is I. A. Ilyin's *Filosofiya Gegelya, kak ucheinye o
konkretnosti Boga i cheloveka* [Hegel's Philosophy as a Theory
of the Concreteness of God and Man] (2 vols.; Moscow:
1918). Abridged German translation: Iwan Iljin, *Die Philosophie Hegels als kontemplative Gotteslehre* (Bern: 1946).

[20] Jean Hyppolite, *Genèse et structure de la Phénoménologie
de l'Esprit de Hegel* (Paris: 1946). The need for a full-scale
scholarly commentary on the *Phenomenology* was noted by
Georg Lasson as early as 1907, in the preface to his centennial
edition: "Gewiss ist ein ausführlicher Kommentar zur Phänomenologie ein wissenschaftliches Bedürfnis" (G. W. F. Hegel,
*Phänomenologie des Geistes,* Jubiläumsausgabe [Leipzig: 1907],
p. xv). In 1924 Richard Kroner repeated the point with greater

mentary, which remains the most careful and useful in any language, draws freely on both Wahl and Kojève and is, in a broad sense, "existentialist" in its orientation.

3. As we have already noted, Heidegger in *Sein und Zeit* makes no reference to the master-slave dialectic, to alienation (in Hegel), to the unhappy consciousness, or to the "death of God."

It seems fair to assume that Sartre and Merleau-Ponty derived their interest in these themes from other sources. The sources, in fact, are fairly obvious: (a) Wahl's 1929 study;[21] (b) Kojève's lectures of 1933–39; (c) the rediscovery of Hegel by such Marxists as Lukács (especially in his controversial and subsequently disavowed work, *Geschichte und Klassenbewusstsein*, 1923); (d) Sartre's and Merleau-Ponty's direct study of Marx's 1844 *Economic and Philosophic Manuscripts*—the "Dead Sea Scrolls of Marxism," as Lewis Feuer has called them. Mention of these last two sources brings us to the existentialist rediscovery of *Marx*.

## III

### *Young Marx Rediscovered*

In the case of Marx there was no need, as there had been with Hegel, for near-total rediscovery. All of

---

emphasis: "Ein Kommentar zur Phänomenologie ist eine heute dringend geforderte Aufgabe, die . . . nur in einem selbständigen Buche gelöst werden kann" (*Von Kant bis Hegel* [Tübingen: 1924], II, 382n). Kojève and Hyppolite between them have supplied a more useful and comprehensive commentary than any of the numerous German scholars who have written on Hegel's philosophy.

[21] Wahl discusses the theme of "the death of God" at some length, with reference to Hegel rather than Nietzsche. The first two chapters in Pt. II of his book are entitled, respectively, "La mort de Dieu" and "La double signification de la mort de Dieu" (*Le Malheur de la conscience,* pp. 69–91).

Marx's works from the *Manifesto* of 1848 on had been readily available since their publication and widely influential at least since the 1880's. Most of Marx's mature works had been translated into French, although thinkers like Sartre and Merleau-Ponty, to say nothing of Wahl, Hyppolite, and Kojève, did not need translations, being entirely at home in German. The "mature" Marx of 1848–83, like the "mature" Engels of 1848–95, had no appeal for existentialists in either Germany or France.[22] *Sein und Zeit* makes no reference at all to Marx. It is doubtful that any existentialist work published before 1932 showed sympathy for, or interest in, Marx's thought. The earliest works to show such sympathy are from the pen of another Paris-based Russian émigré—Nicolas Berdyaev, who as a young man in Kiev and St. Petersburg had flirted briefly with a "Kantian" revision of Marxism and who later, in works, published in Russian in Paris during the 1930's and quickly translated into the major Western languages, including French, embraced the young Marx as a congenial critic of both alienation and objectification. (On the second point, Berdyaev, like Sartre later, misinterpreted Marx, who in fact attacked alienation but defended objectification [*Vergegenständlichung*].)

During the years of the Nazi occupation of Paris, and perhaps earlier, Sartre turned to a serious study of Marx's Paris Manuscripts of 1844.[23] He was drawn

---

[22] In his postexistentialist treatise of 1960, *Critique de la raison dialectique,* Sartre enthusiastically appropriates both Engels and "mature" Marx, stopping short only of the Engelsian universalization of the dialectic to include all of (nonhuman and nonhistorical) nature. Here, as Mrs. Warnock remarks, "it is the fully grown Marx-Engels doctrine of dialectical materialism which has taken over—the very doctrine which, in 1946 [i.e., in the essay, "Materialism and Revolution"] Sartre claimed to find actually [self-] contradictory" (*op. cit.,* p. 156; compare p. 164).

[23] Sartre has told us something about his early encounters with Marx's writings, especially the *German Ideology* and

to them for a variety of reasons: by a general sympathy with Communism, hence with Marxism; by the Hegelian "young-Marx" Marxism of Kojève's lectures; possibly by some of Berdyaev's writings of the 1930's; probably by his study of early Lukács, which in turn was stimulated by Lukács' Rumanian-born disciple, Lucien Goldmann, who had settled in Paris and whom Sartre knew well. Sartre was responsive to the echoes of Hegel's *Phenomenology* in the young Marx, especially the stress on the master-slave dialectic (reformulated by Marx as the dialectic of non-worker and worker) and the theory of alienation and self-alienation. In turn, Sartre was led by his study of Marx (and by Lukács and Kojève) to look more closely and "existentially" at Hegel's own formulations of these themes.

## IV

### Hegel and Marx Existentialized

I suppose that everyone is entitled to his own Hegel and his own Marx. But Sartre's philosophical appropriation and "possession" of both Marx and Hegel are quite extraordinary. Following the lead of Lukács, he Hegelianizes Marx (interestingly enough, Lukács had done this in 1923, nine years before the Paris Manuscripts were published—although there have been rumors that he had access to some of them prior to their publication). Following the lead of Kojève, he Marxianizes Hegel, although in *Being and Nothingness* (1943) he does this less drastically and systematically than Kojève. What Sartre does to both Marx and Hegel,

---

*Kapital.* Since he took them as theoretical statements rather than as incentives to revolutionary *praxis,* he claims to have missed their main point. Compare *Critique de la raison dialectique* (Paris: 1960), pp. 22f. Partial English translation by Hazel Barnes: *Search for a Method* (New York: 1963), pp. 17f. (Hereafter references to the *Critique* will be given as *CRD* with page number.)

and to his own "vintage" existentialism (the vintage
year being 1943), in the huge and difficult first volume
of his *Critique de la raison dialectique* (1960) is a
question to which I shall recur briefly in Section VI.

*Being and Nothingness,* as Marcuse has said, "is in
large parts [sic] a restatement of Hegel's *Phenomenology of Mind* and Heidegger's *Sein und Zeit.*"[24] *Being
and Nothingness* is closer to the *Phenomenology* than
to *Being and Time.*[25] The two books are of about the
same length; both aim at unusual comprehensiveness;
both include much material of a kind not usually
found in philosophical works of their respective periods. Perhaps most striking is the inclusion in both of
historical as well as literary materials: Sartre follows
Hegel in discussing the French Revolution of 1789
and in making several excursions into ancient history.
He rivals Hegel in the number of writers whom he
discusses at some length.[26]

[24] Herbert Marcuse, "Existentialism: Remarks on Jean-Paul
Sartre's *L'Être et le Néant," Philosophy and Phenomenological
Research,* VIII (1947–48), 311.

[25] By a curious coincidence, Heidegger and Sartre were exactly the same age (thirty-eight) when they published their
respective *opera magna.* Hegel was a year younger when he
published the *Phenomenology.*

[26] The *Phenomenology* includes discussions—sometimes without explicit identification of the author in question—of Homer,
Sophocles, Shakespeare, Cervantes, Rousseau, Diderot, Goethe,
and Schiller; *Being and Nothingness* includes discussions of
Sophocles, Rousseau, Balzac, Flaubert, Dostoyevsky, Kafka,
Gide, and Faulkner. This common concern with literary expression of "forms of consciousness" is related to the assumption,
noted by Wahl (with special, but not exclusive, reference to
stoicism, skepticism, and the unhappy consciousness): ". . .
ce que Hegel considère dans la *Phénoménologie,* ce ne sont
pas des philosophies mais des façons de vivre; ou plutôt les
deux ne sont pas séparés" (Wahl, *op. cit.,* p. 7). But the
*Phenomenology* is much more than cultural history plus philosophical anthropology. It also deals—as does Heidegger's *Sein
und Zeit*—with the traditional problems of being, certainty,
truth, law, the order of nature, etc., none of which seems to

*Being and Nothingness,* like the *Phenomenology,*
sets forth "forms or shapes of human consciousness"
(*Gestalten des Bewusstseins*). Indeed one might consider Sartre's detailed analysis of *mauvaise foi*—bad
faith or self-and-other deception—as an attempt to add
a new "form of consciousness" to the Hegelian gal-
axy.[27] The same might be said of the Sartrean treatment of sadism in interpersonal relations—a theme not
touched upon by Hegel. In *Being and Nothingness,*
as in the *Phenomenology,* such *Gestalten* as *mauvaise foi,* "the unhappy consciousness," (*das un-
glückliche Bewusstsein*), and "spirit alienated from
itself" (*der sich entfremdete Geist*) are personified,
acquiring almost mythological status.[28] In both cases
the result is impressive. "Sartre's great inexact equations," as Iris Murdoch has put it, "like those of his
master Hegel, inspire us to reflect."[29]

In *Being and Nothingness* Sartre's basic categories
are Hegelian; they are taken mainly from the *Phenomenology,* with important supplementation from the
*Logic:* for-itself and in-itself, consciousness and self-
consciousness, being and nothingness.[30] Sartre's funda-

---

have interested Sartre in 1943. Compare the comments by
William Barrett in *Irrational Man* (New York: 1958) pp. 221f.

[27] Klaus Hartmann has suggested that Sartrean *mauvaise foi*
may be derived from that "shape of consciousness" which
Hegel in the *Phenomenology* calls *Verstellung* (dissemblance),
as well as from the Kierkegaardian concept of dread. (Compare K. Hartmann, *op. cit.,* p. 55.)

[28] *Ibid.,* pp. 55f.

[29] Iris Murdoch, *Sartre: Romantic Rationalist* (2d ed.; New
Haven, 1959 [first ed., 1953]), p. 114. Of course, Hegel's "inexact equations" are dynamic, his dialectic cumulative and
"progressive," whereas Sartre's "equations" are static, his
"dialectic" noncumulative and, in a sense, circular.

[30] Each of Sartre's key philosophical terms corresponds to a
Hegelian term. The terminological transposition of Hegel from
German into French had been substantially completed—by
Wahl, Kojève, and Hyppolite—when Sartre began his *magnum
opus.* Here is a partial list: *für sich = pour-soi; Fürsichsein =*

mental themes—negation as an ontological factor and the negativity of consciousness—are entirely Hegelian.[31]

However, the use to which Sartre puts his Hegelian categories is radically un- and even anti-Hegelian. His is a truncated dialectic, a dialectic without synthesis, without reconciliation, oddly reminiscent in this respect of the nihilistic dialectic of Bakunin and Lenin. For Hegel, the in-itself and the for-itself are *abstrakte Momente*,[32] that is, one-sided and partial phases of

---

*être-pour-soi; an sich = en-soi; Ansichsein = être-en-soi; anundfür sich = en-soi-pour-soi; An-und-fürsichsein = être-en-soi-pour-soi; Bewusstsein = conscience* (occasionally *Gewissen = conscience*—since the notoriously ambiguous French term *conscience* means both "consciousness" and "conscience"); *Selbstbewusstsein = conscience (de) soi* (the parenthetical "de" in Sartre's words, "ne répond qu'à une contrainte grammaticale" [*L'Être et le Néant* (Paris: 1943), p. 20; hereafter *EN*]; for the remaining 700 pages of the book, Sartre follows this grammatically unorthodox usage); *das Andere = l'autre; der Andere = autrui; aufheben = supprimer et sublimer; Aufhebung = suppression et sublimation; Sein = l'être; das Nichts = le néant.* Sartre occasionally introduces German terms directly into his French text, e.g., Husserl's *Abschattung*, Hegel's *selbständig, unselbständig, Selbständigkeit,* and *Unselbständigkeit.* As Joseph Fell has pointed out, Sartre follows Hegel in using *conscience (Bewusstsein)* and *conscience (de) soi (Selbstbewusstsein)* to designate not states but activities and even agents—as in the "struggle of self-consciousness." Compare Joseph P. Fell, III, *Emotion in the Thought of Sartre* (New York: 1965), p. 156. Of course, Sartre's exotic term *ek-stase,* used in the special sense of "a (futile) gesture of self-transcendence," derives, via Heidegger, from the Greek *ekstasis.*

[31] Compare *EN* 47–52, 511. *Being and Nothingness,* trans. Hazel Barnes (New York: 1956), pp. 12–16, 436. (Hereafter cited as *BN.*) See also K. Hartmann, *op. cit.,* p. 4.

[32] In Hegel *das Moment* (= phase or aspect of a cumulative dialectical process) is clearly distinguished from *der Moment* (= moment of time). In French *le moment* is used indiscriminately for both. English translators of Hegel and of Sartre have used 'moment' in the two different senses, without distinguishing them. *Das Moment* should be rendered either as "dialectical

a dialectical whole, which will be *aufgehoben*—canceled, preserved, and raised to a higher level—and thus reconciled in the concrete$_H$ synthesis of the "in-and-for-itself." For Sartre, the in-itself and the for-itself are irreconcilable; their opposition is unmediatable.[33] Similarly with self and other, and with being and nothingness.[34] In Hegel the self returns to itself out of otherness, including and reconciling the other within itself. For Sartre, self and other stand permanently hostile and unreconciled. His doctrine of the *néantisation* ("nothingizing" or nihilation) of the *en-soi* by the *pour-soi*, whatever sense one may make of it (see below), is certainly not a doctrine of dialectical reconciliation. The result is a distorted Hegelianism; it retains the harsh action of contradiction without the soothing balm of synthesis. And Sartre's is a deeply pessimistic view: every *ek-stase* must fail, every effort by an existing individual to become God, to conquer another's freedom, to assimilate the "massive, viscous, and sickening" *en-soi* is doomed to frustration.[35]

---

phase" or, more precisely if less elegantly, as 'moment$_H$'. Similarly with Hegel's special senses of 'abstract' and 'concrete'. In Hegelian usage 'abstract' means "one-sided," inadequately related, deficiently mediated"; 'concrete' means "many-sided, adequately related, complexly and fully mediated." Unfortunately, Sartre regularly confuses these senses ('abstract$_H$' and 'concrete$_H$') with the quite different Kierkegaardian and even Humean-empiricist senses ('abstract$_K$' and 'concrete$_K$'; 'abstract$_E$' and 'concrete$_E$'). Often he falls into an "ordinary-language" usage, according to which "concrete" means simply "specific" or "particular." For details see my article, "Some Recent Reinterpretations of Hegel's Philosophy," *The Monist*, XLVIII (1964), 40–44.

[33] See the perceptive article by Joseph P. Fell, III, "Sartre as Existentialist and Marxist," *Bucknell Review*, XIII, No. 3 (1965), pp. 63–74, esp. p. 68.

[34] In the dialectical movement of Hegel's *Logic*, being (*Sein*) and nothingness (*Nichts*) are *aufgehoben* in becoming (*Werden*).

[35] There is a kind of subdued and stoical Prometheanism

In general, the defective, destructive, or frustrating
aspects of human existence which in the *Phenomenology* are only *abstrakte Momente*—one-sided and
partial stages in the dialectical development of the human spirit, destined to be definitively *aufgehoben*
—are for Sartre permanent, uneliminable, and unmediatable features of *la condition humaine*. Thus, for
example, the "unhappy consciousness," which for
Hegel is a defective form of the religious consciousness,
is for Sartre an ultimate: "The being of human reality
is suffering. . . . Human reality therefore is by nature
an unhappy consciousness with no possibility of sur-
passing its unhappy state."[36] Similarly with the struggle of self against self, the striving to gain recognition
or respect (*Anerkennung*). This is a stage or mo-
ment$_H$ which gives way to the master-slave relation,
that in turn giving way to the stoic consciousness,
skepticism, the unhappy consciousness, etc. But for
Sartre, "Conflict is the original meaning of being-for-
others."[37] Rejecting Heidegger's category of *Mitsein*
(being-with), Sartre asserts: "The essence of the relations between consciousnesses is not the *mitsein;* it is

---

about the Sisyphus of Camus; Sartre's Sisyphian *pour-soi*, in
contrast, carries no touch of Prometheus. The postexistentialist
Prometheanism of Sartre's *Critique* is essentially Marxist-
Leninist.

[36] *BN* 90. "La réalité-humaine est souffrante dans son être.
. . . Elle est donc par nature conscience malheureuse, sans
dépassement possible de l'état de malheur" (*EN* 134). Wahl
makes Hegel sound, in anticipation, rather close to Sartre when
he writes: ". . . comme en chacun de ces aspects [of human
consciousness] il y a un conflit, on peut dire qu-*en chacun
d'eux nous trouverons cette conscience malheureuse* qui s'est
manifestée sans doute plus nettement à telle ou telle époque,
mais qui se renouvelle sous une forme ou sous une autre *à
toutes les époques de la vie de l'humanité*" (*op. cit.*, p. 94;
italics mine).

[37] *BN* 364. "Le conflit est le sens originel de l'être-pour-
autrui" (*EN* 431).

conflict."[38] In his philosophical play *No Exit*, the celebrated aphorism: "L'enfer c'est les autres" (Hell is
the others) makes the same un-Hegelian point.

Miss Murdoch puts this point vividly when she describes Sartrean "love" as "a battle between two hyp-
notists in a closed room," adding that "other people"
enter Sartre's solipsistic universe "one at a time, as the
petrifying gaze of the Medusa, or at best as the
imperfectly understood adversary in the fruitless conflict of love."[39]

Sartre *begins* with Hegel: each self-consciousness
seeks to be truly *pour-soi* by eliminating all competitors, by reducing each claimant to selfhood to the
status of a mere *en-soi*, a thing or object. But whether
in the short run it succeeds or fails in this attempt,
it must ultimately fail. If it fails in the short run, and
other selves remain as *pour-soi*, they pose a continuing threat to its selfhood. On the other hand, if it
succeeds in reducing all other selves to things (by
killing them), no self will be left to recognize or respect it.[40] Self-respect requires the respect of others
whom the self in turn respects as selves.

This impasse leads to the master-slave dialectic. I
shall not enter into its details, since Sartre—unlike
Kojève—is not interested in them. He is concerned
only to assert, with Hegel—but twisting Hegel's meaning by universalizing and eternalizing what for Hegel
was particular and transitory—that the relation of self
to self is marked by hostility, conflict, the attempt to
destroy and enslave.[41] Sartre agrees with Hegel that

[38] *BN* 429. "L'essence des rapports entre consciences n'est
pas le Mitsein, c'est le conflit" (*EN* 502).

[39] Murdoch, *op. cit.*, pp. 96, 72.

[40] Sartre sees a further, quite clearly neurotic, level of frustration: killing the rival self does not eliminate him completely,
for it fails to destroy his pastness, to make him "never to have
been." His memory remains to haunt and taunt the "victor."

[41] Compare, e.g., ". . . while I seek to enslave the Other,
the Other seeks to enslave me" (*BN* 364). (". . . pendant que
je cherche à asservir autrui, autrui cherche à m'asservir" [*EN*

the attempt to enslave must founder—but not quite
for Hegel's reasons. In Sartre the foundering is, in a
clear sense, nondialectical. In Hegel it is dialectical:
the master becomes other than himself, becomes his
own other, becomes nonmaster and ultimately slave
(of his slave). The slave in turn becomes master of
his master; and the point at which each becomes his
own "other" marks the transition to the new dialectical
phase (moment$_H$) of stoicism, in which the master-
slave distinction is *aufgehoben*.[42] The good stoic can
be indifferently either a master (e.g., Marcus Aure-
lius) or a slave (e.g., Epictetus), because he is not
seriously committed to either role. In the absence of
such a dialectical *Aufhebung* of the master-slave relation in stoicism, the slave's mastering of his master
would generate a "bad," i.e., merely reiterative, infinity.[43]

The question of the role of work in the master-
slave dialectic and in what Lukács and Kojève have
called—following Marx—the "emancipation of mankind" is a theme not pursued by Sartre in his existentialist writings. So I shall not pursue it here; it belongs
in the story of Marxist interpretations and misinterpretations of Hegel, including the "existentialist-
Marxist" interpretations and misinterpretations of Hegel in Sartre's *Critique de la raison dialectique,* to
which I shall return briefly in Section VI.

On another central point Sartre remains somewhat
closer to Hegel; yet he manages to twist the Hegelian
position into something that Hegel would surely have
repudiated. I think that Hegel would have welcomed

---

431].) At this point, too, Wahl appears to want to build a bridge
from Hegel to Sartre. He sees the tendency to "concevoir les
choses sous la catégorie 'domination et escalvage'" as a "trait
fondamental de la conscience humaine" (*op. cit.,* p. 126).

[42] This whole process is lucidly described by Wahl, *op. cit.,*
pp. 119f., 124.

[43] Cf. Jan van der Meulen, *Hegel: Die gebrochene Mitte*
(Hamburg: 1958), p. 305.

Sartre's stress on actuality—"whatever is is actual"[44] —and accepted his concomitant denial of possibility or potentiality as an ontological category. But I think that Hegel would *not* have accepted Sartre's replacement of possibility by "nothingness."

Sartre confuses nonactuality with nonbeing: possibilities are obviously not actual, therefore they are not.[45] Expressed positively, what is merely possible is nothing, a nothingness. For Aristotle's potency (*dynamis*), Sartre substitutes nothingness (*le néant*); for his actualization (*energeia*), nihilation or "nothingizing" (*néantisation*); and for the product or outcome of this process (*ergon*), the "negated" or "nothingized" (*négatité*). This bouquet of neologisms would, I suspect, have a fresher *parfum* in Latin: for *néant* read *nihil;* for *néantisation, nihilatio;* for *négatité, nihilatum.*

Sartre's curious doctrine derives from Heidegger ("Das Nichts nichtet," etc.) at least as much as from Hegel. It is reminiscent of Berdyaev's existentialist doctrine of freedom as rooted in the *Ungrund* or "void

[44] "Tout est en acte" (*EN* 12). Hazel Barnes mistranslates this sentence as "The act is everything" (*BN* xlvi). In this passage Sartre explicitly repudiates any "duality of potency and act" ("la dualité de la puissance et de l'acte"), insisting that "behind the act there is neither potency, nor 'hexis' . . ." (Derrière l'acte il n'y a ni puissance, ni 'exis'. . . ."). Mrs. Warnock comments: "Beings-in-themselves have no possibilities; or rather all their possibilities are realized at once at the moment of creation" (*op. cit.,* p. 62).

[45] I am not persuaded by James Edie's contention that "'pure potency' in the language of Aristotle can be translated into good English as 'nothingness'" (see his contribution to this volume, "Sartre as Phenomenologist and as Existential Psychoanalyst," n. 37). Pure potency or potentiality is nonactual, but it is not nonexistent—not a sheer nonbeing or nothingness. On this point, Kierkegaard, who prized free choice and decision at least as much as Sartre did, remained Aristotelian, analyzing free choice as the actualizing of one among a plurality of possibilities.

of non-being (in Greek *me-on*)." Human freedom, in Berdyaev's words, is "not ontal but meonic."[46] Sartre *may* have been familiar with Berdyaev's position, but his immediate sources were (a) Heidegger and (b) Hegel, as filtered through the Heideggerianizing Hegel-commentaries of Wahl and Kojève. Wahl had said that "for Hegel negativity, freedom, subjectivity, and the process of *Aufhebung* are united."[47] Kojève explicitly "existentialized" Hegel's remarks about the negativity of free human action: "Man," he declared, "is not a being who *is*; he is *nothingness* which *nothingizes* [or *nihilates*] by negating being. Now the negation of being is action." Kojève adds that negativity, as "pure nothingness," is "a real freedom which manifests itself in the form of action."[48]

---

[46] "Freedom," Berdyaev declares, "is rooted in not-being or nothingness" (*Dream and Reality*, trans. Katharine Lampert [New York: 1951], p. 213). The Russian text reads: "svoboda vkorenena v nebytiye ili v 'nichto'" (*Samopoznaniye: opyt filosofskoi avtobiografi* [Self-Knowledge: An Essay in Philosophical Autobiography], [Paris: 1949], p. 232).

[47] "Pour Hegel, négativité, liberté, subjectivité, processus de l'*Aufhebung* sont unis" (*op. cit.*, p. 95, n. 1).

[48] "L'Homme n'est pas un Etre qui *est*: il est *Néant* qui *néantit* par la négation de l'Etre. Or, la négation de l'Etre—c'est l'Action." Negativity, as "néant pur," is a "*liberté* réelle qui . . . se manifeste . . . en tant qu'*action*." (Alexandre Kojève, *Introduction à la lecture de Hegel: Leçons sur la Phénoménologie de l'Esprit professées de 1933 à 1939 à l'École des Hautes* Études [rénies et publées par Raymond Queenau; Paris: 1947], pp. 181, 493.) Kojève also speaks of action as being "négatrice du donné" (*ibid.*, p. 497). It may be worth noting that Kojève—like Nicolai Hartmann (see n. 17)—uses the exact phrase which Sartre was to make the title of his major work: "L'Être et le Néant" (*ibid.*, p. 493n). Kojève makes Hegel sound very much like Sartre when he writes: "Sur le plan 'phénoménologique' la Négativité n'est donc rien d'autre que la *Liberté* humaine. . . ." And again: "La liberté ne consiste pas dans un *choix* entre deux *données*: elle est la *négation* du donné . . ." (*ibid.*, p. 494). All of this, I submit,

Sartre's way of putting the point is even more paradoxical: "Freedom is precisely the nothingness which *is made-to-be* [literally "is be'd"] at the heart of man and which forces human-reality to *make itself* instead of *to be*."[49] Again: "The for-itself is defined ontologically as a *lack of being,* and possibility belongs to the for-itself as that which it lacks. . . . Freedom is the concrete mode of being of the lack of being."[50]

Sartre's position may be seen as a radicalization of Bergson's view (Sartre refers to Bergson more than a dozen times in *Being and Nothingness*): Bergson had denied the ontological status of possibilities as (timeless) structures of nonactuality, asserting that men create their own possibilities and subsequently actualize (some or all of) them.[51] Sartre appears to share

---

is much closer to French existentialism than it is to Hegel's own doctrine.

[49] *BN* 440. "La liberté, c'est précisément le néant qui *est été* au coeur de l'homme et qui contraint la réalité-humaine à *se faire,* au lieu *d'être*" (*EN* 516). Further on Sartre adds that "Freedom . . . is strictly identical with nihilation" (*BN* 567). ("La liberté . . . est rigoureusement assimilable à la néantisation" [*EN* 655].)

[50] *BN* 565. ". . . le pour-soi se décrit ontologiquement comme *manque d'être* et le possible appartient au pour-soi comme *ce qui lui manque.* . . . [La liberté] est le mode d'être concret du manque d'être" (*EN* 652). Sartre adds, punningly, that the possible "has the being of a lack and as a lack, it lacks being. The Possible is not, the possible is possibilized . . . : the possible determines in schematic outline a location in the nothingness . . ." (*BN* 102). (The possible "a l'être d'un manque et, comme manque, il manque d'être. Le Possible n'est pas, le possible se possibilise . . . ; il détermine par esquisse schématique un emplacement de néant . . ." [*EN* 147].)

[51] Bergson attacks those philosophers who consider "freedom a choice between possibles,—as if possibility was not created by freedom itself!" (Henri Bergson, *The Creative Mind,* trans. Mabelle L. Andison [New York: 1946], p. 123). (". . . par liberté un choix entre les possibles,—comme si la possibilité n'était pas créée par la liberté même!" [*La Pensée et le mouvant* (Paris: 1934), p. 132].) Compare Sartre's char-

Bergson's insensitivity to the *aporiai* generated by such a denial of the "objective" or "structural" character of possibility or potentiality. But it must be admitted that in this denial the two Frenchmen have eminent philosophical company—no less than that of Parmenides, Spinoza, and Hegel!

## V

### Alienation and Objectification

I shall not treat the topic of alienation, or the related subtopic of objectification, in detail; it is being treated separately in this volume.[52] I wish only to indicate briefly what Hegel meant by alienation (*Entfremdung* or *Entäusserung*) and by objectification (*Vergegenständlichung*), and the relation between the two; what, in turn, Marx meant by these terms and how he understood their relation; and, finally, what an existentialist like Sartre understands by the terms and their relation.

Hegel in the *Phenomenology* treats alienation in a section entitled "Der sich entfremdete Geist; die Bildung" ("Spirit Alienated from Itself; Culture—[or Education, Formation, "Shaping"]"). The phenomenological reference is not to *absoluter Geist* (Absolute Spirit) but rather to *daseiender Geist* (existing, finite spirit); the historical reference is to seventeenth-century France, a period of extreme cultural formalism, universalism, and sophistication.

Hegel asks how the individual can develop his "natural" powers and gifts, coming to be what he intrinsically and uniquely is. And he answers: by being *gebildet*, shaped and formed by culture—i.e., by acquiring a language, a *"formation littéraire,"* manners,

---

acterization of freedom as "a choice which creates for itself its own possibilities" (*BN* 566)—". . . un choix que se crée ses propres possibilités" (*EN* 654).

[52] See Albert William Levi, "Existentialism and the Alienation of Man," Essay Ten.

mores, etc. To actualize himself as a *particular* individual, a man must, paradoxically, take on *universal* forms. Moreover, these forms are not his creation, indeed are alien to him. Yet historical culture is a wholly human product. Thus men's own historical, collective creations stand massively over against, and alienated from, individual men.

In the Paris Manuscripts, Marx adds to this account of cultural alienation motifs from Hegel's own dialectic of work (taken from the much earlier master-slave stage of the *Phenomenology*); but he simplifies and distorts Hegel's account by omitting the cultural, literary, and linguistic dimensions of alienation, concentrating exclusively upon the economic, social, and —to a degree—psychological aspects of "alienated work" (*die entfremdete Arbeit*). Sartre's version is equally one-sided: it omits the cultural and literary dimensions of alienation, concentrating upon the psychological, and—to a degree—social aspects of "being for others."

As Mrs. Warnock has observed, Sartre's description of bad faith (as a sociopsychological phenomenon) partly echoes the description of alienation in early Marx.[53]

Marx had charged that Hegel confused alienation with objectification and, while praising Hegel's attempt to overcome human alienation, had rejected his parallel effort to overcome objectification.[54] For Marx, every significant action or production (*praxis*) must be an objectification, leaving its permanent, ex-

[53] Warnock, *op. cit.*, pp. 157f. In his "phenomenology of shame" Sartre interprets "the alienation of myself" as (the effect of) an "act of being-looked-at," the result of which is that "I cause myself to learn from outside what I must be" (*BN* 263, 290). (". . . l'aliénation de moi qu'est *l'être-regardé*. . . ."; "*je me fais prendre par mon dehors ce que je dois être*" [*EN* 321f., 350].)

[54] Sartre alludes to Marx's critique of Hegel on this point at *CRD* 20 (English translation: *Search for a Method*, p. 13).

ternal, objective mark on nature and history. Only under capitalism, with its private ownership of the means of production, is productive objectification an alienation. Beyond capitalism alienation will disappear, but objectification will remain as a necessary and permanent aspect of all production.

It should be stressed that existential inwardness, decision, passion—so long as they lack objective expression, so long as they remain unobjectified (*unvergegenständlicht*)—are of no interest or value in Marx's eyes. The process of objectification, the act of objectifying, is incomplete so long as it has not issued in an *objectificatum,* a thing objectified, a product, an *ergon,* in one of Aristotle's senses of that term, namely, the sense in which *ergon* is related to *energeia* as product to process of actualization—as what Hegel and early Marx called *Werk* is related to what they called *Verwirklichung.* For Marx *praxis* stands beyond existence (*hexis*) in virtue of its collective, historical, and objectifying action.

Thus, to Montaigne's question: "What have I done [i.e., made, objectified] today?" Sartre, but not Marx, can reply, with Montaigne, "What, have I not lived [i.e., existed]?" To exist, for Marx—even young Marx —is not enough. To be human, or rather to become human, one must make, must produce—which means that one must objectify, impose an enduring human shape on what is nonhuman.

In *Being and Nothingness* Sartre rejected the positive Marxist evaluation of objectification. (In the *Critique* he accepts it in a vulgarized form that equates objectification with "materialization." See Section VI.) To be sure, for Sartre objectification was never the *bête noire* that it was for Berdyaev, who saw in it a prime threat to freedom, creativity, and the "spirit." What is objectified, for Berdyaev, is alien, hostile, "intolerably banal." Still, Sartre would agree with Berdyaev's claim that "every outward action" is doomed to "tragic failure" because it necessarily involves objectification.[55] In Sartre, as in Berdyaev, the realm of the objectified is the realm of the given—of facticity, inertness, determination.

On Hegel's view, both alienation and objectification must and will be overcome through the dialectical movement of spirit; on Marx's view, alienation, but not objectification, should and will be overcome through the dialectical movement of history; for Sartre, neither alienation nor objectification can be overcome, which is another way of saying that every *ekstase* is doomed to failure and that, in consequence, man is a "useless passion."[56]

---

[55] Berdyaev, *Dream and Reality*, p. 39 (*Samopoznaniye*, p. 51).

[56] *BN* 615. (". . . nous nous perdons en vain; l'homme est une passion inutile" [*EN* 708].) James Edie has argued that *inutile* in this context means not "useless" but noninstrumental —the sense in which Baudelaire called a poem an *objet inutile* (compare Edie's contribution to this volume, n. 41). However, it seems clear from many passages in Sartre that *inutile* means "(necessarily) unsuccessful." A *passion inutile* is one that cannot attain its object. Christ's passion—the effort, through suffering, to become human: temporal, finite, etc.—succeeded; man's parallel passion—the effort, through suffering, to become divine: eternal, infinite, etc.—must fail, since the concept of a divine Being, an *ens causa sui*, is self-contradictory. See also Sartre's assertion that those who believe that they can reconcile or synthesize the *en-soi* and *pour-soi* are "condemned to despair," since "all human activities . . . tend to sacrifice man in order that the self-cause [i.e., God] may emerge and . . . all are on principle doomed to failure" (*BN* 627). (". . . ils sont condamnés au désespoir, car . . . les activités humaines . . . tendent toutes à sacrifier l'homme pour faire surgir la cause de soi et . . . toutes sont vouées par principe à l'échec" [*EN* 721].)

# VI

## Sartre as Marxist

Sartre's "radical conversion"[57] from existentialism to Marxism—a doctrine which he now calls "Knowledge" (*le Savoir*, always with a capital letter) and "the inescapable philosophy of our time"—is not strictly the concern of this paper. However, since I have been examining the relation of Sartre's existentialism to Hegel and Marx, and since the "conversion" might be described as a shift from the position of Husserl and Kierkegaard-Heidegger to that of Hegel and Marx-Engels, I shall comment briefly on the main doctrinal changes between *Being and Nothingness* (1943) and the *Critique de la raison dialectique*, I (1960).

Sartre has always been pro-Communist;[58] his conversion is not political but philosophical—a move from subjectivism to objectivism, from individualism to collectivism, from a theory of individual consciousness to a theory of sociohistorical *praxis*. Sartre has swung from one extreme to another; his new Marxist extreme is reductionist and often vulgarized. Despite a ponderous and complex terminology ("totalized totality" —*totalité totalisée*, the "practico-inert"—*le pratico-inerte*, "dialectic in [sociohistorical] situation"—*la*

---

[57] After graphically portraying the bitter struggle and frustration involved in all interpersonal relationships, Sartre adds enigmatically, "These considerations do not exclude the possibility of an ethics of deliverance and salvation. But this can be achieved only after a *radical conversion* which we cannot discuss here" (*BN* 412n; italics mine). ("Ces considérations n'excluent pas la possibilité d'une morale de la délivrance et du salut. Mais celle-ci doit être atteinte au terme d'une *conversion radicale* dont nous ne pouvons parler ici" [*EN* 484n; italics mine].)

[58] Iris Murdoch shrewdly notes that Sartre is "infected . . . with a certain Trotskyite romanticism, the nostalgia for the perpetual revolution" (*op. cit.*, p. 41).

*dialectique située,* etc.), his position comes close to old-fashioned materialism. The individual is no longer an agent, or *Dasein,* or *réalité-humaine,*[59] but an "organism"—an organism that suffers, runs risks, acts dialectically, "interiorizes" inorganic structures, "materializes itself," etc. Man is now a "material being" (*être matériel*), member of a "material group" (*ensemble matériel*) (*CRD* 166). The world is entirely material; "matter alone holds meanings" ("la matière seule compose les significations") (*CRD* 245).[60] Sartre expresses complete agreement with Marx's statement that the "ideal" (i.e., the "mental" and/or "conceptual") is nothing but the "material, inverted and translated in the human head."[61]

Marx himself was *not* an ontological materialist, as I have argued elsewhere; rather, he was an "economic objectivist," who often confused the terms and concepts 'economic' and 'material'. Sartre as a Marxist materialist comes close not to Marx himself, whether

---

[59] Robert Cumming considers *réalité-humaine* (a much-used term in *EN*) to be Sartre's rendering of Heidegger's *Dasein.* Compare Robert D. Cumming (ed.), *The Philosophy of Jean-Paul Sartre* (New York: 1965), p. 115n.

[60] The bulk of the *Critique* remains untranslated. *Search for a Method,* trans. Hazel Barnes (New York: 1963), contains only the introductory essay (181 pp. in English). The Cumming volume includes sixty-two additional English pages (*op. cit.,* pp. 421–83), translated by Starr and James Atkinson. Aside from its turgid, prolix, and repetitive style, the *Critique* is visually forbidding: the type is small, the pages crowded (fifty lines per page); there are few divisions in the text, relatively few paragraph divisions. Many "paragraphs" are three or four pages long; at least one is more than six pages long (*CRD* 218–24)!

[61] Marx wrote: "Bei mir ist . . . das Ideelle nichts andres als das im Menschenkopf umgesetzte und übersetzte Materielle (*Das Kapital,* I: in Karl Marx, Friedrich Engels, *Werke,* XXIII [E. Berlin: 1962], 27). Sartre quotes a rather free French translation: "Pour moi, le monde des idées n'est que le monde matériel transposé et traduit dans l'esprit [sic] humain" (*CRD* 239, n. 3).

"old" or "young," but rather to Engels, Plekhanov, and Lenin.

Sartre's version of economic theory is almost a caricature, not so much of Marx as of Adam Smith and Ricardo. What sets human history in motion, generating conflict among individuals and groups, is the "contingent but ineluctable [!]" fact of "material [i.e., economic] scarcity."[62] However, the main thrust of the *Critique* is not economic but sociological. Sartre offers an involved theory of (atomic, disintegrated, merely "serial") *collectives*—characteristic of capitalist society—and of their supersession by (cohesive, integrated, "nonserial") *groups*—under "socialism." Sartre's position seems to be a synthesis of Tönnies and Marx: *Gemeinschaft* succeeds *Gesellschaft* through the historical struggle of classes!

Sartre's attitude toward objectification is now close to that of Marx, both young and old (see Section V), and thus close to the position which in *Being and Nothingness* he had repudiated, as entailing the "dogma of the serious [i.e., of the self-righteous and pompous]": "Marx," he wrote then, "proposed the original dogma of the serious when he asserted the priority of object over subject."[63] Like the appeal to determinism, the "spirit of seriousness" involves bad faith. (Cf. *BN* 626; *EN* 721.)

Feasting on historical humble pie, Sartre declares the existential position that he had elaborated in *Being and Nothingness* to have been only an "ideology," in the special and pejorative sense of "a parasitical system living on the margin of Knowledge [i.e., of Marxism], which at first it opposed but into which today it seeks to be integrated."[64]

---

[62] "Instead of the metaphor of indigestion in *Nausea*, we are faced with actual hunger" (Cumming, *op. cit.*, p. 41).

[63] *BN* 580. ("Marx a posé le dogme premier du serieux lorsqu'il a affirmé la priorité de l'objet sur le sujet . . ." [*EN* 669].)

[64] *Search for a Method*, p. 8. ("C'est un système parasitaire

In fact, what we see in Volume I of the *Critique* is not an "integration" of existentialism into Marxism. Rather, the doctrinaire position of Engels and late Marx—*le Savoir*—has simply "swallowed up existentialism."[65]

## VII

### Conclusion

My conclusions may be summarized briefly under three heads:

(1) Although Sartre was stimulated by Hegel's *Phenomenology* and by Marx's 1844 *Manuscripts,* he both modified and misinterpreted key points in Hegel's and Marx's thought—perhaps deliberately, certainly not without precedent (especially the precedent of Kojève's Hegel-commentary). Sartre's is a truncated dialectic; it lacks synthesis and reconciliation and is thus fundamentally un-Hegelian even though it is formulated in explicitly Hegelian categories and concepts.

(2) Sartre takes what for Hegel were low-level, partial, one-sided, abstract$_H$ phases of a continuing dialectical process and lifts them into permanent universality—e.g., alienation, self-alienation, the struggle with the "other," the project of mutual enslavement.

Like Marx, Sartre omits the *cultural* dimension of alienation, which had been central in Hegel's own account, in the *Phenomenology,* of "spirit alienated from itself."

(3) In attempting to assimilate young Marx's theory of alienation, Sartre effected two distortions: first, as he did with Hegel, Sartre treated alienation not as something phenomenologically or historically mediatable and overcomable, but as a fixed and uneliminable feature of *la condition humaine.* Second, he over-

---

qui vit en marge du Savoir qui s'y est opposé d'abord et qui, aujourd'hui, tente de s'y intégrer" [*CRD* 18].)

[65] Warnock, *op. cit.,* p. 176.

looked Marx's insistence on the positive, trans-historical character of objectification, a theme radically incompatible with Sartrean (or any other) existentialism. He tended, as many Marxists have tended—especially among the contemporary existentializing revisionists in Poland, Czechoslovakia, and Yugoslavia—to convert the young Marx into a proto-existentialist. But the youngest possible Marx was in fact no more of an existentialist than the Hegel of the *Phenomenology*—which is to say, he was not an existentialist at all in any meaningful sense of that term.

Since his conversion to Marxism, Sartre, in stressing the (externalizing) objectification of sociohistorical *praxis,* has been forced, in effect if not in so many words, to renounce his earlier existentialist emphasis on the subjectivity of free individuals. His own existentialism has been organically absorbed into his Marxism.

# SARTRE'S "IDEAL" OF SOCIAL UNITY

## *Howard R. Burkle*

My subject is the individual in Sartre's concept of social unity. It is well known that prior to the *Critique of Dialectical Reason,* Sartre was preoccupied with individuals and their freedom, but that now he talks of groups and determining forces. Does this mean, as some critics think, that he has submerged the individual in the collective?[1] Or has he managed somehow to maintain his earlier belief that "at the start of everything lies the initiative of the individual man"?[2] When I speak of the individual, I am thinking of the admirable—even heroic—being which Sartre describes in *Being and Nothingness* and depicts (often "across the grain") in his novels and plays. The true individual is Orestes of *The Flies* and the antithesis of Garcin of *No Exit.* It is the fate of this spontaneous, self-moving, unique ethical agent with which I am concerned.

The position for which I shall argue is that in his concept of the "group" Sartre makes a significant effort to protect the importance of the individual. Whether he succeeds or not, I am not certain; but this is not my concern here. I am concerned rather to clarify his meaning. As I understand it, Sartre conceives of society on the model of an individual. Like Socrates in the *Republic,* but in a very different sense ontologically, he imagines society as the "individual writ large." In an ideal sense, society is an individual endowed as far as possible with qualities of conscious-

This essay was written especially for this edition by Professor Burkle, Grinnell College (Iowa).

[1] Wilfrid Desan, *The Marxism of Jean-Paul Sartre* (Garden City, N.Y.: Doubleday Co., Inc., 1965), p. 293.

[2] *Ibid.,* p. 127.

ness and purposive activity which are analogous to
those possessed by particular men. Even when the resemblance is slight or, as is usually the case, indiscern-
ible, the individual is still important as a center within
which a rebirth of consciousness and creative energy
can take place.

I am aware that this thesis faces difficulties. In some
ways society is too unorganized to be thought of as an
individual, and in other ways it is too mechanical to
be human. And seldom does it proceed in ways that
could be considered intelligent. As Sartre himself observes, individuals in a society are so opaque to each
other that together they lack the intelligibility which
an individual alone has.[3] Hence, to many it will seem
far more realistic simply to accept society as the complicated system of impersonal mechanisms it seems to
be. Nevertheless, I think there is enough in the individuality analogy to make it worth exploring. I shall
approach this subject through the concept of the
"group-in-fusion," which, if I am right, embodies the
ideal of the individual which Sartre is battling to
defend.

## 1. A Sartrean Ideal?

It may seem baldly inconsistent to speak of Sartre's
holding an ideal of social unity. Anyone who maintains, as he does, that nothing is valuable in itself and
that "good" is nothing more than a name for whatever
some human being in fact desires, would seem unable
to assert that one social order is better than any other.
He could say that a certain system is preferable because it most effectively serves some human desire or
because it appeals to the majority aesthetically, but he
could not say that it just is best. Nevertheless, I think
that the term "ideal" is appropriate. It will take the
entire essay to explain this adequately, but this much
can be said now. The whole tone of Sartre's discussion

[3] *Ibid.*, p. 169.

suggests that he does regard one group, the "group-in-fusion," as the paradigm form of society and that he does so for a more substantial reason than that most people happen to like it or find it useful. The reason is that the group-in-fusion is more in accord with the ontology of human freedom: it provides a more creative outlet for human energies, permits individual choice to have greater impact on the course of public affairs, and is more hospitable to individual diversity.

This does not mean that the group-in-fusion is valuable apart from human desire. It is after all because this group satisfies man's desire for an outlet for his inventiveness that he judges it good. Sartre does not give up his conviction that all value is relative to human desire; rather he points to the dialectical relation between the objective conditions in the group-in-fusion and the human desires which flourish under those conditions and confer value upon them by desiring them. In short, the group-in-fusion would have no value if there were no human beings to desire it, but men would not desire it if there were not something about it which satisfies them. In these terms, then—as the mode of society most expressive of spontaneity, diversity, and purpose—the group-in-fusion is the ideal by which actual societies are to be understood and appraised.[4]

### 2. *The "Series"*

We shall concentrate on the group-in-fusion, but since it can be understood only in relation to the other

[4] Robert Denoon Cumming (ed.), *The Philosophy of Jean-Paul Sartre* (New York: Random House, 1965), p. 472. This will stand, I think, in spite of the fact that Sartre says that there is nothing ideal about the totalization which formed the group-in-fusion in Paris in July 1789. Sartre is referring to the motives and some of the actions of the mob: they were angry, afraid, *etc.*, and they shed blood. This sort of behavior is not necessarily incompatible with the sort of idealism discussed in this paper.

groups which Sartre distinguishes, we must deal with them as well. The group-in-fusion is one of perhaps four basic social patterns, the others being the "series," the "group-under-oath," and the "institution." Since the series is the pattern from which the group-in-fusion emerges, we shall begin with it.

In the most general sense, a society as Sartre understands it is a multiplicity of individual human beings held together by common interests. It is important to note from the beginning that the basic units of society are individuals and the bonds of social cohesion are individually rooted desires for common objects. Although these desires often become alienated, that is, separated from individuals and lodged in the group, originally they are rooted in individual needs. Societies differ according to the ways in which they pursue these objects: whether consciously or unconsciously, by inner desire or duty, spontaneously or under compulsion.

A series is a group constituted by interests which are "general," that is, which reside in individuals as parts of the collective. People living in a remote section of a city, say, belong to the series, "Residents of Maplecrest Hills," because by virtue of where they live they need to get the city government to repair the streets, collect the trash more often, improve the bus service, etc. They are one not because of anything they share as persons, but because everyone living in that section is necessarily subject to the needs intrinsic to residency there.

This is not to say that the things desired are general (better bus service obviously is quite specific) but that the way in which they are desired is general. The group has not made them part of its *"praxis"*;[5] that is, they have not consciously desired and sought them.

---

[5] *Praxis* is a technical term meaning essentially purposive activity, effort directed toward some goal consciously entertained. It is to the group what "project" is to the individual in *Being and Nothingness*.

The residents of Maplecrest have not reflected on their isolation and learned to resent it, have not pictured themselves over against the authorities, have not resolved to take steps to obtain their object, have not petitioned and protested, etc. This is the mark of men in series: they are one not through the convergence of their actions but through the impersonal, external features of the group to which they happen to belong. As Sartre puts it, their specific interests are rooted in the "fuller," "deeper" general interests of the social structure.[6]

I have stressed generality as the essential trait of the series not only because Sartre regards it as crucial, but because it is particularly relevant to the case I wish to make for individuality as the ideal of social unity. A series is the least form of society, and its incompleteness or inferiority is due precisely to the lack of individuality in its members and in itself as an association of individuals.

Sartre discusses two other traits, "solitude" and "interchangeability," which are also important to individuality. The series involves "solitude" because its members are related first to the group and only secondarily to each other. Theirs is a "mediated reciprocity," a commonality based simply on the fact that the group has a certain need. Although the need is the same for all, each seeks to fill it alone. Consider a group of Maplecrest commuters waiting for a bus. Their behavior plainly shows that they do not care about each other, but only about the arrival of the bus, the instrument which will satisfy their need to get to work. Although they share this interest, each turns his back on the others and buries his face in his newspaper. This is routine behavior, a customary manifestation of seriality, yet at the same time a free act which each intentionally does to the others. A series is a society in which each excludes the others directly, but joins with them in the impersonal act of catching a bus. Note once more the absence of individuality.[7]

To say that the series involves "interchangeability" is to say that any individual belonging to a given series could be replaced by any other without affecting the group in any important way. Individuals in series are integers, objects moving through space and interacting with other objects. They do not, as distinctive persons, make this society what it is. As Sartre puts it, "Each person is the same as the Others in so far as he is Other than himself."[8]

The basic implication for our subject, the individual, is manifest. In seriality there is hardly any individuality at all, and what is equally important, there is only a minimum of genuine society. People in series may individually be rich in personal qualities and capable of spontaneous and original decisions, but none of this shapes society or is shared by others there.

### 3. The Group-in-Fusion

One of the conditions of the genesis of the group-in-fusion is the loose system of associations we have just examined, for fusion is the dialectical overcoming of solitude, generality, and interchangeability. Another necessary condition is "scarcity," of which ironically there is always enough. One of the major themes of the *Critique* is that men live constantly and inescapably under conditions of scarcity because nature does not contain and men cannot produce enough to supply everyone what he needs. Inevitably, then, men confront each other as competitors; and even more drastically, since what they are competing for are the necessities of life, they meet as mortal enemies. Every man poses the threat of death for every other.[9]

Such is the predicament in which men must live, to

[7] *Ibid.*, p. 458.
[8] *Ibid.*, p. 460.
[9] *Ibid.*, p. 435.

which they must accommodate their societies. Given this innate hostility, it is not surprising that the disjointed and depersonalized patterns of seriality should be so pervasive and that life should weigh so painfully and hopelessly upon the majority of man. Occasionally, however, something happens to alter the dismal pattern: conditions become ripe, a provocation occurs, a few men respond in a new way bringing the "apocalypse" and after it the "group-in-fusion." The apocalypse is the portentous, fluid first phase of the group-in-fusion. The words Sartre uses to refer to it are suggestive of surprise and suddenness. It begins in an "upheaval," is effected by a "lightning stroke of praxis," and spreads by "contagion" and "imitation." Those who are a part of it relate to each other "not as individual or Other, but as a singular incarnation of the common person."[10] All at once some men break through to each other in a community of decisive action. The essence of it is "the sudden restoration of freedom."[11]

Sartre's illustration of this process is, of course, the Parisian uprising of July 14, 1789. The poor of the city were a perfect example of the intense suffering which accompanies scarcity under seriality. Hunger, chronic political unrest, social isolation put them on the verge of insurrection. Then—and this is what triggered the apocalypse—they heard that the army had surrounded Paris. The enemy was all around, physically bounding and grouping them. Suddenly they saw that they had something more in common than misery of body and mind—the need to get weapons and defend themselves. The pivotal factor is that they recognized their plight, saw themselves as together in wanting the same end. In this instant the group-in-fusion was conceived; each of them felt the "individual need as common need."[12]

[10] *Ibid.*, pp. 464, 468, and 470.
[11] *Ibid.*, p. 472.
[12] *Ibid.*, p. 465.

More than any other form of society, the group-in-fusion depends on individual action. Cognitive and conative acts literally bring it into being and sustain it. It is true that individuals also produce seriality by turning their backs on each other, but this is more a matter of inaction, of not engaging in meaningful sociality, than it is a positive creation. By contrast, the group-in-fusion is man's voluntary creation. The right material conditions must be present, but unless some human beings living within these conditions simultaneously understand their situation the same way, desire the same end, and act out these desires in concert, there will be no group-in-fusion. Awareness, choice, and purposive action in an instant can transform the material conditions and create the new society *de novo*. Actually, it would be more accurate to say that the group is the creating rather than the product, for the group-in-fusion is really nothing more nor less than the configuration of consciousness and *praxis* of the constituting individuals.

Let us look at this more closely by considering the "third man" principle which gives the group-in-fusion its structure. What is the third man? Sartre gives the example of a passing taxi driver who notices several men standing at a wall alongside the Seine looking at something in the water. The driver observes that the men are looking in the same direction, making gestures, trying to do something together. In observing this, the driver unifies the group, in the sense that he enlarges it and adds the dimension of awareness to the loose kind of unity it already has. In doing this, he is the "third man."[13]

Now, instead of the lone taxi driver merely looking at strangers, consider the people storming the Bastille, that is, a large number of people who are not merely observing but acting; and imagine each of them serving as third man for all the others. Each by his awareness of the others and by his striving with them for the

13 Desan, *op. cit.*, p. 94.

same goal, unifies them with himself and with each other.[14] There are many centers of consciousness overlapping and interlocking, and many paths of activity converging and co-operating. The many become one without ceasing in the least to be individuals; on the contrary, they remain distinct centers with all their independence and personal difference intact and *enhanced*. They are one not as a thing is one, but functionally: they think, intend, and struggle as one.[15] All relations—individual to individual, individual to group, group to individual—are direct and open. In this sense there are both individuals and an Individual.

## 4. The Group-Under-Oath

The third of Sartre's social forms, the "group-under-oath," is the system which succeeds the group-in-fusion as organization begins to set in. It is what a successful group-in-fusion becomes as its revolutionary impetus wanes and the need for order and routine replaces the need for venture and zeal. It is the pattern into which the group-in-fusion first falls as it loses its urgency and creativity and begins to take on the flesh of an enduring society.

On the surface it resembles the group-in-fusion because it is composed of individuals who are to some extent actively aware of sharing a common project with other individuals; but in the crucial matter of the relation of the individual to the group it is more like the "institution." What is characteristic of the group-under-oath is that it takes itself as the object of its own *praxis*. "It posits itself for itself."[16] No longer, as in fusion, does the group work to bring some new pos-

---

[14] There are details of the third man which add richness to the concept of unity Sartre offers, but we need not go into them here.

[15] Desan, *op. cit.*, p. 139.

[16] Cumming, *op. cit.*, p. 473.

sibility into being, no longer is it revolutionary; now it is dedicated to its own conservation. "The group becomes, in each person, the common objective: its permanence must be salvaged."[17]

At the root of this shift is the disappearance of the external enemy. Once he has been defeated and the danger of attack removed, the community turns its fears on itself. As we noted before, fear is ineradicable because under scarcity every man is the mortal enemy of every other. Although this is temporarily forgotten with respect to intra-group relations while the group-in-fusion is concentrating on the enemy outside, it inevitably returns, bringing with it the "danger of atomization." Now the group must protect itself against those of its members who prefer their own interests to the perpetuation of the group.

Notice that the first step in the formation of a lasting group is the replacement of individual projects by the group project, and the merging of individual centers of consciousness in a group consciousness. Notice too how this alters the quality of the group. It becomes intensely self-aware and fearful about its future, behavior which is remarkably like that of an individual who has been tempted by his inadequacies to doubt his own competence.

At this point the group is making a root choice, whether to lapse into seriality or to consolidate its unity. Its ideal moment, when individuals could follow their own projects yet cohere in perfect harmony with others doing the same, has passed. If the group is to stay together it must choose between the series and the institution. If it chooses the latter, it has only to extend the rudiments of organization already available. The seeds of organization were present in the new group from the beginning, insofar as different individuals performed different tasks in struggling against the enemy: one man was a look-out, another guarded the prisoners, etc. The group-under-oath de-

[17] *Ibid.*, p. 474.

velops this differentiation of function and extends it to other kinds of work. Fixed roles, positions, rules, and laws are laid down; routines, customs, and traditions are established.

The community is then under "oath." It now possesses a group consciousness which binds the individual to the community before all else. This is not, Sartre cautions, a form of social contract, for its validity does not depend on the actual or tacit consent of the governed, but on a habituated sense of duty, a socially conditioned acceptance of the jurisdiction of the group over the life of the individual.

Because the obligation entailed in the oath relates each individual first to the community and then to other individuals by virtue of their role in the community, the oath is called a "mediated reciprocity."[18] The group mediates among individuals. Third man mediation, based on the active consciousness of individuals, has been replaced by institutional mediation. The group has decided that if it is to avoid internal warfare and insure continuity, it must severely curtail the values of individuality.

## 5. *The Institution*

The last of Sartre's four basic social forms is the fully developed "organization"; that is, it is a society which has (1) legitimized and institutionalized self-perpetuation as the overriding concern of all citizens, (2) established the tasks and agencies and distributed the responsibilities needed to carry on the life of the community, (3) set up effective defenses against the disruptions of its own deviant members.

An institution is a thoroughly structured, self-sustaining system, which is more like a machine than an organism and yet not exactly like a machine either. Sartre refers to it in one place as an "inorganic ob-

[18] *Ibid.*, p. 473.

ject,"[19] but in another place he refers to it as *"le commencement de l'humanité."*[20] The point is that although the institution is an overpowering, impersonal
system, it insures the survival of men and thus expresses a solicitude for their well being.

The chief instrumentality by which this feat of social engineering is accomplished is the "terror." Terror
is legitimized violence, an arrangement in which the
recognized leaders are empowered as agents of the
group to coerce or kill whomever they must in order
to preserve the community. The terror embodies the
awful truth that violence is humanly meaningful.[21]
It is France under Robespierre. It is any society which
has faced up to what must be done to unite its citizens and keep them together as a perduring entity.

Although the terror is exercised by the few persons
in power, it is not an expression of only their will or of
some other minority, but of the collective will of all
the individuals making up the community. The institution is a new kind of society, in which the "common
being of the group" has been transferred to the *"praxis*
of the group as such."[22] That is, the group and all the
individuals making it up have their being in the terror.

Although it is obvious that the values of diversity
and spontaneity, which were present in the group-in-
fusion, have been lost, it is also true that something of
value has been gained. Security and survival, which
were in jeopardy in the group-in-fusion, are now available to all. The high-level values of individual freedom have been traded for the less spectacular but
equally important values of social stability. This is
Sartre's point when he describes the institution as the
"reappearance . . . of an interhuman relationship."[23]
Those individuals who have subordinated their de-

[19] *Ibid.*, p. 477.
[20] Desan, *op. cit.*, p. 150.
[21] Cumming, *op. cit.*, p. 481.
[22] *Ibid.*, p. 476.
[23] *Ibid.*

sires to the will of the community in the terror find
their interests fully represented and expressed, and
thus returned to them fulfilled. It is even possible to
say that there is freedom in the institution, the "borrowed freedom" of the "terror-imperative."[24]

In this we see the institution picking its way between seriality and individual *praxis*, the two "negations of the group" which threaten every society.
Since unchecked seriality leads to total loss of individual freedom and unchecked individual *praxis* leads to
total loss of social cohesion, the institution follows a
middle path. It curbs excessive individuality by compelling everyone to make himself an "instrument of
group *praxis*" and at the same time holds the impersonal, mechanical aspects of organization within
bounds by establishing the leaders as embodiments of
the will of the citizens. The institution, thus, is a com-
promise: it lacks the openness and variety which men
as individuals crave, but it avoids the anarchy which
accompanies unqualified individualism. In terms of
the ideals of the Revolution, it achieves a reasonable
level of *fraternité* and *égalité* by giving up some of
the *liberté* which men ideally but impractically desire.

In spite of these reassurances, it cannot be dissem-
bled that, politically speaking, the individual has been
absorbed into the group. Even if we say that he continues as incarnate in the corporate Individual, this
does not change the fact that he lacks the right and
possibility of creative individual action. There is social
unity, there is even community, but there is little of
the sort of individuality we defined earlier.

## 6. *The Epistemology of the Groups*

It is clear enough that the four groups are categories
by which Sartre grasps and analyzes actual societies,
but it is less than clear what relationship they have
epistemologically to the world outside the realm of

[24] *Ibid.*, p. 477.

Sartre's own thinking. Are the categories objective, do they state the essential properties of existent societies and the laws by which they develop and interact? Certainly Sartre is not writing science; he is not giving an empirical description of social facts or of the regularities observed to hold within these facts. Nor is he composing ontology in some Platonic sense: these are not the Ideal realities which material societies imitate. Sartre is writing philosophy—his own sort of phenomenology—in which he describes social phenomena as they appear to intuition.[25] The question of objectivity —whether this is how things really are, how things-in-themselves are—is "bracketed" or bypassed as an insoluble and, thus, meaningless question. Instead, one seeks to understand social phenomena in their "intentionality," that is, in their relation to consciousness.

Thus, Sartre neither simply derives his categories from empirical data nor simply imposes them upon the data. He conceives and uses them in the dialectical interchange between consciousness and the social realities with which consciousness is linked in its situation.

In these terms we should say that there is a certain solid objectivity about the groups; they are conceived on the basis of experience of actual societies of the past and present, and they are designed to fit the societies of any period. But there is also something subjective about them since they tell us what social phenomena mean *to men,* how men are inclined by their interests to symbolize the social patterns they see and

[25] Maurice Natanson, in his *A Critique of Jean-Paul Sartre's Ontology* (Lincoln, Nebraska: University of Nebraska Press, 1951), p. 69, maintains that "the term 'phenomenological', when applied to Sartre's method, is ambiguous and, in certain respects, a misnomer." Natanson takes Husserl as his standard of what is and what is not properly phenomenological, and he is probably justified in doing so. However, Sartre is generally understood as a phenomenologist and we shall follow this customary understanding.

imagine. Sartre sees a certain fluidity in the forms of society, a certain interplay between the necessities of the world and the possibilities which men conceive in their minds and pursue with their bodies and machines.

## 7. The Status of the Groups

Another matter needing clarification is the nature of the interrelationship of the groups as forms of actual societies. Sartre obviously thinks of them both as stages in social change and as types. But are they more than this—an exhaustive classification of the possible kinds of society, perhaps, or the basic structures of society as such?

When we examine the four groups side by side, we notice a certain interesting disparity. Compared with the institution, the group-in-fusion and the group-under-oath are so short-lived that they seem less societies than stages in social change. At one point Sartre actually says that the group-in-fusion *is* seriality in the course of dissolving.[26] And the group-under-oath could plausibly be interpreted as simply the first stage of an institution. This would leave us with two kinds of permanent societies, the series and the institution, and two so-called societies which are actually stages in the establishment of an institution. The interrelation would then be an irreversible cycle, an institution growing out of a series and after a time reverting catastrophically or gradually to a series again. Also it would follow that an institution is the goal of social change, and thus a positive value, while a series, being what remains of a moribund institution, is the opposite.

There is an element of truth in this view, and yet the relegation of the group-in-fusion and the group-under-oath to the status of quasi-societies is unsatisfactory. However fluid and brief they may be, the

[26] Cumming, *op. cit.*, p. 471.

revolutionary groups are still distinct societies. They exist, have their moment of being, and afterward can be remembered, held up as ideal, and used to judge the society then in being. Moreover, the institution and the series, which we have called "permanent," are only relatively that. They too come into being and pass away. Thus, we must conclude that the group-in-fusion and the group-under-oath, although very different because they exist for only brief periods and for special purposes, are nevertheless genuine forms of society.

On other grounds there is also some doubt about the series. It might seem less a kind of society than a pattern of association which is present in different degrees in every society. That is, it might be an ingredient rather than a form of society. The adjectival form "seriality" which Sartre constantly uses as a synonym for "series" suggests precisely this.

Again, there is some truth in this construction, and yet for two reasons we should hesitate to accept it without qualification. First, even though in one respect the series is an ingredient in society (e.g., the seriality which the group-in-fusion is dissolving, or the re-emerging seriality which the institution struggles to control), in another respect it is a society in its own right. Relative to the whole of which it is a part, it may be a mere ingredient, but relative to its own contents and to some other parts of its context, it is a society, albeit a sub-society. Second, it is conceivable that an institution may become so infused with generality, solitude, and interchangeability that it will be changed into a series. Is this not what happened in eighteenth-century France? Had not the proud institution of the monarchy so degenerated that the entire society was a series?

If so, then a series is sometimes a parasitical society living on the other three and sometimes, when it has overcome its host, a society in its own right. As the former, it is the chief provocation to revolution, and as the latter it is the extreme of social degeneracy. A series as such comes into being only when an institution disintegrates radically or when a group-in-fusion fails in its drive toward full organization.

This brief analysis of some of the ways in which the groups are related indicates that each of them is indeed a kind of society but seldom, if ever, exists in a pure form. They appear together in various proportions, patterns of subordination, and temporal sequence, and we must think of them, therefore, as simultaneously: (a) stages in radical social change, (b) structures which coexist in different combinations in every society, and (c) the basic forms of all society. Let us expand briefly on each of these.

### (A) THE GROUPS AS STAGES

Sartre does not believe in progress and certainly has no hope for utopia; thus, the sort of social change which takes place among his four societies cannot be linear or cumulative in any long-range sense. But neither is it cyclical in a fixed way. Societies do not flow from series to institution to series according to some regular rhythm. Although there are the mechanisms and regularities we have been discussing, each society follows its highly unpredictable and idiosyncratic course. An institution may maintain itself for a very long time or for a very brief time; a series may prevail for an instant or continue interminably. A group-in-fusion may grow into a stable society, or give way to another group-in-fusion, or perish letting the newly awakened personal associations fall back into seriality. What happens depends to a large extent on what men choose to do. However, if I am correct in thinking that the group-in-fusion represents the highest social ideal, there will be important differences among the societies in the degree to which men can voluntarily affect their situation. Volition will be most efficacious while men are in the fluid and urgent period of fusion, less so while they are in the stable and relatively satisfying period of institutionalization, and least so while they are in seriality.

## (b) THE GROUPS AS COEXISTING STRUCTURES

Viewed as constitutive elements of a society, the four groups would have the following functions. The institution would be the total society in its ordinary state; it would be the embodiment of whatever stability an organized group has achieved at a given time. Seriality would be one of the "negations of society,"[27] that is, the tendency inherent in every group toward impersonal relationships and the forms produced by this tendency. The group-in-fusion would be the always present but only occasionally active power which institutions have for transforming themselves. The group-under-oath would be the first material product of revolution, the embryo of the new institution.

Viewed thus, seriality and fusion would be the *yin* and *yang* of Sartre's political *Tao*. As immanent patterns never fully actualized, they would function as the negative and positive polarities by which all actual societies are constituted, classified, and evaluated. They would, in a sense, be good and evil contesting for dominance. The closer a society approaches to pure seriality, the more inhumane and more ripe it is for overthrow; and the more it retains of the pattern of pure fusion, the more humane and worthy it is to be preserved. In this case Sartre has not only a social ideal but a principle of social evil.[28] Seriality and fusion are evil and good, respectively, in dialectical tension and support. The triumph of one calls its opposite into being. A too pervasive seriality invites fu-

---

[27] *Ibid.*, p. 475.

[28] It would not be necessary to go as far as Desan, who says (*op. cit.*, p. 264) that a strange form of Manicheanism emerges from the pages of the *Critique*. Seriality could be an endemic tendency away from the ideal, but not a demonic force.

sion, and a successful fusion produces a new material reality with the seeds of seriality which will smother individuality.

On this theory, seriality is present in society not as an evil substance but as the absence of true community. It is in every institution and group-under-oath as the measure of their imperfection: in the latter as the repetitions and routines of everyday living, and in the former as malfunctioning organization. Seriality would not be in the group-in-fusion at all, for as its opposite it disappears at the approach of true community.

### (c) THE GROUPS AS THE BASIC FORMS

Although the four groups are categories covering all possible cases, they do not exclude other ways of classifying societies. Sartre mentions at least two others, the "apocalypse" and the "group-in-opposition," which we treated earlier as moments in the genesis of the group-in-fusion, but which might just as well have been handled as distinct, though evanescent, societies. No doubt others could be identified; it all depends on how finely one wishes to divide the data.

There is also an interesting question about how Sartre's types of society correlate with standard political and economic forms. Do polities with centralized power—monarchies, theocracies, dictatorships—have a greater affinity for seriality than free polities such as the democratic socialist system which Sartre himself prefers? The fact that Sartre's most publicized example of a serialized society is a monarchy, coupled with his strongly aversive comments about Soviet dictatorship, suggests that this might be so. However, he is just as critical of the capitalist Western democracies, and he is on record as once urging the Communists of France to submit themselves unquestioningly to the dictates of the Party. There is no consistent political alignment here. It seems impossible to establish any strict correlation, even theoretically, between the four

groups and particular political-economic systems. Seriality is present and potentially oppressive in every
system. It may abound in both democratic and centralized systems, or it may be controlled. Also a
group-in-fusion may arise in any system. Whenever
the conditions of oppressive seriality and the precipi-
tating appearance of the enemy coalesce, the apocalypse may come. The determining factor is not the
formal political and economic arrangements, but the
response of the people. The crucial factor is always
what men choose to do.

## 8. *The Ideal*

Perhaps the most serious objection to the position I
have been developing is that this ideal of social unity
seems entirely impracticable. It is all very well to write
essays about the revolutionary Third Estate of Paris
and to dream romantic visions of crowds of exultant
men and women surging toward the Bastille, their
pikes held high in a gesture of perfect solidarity and
individual courage; but this has little connection with
the gray details of everyday social reality. This har-
monic anarchy, this anarchistic harmony, is simply too
fantastic to be taken seriously as a depiction of social
reality, or even as a meaningful ideal which could be
used to fashion an actual community.

Moreover, Sartre seems to recognize this himself.
He explicitly admits that the group-in-fusion "cannot
have the ontological status claimed in its praxis";[29]
and more than once he speaks of the "impossible
unity" of the unorganized society.[30] Would it not be
better to reduce the group-in-fusion to a minor place
and admit that the values of individualism, however
precious, must be set aside as largely incompatible
with orderly political life? There would still be a place
for eccentricity, uniqueness, independence, and the

[29] Cumming, *op. cit.*, p. 475.
[30] *Ibid.*, p. 476.

like in private matters and in the realm of culture. Indeed, they might flourish there, in what men think, and write, and paint, *because* they have not been inserted into the political sphere, where they do not belong.

In one sense, this point cannot be denied, and it is very close to the position Sartre has adopted. He is as aware as anyone of the restrictions which must be put on personal liberty. Indeed, has he not said so much about this that some think he has abandoned his original convictions about the preeminent worth of individual freedom? However, in another sense this objection about the impracticability of the individualistic social ideal misses the point. For Sartre, a worthy ideal is not one which can be easily actualized, nor even one that can be actualized after an arduous struggle, but one so demanding and lofty that even the most heroic effort could not translate it into full, or even approximate, reality. An ideal must be a virtual impossibility, a possibility which stands in the most excruciating opposition to actuality.

For Sartre, ideals add a dimension of infinity to the world of objects. They make the present with its dead weight of pastness receptive to the future. Through human agents reaching for ideals the present can respond to possibilities and become the future. This is the sort of dynamism which the group-in-fusion exhibits. It is an actual occurrence and yet, historically speaking, it is a phantom. The combination of perfect individuality and perfect community comes, or almost comes, for an instant and then passes. The rigid, constricting realities of society melt suddenly and permit individuals to be individuals and at the same time enjoy the sense of comradeship and mutuality with other human beings for which they are constantly longing. The magic instant of the surging group-in-fusion is as close as Sartre's humanity will ever get to heaven. In the enthusiasm to breach the walls of the Bastille, the grinding pains of the real world are transcended: hunger is forgotten, death is ignored, scarcity is negated, and isolation is overcome. The other man, my enemy, is suddenly so much my friend, so close to me that I literally cannot tell where he begins and I end. Here, in the moment of fusion, Sartre finds the means to escape the nightmarish "Look" of the "Other" which he vainly struggled to overcome in non-political ways in *Being and Nothingness*.

It is enough for Sartre that the ideal pass close to earth, that men by their *praxis* bring it close enough to soften the rigid forms of actuality and stir up their own sluggish desires for a better world than they otherwise would have. The ideal may be impossible, but it is not unreal; it may be impractical in itself, but it is not impractical in its effects. The group-in-fusion, though nothing as compared with the institution, is a potent factor. It is an event in which society approaches ethical accountability and achieves a measure of political creativity.

In this, does not the group-in-fusion prove to be significantly similar to the creative individual human being? What is the *pour-soi* except a nothingness rooted in actuality, a capacity of human actuality for becoming other than it is, an openness to possibility which gives man such dignity and grandeur as he possesses. If, in the group-in-fusion, society has a similar capacity, it can never justify its inhumanity nor forget its proper subservience to human well-being.

# PRAXIS AND DIALECTIC
# IN SARTRE'S CRITIQUE

*Anthony Manser*

The stated aim of the *Critique de la raison dialectique* is to establish the foundations of dialectical reason. The title obviously invites, and is meant to invite, comparison with Kant's *Critique of Pure Reason*. But whereas it is possible to exhibit the plan on which Kant intends to proceed, however difficult it may be to follow the details of it, in the case of Sartre's book it is hard to find any organization of the material. Many of the severe judgments which have been passed on the work are partially due to this problem. What I want to do in this article is both to retract some of my earlier criticisms[1] and to take a closer look at the way in which Sartre "founds" the dialectic at the beginning of the text. Even here the organization of the book is misleading; the first section, entitled "Questions de méthode," is an article Sartre had previously published on the relations between Marxism and Existentialism. He says (p. 9) that logically this should come after the bulk of the work. Clearly it is of a different order from the rest, and of much less philosophical interest. In it he claims that Existentialism is only an ideology compared to Marxism, but the kind of Marxism that appears in the *Critique* proper is very different from the orthodox variety, in fact appears to involve a denial of many Marxist tenets. I intend to ignore both "Questions de méthode" and the precise relation of Sartre to Marxism.

This essay was written especially for this edition by Mr. Manser, the University of Southampton.

[1] All references to the *Critique* itself will be given in brackets in the text. Other references are at the foot of the page.

Sartre claims that dialectical reason is superior to "analytic reason," which is this term for what is normally called "reason" in philosophical discussions. He seems to think that the idea of "founding" analytic reason makes sense because that reason is conceived as a linear process, springing from some given starting point, the "given." Part of the trouble here is that the myth of "foundations" is, as so often, bedeviling philosophic thinking. Many philosophers have believed that unless we have some firm base from which to start, the edifice of knowledge will be in danger of collapse, and it is hard to get rid of this idea. Popper suggested a metaphor to try and soften the force of this notion, that of a building constructed on piles in soft ground. To go higher it is necessary to drive the piles in deeper, though not in the hope of reaching bedrock, only to support the higher edifice. This metaphor may help to remove some part of the idea of "foundations," but some still remains; there are "foundations" for knowledge, though not of the same type hitherto envisaged. Whether this notion of a firm starting point is necessary to ordinary knowledge or not, Sartre agrees with Hegel and Engels that the dialectic is circular (cf. p. 155), and this can only mean that there can be no starting point for it, we can begin where we please and eventually come back to the place where we began. No place in the circle is especially privileged. If dialectic is to be separated from ordinary reason in this way, then there would seem to be a distinction. But Hegel, Marx and Sartre all connect dialectic with history, which would seem to be an example of a linear process; what happens now may depend on what happened earlier and the reverse never occurs.

Thus even at the beginning of the examination of "dialectical reason" we seemed to be faced with the kind of confusion which many philosophers have claimed is endemic in all attempts to talk of the dialectic. It is partly for this reason that it is impossible to give a definition of the term. But it does not follow that Sartre cannot make something useful of the notion, as I shall try to show. One caution needs to be inserted at the outset; neither Hegel nor Sartre ever makes use of the triad "Thesis, Antithesis, Synthesis." In fact they could not if they wished to remain true to what they hold the dialectic to be; they would both claim that this was an attempt to reduce dialectical reason to analytic. One of the motives for attempting to produce a "dialectic" instead of being satisfied with ordinary logic is the problem of the emergence of novelty. There seem to be two ways of dealing with a new idea. The first is to trace its origin, to show how it emerged from old ideas, to reduce it to a combination of these. This in some way destroys the novelty. Sartre claims that this way is typical of analytic reason, of the natural sciences, though he admits that in the appropriate area it is successful. We might say, crudely, that the typical empiricist procedure is to show that something which at first sight seems novel is really a combination of well-known elements. Reason is analytic here in the sense that it divides the problem up as Descartes suggested as the second move of his method. It is also necessarily atomistic; any solution will have to be in terms of those pieces, and a final solution will only be reached when the pieces are "ultimate" or "fundamental," though this does not mean that further investigation may not result in breaking down the "fundamental" bits into more fundamental ones.

If this is taken to be the right way of proceeding, to be the nature of "reason," then there must be such foundations both at the mental and the physical level. The empiricist approach to knowledge demands a stopping place at the "elementary" constituents of thought, be they simple ideas, sense-data, or whatever. Similarly, the scientific approach will lead to "atoms" in the sense of irreducible particles. In this latter case, it is not clear that there can, in theory, be a final unanalyzable element—only elements which have not yet been analyzed. In the case of the mind,

there may well be reasons given as to why simple
ideas or sense-data are the necessary starting point.
But in either case the ultimate elements will constitute the *foundation* of the rest of knowledge. For a
certain conception of knowledge, the myth of foundations is a necessary myth. Sartre argues that just as
there is a parallel between the empiricist theory of
knowledge and the way nature is thought to operate,
so there will be a parallel between what is studied by
dialectic and the dialectic itself. Following Marx, he
says: "I affirm both that the process of knowledge is
dialectical, that the movement of the object (whatever it be) is *itself* dialectical and that these two dialectics are only one" (p. 119).

One way, then, of coping with novelty is to show
that it is not really novel, only a recombination of old
elements. The other way is to make it a mystery, the
result of some kind of "leap." The romantic conception of the "genius" in art is an obvious example. More
germane, perhaps, is the way of looking at the history
of science which has recently become popular. Science used to be looked on as an ordered and reasoned
progress, at least from its origins in Galileo and New-
ton; the new way, exemplified by Kuhn, talks in terms
of "scientific revolutions," the sudden emergence of a
new way of thinking which is irreducible to the old.
In Kuhn's own words: ". . . scientific revolutions are
here taken to be those non-cumulative developmental
episodes in which an older paradigm is replaced in
whole or part by an incompatible new one."[2] He later
compares them to "changes in world view," and to the
switch from seeing a duck-rabbit as a duck to seeing
it as a rabbit.[3] Also he talks of the switch as being made on the basis of "faith" or on "aesthetic
grounds."[4] To talk in this way is to deny that an analysis is possible, and hence there can be no "logic of

[2] *Structure of Scientific Revolutions,* Chicago, 1962, p. 91.
[3] *Ibid.,* p. 110.
[4] *Ibid.,* p. 157.

discovery" in the sense of a set of teachable procedures which can be used to initiate new ideas.

There is a tendency to look upon any attempt to make sense of a new idea or discovery as an attempt to "explain" it in the analytic sense of the word. This is why to many of Hegel's followers it appeared that what he was doing was giving a new kind of logic in his effort to comprehend history. Of course this is what he was doing, but they took the new logic to be a variant of the old and hence something which could be reduced to a set of mechanical moves, the famous "triad." It is natural to us to think of logic in the ordinary sense as a set of mechanical moves. One of Sartre's points in the *Critique* is that the tendency to model our minds, or the activity of reason, on machines is part of a general alienation in our society, which makes the human product, the machine, take priority over its makers. The machine becomes the master and the servant of the machine a kind of appendage to it (cf. p. 230). In highly developed countries like our own it is easy to forget the change in the way of life caused by the introduction of machines and factories. For example the idea of punctuality hardly exists before the factory; it is machinery, in the first instance, which requires rigid adherence to a schedule. In fact Sartre sees a close connection between "analytic reason," modern science and industry. In this connection it is perhaps significant that Adam Smith's famous description of the mass production of pins seems the counterpart in the material mode of Descartes' second rule: ". . . to divide up each of the difficulties which I examined into as many parts as possible, and as seemed requisite in order that it might be resolved in the best manner possible."[5]

Sartre cannot, and does not try to, deny the enormous success of analytic reason in its proper sphere, that of the natural sciences; he merely claims that there is no intelligibility in it (cf. p. 160). Dialectic

[5] *Discourse on Method,* Part II.

reason has nothing to offer in these areas. But intelligibility is to be expected in the study of human activities, in history and sociology, and it is here that the dialectic comes into its own. A rather similar claim for the importance of understanding in the social sciences has been advanced in this country by Peter Winch, in his book *The Idea of a Social Science*,[6] though the terms in which he makes this claim are very different. Like Winch, Sartre insists that this understanding is not a matter of feeling or sympathy; it is in no way irrational (cf. p. 161). The difficulty of using natural science to deal with the realm of the social is that "natural science has the same structure as a *machine*" (p. 147). But both machines and science are human creations; using machines as models for human behavior seems to make the creator depend on the created. One difficulty in making a strong analogy between machines and organisms is that all machines built so far require human intervention in their operation, whereas organisms can operate by themselves. One biologist, commenting on this, remarks: "This situation creates a curious dilemma: a machine theory of life would require that living organisms, like lifeless machinery, must require external controls, whereas vitalists ought to believe that life—unlike any known machinery—may perhaps run without human participation. . . . It will be noticed that these propositions are a reversal of the usual more superficial attitudes; traditionally mechanists say that life runs 'quite by itself like a machine'. . . ."[7] So far there is no machine that can repair itself and construct further machines.

For Sartre the starting point of understanding, and hence of the dialectic, is human *praxis*, which is his general term for human activity in all forms. To understand what happens in history or in society, he

[6] *The Idea of a Social Science*, London, 1958.
[7] H. Kalmus, "Axioms and Theorems in Biology", in *Nature*, April 20, 1963, p. 241.

claims, one must first get clear about what any man does. It is in this sense that he starts, indeed has to start, his work with a consideration of the isolated individual. But this is a conceptual, not a historical, starting point, and those who have read the *Critique* as giving some kind of account of how societies evolved from individuals have missed the logical structure of the work. The switch to *praxis* is not such a radical departure from *L'Être et le Néant* as might at first appear: "The very transparency of *praxis* . . . has as its origin the inseparable liaison of negation (which totalizes in *situation* what it denies) and of the project which is defined by relation to the abstract *whole*—which is still formal—which the practical agent projects into the future and which appears as the re-organized unity of the negated situation" (p. 149). *Praxis* is both negation and project, though it is also totalization; in a sense the latter term is another way of putting the same point. Many so-called "things" are really "totalizations," not inert objects existing in themselves but wholes whose existence depends on our attitudes and activities. "The synthetic unity of a house is not simply the work that constructed it, it is also the act of living in it: considered in itself it returns to inert multiplicity" (p. 138). It is by looking on it as a house, as a place to dwell in, that we make it into one; if we come to look on it in a different way, e.g., as an obstacle in the path of a new road, it becomes merely a certain collection of matter which has to be removed. A whole consists of a set of parts which are internally related in the sense that the parts take their character from the whole of which they are parts. This kind of relation, Sartre believes, is one which cannot be treated by "analytic reason" but only by the different technique of the dialectic. In fact "dialectic" might be defined as the study of such "wholes." The world is a "human world" in that by our *praxis* and projects we divide it up and put it together into an organized environment, both physically and mentally. For in order to act on the world, I must first "totalize" the field in which I am going to operate. But we cannot do this just as we please, for others before us have divided it up; there is the realm of the "practico-inert."

If we are in a realm of wholes and of a circular dialectic, then making the individual the conceptual starting point would appear to be wrong. We feel that the circularity in question ought to involve the individual being as much a product of his society as it is of the individuals which compose it. But if Sartre does carry over such notions as "negation" and "project" from *L'Être et le Néant*, then the individual is genuinely primary. It is clear that Sartre does give priority to the individual; indeed, a large part of the second section of the *Critique* is taken up with denying that a collection of men can "do" things in the way an individual can. Sartre distinguishes between a "constitutive" and a "constituted" dialectic, the latter being the almost illusory result of a number of individuals acting together. Only the former is really "dialectic." Part of what Sartre wants to claim is that men make their own chains, rather than being chained by an existing society. It is thus clear why, to many critics and particularly those from the Marxist side, the *Critique* has seemed only a development of *L'Être et le Néant*, where the individual was completely free whatever the circumstances. There is, however, a genuine circularity involved, but a different one from the simple relation of the individual to his society. One reason why Sartre cannot accept such a simple circle is that he wishes to deny that the individual and society are equally identifiable entities, exist on the same level. A society for Sartre is only individuals acting together.

I compared Sartre's demand for intelligibility in the study of society to a similar demand by Winch. Throughout the *Idea of a Social Science*, the latter stresses that we must *understand* what men do in order to explain their actions, and this understanding involves a recognition of their behavior as meaning-

ful. Without such recognition it would be impossible
to divide up a set of human movements into separate
actions. The same would seem to apply to animal behavior, in that unless we possess some teleological
notions it would be impossible to divide up the movements of an animal into separate sequences; we would
only have a continuum of motion. Winch tends to
concentrate on language as the type of meaningful
behavior; Sartre's notion of *praxis* is wider, but it includes language as a special case. To some critics,
Winch's approach has seemed idealistic; the following
quotation will show why: "I have also tried to show
that social relations really exist only in and through
the ideas which are current in society; or, alterna-
tively, that social relations fall into the same logical
category as do relations between ideas."[8] It is clear
that to a Marxist this could count as explaining the
infrastructure by means of the superstructure; to such,
social relations are the product of economic relations
between men. Sartre gives a different objection, though
one which for him would also be described as "Marxist," though not one which is so easy to state. Sartre
says: "In other words, Hegel ignored matter as that
which mediates between individuals. Even if we adopt
his terminology, we must say that each consciousness is the reciprocal of the Other, but that this reciprocity can take an infinite number of different
forms—positive and negative—and that it is the mediation of matter which decides the forms it will take
in any concrete case" (pp. 192–93). Sartre is trying to
explain the apparent dependence of ideas on the
economic state of society whilst not reducing them to
mere "reflections" of that state. He could not admit
such a determinism; *praxis* is free. Further, there is an
anarchist element in Sartre's thought; he sees any rule
as something which artificially restricts men, as in itself alienating. Winch seems to equate meaningful
and rule-governed behavior, so to him any such no-

[8] *Op. cit.*, p. 133.

tion is nonsensical. The example of animal behavior was meant to suggest that there is meaningful behavior which is to suggest that there is meaningful behavior which is not rule-governed, that some actions can only be understood in terms of their end without reference to rules. For Sartre, *praxis* comes before rules and is thus prior to language; in fact, for him language is a special case of *praxis*. Hence it is impossible to understand *praxis* on the basis of language; we must proceed in the opposite direction. This claim is related to the Marxist one about the relation between infra- and superstructures, but is more sophisticated and leads to a denial of many Marxist dogmas, such as economic determination. Sartre, with Marx and contrary to the Marxists, wishes to state that "Men make their own history. . . ."

The full quotation runs: "Men make their own history, but they do not make it just as they please; they do not make it under circumstances chosen by themselves, but under circumstances directly encountered, given and transmitted from the past. The tradition of all the dead generations lies like a nightmare on the brain of the living."[9] That which constitutes the "tradition of all the dead generations" is what Sartre calls the "practico-inert," past *praxis* embodied in matter which now regulates or alters our lives, either in the form of changed physical conditions—he instances the floods that devastated large areas of China from the continual deforestation of innumerable peasants, each trying to improve his own situation—to those "exigences"—demands or necessities—which are incorporated in matter and which regulate our lives. The feeling of oppression generated by these, even by public language itself, must be grasped in order to understand the *Critique;* it is brought out well by the following: "From this point of view, it must be said that the practico-inert field *exists,* that it is *real* and that nevertheless free human activities are not suppressed,

---

[9] *18th Brumaire of Louis Napoleon.*

*not even altered* in their transparency as projects in
the course of realization. The field exists: in fact it
surrounds and conditions us; I have only to look out of
the window: I shall see cars which are men and whose
drivers are cars, a policeman who is directing the traffic at the corner of the street and, further away, auto-
matic regulation of the same traffic by red and green
lights, *a hundred exigences* which point to me, pedes-
trian crossings, notices giving orders, notices which
forbid; collectives (a branch of the Crédit Lyonnais, a
café, a church, apartments and also a seriality made
visible: people are queuing in front of a shop), instruments (announcing in congealed voices the way to
use them, pavements, roads, taxi-stations, bus-stops,
etc.). All these entities—neither things nor men, practical unions of man and an inert thing—all these appeals, all these demands do not yet concern me directly. In a moment I will descend into the street and
I will become *their thing* [he adds a footnote: It is
obvious that I am in my apartment the thing of other
things (furniture etc.).], I will buy that collective,
a newspaper and the whole practico-inert which surrounds me and points to me will be revealed *on the
basis* of the total field, that is to say of the World . . ."
(pp. 362–63). But it is only through my *praxis,* my
free actions, that these demands and necessities get a
grip on me. Nevertheless, my *praxis* is, as it were, re-
fracted and hence distorted through them. They are
human products, but I am in a sense their product
in that they define and limit the possibilities of my
life. There are still an infinite variety of courses open
to me, but others are closed. In this sense men are "the
products of their products"; it is not society which acts
on man, it is the products of society.

This is a specification of the central dialectic discovery that "man is mediated by things to the extent
that things are mediated by man" (cf. p. 165). This
is partly because man is an organic creature who depends on other organic or inorganic matter in order
to survive. This dependence is revealed in need (*be-*

*soin*), which is even at this level "negation of the negation and totalization" (pp. 166). Sartre takes over this "law" of the dialectic from Engels, but transforms it radically in doing so (cf. pp. 168–69). There can be no negations in nature because "There can be no *resistance* and, consequently, no negative force except in the interior of a movement which is determined *as a function of the future*, that is to say of a certain form of integration." (p. 169). This is closely related to the argument of *L'Être et le néant:* even to talk of things being destroyed by natural events is already to take up a human viewpoint; in nature itself there are merely changes, though even to say this is perhaps to trespass beyond the bounds of sense; negation only comes into the world via man. But in that book negation was a specification of a general "nihilation" which defined the *pour-soi;* here we meet with negation at what might be called a "lower" level, that of man as a biological organism. But it is still a question of man; Sartre does not want to say that an animal "negates" in any sense. And this is because it is a matter of "need" which has to be recognized as such, is self-conscious.

To say that need is a feeling of lack is already to introduce negation; hence the attempt to satisfy that need is the negation of the negation. But why should not this be a simple return to the starting point? Why should the negation of a negation lead to a new situation? Engels thought this was just a fact about the way in which the world worked, but Sartre argues that it only occurs in special circumstances (cf. p. 173). These arise when "totalization" is involved, when the negation is "interiorized." There can be a simple circle of need and satisfaction, for example among certain primitives who "have no history" (p. 203). These do not negate their situation, or rather there is no proper situation for them because they have no *praxis*, only an *"exis."* For *praxis* involves seeing the situation as a whole (totalization) and working to change it. Perhaps this is better put in one stage rather than two: the only way in which the situation is revealed as a situation is by the act of trying to change it. *"Work,* of whatever kind, can only exist as totalization and the overcoming of contradiction" (p. 173).

But work or *praxis* in this sense has the important property of making use of the "inertia" of nature to attain the end. The tool is just a piece of inert matter whose very inertness is used; the hardness and weight of a stone enable it to function as a hammer. To see an object as a potential tool is to transcend it as it is in itself toward certain human ends. This is totalization and negation, and these are already "internal" relations, as is seeing something as a whole. Thus for Sartre internal relations are logically prior to language. Indeed, for him language is a special case of tool-using, for "The word is a material object" (p. 180) in the sense that considered in itself it is just a set of vibrations in the air or black marks on white paper. But to look upon it as only these is to fail to see it as a word. To do that involves seeing the noises or marks as having internal relations to one another, relations which make them the words that they are. Thus *praxis* is basic.

Here I must again stress that Sartre is not putting forward a historical account; he is claiming that any piece of *praxis* can be seen as dialectical, as involving totalization and hence internal relations. "In the activity of work it is necessary that the unity of the practical field be first realized in order that the worker can pass to the analysis of the difficulties. This 'analysis of the situation' operates by the methods . . . of analytic reason; it is indispensable but it already presupposes prior totalization" (p. 176). But this "concrete experience" of each one of us is for Sartre "abstract" because working in solitude is something which itself has a "historical and social determination" (p. 178). As far as his account goes, it could be the case that men had always existed and acted. It is logical priority which is at issue, just as in an explanation of

the logical nature of language there is no need to discuss its origin.

The very act of changing the environment reflects back on the changer and alters him in turn. This
may occur in obvious ways, as in the case of the
Chinese peasants, or in more subtle ones, as with the
discovery of gold in Spanish America which led to the
bankruptcy of Spain. By making use of matter, man
is laying himself open to alienation, the possibility of
becoming the product of his own product. The world
is not just inert, it is also "practico-inert": "History,
considered at this level, has a terrible and desperate
meaning; it appears, in fact, that men are united by
this inert and demoniacal negation which steals their
substance (that is their work) from them to turn it
against them in the form of an *active inertia* and an
exterminating totalization" (p. 200). Sartre spends
much space discussing this, and showing how it can
be dialectically understood. The Chinese floods are
a simple case, but the forms of alienation which are
uppermost in our society, for example, those features
which led Simone Weil to see technology as the modern form of oppression, require more space to deal
with than is available here.

To say that relations between men are mediated by
matter sounds paradoxical; to most people it is just a
matter of recognizing others as persons like ourselves
and being attracted to them by some kind of instinct.
And if it is pointed out that hostility between men is
just as much a fact as amity, the theory of an instinct is modified to fit the facts. Sartre wants to
show why relations between men take the form they
do, though he admits that the actual relations between men at a given moment are due to historical
circumstances, but not the fact that there are such relations. There is a prior recognition of the other as a
person. For if human relations were just the product of
history, men would be its products, not also its pro-
ducers. Sartre's first question here is what is it to recognize another *as a man?* The answer is to see him as a

being with a *praxis*. He adds that even to deny the full humanity of someone is already to recognize him as a man: ". . . *to treat a man like a dog* one must first see him as a man. The secret sickness of the master is that he is perpetually compelled to take into consideration the *human reality* of his slaves (whether he counts on their skill or their understanding of situations, or whether he takes precautions against the permanent possibility of revolt or escape) at the same time as refusing them the political and economic status which defines a human being *at that time*" (pp. 190–91). To see a man as possessing *praxis* is not necessarily seeing him as having the same *praxis* as oneself, though of course it may be. In that case, the immediate reaction would be one of hostility, given that we exist in a world of scarcity. Man may appear to man as the "anti-man," the "bête carnassière et féroce" (p. 187; this phrase also occurs in Sartre's play *Les Séquestrés d'Altona*). Even if his *praxis* is directed to a different end, he is still "totalizing" the world in a different way, and this may seem a challenge to my totalization. It has often been claimed that the "look" which revealed the existence of the other in *L'Être et le Néant* is basically hostile; in the *Critique* Sartre is trying to explain what he takes to be a basic fact that any original relation of man to man is one of hostility (p. 192).

Of course he does not deny that there are cases where men work together for an end, but he questions the status of this common activity. He wants to say that each is working to attain his own end, and hence thinking of the other as a tool which is necessary for the job. But the reason why he says this is his views on human individuality. It seems for him a logical point that each must have his own *praxis;* even where the case for a common *praxis* is strongest, that of the "groupe en fusion," there is only an appearance of common *praxis*. For a group or a mob does not survive the achievement of its "end," whereas a genuine organism does (cf. pp. 411–12). Just as each individual is tried for his part in a mob action, so each had his own *praxis*, which, as the result of particular circumstances, happened to coincide with the others.

Because man is basically *praxis*, this must also be responsible for human relations. Some human relations may come into being by the mediation of a third party. Sartre instances the taxi-driver who sees a collection of people watching the same event. For each of them, the presence of others is a hindrance; each's attention is directed to the event itself. But the third who sees them imposes a unity from the outside. This unity may take on a different form if they see that they are observed; he has united them into an "us." They in turn may interiorize this, perhaps in the form of a feeling of hostility to him, into a feeling of "we," as when the quarreling husband and wife turn together on the outsider who intervenes. Sartre claims that there is a constant interplay between a direct relation between two (or more) individuals and a relation which depends on the presence of a third party: "The binary formation, as immediate relation between man and man, is the necessary foundation of any ternary relation; but inversely the latter, as mediation of man between men, is the basis on which that reciprocity is recognized as a reciprocal liaison. If the Idealist dialectic abused the notion of the triad, it is mainly because any *real* relation of men amongst themselves is necessarily ternary. But this trinity is not a meaning or an ideal character of human relations: it is inscribed in *being*, that is to say in the materiality of individuals" (p. 189). There cannot be a relation between two isolated individuals, because each exists in a pre-existing world of men. Hence any relation which is established between them is one which can be seen or constituted from outside by another. This of course gives rise to possibilities of alienation—others may alter what I thought the relation was.

In the last resort it is matter which is the basis of all human relations, in the double sense that men are also material objects and that their *praxis* is the chang-

ing of the material world. If man is a being defined
by *praxis*, then this must be the foundation, in some
sense, of all that he does and that happens to him. But
this is not simply a result of the individual's *praxis*
because this is modified by the contingent existence of
others' *praxis*, both present and past. What happens
at any moment can only be made intelligible by looking at the constant interplay of man, man and the
practico-inert, because each individual is born into a
world of men, a world which is already formed by previous generations. Individual *praxis* is the logical starting point (or limit) of explanation, but the explanation
of a particular event can only be given in terms of the
dialectical relations it has with the milieu. In other
words, there can be no explanation of *praxis* in itself; it is just the original relation of man to the world.
In this it is like the "original upsurge" of the *pour-soi*
in *L'Être et le Néant*. To account for the forms that
*praxis* takes at any time we have to use the methods
of the dialectic, because *praxis* involves internal relations. And this explanation will be circular in the sense
that there is no necessary starting-point for it.

I have endeavored to set out the way Sartre conceives of dialectic. Lévi-Strauss criticizes him for failing to notice a "curious paradox; for the work entitled
*Critique de la raison dialectique* is the result of the
exercise by the author of his own analytic reason:
he defines, distinguishes, classes, and opposes. This
philosophic treatise is not of a different nature from
the works which he discusses and with which he enters
into a dialogue, even if to condemn them. How could
analytical reason be applied to dialectical reason, if
they are defined by mutually exclusive characteristics?"[10] In one sense, Lévi-Strauss is right; the book
does not apparently differ from other works of philosophy. Similar points have been raised before in the
history of philosophy against those who tried to make
a distinction between, for example, the Understand-

[10] *La Pensée sauvage*, Paris, 1962, p. 325.

ing and the Reason, between *Verstand* and *Vernunft*.
If our normal language is structured by the understanding, or by analytic reason, then it would seem
impossible to use it to talk of the realm of Reason
or of the dialectic. The only solution would seem to be
to use a different language, but this would give rise to
the problem of how such a language could be learnt
or understood. Perhaps Heidegger is the only philosopher who has been consistent in this respect, and
the problem of understanding him arises from the fact
that he speaks in the language of Reason.[11] A high
price has to be paid for such an attempt, and it is
obvious that Sartre is not a man to risk failure to com-
municate in this way. The *Critique* may be hard to
understand, but there are arguments in it which
can be followed; it does not read like a work of
Heidegger.

There is a temptation to say that Sartre and others
are forced to proceed in this way by the structure of
language. But if they can proceed with any success,
then it would seem that another logic or language was
not needed. If our language is such that we cannot
speak in it of certain things, then the right and only
course is to remain silent about them. But there are no
mentionable matters which we cannot discuss in our
ordinary language. We are quite able to talk of wholes
which are "more than the sum of their parts" even if
they do not seem to fit the categories of normal logic.
Part of the trouble here is a wrong notion of logic;
it is thought of as if it independently provided rules
of language, instead of the rules being extracted from
the language itself. Ordinary talk can cope with both
"dialectical" and "analytical" arguments. Trouble
only arises when these are hypostatized into "faculties,"
separate sections of the mind or of Reason. If we make
an impassable gulf between two parts of the mind or
sorts of reason, then it is not surprising that there

---

[11] I owe this point, indeed much of this paragraph, to a
private communication from Professor Körner.

is no way of getting from one to the other. That we can talk of wholes and of internal relations is evidence that there is no such gulf.

For what is the core of Sartre's argument that "analytic reason" is incapable of coping with human history? I have already mentioned that his claim is like Winch's that the social sciences cannot be studied by the same methods as the physical sciences. This means that what is under attack is not "the way we talk" but a certain *theory,* namely that the only way of proceeding in science is that followed so successfully by physics. Insofar as Descartes and other philosophers can be seen as setting out the basis of this method, and claiming that this is reason, it is they who are under attack. In a sense Sartre has a justification for calling the period of philosophy from Descartes to Kant the period of the dominance of Descartes, for it is he who sets the scene for subsequent philosophers by providing the problems with which they had to deal and by stressing a certain notion of "knowledge" which formed the standard. When Sartre says that the dominant philosophy of the present time is that of Marx, he means, similarly, that it was Marx who raised the problems for the next stage of philosophizing by turning attention from the natural sciences to the social. And if the social sciences provide the particular problems of modern thought, this is because they are not amenable to the methods used in the previous period. But there is no reason, as Sartre agrees, to discard these methods where they are successful; all we have to do is to introduce new ones for dealing with society. In a way such new methods are bound to appear odd to those versed in the old, because if they did not differ in some important sense they would not be new methods. Further, they cannot be reducible to the old, otherwise there would be nothing new about them. It is at the level of philosophical accounts that the quarrel arises. Sartre frequently contrasts "analytic" and "dialectic" reason, and even claims that the latter is "superior" to the former.

But he does not claim that these are separate "faculties" of the mind or separate kinds of language. So he does not have to claim that a special language is required for the dialectic. The resources that we already possess are adequate; it is only certain philosophic theories that blinded us to this.

In conclusion, I must point out that in this paper I have been primarily concerned with expounding what Sartre has to say; I have not tried to criticize it. This is not because I believe that it is immune to criticism, but because only when what is being done is clearly seen can criticism begin. Most of what has been written on the *Critique* seems to me to spring from misunderstandings. It is an important work, and without a firm knowledge of what it says, worthwhile criticism is impossible.

# SARTRE AND THE HUMANIST TRADITION IN SOCIOLOGY

*Michael A. and Deena Weinstein*

Sartre's work on the relationships among human beings and societies can be considered productively from
a variety of critical perspectives and points of view.
Wilfrid Desan and Walter Odajnyk have situated Sartre's *Critique of Dialectical Reason* in the framework
of Marxist social philosophy and have judged Sartre's
attempt to humanize contemporary Marxism with the
existentialist notion of freedom as a failure.[1] Mary
Warnock and James F. Sheridan, Jr., have juxtaposed
the ideas developed in *Being and Nothingness* and
those presented in the *Critique*.[2] Warnock has argued
that Sartre underwent a "radical conversion" from a
philosophy of freedom to Marxist sociology. Opposing this view, Sheridan has maintained that a single
fundamental project unites both works. The perspectives elaborated by the recent British and American commentators are useful in furthering understanding of Sartre's writings. Sartre declares himself a
Marxist, and it is surely appropriate to explore the
relationships of his work to the Marxist tradition. Sar-

This essay was written especially for this edition by Michael
A. and Deena Weinstein, Purdue University.

[1] Wilfrid Desan, *The Marxism of Jean-Paul Sartre* (Garden
City: Doubleday and Company, 1966). Walter Odajnyk, *Marxism and Existentialism* (Garden City: Doubleday and Company,
1965).

[2] Mary Warnock, *The Philosophy of Sartre* (London: Hut-
chinson University Library, 1965). James F. Sheridan, Jr.,
*Sartre: The Radical Conversion* (Athens: Ohio University
Press, 1969).

tre claims that the existentialism of *Being and Nothingness* and the Marxism of the *Critique* are mutually supportive, and it is certainly proper to investigate whether or not his claim is correct. Interpreting the *Critique of Dialectical Reason* in the contexts of Marxist social philosophy and the entire body of Sartre's writings produce insights into the purposes of the *Critique* and the meaning of many concepts developed within it. However, Marxist social philosophy and Sartre's early existentialism do not constitute the only frames of reference for interpreting the *Critique*. Sartre's writings on the human being and social units can also be analyzed in the context of the humanist revolt against abstract and formal sociologies that is under way in both Europe and America. Sartre's effort is one among several dialectical sociologies that have appeared recently in the West. These humanistic and dialectical sociologies share important resemblances in method and object, although they differ widely in substance and concept. A comparison of Sartre's *Search for a Method* and two American attempts to develop a method for a humanistic sociology will reveal a unity in the dialectical revolt against formalism that surpasses such traditional categories as "Marxism" and "scientific sociology."

Perhaps the most striking resemblance between Sartre's methodological writings and the work of the American humanists is that both bodies of literature can be most readily defined initially by their opposition to sociological theories that are currently dominant in different parts of the world. The characteristics that Sartre imputes to official Soviet Marxism and the qualities that American humanists like C. Wright Mills and Barrington Moore attribute to structural-functional theory and empirical sociology reveal the first moment of the humanist revolt. The basis of Sartre's disagreement with official Soviet Marxism is his affirmation of the unity of theory and practice as a goal of sociology and social philosophy. For Sartre, official Soviet Marxism has been defined by a split be-

tween theory and practice that has resulted in an unprincipled empiricism in action and an abstract formalism in thought. Sartre's aim is to develop a method
that will once again make the unity of theory and
practice possible in the Marxist tradition. The basis
of the American humanist's disagreement with empirical sociology and structural-functionalism is a
commitment to the development of a sociology that is
relevant to the alleviation of significant problems of
human existence in the present age. For C. Wright
Mills and Barrington Moore, American sociology has
been split between an empiricism that provides information for bureaucratic decision-makers and an abstract conceptualism that at best produces elegant systems of abstractions and at worst provides a justifying
ideology for power elites and vested interests. The
American humanists search for a method that will
unite concerns with generalizing power and attention
to fact. In their most general aspects, the projects of
Sartre and the American humanists consist in reviving
the classical tradition of sociological analysis in such
a way that it will be relevant to the structural and
psychological problems of the post-modern era, or
what C. Wright Mills calls the Fourth Epoch.

The official Soviet Marxism that provides Sartre
with the reason to search for a method is itself defined
primarily by a method. Sartre sketches a sociological
explanation for the split between theory and practice
that he finds in contemporary Marxism. When Marxism, the philosophy that wants to change the world
because "it is and wants to be *practical*," became the
official theory of the Soviet Union, theory was divorced from practice.[3] The Soviet Union was confronted with the tasks of defense against encirclement
and rapid industrialization. In order to carry out these
tasks the leadership of the Communist Party of the
Soviet Union (CPSU) attempted to maximize the in-

[3] Jean-Paul Sartre, *Search for a Method* (New York: Vintage Books, 1968), p. 22.

tegration of the Soviet population. Part of the process of integration involved the suppression of dissent and criticism. The conflict engendered by discussion might diminish intra-group solidarity and, thus, the Party leadership reserved the right to "define the line and to interpret the event."[4] Practice became an unprincipled empiricism geared to tactical advantage and theory became a static formalism. This kind of explanation is familiar in American sociology, particularly in theories of political elitism. For example, S. M. Lipset has noted that anti-democratic tendencies in American labor unions are partly due to the need for conflict groups to maintain intra-group solidarity.[5] Such explanations are usually derived from theories stressing the centrality of political conflict and have been a staple of such anti-Marxist writers as Mosca, Pareto, and Michels. However, the argument takes a novel twist in Sartre's hands. Once a leadership group exercises its right to define the line and to interpret the event, it must devise a method through which definitions and interpretations are developed. It is the method of "placing" that impels Sartre to search for a new method.

Sartre declares that contemporary Marxist theory is made up of formalized abstractions that he calls "general particularities." Both the Soviet Marxists and their opponents like the Trotskyites employ in their social analyses terms like "bourgeois idealism" and "bureaucracy." There is a pretense that these terms refer to particular historical situations, events, and units. However, they are "purely formal" unities of "abstract, universal relations."[6] Armed with an arsenal of "general particularities," analysis for the Marxist becomes a matter of "placing." Particular historical events are denuded of their detail and their relations

[4] *Ibid.*

[5] Seymour Martin Lipset, *Political Man* (Garden City: Doubleday and Company, 1963), pp. 387–436.

[6] Sartre, *Search for a Method*, p. 24.

with other events and are classified as instances of a
"general particularity." The classical Marxist search
for the whole in its parts becomes the "terrorist practice of 'liquidating the particularity.'"[7] Sartre terms
the method of placing events under general particularities a form of Scholasticism. The method of placing is anti-empirical because its "sole purpose is to
force the events, the persons, or the acts considered
into pre-fabricated molds."[8] The Marxist becomes
deadened to new experiences and his interpretations
are revealed as attempts to reduce the present and
the future to the past. Although Sartre never makes
the connection fully explicit, we can surmise that the
method of placing is the intellectual expression of a
leadership group attempting to preserve and extend
the integration of a population in conflict with other
collectivities. We may add that Sartre's commitment
to Marxism perhaps prevents him from recognizing
that the method of placing functions to further the
maintenance of a leadership group that met concrete
social challenges in the past, but is incapable of meet-
ing them in the present. Such a leadership group will
use the method of placing in an attempt to reduce the
novel situations of the present to situations that it has
already surpassed. Along with the method of placing
and the units termed general particularities goes a
crude empiricism in practice. Behaviorism and Pav-
lovianism are the practical counterparts of ideological
and official Soviet Marxism.

Like Sartre, the American humanists define their
revolt as an opposition to a method. Parallel to
Sartre, Barrington Moore charges American sociologists with developing a "new scholasticism." Of course,
Sartre and the American humanists criticize in different contexts and, thus, their attacks are not exactly
the same. Sartre is criticizing the methods of intellec-
tuals formally affiliated with political movements

[7] *Ibid.*, p. 28.
[8] *Ibid.*, p. 37.

and even actual regimes. Marxist analysis is geared
to interpreting day-to-day social and political conflicts,
and it unabashedly takes sides in these conflicts.
Sartre does not oppose these two aspects of Marxist
analysis. He aims at improving the interpretation of
historical events so that the analysis will be a more
effective weapon in the battle for liberation. The
American humanists criticize the methods of social
scientists who attempt to separate their political
affiliations from their research. In their professional
work American social scientists usually claim that
they neither provide interpretations of particular social and political conflicts nor take sides in such conflicts. Rather, they claim to describe universal social
processes and to maintain scientific objectivity. Thus,
the issue of value-neutrality in social studies has been
very important to American humanists. We will not
analyze the humanist's critique of value-neutrality,
but will concentrate on the criticisms of social science methods. Considering the differences in contexts, the similarities among Sartre and the American humanists are all the more striking.

The divorce of theory and practice that Sartre finds
in contemporary Marxism is paralleled by a polariza-
tion of methods, or a separation of theory and research, that the American humanists discover in
current sociology. Barrington Moore identifies two
tendencies in contemporary American sociology. The
tendency of "empirical fact-gathering" is founded on
the rationale that "by getting positive answers to a
series of small problems we will wake up some fine
day with a conclusive answer to the big problems."[9]
The tendency of elaborating "analytical categories" is
based on the rationale that any description of the
"facts" implies a system of general categories and that
it is wise "to make these categories and hypotheses as
explicit and logically watertight as possible" so that

[9] Barrington Moore, Jr., *Political Power and Social Theory*
(Cambridge: Harvard University Press, 1958), p. 92.

research will test the tenability of theories.[10] Moore sees no reason why empirical studies that are severely restricted in space, time, and subject should eventually produce answers to major sociological questions. However, he is even more critical of formal theories. Analytical theorists tend to support their theories by the method of "illustration." Moore remarks that "any concept can be 'illustrated' somehow or other, and facts picked up off the table and put into pigeon holes."[11] The method of illustrating is essentially the same as the method of placing. In both cases historical events are detached from their relations to other events and divested of most of their particular characteristics so that they can be classified under categories that have already been formulated. While the method of illustrating may not function to maintain a political leadership group, perhaps it does help to preserve the positions of professional elites in the social sciences by masking the obsolescence of their work.

C. Wright Mills identifies as abstracted empiricism and grand theory the two tendencies that Barrington Moore described. Abstracted empiricism is Moore's empirical fact-gathering with the addition of the claim that this sort of research is usually performed at the behest of wealthy and powerful bureaucratic groups which need information upon which to base decisions. These groups are interested in controlling workers, consumers, inmates or conscripts, and they are not concerned with theoretical interpretations. Abstracted empirical research provides information to large organizations and cloaks itself in the garb of experimental science. Mills describes grand theory in very Sartrian terms as a fetishism of Concepts. Criticizing the structural-functionalism of Talcott Parsons, Mills remarks that the grand theorists are "possessed by the idea that the one model of social

[10] *Ibid.*, p. 97.
[11] *Ibid.*, p. 100.

order" they have developed "is some kind of universal model."[12] The abstract universality of grand theory prohibits its use as a means of analyzing problems of substance. For Mills, as well as for Moore, grand theory removes social occurrences from their historical relations and classifies them as instances of predefined general ideas. The method of placing or illustrating is as much a source of revolt for Mills as it is for Sartre and Moore. Whether or not Soviet and European Marxism, and American sociology, are actually characterized by the method of placing or illustrating in their theoretical moments, Sartre and the American humanists believe that they have discovered such a conservative method at the heart of the literature. They respond to the problem of method by proposing new methods.

Five distinctive characteristics describe the methods that the humanists develop as replacements for the regnant approaches in East and West. The new methods stress a historical rather than a universalistic approach, multi-variate sociological analysis rather than single-factor social theory, empirical and dynamic methods instead of the method of placing or illustrating, concern with totalization instead of interest in fully defined totalities or pluralistic models, and an emphasis on the practical rather than on the contemplative. These five hallmarks of the methods suggested by Sartre and the American humanists should not be interpreted as separate from one another. Sartre and the American humanists are reacting to sociologies that have set up walls of separation between research problems, concepts, and the most basic moments of sociological activity. The abstracted empiricism of Mills, the empirical fact-gathering of Moore, and the unprincipled empiricism of Sartre are all terms referring to a situation in which the context of research or decision-making is drastically limited by

[12] C. Wright Mills, *The Sociological Imagination* (New York: Grove Press, 1961), p. 98.

space, time, subject, and goal. Problems are given restricted and artificial definitions, and piecemeal solutions are attempted. The objective of unprincipled
empiricism is expedient adjustment by leadership
groups to threatening conditions. The new methods
will be attempts to relate specific problems to one
another and to more general tendencies in social
structure. The grand theory of Mills, the analytical
categories of Moore and the orthodox Marxism of
Sartre are all terms referring to sociological theories
characterized by self-contained and watertight categories under which observations are classified and
evaluated. Like unprincipled empiricism, grand theory also deprives events of their relations to one another. Historical occurrences are revalued as instances
of general ideas. The new methods will aim at producing more fluid and flexible concepts. Finally, the
most serious separation discovered by the humanists
is the one between theory and practice, or theory and
research. While practice and research are viewed
as responses to atomized and artificially restricted
problems, and theory is seen as the elaboration of
empty analytical categories, theory and practice are
viewed as entirely divorced from one another. The
final objective of the new methods will be the unity
of theory and practice. Thus, the five characteristics of
the new methods can most usefully be seen as facets
of a single procedure. Each facet depends upon the
others for its full meaning. Speaking long enough
about any one characteristic will result in a discussion
of the others. Perhaps this is inevitable when dialectical methods are under consideration.

### Historical Approach

In his "New Scholasticism and the Study of Politics,"
Barrington Moore remarks that perhaps the best a
sociologist can do "at any given moment in history is
to draw out the potentialities of the social forms
that exist before us in such a way as to set up a criti-

cal standard for evaluating the status quo."[13] This statement sums up the concern with developing a historical approach to sociological inquiry that comprises the most evident hallmark of the new methods of Sartre and the American humanists. Unprincipled empiricism and grand theory banished history from sociological study in two different ways. Unprincipled empiricism reduced the contexts of research and decision-making to such narrow frames of space and time that any vision of broad historical changes was lost. Events were situated neither laterally nor in their backward and forward tensions. They were viewed as problems, each to be solved on its own terms or in the terms of leadership groups. Grand theory removed history from sociological study by its claim to categorize universal social processes. Qualities of events that did not have relevance to the category system of the particular grand theory were deemed trivial appearances and were "liquidated" as the event was subsumed under one of the categories. In opposition to the depreciation of history by unprincipled empiricists and grand theorists, Sartre and the American humanists have proclaimed the radically historical character of their new methods. Not only do the humanists claim that space and time frames should be extended in empirical research, and that the analysis of particular structural types should be added to the description of universal social processes in theoretical studies; they doubt that any significant sociological principles can be applied in the study of more than one historical era. For Moore, this means that the sociologist should attempt to draw out the potentialities of the social forms that exist before him and try to set up a critical standard for evaluating the status quo. Sartre and Mills make comparable statements. Sartre's principle that a philosophy "remains efficacious so long as the *praxis* which has engendered it, which supports it, and which is clari-

---

[13] Moore, *Political Power*, p. 108.

fied by it is still alive," reveals a radically historical approach.[14] This opposition, through a historical approach, to formalism and brute empiricism is perhaps behind Sartre's extreme statement that any going beyond Marxism in the present era is "at worst only a return to pre-Marxism; at best, only the rediscovery of a thought already contained in the philosophy which one believes he has gone beyond."[15] For Sartre, as long as scarcity of economic goods obtains, the *praxis* that engenders Marxism will remain alive. While not as radical as Moore and Sartre, Mills also favors a historical approach. He suggests that sociologists conceive types of social structure in terms of institutional orders and relate the outlines of these orders in "a set of 'working models' which are used to make us more aware, as we examine specific societies at specific times, of the links by which they are 'tied together.' "[16]

The claim that significant sociological principles cannot be applied in more than one historical era is subject to serious question. Is it not the case that the discussions of the humanists presuppose sociological principles that are applicable to more than one historical period? When Sartre argues that a philosophy is relevant so long as the *praxis* that engendered it remains alive, is he not implying that *praxis* is a defining quality of human existence over all historical periods? Further, when he adds that Marxism cannot be surpassed as long as scarcity of economic goods obtains, is he not saying that the relationship of the quantity of economic goods and their distribution to human need is important for understanding social life over all historical periods? The same questions can be raised with reference to the work of Mills. When he advises sociologists to conceive types of social structure in terms of institutional orders, is he

14 *Ibid.*, pp. 95–96.
15 Sartre, *Search for a Method*, p. 7.
16 Mills, *The Sociological Imagination*, pp. 44–45.

not implying that institutional orders such as the
economic and political appear in all historical periods? Further, is he not saying that the study of social structure is important for understanding social
life over all historical periods? With regard to
Moore's proposal, is he not saying that "social forms"
always have potentialities that can be evaluated according to a critical standard? In summary, is it not
the case that while the humanists attempt to oppose
the universalism of grand theory with a radical historical approach, they must introduce an implicit
grand theory in their very description of the historical
approach? These questions miss the point of the humanist's enterprise. They are not concerned with
claiming that no sociological principles are applicable
across historical periods. Rather, they claim that no
significant sociological principles are applicable across
historical periods. The important task is to define the
humanist's criteria of significance, and this task can
only be accomplished by considering the other four
hallmarks of the humanist method. The radicality of
the humanist's historical approach is relative to the
other facets of the humanist method. The humanists
are by no means traditional historicists. In fact, Mills
places the historicists on a par with grand theorists because they produce "a trans-historical strait-
jacket into which the materials of human history are
forced."[17] Another possible criticism of the humanist's
historical approach is that the notion of historical era
has not been given a definition independent of a social situation in which a single set of significant sociological principles can be applied. Under this interpretation, the humanists would be saying that in
time, social situations tend to change in respects important enough to require new theoretical categories
for their adequate analysis. There is no reason why
this interpretation should not be upheld, especially
since an independent definition of historical era would

[17] *Ibid.*, pp. 22–23.

imply an ambitious trans-historical theory of society. This does not mean that the problem of determining the conditions in which a theory is judged as adequate by the humanists can be resolved easily. As in the case of criteria for significant sociological principles, the criteria for determining the adequacy of theoretical units can only be determined by investigating the other facets of the humanist method.

## *Multi-Variate Analysis*

The second facet of the humanist method is involved with the multi-dimensional character that Sartre, Mills, and Moore find in historical events. The emphasis on multi-variate analysis is a reaction to the single-factor explanations of social phenomena offered by orthodox Marxists and structural-functionalists. While the content of the charges that Sartre and the American humanists bring against the regnant sociologies differs widely, the similarities in the form of attack are striking. Mills argues that the structural-functionalism of Parsons reduces all historical events to instances of conformity to or deviance from a normative order and a value hierarchy that is supposedly widely shared within a given society. He accuses Parsons of mistaking the ideological legitimations of a social structure with the social structure itself and cautions that sociologists should not avoid investigating economic, political, and military structures of domination.[18] While Mills accuses the grand theorists of dissolving social structure into superstructure, Sartre argues that orthodox Marxists reduce all historical events to manifestations of the structure. He maintains that contemporary Marxists have dissolved men in "a bath of sulphuric acid" instead of studying them in depth. Their strategy has been to refer all events, including Sartre's philosophical writings, to economic contradictions and to conflicts of material

[18] *Ibid.*, p. 42.

interests. Sartre claims that an "unprejudiced examination of the historical object" will determine in each case whether or not "the action or the work reflects the superstructural motives of groups or of individuals formed by certain basic conditionings."[19] Economism will not provide an adequate analysis of all human productions. The novels of Gustave Flaubert and the history of phenomenology from Husserl to Sartre are not merely the expression of conflicts within the system of economic production, but also reflect factors in biography and partly autonomous cultural development. In form, Moore's critique of reductionism is similar to the attacks of Mills and Sartre. He charges the structural-functionalists with underemphasizing the autonomy of personality and culture, and with making these factors dependent upon the activities that are supposedly necessary to maintain a social system. Sartre and the American humanists are united in their condemnation of the reduction of multi-dimensional historical events to a single level of analysis.

Despite the differences in content among the sociologies that Sartre and the American humanists attack, both the form and the content of the modes of analysis that they recommend as replacements are strikingly similar. Each of them is committed to both a multi-variate analysis that does not reduce all of the aspects of a given historical event to a single factor and an emphasis on the centrality of social structure. Further, Mills, Sartre, and Moore all view proper sociological analysis as an investigation of the intersection of the concrete human being, the social structure in which he acts, and the history of social institutions. Sartre is perhaps the writer who has attempted to be most explicit in defining the new method. Borrowing from Henri Lefebvre, Sartre develops a "progressive-regressive" method. While there are many ambiguities in Sartre's discussion of this method, it is

[19] Sartre, *Search for a Method,* p. 42.

clear that it takes structure, person, and history as the primary variables. Sartre remarks that both a horizontal complexity and a vertical complexity characterize human groups. The horizontal complexity corresponds to what sociologists usually call social structure. It refers to the relations of the group to major social institutions and the techniques through which the group carries on work. The vertical complexity refers to the historical situation of the group. It involves practices that survive from the past and the sequence in which various institutions were formed. The vertical and horizontal complexities are not well defined by Sartre and he moves immediately to stating the several stages of the progressive-regressive method as Henri Lefebvre developed them. The first phase of the method is descriptive. The sociologist observes an event with the guidance of a general theory. The second phase is analytico-regressive. Here the sociologist attempts to "date" the event by situating it in history. The third phase is historical-genetic. Here the sociologist attempts to "rediscover the present," which is now elucidated. Sartre remarks that Lefebvre's method needs no further elaboration. He claims that "this method, with its phase of phenomenological description and its double movement of regression followed by progress, is valid . . . *in all the domains of anthropology.*"[20] This remark is troublesome because Lefebvre seems to advocate description guided by a general theory while Sartre seems to favor an initial phase of "phenomenological description." This difficulty seems to be resolved in favor of description guided by a general theory. This general theory is structural and Marxist: "The structures of a society which is created by human work define for each man an objective situation as a starting point. . . ."[21] Thus, the first phase of Sartre's method is situating an event in the social structure.

[20] *Ibid.*, p. 52n.
[21] *Ibid.*, pp. 92–93.

The second phase is relating biography to the structure, enhancing Marxism with existential psychology. The final phase is integrating structure and biography into a historical movement. Sartre describes the method succinctly: ". . . it will progressively determine a biography (for example) by examining the period, and the period by studying the biography. Far from seeking immediately to integrate one into the other, it will hold them separate until the reciprocal involvement comes to pass for itself and puts a temporary end to the research."[22] How a "reciprocal involvement comes to pass for itself" is not in question at present. Sartre does not pretend to advocate natural science methods, and in this essay we are concerned with situating Sartre in a sociological movement rather than with examining the validity of his method. What is most significant for our purposes is Sartre's definition of sociology as the study of the intersection of social structure, history, and biography.

In describing the sociological imagination, or the pattern of thought most appropriate for working in sociology, C. Wright Mills comments: "The sociological imagination enables us to grasp history and biography and the relations between the two with society."[23] For Mills, there are three major questions that the sociologist should pose. First the sociologist should attempt to determine the structure of the society under study. Second, he should try to define where this society stands in human history. Finally, he should attempt to find out what varieties of men and women prevail in the society. Mills sees the most fruitful distinction in sociology as that between "personal troubles of milieu" and "public issues of social structure."[24] Ideally, sociologists should "locate" the individual, as a "biographical entity," within various interpersonal milieux, and then locate these milieux

---

[22] *Ibid.*, p. 135.
[23] Mills, *The Sociological Imagination*, p. 6.
[24] *Ibid.*, p. 8.

within the social structure.[25] Mills climaxes his discussion with a program for multi-variate analysis that
is almost the same as Sartre's description of the
progressive-regressive method. Mills states that in the
study of contemporary society it is a "good rule first
to explain its contemporary features in terms of their
contemporary function."[26] This is equivalent to Lefebvre's suggestion that the sociologist first grasp the
horizontal complexity of a community, and Sartre's
statement that the first moment of sociological analysis
is situating the event in a structure. Mills proceeds
to recommend a second phase of analysis: "One
works back to the genetic, biographical causes only
after having exhausted the contemporary features and
setting of the character."[27] This is equivalent to Lefebvre's suggestion that the sociologist grasp the vertical complexity of a community only after he has understood the horizontal complexity, and Sartre's
statement that biographical and historical studies succeed structural descriptions. Mills's recapitulation of
the method is much like Sartre's in both content and
difficulties. He declares that the "classical social science" he wishes to revive neither builds up generalizations from microscopic analysis nor deduces explanations from abstract concepts. Rather, classical
sociologists "try to build and to deduce at the same
time, in the same process of study, and to do so by
means of adequate formulation and reformulation of
problems and of their adequate solutions."[28] Again,
what "adequate" formulation, reformulation and solution of problems means, in operational terms, is not
under discussion here. We are primarily concerned
with the convergence in content and form of the
multi-variate analyses proposed by Sartre and the
American humanists. For Moore, the moments of a

25 *Ibid.*, p. 161.
26 *Ibid.*, p. 154.
27 *Ibid.*, p. 155.
28 *Ibid.*, p. 128.

new method of multi-variate analysis resemble those described by Sartre and Mills. He counsels sociologists to situate an event in the social structure and then work back to personality and cultural factors to explain why "a particular individual or group of people refuses to adapt to the imperatives of a specific social system or situation."[29] Moore describes his method as perceiving "the general in the atypical or even the unique, resolving in this fashion the tension between universals and particulars."[30] For example, Marx captured the general features of nineteenth-century capitalism by studying the special case of the English economy. Like Mills and Sartre, Moore believes that sociologists should study the historical evolution of social structures, as well as the limits and possibilities of human behavior.[31] Again, the two themes of a progressive-regressive method and a study of the interraction of social structure, history, and biography are dominant.

## Empirical and Dynamic Methods

If Sartre and the American humanists advance methods that are historical in approach and multi-variate and dialectical in analysis, their studies are also empirical and dynamic. Sartre's initial critique of orthodox Marxism and the attacks of Mills and Moore on structural-functional theory were based on opposition to the method of placing or illustrating. The Marxists tended to denude events of their horizontal and vertical complexities so that they could be placed under the categories of a static theory. Empiricism was limited to capturing a discrete event. Succeeding the moment of capture analysis was done on a level of abstraction. Since the abstractions did not change as

[29] Moore, *Political Power*, p. 103.
[30] Maurice Stein and Arthur Vidich (eds.), *Sociology on Trial* (Englewood Cliffs: Prentice-Hall, Inc., 1963), pp. 87–88.
[31] *Ibid.*, p. 88.

actual social situations altered, the static Marxism became less and less effective as a tool of sociological and political analysis. The intellectual terror of liquidating particularities became more and more severe. According to Moore and Mills, structural-functionalists tended to deprive events of their relations to social structure and of their historical relations so that they could be made to appear as examples of conformity to or deviance from a normative order and a value hierarchy. Again, those empirical inquiries that took place were limited to the seizure of discrete events. Once the seizure had been accomplished, the event was absorbed into one of the categories of the grand theory. The progressive-regressive analyses of Sartre and the American humanists are attempts to free sociology of static formalism.

In his criticism of structural-functional theory, Moore describes how the formalists might treat a problem in political sociology: "dictatorship and democracy would be separated into airtight compartments with carefully worked out definitions of each. Then other facts would be sorted into neat piles labeled 'dictatorship' and 'democracy.'"[32] He remarks that such a method would make invisible the whole process by which one social structure changes into another. Moore recommends that sociologists become more like historians. They should be more empirical and examine "each piece of potentially useful data" to see how it bears on the problems that they are studying. They should relate each new piece of information to the knowledge that they have previously acquired and thereby gain the cumulative insights of a dynamic analysis. Mills makes similar statements. He asserts that the empiricism of everyday life is characterized by stereotypes and conceptions of a given society. If the sociologist attempts to free himself from these stereotypes by doing isolated statistical studies, content will swallow idea. If he attempts

[32] *Ibid.,* p. 78.

to free himself through grand theory, idea will swallow content.[33] The proper method is to take up substantive problems "on the historical level of reality" and effect a continuous interplay between exploration of new data and integration of that data into flexible theoretical structures.[34] Sartre also favors an empirical and dynamic method. He accuses Lukács of failing to derive his concepts "from experience—or at least not from the new experiences which (he) seeks to interpret."[35] Like Mills, Sartre believes that the investigation of new data and the theoretical interpretation of these data should be a continuous process. It appears that the basic feature of an empirical and a dynamic method is that it constantly alters and perhaps sometimes destroys existing sociological theories in the interest of making theory applicable to changing social situations. The progressive-regressive method seems to involve the continuous invention of new names and conceptual relations to describe novel experiences and social forms. However, the claim that the progressive-regressive method is empirical and dynamic remains abstract until the activities of theorizing and "doing sociology" have been described. In a difficult discussion, Sartre calls the proper sociological activity "totalizing." Mills presents a description of the "sociological imagination" that is similar to Sartre's discussion of totalizing, but less difficult to follow. We now turn to the core of the methods developed by Sartre and the American humanists—the sociological *praxis*.

### Totalizing Concerns

Mills develops his discussion of the sociological activity around the Marxian "principle of historical specificity." He interprets this principle to state that

[33] *Ibid.*, p. 124.
[34] *Ibid.*, p. 128.
[35] Sartre, *Search for a Method*, p. 37.

"any given society is to be understood in terms of the specific period in which it exists."[36] This seems to be merely a definition of the historical approach that we have previously identified in the works of Sartre and the American humanists. In fact, Mills even recognizes at this point that he has difficulty elaborating an independent definition of a historical period. However, he claims that despite this difficulty, "the institutions, the ideologies, the types of men and women prevailing in any given period constitute something of a unique pattern."[37] He further argues that within this pattern "various mechanisms of change come to some specific kind of intersection."[38] The sociological *praxis* can be defined as the effort to grasp the pattern that characterizes one's age and apprehend the mechanisms of change. There are no trans-historical laws of society because historical change is change of unique social structures: "Just as there is a variety of social structures, there is a variety of principles of historical change."[39] Mills states that the job of the social scientist is to make the social structure explicit and to study it as a "whole."[40] If there is any specifically sociological work, it is "the continual effort to relate" features of a society to others "in order to gain a conception of the whole."[41] It is important that Mills does not attempt to grasp the "whole" by placing a grid of preconceived categories over social reality. Instead, he is engaged in a "continual effort" to relate different facets of a changing social situation into a pattern. He carefully distinguishes his sociological *praxis* from the activities of traditional pluralists and holists. The pluralism that underlies abstracted empiricism claims that the

---

[36] Mills, *Sociological Imagination*, p. 149.
[37] *Ibid.*
[38] *Ibid.*
[39] *Ibid.*, p. 150.
[40] *Ibid.*, p. 79.
[41] *Ibid.*, p. 137.

causes of events are numerous, scattered, and minute.
There is no whole to aim at and the sociological
*praxis* consists of analyzing problems that are severely
restricted in their horizontal and vertical complexities.
In the Millsian *praxis,* one relates parts to each other
in an effort to gain a conception of the whole. Mills
links the pluralist doctrine to justifications for piecemeal reform of the social structure.[42] Mills is equally
opposed to traditional holism, in which society is
viewed as an integrated organism. Mills views social
structure as a dynamic complex of trends, and the
aim of the sociological *praxis* becomes seeing several
major trends together as "moving parts of the total
structure of the period."[43] Mills does not believe that
social scientists can give adequate descriptions of
fully defined social totalities. Social structure is constantly changing, and the sociologist should be continuously "totalizing." In the process of totalization
one may grasp only a fragment, and his attempt may
be biased. However, the risk of attempting to grasp
the moving whole is less than the risk involved in
losing consciousness of the whole or pretending that
it is a finished totality. Like Mills, Moore attacks both
pluralism and holism. He argues that the pluralist
assumption that historical data form separate and
discrete units is incorrect. Social phenomena are always found in relation to one another and while in
any particular study one can only examine some of
the data and trace some of the relationships among
them, he should attempt to "make a connection between the parts and the whole."[44] By no means, however, is this whole a fully defined totality. Holists
tend to project relationships that they have discovered at a certain time and place unjustifiably into the
future. For Moore, the sociologist should look at
atypical practices as well as typical social patterns so

[42] *Ibid.,* p. 85.
[43] *Ibid.,* p. 153.
[44] Stein and Vidich, *Sociology on Trial,* p. 79.

that he can find "the seeds of possible future developments."[45] He notes that there is a tendency for "the various institutions and beliefs in any society to hang together in at least a roughly coherent fashion."[46] This is the whole that Mills attempted to grasp. Moore adds that along with the tendency toward mutual adjustment among institutions in a society goes continual disruption of these forms. As in Mills, the sociologist should attempt to totalize a continuously changing history.

Despite his difficult language, Sartre seems to recommend the same sociological *praxis* as Moore and Mills. He claims that the "ruling principle" of his inquiry is "the search for the synthetic ensemble, each fact, once established, is questioned and interpreted as part of a whole."[47] While the sociologist should be guided by Marxist theory, in the sense that he is concerned with determining the structural significance of events, he also "seeks to discover the totality by means of the facts."[48] Thus, Sartre rejects both pluralism and holism. He charges pluralism with dividing men into watertight groups and losing any sense of the total. Since it contains no attempt to apprehend the vertical and horizontal complexities of events, it prevents one from understanding dialectical totalization. The attempt to grasp the whole by relating together facts that have been situated in a structural theory is abandoned for the statement of unresolved paradoxes and conflicts.[49] Sartre is equally opposed to holism. He accuses the Gestalt sociologists, in particular Kurt Lewin, with affirming the radical autonomy of the object of study. First, Lewin asserts the ontological autonomy of the object by claiming that the group is a concrete whole with

45 *Ibid.*, p. 89.
46 *Ibid.*, p. 90.
47 Sartre, *Search for a Method*, p. 26.
48 *Ibid.*
49 *Ibid.*, pp. 19–20.

properties separate from those of its parts. Second, he asserts the methodological autonomy of the object by claiming that every sociological law "is a structural law and expresses a function or a functional relation between the parts of a whole."[50] According to Sartre, Lewin has banished history from sociological inquiry, and has substituted a "unity already made" for a "unity in the process of being made."[51] From another viewpoint, Sartre claims that the holists are confined to the study of horizontal complexities and ignore vertical complexities. The sociologist must attempt to make history known, incident by incident, as a complete experience. His task is to recognize "the irreducible originality of . . . social-political groups . . . and to define them in their very complexity, in terms of their incomplete development and their deviated objectification."[52] The method of placing will not do. Totalization attempts to capture wholes-in-the-making, and these are the only social wholes. *Praxis* always outruns itself at the same time that it is limited. New activities are expressed in outworn terms; new terms are ambiguous because the actions that they signify are limited by the structural possibilities. The sociological *praxis* is a continuous effort to cast light on the "struggle in the dark," that defines social activity, by relating events to one another in a structural investigation. The notion that events must always outrun any description of a totality, and that the sociological *praxis* consists in a continuous activity of totalization is at the heart of the methods of Sartre and the American humanists. Rather than viewing Sartre's undertaking as an attempt to synthesize existentialism and Marxism, and seeing the American humanist's enterprise as an effort to introduce the study of conflict and social change into American sociology, one can usefully view the

[50] *Ibid.*, p. 69.
[51] *Ibid.*
[52] *Ibid.*, p. 123.

works of both the American humanists and Sartre as attempts to surpass the methodological debate between holists and pluralists by introducing the method of totalization. Whether or not Mills and Moore have recaptured the "classical tradition" in sociology, and Sartre has revived authentic Marxism, the convergence of methodological critiques against regnant methods is striking. Even more significant is the convergence of methodological proposals. It remains for us to discuss the fifth facet of the new method—the purpose that totalizing activity is supposed to realize.

### Practical Emphasis

The historical approach, multi-variate and tripartite analysis, empirical and dynamic methods, and totalizing concerns of Sartre and the American humanists are finally justified by their bearing on the general social *praxis*. It is in the purpose of totalizing activity that the early questions about the nature of a significant sociological principle and the definition of a historical period are partially resolved. Moore gives perhaps the clearest statement of the purpose of totalizing: "Uniformities in social behavior become significant for us only when they concern important problems, such as freedom and compulsion. What is important is not a matter of subjective whim, but is the consequence of a specific historical situation."[53] Moore remarks that the study of society through the new method reveals that neither voluntarism nor determinism provides an adequate interpretation of history. Historically, nearly all human beings have been "confronted with the overwhelming weight of a society they as individuals did nothing to create."[54] Thus, throughout history the alternatives for human beings have been severely restricted. This judgment

[53] Stein and Vidich, *Sociology on Trial*, p. 77.
[54] *Ibid.*, p. 86.

is the origin of Moore's remark that the best a sociologist can do is to draw out the potentialities of
the social forms that exist before him. The purpose
of the sociological *praxis* is the discovery of possibilities and opportunities for human freedom within the
social *praxis*. Sociology not only debunks myths; it
also describes possibilities for action through the process of totalization. This discussion provides a clue to
the solution of the problems of sociological significance and the definition of a historical period. While
the idea of sociology as the study of the intersection
of history, biography, and structure applies across
historical periods, even more important is the implication that the problem of human liberation has characterized all historical periods thus far. Significant
sociological principles describe the possibilities for
liberation from dominations and for increasing alternatives of human choice within specific social structures. These significant principles are deemed relative
to given historical periods because the humanists believe that the modes of liberation and enhancing
alternatives change over time and space. This judgment is essentially empirical rather than ontological.
Insofar as modes of domination and liberation change,
sociology must change. This makes it quite difficult to
define neatly a historical period. Modes of domination
and liberation are complex, and some aspects of them
may change at different rates than others. Part of the
meaning of sociology as totalization is an effort to
apprehend these various rates of change and their
bearing on the social structure as a whole-in-the-
making. Perhaps the best definition of a historical
period is a time frame in which a single general mode
of liberation applies. When a means to liberation
does not gain progressive results, a new historical
period has come into being. This is essentially the
position of C. Wright Mills, who argues that we currently live in a post-modern "Fourth Epoch" characterized by the condition that "increased rationality

may not be assumed to make for increased freedom."[55]
Thus, the problem of liberation in the Fourth Epoch
has a new dimension—there is the possibility that
human beings can be turned into cheerful robots.[56]
However, within this specific historical situation the
ultimate objective of the sociological *praxis* remains
the continual translation of "personal troubles into
public issues, and public issues into the terms of their
human meaning for a variety of individuals," so that
actors will have the maximum opportunity "to formulate the available choices, to argue over them—and
then, the opportunity to choose."[57] Essentially the
same points are made by Sartre. He neatly summarizes
his conception of the goal of the sociological *praxis:*
"Our historical task, at the heart of this polyvalent
world, is to bring closer the moment when History
will have *only one meaning,* when it will tend to be
dissolved in the concrete men who will make it in
common."[58] Thus, the last facet of the methods proposed by Sartre and the American humanists is a
concern with the attainment and extension of human
freedom within social structures. Only the foundation
and justification of these methods in human *praxis*
can account for the historical approach, multi-variate
analysis, empirical and dynamic methods, and totalizing concerns of Sartre and the American humanists.

The root of the humanist method in human *praxis*
and its justification in terms of enhancing freedom,
leads to a serious question. In *Social Life and Cultural Change,* Don Martindale has registered a criticism of Mills that applies to all of the humanist sociologists discussed here. Martindale claims that the
only general aspects in Mills's work are moral judgments. These moral absolutes give "the social scientist

---

[55] Mills, *Sociological Imagination,* p. 167.
[56] *Ibid.,* p. 171.
[57] *Ibid.,* pp. 187, 174.
[58] Sartre, *Search for a Method,* p. 91.

ability to transcend his milieu."[59] However, this transcendence is neither scientific nor rational. Sociology
is abandoned "as a strictly scientific enterprise," and
it is transformed into a "sociopolitical program."[60] According to Martindale, Mills leaves the sociologist
with the trans-rational task of complaining against
those in power, informing those who are not in power
about the activities of the powerful, and "evaluating
the epoch."[61] Martindale seems to be saying that one
must accept the goal of human liberation before he
can use the methods recommended by the humanists.
Only the moral criterion can save studies done with
this method from losing general import. This criticism
seems to be based on a misunderstanding of the methods proposed by Sartre and the American humanists.
These methods are rooted in the notion of a human
condition, and not in a trans-historical moral judgment. If the human condition situates an actor with a
biography in a historically specified social structure,
this does not mean that the sociologist must guide his
work by the principle of enhancing human freedom.
The humanists are committed to recognizing human
*praxis* as a fact. They are not bound by their method
to prefer liberation to domination. That Sartre and
the American humanists justify their method as a moment in the struggle for liberation is independent of
the use of the method itself. It is not at all clear that
they recognize this independence. After all, their
moral commitments to liberation from intellectual terror were important factors in the search for a method.
However, it should be clear that totalization can discover possibilities for domination as easily as it can
discover possibilities for liberation. Insofar as Sartre and the American humanists have developed a
method, they have developed a tool that can be used

[59] Don Martindale, *Social Life and Cultural Change* (New
York: D. Van Nostrand Company, 1962), p. 482.

[60] *Ibid.*, pp. 482–83.

[61] *Ibid.*

for a variety of goals. Thus, the humanist method is general because it recognizes human *praxis* as a fact and studies human activity in relation to the intersection of biography, structure, and history. It is not rendered general by a moral judgment, though it is justified by one. Criticism of the method would best proceed by accepting it as a serious attempt to render adequate descriptions of social change and its direction. From there one might attempt to find out how one could verify results obtained by using the method. Such a critical examination is not in place here. The purposes of this essay were first to show that there is a humanist method and, second, to show a convergence between the work of Sartre and the studies of two American sociologists. With the definition of the several facets of the humanist method and the comparative study of the three writers, these tasks have been accomplished.

The advantages of situating Sartre's work in the context of sociological methods are several. First, it highlights aspects of Sartre's work that are not emphasized in studies where the context is existentialism or Marxism. Among these neglected aspects are the historical approach and the multi-variate analysis. Second, it lends evidence to support the hypothesis that Sartre's sociological writings are part of a revolt against formalism that is under way throughout the West. At this juncture it is impossible to "totalize" ourselves and identify the structures which support both official Soviet Marxism and American structural-functionalism. Neither Sartre nor the American humanists use their methods to identify new social forms and problems of liberation. However, their very convergence sets the stage for such a study.[62] The whole is no longer found within nation-states, but has become world-wide. Of course, just as comparison with

[62] See Michael A. Weinstein, "Politics and Moral Consciousness," *Midwest Journal of Political Science*, May 1970, for an attempt to use the method described in this essay.

American sociologists allows Sartre to transcend Marxist particularism, comparison with Sartre takes the American humanists beyond the confines of American sociology. Finally, describing Sartre as a methodologist makes his work available as a contribution to sociology. It is his possible contribution to the sociological *praxis* that inspires this essay.

# BIBLIOGRAPHY

The list of Sartre's works given here is not complete. The more important works, both literary and philosophical, are given in chronological order. In the second part of the bibliography, a few books and articles about Sartre are listed which are likely to be useful, but, again, no attempt has been made at completeness.

## I. Sartre's writings:

*La Transcendance de l'égo: Esquisse d'une description phénoménologique,* Recherches Philosophique VI, Paris, 1936.

*The Transcendence of the Ego,* trans. F. Williams and R. Kirkpatrick, Farrar, Strauss, and Giroux, Noonday Press, New York, 1957.

*L'Imagination, étude critique,* Felix Mian, Paris, 1936.

*Imagination: A Psychological Critique,* trans. F. Williams, University of Michigan Press, Ann Arbor, 1962.

*La Nausée,* Gallimard, 1938.

*Nausea,* trans. L. Alexander, New Directions, New York, and London, 1949.

*Esquisse d'une théorie des émotions,* Hermann, Paris, 1939.

*Sketch for a Theory of the Emotions,* trans. P. Mairet, London, 1962.

*Le Mur,* Gallimard, Paris, 1939.

*Intimacy,* Berkley Publishing Corp., New York, 1949.

*Intimacy,* trans. L. Alexander, Neville Spearman, London, 1949.

*L'Imaginaire: psychologie phénoménologique de l'imagination,* Gallimard, Paris, 1940.

*The Psychology of the Imagination,* The Citadel Press, New York, 1961; London, 1949.

*L'Être et le Néant: essaie d'ontologie phénoménologique*, Gallimard, Paris, 1943.

*Being and Nothingness*, trans. Hazel Barnes, Methuen, London, 1957; The Washington Square Press, New York, 1965.

*Les Mouches: drame en trois actes*, Paris, 1943 (first performance). Théâter 8, 1941.

*The Flies*, trans. S. Gilbert, Hamish Hamilton, London, 1946; Alfred A. Knopf, New York, 1962.

*Huis clos: pièce en un acte*, Paris, 1944. Théâter 7, 1945.

*No Exit*, Alfred A. Knopf, New York, 1947.

*In Camera*, trans. S. Gilbert, Hamish Hamilton, London, 1947.

*L'Existentialisme est un humanisme*, Nagel, Paris, 1946.

*Essays in Existentialism*, The Citadel Press, New York, 1967.

*Baudelaire*, précedé d'une note de Michel Leiris, Gallimard, Paris, 1947.

*Baudelaire*, trans. M. Turnell, New Directions Publishing Corp., London and New York, 1949.

*Situations* I (including: Une idée fondamentale de la phénoménologie de Husserl: "L'Intentionalité" (1939), "L'homme et les choses" "La liberté Cartesienne" (1946), and other essays), Paris, 1947.

*Situations* II (including "Qu'est-ce que la littérature?" [1947], and other essays), Paris, 1948.

*What Is Literature?* Harper & Row, New York, 1949.

*Les Mains sales:* pièce en sept tableaux, Gallimard, Paris, 1948, (first performance).

*Crime passionnel,* trans. Kitty Black, Hamish Hamilton, London, 1949.

*Situations* III (including "La république du silence" [1944], "Paris sous l'occupation" [1944], "Matérialisme et révolution" [1946], "Orphée noir" [1948], and other essays), Paris, 1949.

*Black Orpheus*, University Place Book Shop, New York, 1949.

*Le Diable et le Bon Dieu:* pièce en trois actes et onze tableaux, Paris, 1951 (first performance).

*The Devil and the Good Lord,* Knopf, New York, 1960.

*Les communistes et la paix (Temps Modernes* nos. 81, 84, 85, 101), 1952–54.

*Communists and Peace,* George Braziller, Inc., New York, 1968.

*Saint Genet: Comédien et Martyr,* Gallimard, Paris, 1952.

*Saint Genet: Comedian and Martyr,* trans. Frechtman, Braziller, New York, 1963.

*Critique de la raison dialectique,* Volume I, Gallimard, Paris, 1960.

*Merleau-Ponty vivant (Temps Modernes,* 184, 185), 1961.

*Les Mots,* Gallimard, Paris, 1964.

*Words,* Braziller, New York, and Hamish Hamilton, London.

*Situations* IV (including "Portrait du Colonise" (1957), "Nous sommes tous des assasins" (1958), and other essays), Paris, 1964.


II. *A Selection of Writings about Sartre (arranged alphabetically):*

Jeanson, Francis, *Le problème moral, et le pensée de Sartre,* Editions du Nyrte, Paris, 1947.
　　*Sartre par lui-même,* Editions du Seuil, Paris, 1954.

Laing, R. D., and Cooper, D. G., *Reason and Violence,* New York (Barnes & Noble) and London, 1964.

Manser, Anthony, *Sartre,* Athlone Press, London, 1966.

Merleau-Ponty, Maurice, *Humanisme et Terreur,* Gallimard, Paris, 1947.
　　*Humanism and Terror,* Beacon Press, 1969.
　　*Sens et non-sens,* Nagel, Paris, 1948.

    *Sense and Nonsense*, Northwestern University Press, Evanston, 1964.

    *Les aventures de la dialectique*, Gallimard, Paris, 1955.

Murdoch, Iris, *Sartre, Romantic Rationalist*, Bowes and Bowes, Cambridge, Yale University Press, New Haven, 1953.

Thody, Philip, *Jean-Paul Sartre: A Literary and Political Study*, Macmillan, London, 1960.

Warnock, Mary, *The Philosophy of Sartre*, Hutchinson, London, 1965, and Barnes & Noble, New York, 1967.


Various authors:

*Journal of the British Society for Phenomenology*, Vol. I, No. 2, "Jean-Paul Sartre, Perspectives, In Honor of His 65th Birthday," London, 1970.